The Quest for Human Nature

The Quest for Human Nature

What Philosophy and Science Have Learned

MARCO J. NATHAN

OXFORD
UNIVERSITY PRESS

Oxford University Press is a department of the University of Oxford. It furthers
the University's objective of excellence in research, scholarship, and education
by publishing worldwide. Oxford is a registered trade mark of Oxford University
Press in the UK and certain other countries.

Published in the United States of America by Oxford University Press
198 Madison Avenue, New York, NY 10016, United States of America.

© Oxford University Press 2024

All rights reserved. No part of this publication may be reproduced, stored in
a retrieval system, or transmitted, in any form or by any means, without the
prior permission in writing of Oxford University Press, or as expressly permitted
by law, by license, or under terms agreed with the appropriate reproduction
rights organization. Inquiries concerning reproduction outside the scope of the
above should be sent to the Rights Department, Oxford University Press, at the
address above.

You must not circulate this work in any other form
and you must impose this same condition on any acquirer.

Library of Congress Cataloging-in-Publication Data
Names: Nathan, Marco J., author.
Title: The quest for human nature : what philosophy and science
have learned / Marco J. Nathan.
Description: New York, NY : Oxford University Press, [2024] |
Includes bibliographical references and index.
Identifiers: LCCN 2023040357 (print) | LCCN 2023040358 (ebook) |
ISBN 9780197699256 (paperback) | ISBN 9780197699249 (hardback) |
ISBN 9780197699263 (epub)
Subjects: LCSH: Humanity. | Philosophy and science.
Classification: LCC BJ1533.H9 N38 2024 (print) | LCC BJ1533.H9 (ebook) |
DDC 179.7—dc23/eng/20231031
LC record available at https://lccn.loc.gov/2023040357
LC ebook record available at https://lccn.loc.gov/2023040358

DOI: 10.1093/oso/9780197699249.001.0001

Dedicated with love to the new generation of the Nathan family:
Martina, Virginia, Alexander, Nicoló, Jacob, and Laila.
Whatever your nature turns out to be, may it never change!

πολλὰ τὰ δεινὰ κοὐδὲν ἀνθρώπου δεινότερον πέλει.
τοῦτο καὶ πολιοῦ πέραν πόντου χειμερίῳ νότῳ χωρεῖ,
περιβρυχίοισιν περῶν ὑπ᾽ οἴδμασιν. θεῶν τε τὰν
ὑπερτάταν, Γᾶν ἄφθιτον, ἀκαμάταν, ἀποτρύεται ἰλλομένων
ἀρότρων ἔτος εἰς ἔτος ἱππείῳ γένει πολεύων.

Many wonders there be, but naught more wondrous
than man; Over the surging sea, with a whitening south
wind wan, Through the foam of the firth, man makes his
perilous way;
And the eldest of deities Earth that knows not toil
nor decay Ever he furrows and scores, as his team, year in
year out,
With breed of the yoked horse, the ploughshare
turneth about.

—Sophocles, *Antigone*, translated by F. Storr (1912)

Contents

Preface	ix
1. What's at Stake?	1
2. A Science of Human Nature?	21
3. Is There a Human Nature?	61
4. What Makes a Trait Innate?	96
5. Are We Genetically Determined?	128
6. Oppression or Emancipation? Part (i): Human Races	165
7. Oppression or Emancipation? Part (ii): Sex and Gender	200
8. Normality: Facts or Politics?	233
9. Should We Be Concerned about Enhancing Our Nature?	266
10. Can Science Explain Human Nature?	295
References	329
Index	349

To illustrate the general approach, here is a pattern in need of elucidation. Why is pornography so male-dominated? Why is it that most adult-oriented material is produced with an audience of men in mind and is intended primarily for male consumption? In the late 1970s, when Symons was writing, the trend in the sexuality literature was to minimize biological differences in erotic arousal between men and women and to attribute these findings to the sociopolitical repression of females. From this perspective, women are no less aroused by pornography than are males. But female sexuality is culturally repressed, much more so than its male counterpart.

Symons favors a different explanation, grounded more in biology. While many women respond sexually to porn in experimental settings, he maintains, few seek it "in the wild." Such evidence, Symons continues, demonstrates what has long been known. First, women are capable of being aroused by erotica, mainly via the subjective process of identification with female characters. Second, once sexual activity is underway, women have the potential to be as strongly aroused as men. Yet, this need not imply that women fail to respond to pornographic material like men because they are repressed or in need of emancipation. Rather, Symons rejoins, this reflects the crucial difference between surfing the web at home, in private, and agreeing to participate in an experiment. Porn in psychological studies simulates an actual sexual interaction to which participants have previously consented and are willing to engage in, by agreeing to the study. Hence, erotic arousal replicates ordinary responses during sexual interactions. In contrast, spontaneously seeking out porn requires taking the initiative. This could explain why, while women have the potential to be strongly aroused by pornography, they seldom actively pursue it. It also captures women's general lack of sexual response to male nudity. Failing to grasp such basic facts, Symons says, has led to neglect of significant sexual differences between genders:

> In my view, as long as the matter is phrased in terms of hyper vs. hypo-sexuality (with hypersexuality assumed to be good or desirable), and as long as evidence for sex differences in sexuality is felt to be necessarily detrimental to women, experiments will continue to be designed, and their results interpreted, to emphasize similarities

42   THE QUEST FOR HUMAN NATURE

between men and women, and the everyday world will continue to suffer neglect. (Symons 1979, p. 170)

Is there a better alternative? Symons' ultimate explanation for sexual behavior follows a familiar pattern. Since males can impregnate females at virtually no cost in terms of time and energy, natural selection favors the basic male tendency to be sexually aroused by the sheer sight of females, proportionally to perceived reproductive value via visual cues. For a male, any random mating pays off reproductively. Human females, in contrast, invest a substantial amount of energy and incur serious risks by becoming pregnant. Hence, the circumstances of impregnation are extremely important to female reproductive success, much more than for their male counterparts. Nubile females seldom have problems encountering a willing sexual partner, so the task is to find the fittest available male, always factoring risk, and to maximize the returns on sexual favors. Being sexually aroused by the sheer sight of males would promote random mating, undermining these aims. It would also waste time and energy that could be spent in economically significant activities and nurturing children. All this encapsulates why visual sexual arousal would be detrimental for women.

Analogous arguments are advanced to explain the practice of covering nudity with clothes which, according to Symons, has divergent explanations across the sexes. Deliberate male display to unfamiliar women is perceived as threat. Female exposure to a male could be taken as unsolicited sexual invitation. Similarly, women and men have different reasons guiding choice of clothing. Female reproductive value can be assessed more accurately from physical appearance than a male's reproductive value, leading females to display themselves more openly. In contrast, men dress drably to appear more attractive to women. Explicit attitudes on the part of men are often a dislikable sign of promiscuity. Incidentally, this captures the tendency of homosexual men to dress more flamboyantly. They face the same challenge of heterosexual women, appearing sexually attractive to males, who assess attractiveness primarily based on physical appearance. *Und so weiter.*

All this purports to show that mechanisms of attractiveness are less variable or culture-dependent than most people surmise. The key to human sexuality is to conceive it as an adaptation, shaped by our evolutionary past:

If one argues, as so many people continue to do, that behavior must be caused either by the genes or by the environment, and that any exception to a general rule demonstrates environmental causation (unless the exception can be shown to have a genetic basis), one can deny the existence of any genetic influences on human sexual preferences. But if one acknowledges that behavior and psyche result from the interactions of genes and environments, and that human genes were selected on the basis of their ability to perpetuate themselves within a limited range of environmental circumstances, then, despite exceptions, one can interpret the cross-cultural regularities in standards of physical attractiveness as powerful evidence for "innate" dispositions. (Symons 1979, p. 200)

This illustrates the overarching strategy of sociobiologists and evolutionary psychologists to capture sexual behaviors. Parallel accounts are sought for other significant aspects of sociality, from intelligence to xenophobia. The issue now becomes whether this strategy holds water.

§2.5 Carrying Wilson's Torch

Not everyone merrily jumped on Wilson's bandwagon. Sociobiology came under fire in the 1980s. The main charge was that it provided a drastically simplistic and stereotypical depiction of social conduct, overlooking diversity of behaviors in human and non-human species alike. This led to public distancing from its excesses. Overwhelmed by critique, sociobiology morphed into new fields, such as Darwinian anthropology, human behavioral ecology, cultural evolution, and evolutionary psychology. The aim of this section is threefold. First, it presents these revamped approaches. Second, it clarifies the rationale for moving away from sociobiology. Third, it explains the subtle albeit significant shift from sociobiology to its descendants.[14]

---

[14] Summarizing in a few paragraphs decades of overlapping but independent research is no trivial task. My discussion draws from various quality surveys, such as Griffiths (2008), Mameli (2008b), Laland and Brown (2011), Garson (2015), and Lewens (2015b).

44   THE QUEST FOR HUMAN NATURE

First, let's focus on *human behavioral ecology*, an offshoot of Darwinian anthropology.[15] Its starting point is the observation that humans have faced an array of changing environments over their long evolutionary history. Consequently, the argument runs, humans should not be expected to have developed a plethora of specialized mental abilities that can be adapted and applied to a broad range of circumstances. Phenotypic and behavioral plasticity, coupled with optimality models and other mathematical tools, provide powerful resources to shed light on the evolution of our bodies and minds. The extent to which the human mind should be conceived as modular will be further assessed in Chapter 4. However, human behavioral ecology does not explicitly present itself as a "science of human nature." Hence, we shall not discuss it in detail here.

A second, different development in the wake of sociobiology comes from *cultural evolution*, a movement that emerged in the 1970s and 1980s, pushing for greater recognition of the power of culture as an independent driving force. The guiding thought—which harks back to the insights of Darwin as well as early followers such as Morgan, Baldwin, and James—is that many cultural entities, from artifacts to linguistic expressions, follow a phylogenetic trajectory of their own. A preliminary challenge in sharpening this intuition involves turning the platitude that culture evolves, in the broad sense of "changes over time," into a substantive and testable hypothesis.

Following Lewens (2015b), we can distinguish three strands of cultural evolution. First, the *historical* approach sets out to understand how various forces have contributed to the transformation of earlier states into later ones. This formulation faces a basic challenge. Applying the "evolutionary" label to all approaches offering a historical genealogy of cultural patterns effectively turns any diachronic view of culture into an "evolutionary" theory. This makes little sense of modern debates. The second, *selectionist* derivation of cultural evolution purports to enrich this general historical characterization by maintaining that the very conditions required for natural selection to

---

[15] An early perspective on human behavioral ecology can be found in Irons (1979). More recent developments include Smith and Winterhalder (1992), Cronk et al. (2000), and Tomasello (2022).

occur in the biological realm—from abundant variation to faithful reproduction to differential reproductive success—are also discernible in the cultural sphere. The third strand of cultural evolution is the *kinetic* one, grounded in the observation that the human ability to learn from others can lead to changes at the population level.

In short, cultural evolutionists of all three sorts bring together sophisticated mathematical models and field observations to test a host of empirical hypotheses regarding the co-evolution of genes and culture.[16] In recent publications, scholars such as Boyd (2018), Henrich (2016, 2020), and Tomasello (2019) have emphasized the uniqueness of our species, in terms of both geographical range and biomass.[17] The key to unraveling the secret of our success, these cultural evolutionists insist, lies not in our brains, our individual intelligence, but in our *culture*, which cannot be understood as separate from biology. Culture arises in response to adaptive challenges that triggered high forms of cooperation and the transmission of knowledge across generations. Brains alone fail to explain our capacity to adapt to a wide range of circumstances. How does adaptive culture knowledge work? Whereas evolutionary psychologists stress that we adopt beliefs and practices that we deem beneficial, cultural evolutionists favor a different answer: we adopt beliefs and practices because this is what people around us do.

In what follows, our main focus will be a third research program that explicitly purports to apply Darwin's original insights to the study of the human mind: *evolutionary psychology.* There are two reasons for this choice. First, evolutionary psychology is closer to original sociobiology than any other offshoot. Second, and more important, evolutionary psychology has been more explicit than either human behavioral ecology or cultural evolution in its intent to embrace and

---

[16] Modern approaches to the co-evolution of genes and culture have been independently pioneered by Cavalli-Sforza and Feldman (1981) and Lumsden and Wilson ([1981] 2005). Selectionist approaches, which hark back to Darwin, have been articulated more recently by Campbell (1974) and Basalla (1988). The kinetic theory, in turn, is developed by Boyd, Richerson, and Henrich (Boyd and Richerson 1985, 2005; Henrich and Boyd 1998; Henrich 2016; Boyd 2018). Critical discussions of cultural evolution can also be found in Sperber (1996), Sterelny (2012), Dennett (2017), and Heyes (2018).

[17] Other insightful yet accessible overviews of the biology underlying human uniqueness can be found in Gazzaniga (2008) and Sterelny (2012).

46 THE QUEST FOR HUMAN NATURE

develop a true "science of human nature." Allow me to elaborate. As noted above, human behavioral ecologists are not especially interested in human nature per se. Many cultural evolutionists, in contrast, seek an explanation of human uniqueness, which brings up the issue of our biological underpinnings. Nevertheless, human nature, when mentioned at all, is not introduced as a concept in need of articulation. To wit, Henrich (2016, p. xii) explicitly states: "I'm more convinced than ever that to understand our species and to build a science of human behavior and psychology, we need to begin with an evolutionary theory of human nature." Nevertheless, the notion of human nature at play is never defined or outlined in any detail. It appears to be a background assumption, an undefined primitive, a conceptual springboard for raising questions about cultural evolution. Evolutionary psychologists, such as Buss, Cosmides, Tooby, and Pinker, in contrast, are much more explicit in outlining our biological underpinnings and their implications for our one true nature. In this regard, we shall focus on evolutionary psychology as carrying Wilson's torch.

Before cruising along, a preliminary clarification in is order. The label "evolutionary psychology" is ambiguous. Broadly construed, it may refer to any evolutionary study of mind. On a narrower reading, it picks out a specific research program often associated with scholars such as Cosmides, Tooby, Pinker, and Buss. In what follows, I try to avoid confusion by reserving "evolutionary psychology" for the second, more specific version.

Contemporary evolutionary psychologists often brush off the resistance to sociobiology based on a combination of parochial ideology and crass misunderstanding:

> Part of the controversy stemmed from the nature of Wilson's claims. He asserted that sociobiology would "cannibalize psychology," which of course was not greeted warmly by most psychologists. Further, he speculated that many cherished human phenomena, such as culture, religion, ethics, and even aesthetics, would ultimately be explained by the new synthesis. These assertions strongly contradicted the dominant theories in the social sciences. (Buss 2019, p. 17)

In fairness, Buss also notes that "[d]espite Wilson's grand claims for a new synthesis that would explain human nature, he had little empirical evidence on humans to support his views. . . . Although scientific revolutions always meet resistance, often from within the ranks of established scientists . . . Wilson's lack of relevant scientific data on humans did not help" (2019, p. 17). Yet, after this nod, Buss quickly moves on to state that "part of the resistance to the application of evolutionary theory to humans is based on several common misconceptions. Contrary to these misconceptions, evolutionary theory does not imply genetic determinism. It does not imply that we are powerless to change things. It does not mean that our existing adaptations are optimally designed" (2019, p. 19).

While there is surely some truth to all these points, it is crucial to keep them distinct and avoid muddying the waters. First, there is no shortage of petty academic disputes turned sour into full-fledged turf wars. Second, evolutionary theory has a long history of misinterpretation that sadly persists to the present day. Having said this, many critics of sociobiology—including all the ones discussed in ensuing sections—were not protecting their own discipline and are hardly confused about the basics of evolution by natural selection. Rather, the chief complaint was the lack of solid data backing up the sensationalism. The strong correspondence between genes and behaviors posited by sociobiology simply lacked experimental support. And Wilson's choice of targets did not help either. Before coming to terms with the alleged facts that human beings are naturally xenophobic and that men have an evolved tendency to rape, we better have darn good evidence!

With this in mind, we can turn to our third and final task, namely, explaining the shift from sociobiology to evolutionary psychology. What was novel and what remained constant? The main transition from the original discipline to its intellectual progeny concerns a shift in explananda, that is, in the objects of explanation. Whereas sociobiology purported to explain human *behaviors* directly, by ascribing to them adaptive significance, evolutionary psychologists draw attention to the *cognitive mechanisms* underlying the behaviors in question.[18] To

---

[18] An explicit acknowledgment of the crucial role of the mind as mediating the relation between genotype and behavior can be clearly discerned in Lumsden and Wilson ([1981] 2005).

48   THE QUEST FOR HUMAN NATURE

fully appreciate this claim, we need to briefly look deeper into the notion of a cognitive mechanism.

An *evolved psychological mechanism*, in brief, is a set of mental processes in an organism, which evolved because of a specific adaptive advantage. More precisely, an evolved psychological mechanism has the following six properties. First, it exists in its current form because it solved a specific problem of survival and reproduction recurrently over the evolutionary history of the species. Second, an evolved psychological mechanism is designed to take in a narrow slice of information. Third, the input of an evolved psychological mechanism "tells" an organism the particular adaptive problem it faces. Fourth, the input of an evolved psychological mechanism is transformed into output through decision rules or procedures. Fifth, the output of evolved psychological mechanisms can be cognitive activity, information shared with other mechanisms, or manifest behavior. Sixth and finally, the output of an evolved psychological mechanism is directed toward the solution to a specific adaptive problem:

> In summary, an evolved psychological mechanism is a set of procedures within the organism designed to take in a particular slice of information and transform that information via decision rules into output that historically has helped with the solution to an adaptive problem. Psychological mechanisms exist in current organisms because they led, on average, to successful solutions to specific adaptive problems for that organism's ancestors. (Buss 2019, p. 46)

Evolved psychological mechanisms include neural circuitries designed to select nutritious foods and healthy mates, as well as more specialized modules like morning sickness, the heightened sensitivity and nauseous reaction to selected foods that many pregnant women experience, typically, during the first trimester. Incidentally, this common moniker is a misnomer, as "morning sickness" can strike at any time, day or night.[19]

The functional identification of evolved mechanisms purports to carve the mind at its joints. Just as our bodies contain thousands of

---

[19] These cases are developed in Cosmides and Tooby (2013) and Buss (2019, Ch. 3).

specialized mechanisms, the mind must also encompass myriad task-specific modules. Unlike human behavioral ecology, evolutionary psychology explicitly privileges problem-specificity over generality because universal strategies fail to guide organisms to correct adaptive solutions. Even when they do, they may lead to costly errors. And what constitutes a successful solution differs from problem to problem. Since unique tasks require specific fixes, organisms confronted with various problems require an array of strategies.

Importantly, the observation that a mechanism has led to a successful solution in the evolutionary past may or may not lead to an effective strategy today. Our preference for sweet foods may have been an important adaptation at a time when caloric intake was a challenge, whereas it may lead to pathological conditions in the present environment, from obesity to diabetes. As evolutionary psychologists Cosmides and Tooby (2013, p. 91) famously put it, "our modern skulls house a stone-age mind."

In conclusion, evolutionary psychology presents itself as a scientific synthesis of modern evolutionary biology and its cutting-edge tools—inclusive fitness, parental investment, sexual selection, and the like—with current psychology and its focus on information-processing modules, the study of artificial intelligence, and the (allegedly) universal expression of emotions:

> Evolutionary psychology is an *approach* to psychology, in which knowledge and principles from evolutionary biology are put to use in research on the structure of the human mind. . . . In this view, the mind is a set of information-processing machines that were designed by natural selection to solve adaptive problems faced by our hunter-gatherer ancestors. (Cosmides and Tooby 2013, p. 83)

The chief goal of this research program is to evaluate the presence of adaptation or absence thereof. More specifically, evolutionary psychology is geared toward two broad aims. First, it purports to discover previously unsuspected links between manifest behavior and features of human biology, pertaining to survival or reproduction. Second, it focuses on adaptive function. Like its intellectual predecessor—sociobiology—evolutionary psychology stresses that natural selection

50 THE QUEST FOR HUMAN NATURE

occurs rather slowly. From this well-established observation, it infers the much more controversial thesis that the traits we observe in extant populations are hardly optimal for current circumstances. Hence, the key to characterizing the human mind, as it is presently constituted, is to understand the adaptive problems faced by our ancestors. We are adapted to past conditions, not present ones. These considerations raise an important, pressing concern. Is evolutionary psychology, at bottom, just a revived form of sociobiology in disguise, as Wilson himself suggests in the passage quoted in this chapter's epigraph?

§2.6 Cautionary Voices

The previous pages introduced sociobiology and its intellectual progeny. Specifically, §2.3 discussed the emergence of sociobiology. §2.4 distilled its core explanatory argument and applied it to human sexual behavior. §2.5 discussed the transition from sociobiology to evolutionary psychology. This section voices some skepticism concerning both research programs.

Recall the general structure of the main sociobiological argument. Sociobiological explanations begin by identifying a pattern of behavior deemed universal. This universality is then accounted for by positing some evolutionary advantage. The third and final step is to explain the evolvability of the adaptive behavior, or of the mechanisms producing the behavior, by positing some genetic basis. This strategy is found in virtually identical guise within evolutionary psychology, with the proviso that the explanation of allegedly universal behaviors is now mediated by the postulation of evolved psychological mechanisms.

How successful is this strategy? The story is meant to apply to all sexually reproducing organisms. Specifically, the more disparity one finds in the contributions of males and females in a species, the more effective the narrative should become. Indeed, this strategy has provided some insight into mating behaviors in nature. But how much can it really explain?

Based on these preliminary observations, we can ask what kind of behavior we should witness in sexually reproducing species like humans. Intuitively, males can be expected to be more inclined toward

A SCIENCE OF HUMAN NATURE? 51

promiscuity, whereas females should tend toward monogamy. Things, however, are not quite that simple.

When it comes to mate selection, what we behold in the wild is enormous diversity among species in degrees of promiscuity vs. monogamy across both sexes.[20] Echoing Wilson, let's restrict our attention to some of our closest evolutionary cousins. Chimpanzees and bonobos are typically highly promiscuous. Silverback gorillas, in contrast, display a different social structure, in which dominant males tend to enjoy virtually exclusive access to sexual partners. What conclusions should we draw for our own species? At a minimum, a cautionary tale is appropriate. Describing mating behavior and generalizing it into patterns requires careful observation. None of this sounds remotely shocking. So, where exactly could the basic sociobiological argument have gone astray? Once we take a deeper look, it becomes clear how potential pitfalls arise at virtually every turn.

First, universality calls for careful scrutiny. Consider the claim that human males are "naturally promiscuous." What exactly is the proposal here? On the one hand, the thesis cannot be that all men invariably display promiscuous behaviors, which is clearly false. Evolutionary psychologists are perfectly aware of variations in human behavior, sexual conduct included. Still, they believe that the degree of variation is heavily overestimated, overlooking general patterns of behaviors. The challenge is turning this intuition into a substantive empirical hypothesis. Cashing out the tenet as holding that human males sometimes display dissolute tendencies, the claim becomes true, albeit trivial, uninteresting. Presumably, the conjecture under scrutiny is that men reliably display indiscriminate sexual behavior under particular circumstances. Now, this is an interesting assertion, worth investigating. Yet, the universality of this pattern cannot simply be assumed. In order to properly test it, we would need to fix the social environment and seek reproductive skew. According to the hypothesis under scrutiny, having fixed the social environment, we will find a consistent difference in the sexual behavior of males and females, with the former more inclined toward indiscriminate exploration. Assessing

---

[20] Much of the following discussion is inspired by Kitcher (1985a), Dupré (2001), and Buller (2005).

52 THE QUEST FOR HUMAN NATURE

this requires determining what exactly counts as "promiscuous behavior," under what specific conditions the behavior in question is expected to emerge—which environments should be held fixed—and what observed frequency pattern would legitimate claims of universality. None of this is straightforward.

And coming up with a clear empirical hypothesis is only the beginning. Suppose that we could successfully establish a plausible, testable, universal behavioral pattern. Still, a second difficulty besets the tenet that the behavior under scrutiny confers a genuine evolutionary advantage, the second step of the sociobiological argument. Here is a simple example.[21] Given the discrepancy in parental investment, it may seem obvious that it would always be beneficial for men to desert the mothers of their children and seek other sexual partners. This, however, is far too simplistic. Whether paternal desertion is advantageous, from an evolutionary standpoint, depends on a series of factors. What is the probability of finding a new sexual partner? What are the chances of encountering a rival, the likelihood of fending them off, and the cost of doing so? What are the odds that offspring will survive if raised by a single parent, or without parents? To further complicate things, the optimal strategy will depend on the actions of other males in the territory. If most rivals are seeking sexual opportunities, any given male may do better staying at home and contributing to the upbringing of their own offspring. In short, behaviors can be explained in terms of evolutionary advantages, at least in principle. Nevertheless, working out the details of how reproductive benefits are gained and ruling out alternative hypotheses is a gargantuan task.

A third challenge undermines the presupposition that selection can work only where there are genes to select, the final step of the standard sociobiological strategy. Assume for the sake of the argument that, with much work, we have successfully established a male tendency to desert their partners as a universal pattern across human populations. Further suppose that we could pinpoint the evolutionary advantage

---

[21] This example was originally developed by Kitcher (1985b). Kitcher's point, concerning the flexibility of sexual strategies in humans and other animals, has been expanded by Gowaty (2008) and Gowaty and Hubbell (2013) and, more recently, by Barker (2015).

it bestowed upon our hunter-gatherer ancestors in the savannah, our so-called *environment of evolutionary adaptedness*, "EEA" for short. Can we expect these evolved mechanisms to produce the same patterns of behavior in contemporary settings? Unfortunately, the answer is negative. We cannot straightforwardly assume that a single genetic makeup will trigger analogous behavior in radically different contexts. Mental structures evolved in the EEA may or may not have retained their original function. Hence, the underpinning of universal adaptive behaviors, genetic or otherwise, cannot be assumed. It must be established—which constitutes yet another painstaking task.[22]

Upon further scrutiny, the relationship between ecological and social environments from our evolutionary past, and the ones of our contemporary world, is more complex than it is often assumed. "Trophy wives" deficient in manners or intelligence are nowadays more often ridiculed than envied. Modern standards of attractiveness transcend long-term relations or the bearing of children. Many people seek casual or homosexual liaisons. From this standpoint, regardless of evolved psychology, huge variation in sexual behavior across individuals and populations should hardly be surprising. As Dupré (2001) quips, the maladapted mind is perhaps constantly and uncontrollably driven by atavistic urges from a bygone past. The healthy mind, navigating effectively the complexities of modern life, is an altogether different matter.

Critics such as Kitcher, Buller, and Dupré have expressed similar reservations regarding another methodological strategy widely employed across sociobiology and evolutionary psychology: the comparison of conduct among humans and other species. Sociobiologists have frequently been accused—often not without reason—of supporting their conclusions concerning people by appealing to any convenient analogy, no matter how tenuous, to non-human organisms. To illustrate, scorpionflies and ducks figure in discussions of the biological roots of rape. However, the behavior of coupling *Mecoptera* is only loosely connected to human rapists. Evolutionary psychologists are admittedly less reliant on these crude comparisons than are sociobiologists. Still, animal images continue to play a rhetorical role.

---

[22] Smith (2019) further maintains that this task, dubbed the matching problem, is not methodologically feasible, making evolutionary psychology "impossible."

54   THE QUEST FOR HUMAN NATURE

Buss (1994), for one, compares women to weaverbirds who prefer males with desirable nests, and likens men using resources to lure partners to male roadrunners offering up a hard-won kill.

A further common objection to early sociobiology was its massively simplistic account of human conduct. In response, modern evolutionary psychology allows for more nuanced behavioral strategies. In doing so, it exposed itself to the old charge that heavily adaptationist explanations are *unfalsifiable*.[23] Developing this point, Dupré observes how the sociobiological emphasis on heterosexual male promiscuity borders on inconsistency since the total number of matings is identical for males and females. Evolutionary psychologists responded by replacing early monolithic theories of sexual predilections with a repertoire of evolved mating behaviors, such as an appeal to rape as a last-resort alternative. The basic idea is that, in addition to psychological mechanisms promoting pair-bonding, humans have alternative strategies for engaging, under appropriate conditions, in casual sexual liaisons. From a purely evolutionary perspective, it may make sense why men would have evolved this strategy. But why should women cooperate? Evolutionary psychology has a cottage industry of "economic" explanations for female proclivities toward casual sex. These range from women gaining insurance against the provisioning inadequacies of their principal mate, to seeking genes from different sources, to the so-called "self-appraisal theory," where casual liaisons allow women to appraise their "market value" so that they do not sell themselves short. Given the high stakes, we better have strong evidence in support of these claims.

All these considerations reveal how easy it is to concoct evolutionary just-so stories of varying plausibility. The related attempt to accommodate the empirical variability of human behavior has led to the introduction of increasingly flexible auxiliary assumptions. If a behavior is believed to be more or less universal across cultures, the reason must be that it has evolved. If there are exceptions, it is because there is sensitivity to cultural influences. But once cultural influence is allowed to enter the game, any amount of variability will be explicable within

---

[23] For a classic, scathing account of this objection, see Gould and Lewontin (1979).

the paradigm. A theory that explains everything explains nothing—at least until it puts forth successful predictions. Dupré joins Kitcher and fellow critics in concluding that these tales should be treated with caution, especially when a series of alternative hypotheses are available to account for the same behaviors.

In sum, the argument first provided by sociobiology, subsequently refurbished by evolutionary psychology, is less airtight than it initially appears. The charge is not that these conclusions are false. The worry rather is that these explanations may be overly rash and simplistic. With these concerns in mind, to provide a clear and fair assessment of evolutionary psychology, it is important to clarify what exactly is at stake.

First, some readers may be under the impression that criticizing evolutionary psychology is tantamount to questioning that our mind and brain are the product of evolution. After all, what is the alternative, a "non-evolutionary" psychology? This reaction—encapsulated by Anne Campbell's oft quoted quip according to which naysayers believe that "evolution stops at the neck" (2002, p. 13)—completely misses the mark. As we saw in §2.5, sophisticated critics of sociobiology and advocates of alternative accounts hardly ignore the rudiments of evolutionary theory. No serious scholar any longer denies that humans are the product of evolutionary forces. The controversial question is not "Are brains evolved?" but, rather, "At present, can we provide plausible adaptationist explanations of human behavior?" As we have seen, the answer to this latter issue is far from settled.

A second, related confusion concerns the range of available options. Evolutionary psychology is often marketed as the only viable alternative to the old image, harking back to John Locke, that the human mind is an indefinitely malleable *tabula rasa* or "blank slate" ready to be chiseled by culture.[24] To be sure, some twentieth-century scholars have defended the virtual omnipotence of cultural evolution, or have gotten close to it. Without getting bogged down in technicalities, radical forms of environmentalism have been rightly ruled out. Yet, presenting evolutionary psychology as the *only* alternative to a blank

---

[24] This distortion is fueled by both Pinker (2002) and Cosmides and Tooby (2013).

56 THE QUEST FOR HUMAN NATURE

slate poses a false dichotomy. The modularity of mind—debated in psychology[25]—comes on a spectrum, with evolutionary psychology merely occupying one spot, toward the specialization extreme.

Third, no scholar worth their salt claims that all evolutionary psychological hypotheses are bogus. Even firm critics acknowledge that some discoveries are, indeed, interesting and surprising. For instance, there is now strong evidence, based on variants of the influential "Wason selection task," that people are better at performing logical inferences when the subject matter is the application of familiar social conventions, as opposed to abstract rules. In the famous scenario envisioned by Wason in 1966, subjects are shown a set of four cards placed on a table, each of which has a number on one side and a colored patch on the other side. The visible faces of the cards show 3, 8, red, and brown. The question is which card(s) one must turn over in order to test the truth of the proposition that if a card shows an even number on one face, then its opposite face is red. While many subjects tend to struggle in providing a solution, the difficulty evaporates when the same task is posed in less abstract terms, such as making sure that underage kids are not consuming alcoholic beverages at a bar.

Still, there is a wide theoretical gap separating the identification of an intriguing explanandum from the firm postulation of specialized, innate, mental modules dedicated exclusively to the solution of specific tasks. Assume, for the sake of the argument, that evolutionary psychologists are correct in positing—controversial—robust patterns characterizing the behavior of men and women, such as the hypothesis that males tend to prefer somewhat younger females, whereas females tend to select slightly older males. Nevertheless, before inferring the existence of mental modules in males the function of which is to measure the waist-to-hip ratio of prospective female sexual partners with a consistent preference for 0.7, we need stronger, more conclusive evidence. As Dupré (2001, p. 428) aptly puts it:

> This is not, of course, an argument against there being a biological component to what is, certainly, an evolutionary fundamental social

---

[25] See, for instance, Fodor (1983), Anderson (2014), and Zerilli (2019).

A SCIENCE OF HUMAN NATURE? 57

relationship. I do want to insist, however, that the evidence under consideration licenses no compelling conclusions about the innate structure of the mind.

In conclusion, on the colorful sketch provided by Buss, among others, women seek help and resources and thus prefer older men of higher status. Men, in turn, search for beauty—an external cue for high fertility—and fidelity. Both sexes have evolved a host of sexual strategies to achieve their goals. Men are ascribed an evolved tendency to kill unfaithful wives, under appropriate circumstances, to prevent reproductive resources being diverted to an evolutionary rival and to treat women as property.[26] Others, such as Sperber and his collaborators, buy into massive modularity and evolved adaptation without buying into these more or less specific modular hypotheses. But, in general, evolutionary psychology, like sociobiology long before it, sketches a bleak depiction of human beings. If this is who we humans are, we'll come to terms with it. But, given the dire implications of this unfavorable portrait, we better have darn good evidence before throwing in the towel and meekly acquiescing. It's not clear that we're quite at that point, at least as of yet.

§2.7 Revolution or Red Herring?

Time to tie up some loose ends. Fathoming the depths of human body and mind is hardly a new endeavor, harking back at least to Plato, Aristotle, and many of their early commentators. Since then, countless thinkers have attempted to unlock the mystery of who we are, from Augustine to Shakespeare, from Siddhartha Gautama to Wollstonecraft. But it was only in the wake of Darwin's groundbreaking insights that humans began to be viewed as the product of evolution, paving the way for a scientific analysis of human nature. This too was a long-winded process. In the words of a contemporary scholar: "Only within the past few decades have we acquired the conceptual tools to

---

[26] The first example comes from Buss (1994); the second from Wilson and Daly (1992).

58 THE QUEST FOR HUMAN NATURE

synthesize our understanding of the human mind under one unifying theoretical framework—that of evolutionary psychology" (Buss 2019, p. 4). Indeed, several authoritative venues, from the *New York Times* to *Scientific American*, frequently provide a platform for provocative claims about the evolutionary shaping of human agency. Lay readers may thus be forgiven for getting the impression that we now know quite a bit about this topic. But it is worth asking whether we really do.

Sociobiology first and evolutionary psychology later presented themselves as the "new science of the mind" and the "new science of human nature." Echoing this sentiment, in the preface to *The Blank Slate*, Pinker (2002, p. xi) provides a glowing panegyric suggesting:

> [T]he new sciences of human nature can help lead the way to a realistic, biologically informed humanism. They expose the psychological unity of our species beneath the superficial differences of human appearance and parochial culture. They make us appreciate the wondrous complexity of the human mind, which we are apt to take for granted precisely because it works so well. They identify the moral intuitions that we can put to work in improving our lot. They promise a naturalness in human relationships encouraging us to treat people in terms of how they do feel rather than how some theory says they ought to feel. They offer a touchstone by which we can identify suffering and oppression wherever they occur, unmasking the rationalizations of the powerful. They give us a way to see through the designs of self-appointed social reformers who would liberate us from our pleasures. They renew our appreciation for the achievements of democracy and the rule of law. And they enhance the insights of artists and philosophers who have reflected on the human condition for millennia.

Awesome, I'm sold, count me in! So, what exactly have we discovered? In *On Human Nature*, Wilson develops his original insights and articulates a conception of human nature that boils down to three core tenets.[27] First, the key to understanding our nature lies in our genes, which have been shaped by natural selection for most of our evolutionary past with little contribution from cultural processes. Second,

---

[27] For excellent reconstructions of Wilson's argument, especially his conception of the relation between genes and behaviors, see Flanagan (1991, Ch. 7) and Richerson (2018).

these genes powerfully influence our biological and psychological development, regardless of unquestionable variations, individual differences, and personal idiosyncrasies. Third and finally, cultural evolution and the effects of forces such as reason are relatively recent phenomena in our phylogenetic history. Consequently, their effects on our universal architecture are bound to be marginal. We are adapted to past not present conditions. In this sense, humans have been described as having a "stone age mind."

These ideas, originally developed by sociobiologists, remain prominent across evolutionary psychology and cognate fields, from Darwinian anthropology to human behavioral ecology. Once again, Buss (2019, p. 43) is quite explicit on this score: "All species have a nature; that nature is different for each species. Each species has faced somewhat unique selection pressures during its evolutionary history and therefore has confronted a somewhat different set of adaptive problems. . . . All psychological theories require at their core fundamental premises about human nature." As discussed throughout this chapter, evolutionary psychology provides a heavily adaptationist analysis of the human mind as a collection of evolved information-processing modules. The study of human nature has thus shifted focus from overt patterns of behavior to the underlying psychological mechanisms. Setting this subtle—albeit significant—tweak aside, the overarching assumption corresponds to Wilson's original insights. At the same time, critics are quick to point out, evolutionary psychology has also inherited the incendiary rhetoric and methodological flaws of its predecessor. Revolution or red herring? The jury is still out on this one. Nevertheless, some caution is advisable, indeed recommended, a sound piece of advice that is not heeded often enough.

Providing a comprehensive assessment of the successes and limitations of sociobiology and evolutionary psychology transcends both my interest and my professional competence. The crucial issue, from our present standpoint, is whether current science provides the resources for unlocking *human nature* and, if so, what exactly it has discovered. Again, we need to tread carefully as the question is less clear-cut than it may initially appear. We should all agree that humans, like any other species, are the product of natural selection in combination with other evolutionary forces. But what, exactly, is the outcome of this process?

60 THE QUEST FOR HUMAN NATURE

What is this human nature that many authors—from Wilson to Pinker, from Buss to Boyd, to Cosmides and Tooby—enthusiastically point to? The answer is hardly obvious. Intellectual progress requires breaking down overarching slogans into precise testable hypotheses. In a nutshell, we need a working definition of human nature.

Chapter 3 begins the framing of our object of explanation. How should human nature be understood, what does an analysis of human nature purport to capture, and does anything substantive correspond to these accounts? While there are various extant proposals, none of them is unassailable. Confronted with hard challenges in providing a general definition of human nature that is both empirically viable and satisfies its core theoretical desiderata, we'll search for more tractable scientific proxies. Specifically, we'll strive to make some sense of the identification of human nature with a set of "innate" traits (Chapter 4) and the claim that our genetic endowment determines who we are (Chapter 5). Unexpected conclusions await us all along the way. But now I'm already getting ahead of myself. First and foremost, we need to set up our explanatory target. What is this pesky concept of human nature?

3
Is There a Human Nature?

The only thing that one really knows about human nature
is that it changes.
—Oscar Wilde, *The Soul of Man under Socialism*, 1891

§3.1 Charting the Territory

Quick recap of our journey so far. Chapter 1 provided an informal introduction to our main topic—human nature—and its hallowed intellectual history. For a long time, human nature could not be grounded in full-fledged empirical studies. Even proto-naturalistic approaches from the eighteenth century remained rather unsystematic. Chapter 2 discussed the rapid shift in the wake of Darwin's theory of evolution by natural selection, which provided an organizing framework, a springboard for advancing a true science of human nature. By the 1970s various researchers started arguing that, after centuries of relatively unsuccessful philosophical stints at capturing who we are, it was high time for biologists, psychologists, and other natural scientists to take matters into their own hands.

The first structured attempt to explain behavior and culture in naturalistic terms was the discipline of sociobiology. Sociobiologists strived to spell out a macroscopic view of humans, distancing themselves from the overly anthropocentric methodology of traditional sociology and anthropology. Sociobiology viewed the influence of our genetic endowment on our body, mind, and behavior as the gateway to human nature. This approach was explicitly grounded in evolutionary theory. In Wilson's own words, his genetic hypothesis has a "Darwinian heart." According to many of its proponents, sociobiology provided novel,

The Quest for Human Nature. Marco J. Nathan, Oxford University Press. © Oxford University Press 2024.
DOI: 10.1093/oso/9780197699249.003.0003

62 THE QUEST FOR HUMAN NATURE

deeper, more persuasive explanations of significant social conduct like incest taboos and hypergamy.

Undermined by fierce critique, sociobiology morphed into a host of new fields, such as Darwinian anthropology, human behavioral ecology, and cultural evolution. Sociobiology's most direct descendant—evolutionary psychology—retained the adaptationist character of its intellectual precursor but shifted its explanatory target from adaptive behaviors to underlying cognitive mechanisms. From this perspective, the key to unlocking our human nature is pinpointing the adaptive problems faced by our stone-age ancestors. Our mind, evolutionary psychology suggests, is a collection of myriad specialized encapsulated modules adapted to past conditions, as opposed to current ones. Despite this shift, naysayers invite us to ask whether we are just rehashing old mistakes.

As noted, a comprehensive overview—let alone a critical assessment—of evolutionary psychology and cognate fields transcends the scope of this work. My present aim is narrower. Evolutionary psychology, like its predecessor, routinely presents itself as the "new science of human nature." It is only fair to ask whether we finally have a science of human nature. Now, surely, the bombastic slogans of Wilson and his followers should be taken with more than a grain of salt. Mesmerized by elegant prose, it is tempting to blend basic facts about animal behavior and evolution with more contentious tenets. We undoubtedly have lots in common with apes and other phylogenetic cousins. Likewise, biology and culture alike set us apart from them. Still, it is a huge leap to the conclusion that it is our genetic endowment which shapes who we are. This is not to deny, of course, that empirical studies of social behavior have yielded promising results. But the issue of whether and how biology unveils *human nature* is much deeper, more nuanced, and more problematic. If sociobiology's ambitious quest has been successful, what has it discovered? If it is doomed to failure, why has it fallen short? To answer these questions, we need to zoom in and focus more explicitly on our object of study, what it is that we are trying to capture and explain.

With this goal in mind, the principal focus of the present chapter is our pesky explanatory target: human nature. What is it? Does it even exist? The ensuing pages examine three influential views. Our point of departure, in §3.2, is a popular essentialist stance according to which human nature consists of a set of intrinsic defining properties that all and only humans share. Such non-relational essences, it turns out, are quite demanding. Hence, finding an appropriate set of necessary and sufficient conditions for human nature is hardly a promising strategy. §3.3 introduces a suggestive analogy, conceived by evolutionary psychologists to motivate the belief in a shared human nature: the *argument from Gray's Anatomy*. The following two sections consider two ways of fleshing out this preliminary intuition. §3.4 outlines a *natural state model*, according to which human nature is only intended to capture what it means to be a "normal" person. §3.5, in turn, considers an array of *"field guide" conceptions of human nature*. §3.6 concludes by framing the theoretical role of human nature. Field guide conceptions provide a viable, scientifically kosher definition of human nature. Nevertheless, as we shall see, such "thin" accounts fall short of prominent desiderata than any robust, "thick" conception of human nature—especially one purporting to ground accurate empirical descriptions and adequate normative prescriptions à la Chomsky—should satisfy.

§3.2 Essentialist Strategies, Plato to Platinum

Numerous philosophers, as well as scientists across various fields, have asserted that all human beings are fundamentally alike, that we all share one true nature. Recently, as discussed in the previous chapter, it has become fashionable to search for this core sameness in our biology. Yet, what exactly constitutes a "human nature" is seldom articulated. How should this core tenet be parsed?

A tempting preliminary suggestion is to characterize human nature as the *totality of human behavior*. Humans engage in a range of activities. Some people are violent; some are kind; some play chess; some enjoy cooking. Insofar as any of us partake in these occupations, they all belong to our human nature. If my neighbor happens to love watching paint dry, this too is included in human nature. Is this an adequate definition? This is a tricky question. In fairness, anyone is free to define terms as they like. At the same time, one must live with the consequences of such choices. If human nature is characterized as

64   THE QUEST FOR HUMAN NATURE

the totality of our behavior, the concept is deprived of any theoretical meaning. Thus construed, human nature becomes shorthand for life in general and a straightforward implication of the existence of beings like us. It is too broad and all-encompassing to be operationalized, studied, or assessed. For this reason, few—if any—scholars define human nature as the totality of human behavior.

Let's try out something different. Traditionally, the concept of human nature is taken to refer to a proper subset of human traits or conduct deemed characteristically human. What fits this bill? On its standard reading, defining properties must satisfy three conditions. First, human nature refers to *distinctively* human characteristics: a set of features that jointly or individually set us apart from other species. Second, the quintessential human nature must be *universal* within our species, that is, possessed by all humans. Third, human nature is typically taken to refer only to *biological* characteristics. Biological nature is contrasted with cultural influences, viewed as unnatural impositions that transform, repress, or corrupt our identity. This insight has a long-standing tradition, harking back at least to Hume's *Treatise,* where it is argued that human nature must pick out what is "firm and solid" or that which has deep roots in our "internal constitution" regardless of what explains the entrenchment of these traits. This third feature—the biological, non-cultural dimension of human nature—is frequently dropped, since the dichotomy biology vs. culture, nature vs. nurture, has come to be viewed with suspicion in contemporary discussions. Culture is nowadays viewed as just another expression of who we are. Whether kids grow up playing tennis or ice hockey may be the result of the environment in which they are raised. But it can equally be seen as the expression of an ingrained need to play sports and engage in social interactions, as well as individual preference and talent. The re-lation between biology and culture is better described as symbiotic.[1]

---

[1] On the interpenetration of genetic and cultural influences in human evolution, see the debates over cultural evolution from §2.5 (Richerson and Boyd 2005; Lewens 2015b; Henrich 2016; Boyd 2018; Laland and Brown 2011, 2018). For a more general discussion of what Keller (2010) dubs the "mirage of a space between nature and nurture," see also Ridley (2003), Buller (2005), and Tabery (2014). Attempts to resurrect some facets of the distinction between biology and culture can be found in Machery (2008) and Kronfeldner (2018).

IS THERE A HUMAN NATURE? 65

So, following this trend, we'll take a blend of the first two conditions as our preliminary working definition. Human nature refers to features that are *universally* and *distinctively* human.[2] This idea requires some elaboration.

Based on the conception just delineated, human nature corresponds to a set of universal biological or psychological characteristics that define us uniquely as a species. The follow-up becomes whether there are traits or behaviors which are universally and distinctively human and, if so, what these could be. The intuition underlying our preliminary definition of human nature can be cashed out in terms of *essentialism*, the tenet that selected features define membership into kinds. Essentialism has a long and prominent history in Western thought, harking back to Plato's *eide*, ideas. Yet here we shall introduce the doctrine in its contemporary guise. At the most general level, essentialism says that entities belong to a kind just in case they share all the essential, defining features.

Essentialism can be effectively illustrated with examples from chemistry. Suppose that I want to figure out whether the old pocket watch I inherited from my grandfather is really made of platinum. Clearly, it is not enough that it looks, feels, or weighs appropriately. To be sure, I need to consult an expert. What would a jeweler well-versed in atomic chemistry do? Presumably, they will assess the atomic structure of my watch. The rationale is intuitive. All platinum atoms must have atomic number 78. If most molecules constituting my watch have such atomic structure, then, yes, it is made of platinum. The thought is that having atomic number 78 is both necessary and sufficient for a metal to be platinum. As such, atomic number 78 is the essence of platinum. That's where the buck stops.[3]

---

[2] Buller, from whose insightful discussion I am freely borrowing, presents this as the working definition of evolutionary psychology: "In sum, then, according to Evolutionary Psychologists, human nature consists of a set of psychological adaptations that are presumed to be universal among, and unique to, human beings" (2005, p. 423). Whether evolutionary psychologists are committed to such characterization remains controversial (Machery and Barrett 2006). Nevertheless, Buller's conditions capture well a popular vernacular conception of human nature. Hence, in what follows, I take it as such.

[3] I am admittedly and deliberately ignoring isomers and other complications, for the sake of simplicity. As Ramsey (2018) notes, the molecular formula of hematite, Fe_2O_3, does not identify hematite uniquely as it can occur in polymorphs such as maghemite.

66 THE QUEST FOR HUMAN NATURE

Let's focus on essences. In general, an essence is a set of necessary and sufficient conditions for belonging to a kind. One may think of an essence as a universal and distinctive property shared by all and only members of the category in question. At the same time, it is crucial to emphasize that not just *any* universal and distinctive property will do the trick. Consider, once again, the property *being platinum*. Clearly, all and only pieces of platinum have the property of being platinum. Nevertheless, it feels much like cheating to say that being platinum is the essence of platinum. Or take the following suggestion: "x is platinum if and only if an expert would identify x as platinum." If experts are reliable enough, we can suppose that all and only pieces of platinum have the property of being identifiable as platinum by those competent in the field. Again, this does not feel like a real discovery, but a hocus pocus, a cheap trick. Something has gone south. Simply put, true essences are not merely universal and distinctive properties. In addition, they must be *non-accidental* and play an *explanatory* role.[4] Both claims are worth explicating.

Oversimplifying a bit, an "accidental generalization" can be defined as a universal statement that happens to be true but could have turned out to be false. Suppose that my grandfather was an avid watch collector. It so happens that all the watches he bought in 1977 are platinum. This being so, the statement "All watches Grandpa bought in 1977 are platinum" is a true one. But note, while this happens to be true, it could have been false. Pops could just as well have decided to purchase a gold watch that same year without overtly violating any obvious constraint. The generalization "All platinum has atomic number 78" is also a true one. Yet, this is hardly a mere accident. There is some nomological—that is, law-like, necessary—connection between being platinum and having atomic number 78. This law-likeliness allows us to make informed predictions regarding the molecular composition of pieces of platinum, both observed and unobserved.

Moving on to the second desideratum, for essences to be explanatory they must specify what constitutes an entity of the relevant kind. It

---

[4] A seminal discussion of the difference between laws and accident is Goodman (1955). A solid overview of why essences must be nonaccidental and explanatory is Sober (2000).

is not enough for an essence to correctly pick out all pieces of platinum. An essential attribution must also account for what makes a scrap of metal an instance of the platinum kind, a valued member of the precious metals club.

These considerations raise a substantial follow-up. In order to be explanatory along the lines just discussed, must an essence be *intrinsic* to the kind, or may it also be *extrinsic*, that is, relational? Allow me to develop this point further. Let's say that an entity *e* has an intrinsic property *i* just in case whether *e* instantiates *i* depends only on *e* itself, independently of any contextual feature. Thus, for instance, for a person to have a certain mass, height, or two kidneys are all intrinsic properties. In contrast, being a cousin, being shorter than the Eiffel Tower, and being within three hundred miles of the International Space Station are extrinsic, relational properties. To wit, whether I am within three hundred miles of the ISS doesn't just depend on where I am, but also on where the ISS happens to be orbiting at that exact time.

This is pertinent to our present discussion because, as we shall shortly see, it is highly disputed that biological species have intrinsic essences. In contrast, many biologists and philosophers of biology accept that species may well have historical essences of relational ilk. Species are typically classified based on their genealogical nexus, their position on a cladogram, or other sorts of phylogenetic relations. Whether or not historical phylogenetic relations should count as bona fide explanatory essences is an interesting issue that, however, transcends the scope of this work.[5] The important point, for our present purposes, is that all the arguments surveyed in this section are directed against essentialism of the *intrinsic* kind. A discussion of whether a conception of human nature grounded in the evolutionary trajectory of our species is robust enough will be postponed until §3.5.

With this distinction between intrinsic and extrinsic properties under our belts, we can move on to ask if there are intrinsic biological

---

[5] For a discussion of whether species have historical essences, see Griffiths (1999) and Godman and Papineau (2020). The thesis that relational essences lack explanatory power has been articulated by Devitt (2008, 2010, 2023), who advocates a form of biological essentialism that is partly non-relational. Devitt's resurrection of intrinsic multimodal biological essentialism has attracted much criticism (Barker 2010; Ereshefsky 2010; Lewens 2012; Leslie 2013; Slater 2013; Sterelny 2018; Godman et al. 2020).

68 THE QUEST FOR HUMAN NATURE

essences. Specifically, the issue is whether species are "natural kinds" like chemical elements and whether they reflect real, objective categories in the world unified by defining properties. Is belonging to *Homo sapiens* analogous to being made of platinum? To answer this question, we must determine whether there are universal and distinctive biological human features.

Intuitively plausible candidates for intrinsic human essentials include having a circulatory system, breathing oxygen, and digesting food. Unfortunately, none of these characteristics will do. This is because, although all humans allegedly share them, these features are hardly exclusively ours. Many other species have hearts, stomachs, and lungs. Some may therefore be inclined to search for more specific properties belonging solely to humans. Could we point to a uniquely human blood type? Or, perhaps, the ability to speak Korean? This won't work either, as not everyone has the same blood type or speaks Korean. It looks like we've taken a wrong turn. We are looking for a trait, or set of traits, that all humans have and no non-human shares. If these are to be found, it will have to be elsewhere.

The obvious strategy is to look into our DNA. Back in the year 2000, some readers may recall, researchers were finally able to sequence the human genome. This implies the existence of a *human* genome, a genetic sequence that is unique to our species. Maybe that could be our human essence. Let me provide a succinct rejoinder—additional details will be postponed until Chapter 5. The *genome* of an organism can be defined as the entirety of the hereditary information encoded in its DNA—or, for some viruses, RNA—including both coding and non-coding sequences. Each genome is strictly unique. My genome is unlike the one of my goldfish, but it is also different from yours. No two individual humans have the same DNA. The closest it gets is with homozygous twins. But even identical twins will have tiny genetic differences, due to random mutations. This being so, in what sense can we talk about a "human" genome? Well, the brief answer is that, despite the variation just noted, my genetic endowment will be much closer to yours than to the one of my goldfish. And geneticists can abstract these similarities to idealize a prototypical human genome closely resembling the DNA of all humans. Yet, this will not solve our problem. As mentioned above, intrinsic essences are quite demanding.

Similarities ain't gonna cut it. While there are distinctive human characteristics, none of them is *universally* human. Vice versa, while there are universal human properties, none of them is *distinctively* human. Hence, no genetic sequence is shared by all of and only us. More generally, there are no intrinsic essences, no sets of biological traits shared by *all and only* members of a species. Mic drop.

Some frustrated readers will likely protest. Focusing on genetics, they retort, is a blunder. What makes us who we are is not biology but psychology. There surely must be mental traits that are universally and distinctively human. Thus, let's see if we can find a cognitive human essence. On the one hand, it is not hard to think of mental properties that only humans share. No other animal can read, process complex syntax, or learn advanced algebra. Still, not all humans enjoy these capacities. Consider infants, or people who are heavily cognitively impaired, or patients in deep comas. It would be preposterous to exclude all of them from our species. On the other hand, with ingenuity, we could search for some psychological feature that all humans possess—disliking pain, perhaps? But, even setting masochism aside, these features are not distinctively human. Many other species avoid pain. Cutting to the chase, psychology is in no better position than biology. There seems to be no human psychological essence; no set of neurocognitive properties is shared by all and only human beings.

A similar point pertains to social properties. As Hull (1986) anticipated, looking for distinctness and universality intuitively seems more promising in the social sciences than in the natural sciences. But this may just be a function of vagueness. It is hard to maintain that all and only humans have the same blood type or genetic profile because these claims can be—and have been—factually disproven. In contrast, the hypotheses that an organism, human or otherwise, is "rational," has the capacity to lie, or feels guilt are harder to operationalize.

Let's draw some general morals. It is plainly false that all organisms belonging to *Homo sapiens* are essentially the same, in the sense of sharing necessary and sufficient intrinsic properties for species membership. Any character universally distributed across a species is also possessed by other organisms. Conversely, any feature unique to a species is unlikely to be universal across the clade. As Hull (1986, p. 6) elegantly articulates: "If evolutionary theory has anything to teach us

70   THE QUEST FOR HUMAN NATURE

it is that variability is at the core of our being . . . our own essentialist compulsions notwithstanding." Ghiselin (1997, p. 1) puts it even more bluntly: "What does evolution teach us about human nature? It teaches us that human nature is a superstition."

Some remain unconvinced. The problem, a revamped objection runs, is focusing on single traits. We should look instead for *multimodal* distributions, *clusters* of traits. Organisms belong to a particular biological species because they possess enough of the relevant or more important properties. Hull's classic essay preempts this rejoinder too. It is easy to find phenotypic patterns that remain relatively stable across species. Humans, after all, tend to look and behave in a certain way. But these aleatory characteristics, these multimodal distributions, cannot work as intrinsic essences. They do not capture species membership. Clusters of properties, unimodal or multimodal, change over time. Species evolve and both phenotypic and genetic variation are crucial for selection. Diversity exhibited by any species is a function of both regularities, which characterize selection processes, and stochastic historical contingencies. Yet, as Darwin realized, this variation is hardly accidental. Without it, evolution would grind to a halt. "*Which* variations characterize a particular species is to a large extent accidental; *that* variations characterize species as such is not" (Hull 1986, p. 3).[6]

In conclusion, are there unique traits that all and only humans share? Much depends on how loosely we are willing to define them. But none of them constitutes a viable intrinsic human essence. Variation is a core feature of evolution. Hence, if human nature is identified with the idea of a human essence—biological, psychological, social, or otherwise— it is hard to see how there could be a human nature. Should we conclude then that there is no human nature tout court? This would be premature. Let's seek a better definition.

---

[6] If variation is rampant throughout the biological kingdom, some may worry, how is systematics even possible? How does the classification of species deal with variation? A widespread answer is *genealogy*. Any organism that is part of an ancestor-descendant network belongs to that species even if atypical or "aberrant." Genealogy and character co-variation do not always coincide. Still, atypical individuals are members of the species. Conversely, phenotypically similar organisms are not necessarily conspecifics.

§3.3 Gray's Anatomy

The previous section explored the most intuitive, clear-cut, and widespread conception of human nature. From this standpoint, human nature is constituted by the essence of being human, that is, a set of intrinsic conditions that are necessary and sufficient for belonging to our species. These are characteristic properties jointly satisfied by all and only human beings.

Is human nature intrinsically tied to human essence? As anticipated, this is a tricky question. On the one hand, everyone is entitled to define concepts as they wish, as long as they are clear and consistent, without the semantic patrol pulling them over. On the other hand, we need to live with the consequences of our terminological choices. The implications of straight-up essentialism are dire. Echoing Hull, a variety of authors have convincingly argued that no suitable intrinsic characteristic, biological or psychological, is shared by all and only humans. And, even if we were to find one, it would be a haphazard coincidence from an evolutionary point of view. In the end, if human nature is plainly identified with human essence, we must come to terms with the conclusion that either there is no human nature or that several fellow humans who lack the essence, the defining condition, must be excluded from humanity. Neither option is especially palatable.

Almost four decades after the publication of Hull's classic essay "On Human Nature," these observations have become if anything more deeply entrenched. Few scholars, especially empirically inclined ones, advocate forms of biological or psychological essentialism. Does this mean that we need to give up on the existence of a human nature? That would be too rash. Most contemporary authors who purport to study human nature realize that what they are talking about is no bona fide human essence. This should come as little surprise. As we saw in Chapter 2, Wilson wisely steered clear of crude essentialism. The key to human nature lies within our genetic endowment. But no specific gene, set of genes, or sequence of nucleotides is essential for being human. His intellectual disciples, evolutionary psychologists, followed suit, identifying human nature as a collection of evolved psychological mechanisms, without any explicit pretension of characterizing these as individually necessary and jointly sufficient defining properties.

72 THE QUEST FOR HUMAN NATURE

But then the issue becomes: in what sense do genes or psychological mechanisms constitute our human nature? The two ensuing sections cash out two strategies for defining human nature without falling prey to naïve essentialism. Before doing so, however, it will be illuminating to address a preliminary issue. What reasons do we have, from a biological or psychological standpoint, to even believe in a human nature to begin with?

Some evolutionary psychologists offer an intriguing analogy purporting to motivate the existence of a universal human nature: the *argument from Gray's Anatomy*.[7] Human beings, the suggestion runs, share anatomy and physiology. This general "architecture," gradually evolved over myriad generations by the process of natural selection, is what young kids get acquainted with when they learn that humans have two hands, two eyes, two lungs, and one heart. Medical students examine this blueprint in much greater detail. One of the most widely adopted textbooks in medical schools, first published by the British physician Henry Gray in 1858, is titled *Gray's Anatomy*, whence the name of the argument. Incidentally, this is also the origin of the—misspelled—title of the popular TV series.

None of this is especially contentious. The controversial argument in support of a common human nature emerges once we draw an analogy between physical and mental traits. Evolution by natural selection has shaped our bodies. Likewise, natural selection has also molded our minds. Hence, we should expect selection to have designed a system of psychological mechanisms that are just as universal as the anatomical and physiological adaptations depicted in textbooks. And this neurocognitive substrate, the suggestion runs, may well be the very foundation of human nature we have been looking for. This is the gauntlet thrown down by evolutionary psychologists, the driving force behind the argument from Gray's Anatomy.

The idea of a universal human psychological architecture, mirroring our shared anatomical structure, is hardly unassailable. The argument from Gray's Anatomy can be—and has been—challenged on several

---

[7] This analogy was originally advanced and defended by Tooby and Cosmides (1992).

IS THERE A HUMAN NATURE? 73

grounds. Here are five concerns that aim to undermine the simile under scrutiny.[8]

First, the hypothesis at hand—the argument from Gray's Anatomy—is grounded in a parallel between human anatomy and psychology. Some find this connection tenuous. Whereas our anatomy has gradually adapted to relatively stable environments, the objection runs, the human mind has evolved to be responsive to rapidly changing conditions. In addition, most selection pressures on the mind are social, and social pressures are less uniform than environmental ones. Hence, from the observation of a universal human anatomical architecture, we cannot straightforwardly infer the existence of a corresponding psychological one. Further evidence is required.

Second, the argument from Gray's Anatomy gains traction from the postulation of anatomical similarities across people at a relatively broad scale. But uniformity at coarser levels hardly implies uniformity at finer ones. The highly specialized micro-modules posited by evolutionary psychologists are much more detailed than any multifunctional anatomical structure observed in the body that is widely shared across humans. In short, to support the existence of universal psychological adaptations, one would need to provide evidence of psychological uniformity at a grain much finer than the one licensed by the argument from Gray's Anatomy.

Third, an appeal to common anatomy warrants no specific conclusions concerning distinctively human universals. Broad human anatomical structures—like having two eyes or two kidneys—are widely shared across non-human species in the primate order and, in some cases, entire classes of Mammalia and vertebrates. We could perhaps paraphrase this objection as questioning whether we are justified in identifying an overarching human architecture, whether anatomical or psychological, with our own true human *nature*. And the answer to this question remains rather murky.

Fourth, any alleged "universal human architecture" has been shaped during the entire history of our lineage, including ancestors we share with evolutionary relatives. It doesn't follow that any species-specific

---

[8] A version of these five objections is articulated and defended by Buller (2005).

74 THE QUEST FOR HUMAN NATURE

adaptation has emerged during our comparatively recent evolution. On the flip side, if cognitive adaptations have been gradually built throughout our phylogenetic history, it isn't clear why they should be counted as part of our *human* nature.

This brings us to a fifth and final counterargument. Strictly speaking, there is no anatomical or physiological blueprint shared among all and only humans, accurately represented by *Gray's Anatomy* or analogous textbook. The posited structural identity is a useful idealization. When depicted at a finer scale, it becomes evident that we're not all cast from the same mold. Hence, there is no reason to believe in a single psychological blueprint that describes us either, contrary to what evolutionary psychologists would have us believe.

In conclusion, this section examined an influential analogy supporting the existence of a shared human nature: the argument from Gray's Anatomy, as well as five skeptical rejoinders. Assessing its plausibility lies beyond the scope of this work. The relevant observation, for present purposes, is that evolutionary psychology often presents itself as the "new science of human nature." And yet, the presupposed notion of human nature cannot be the strong form of intrinsic essentialism introduced in the previous section. Various authors have revamped Hull's arguments, claiming that the idea of a universal human nature, conceived along evolutionary-psychological lines, is deeply antithetical to a Darwinian conception of our species. It is an old myth whose time has passed and should finally be discarded. This may well be true. But Hull's critique of essentialism is not going to cut it here. Henry Gray, the original author of the textbook, knew perfectly well that not all human beings have two arms or two kidneys. The same can be said about contemporary advocates of human nature. The question becomes how to reconcile the idea of a universal human architecture—anatomical or psychological—with the truism that not all members of *Homo sapiens* fit the bill. The next two sections explore two strategies for addressing atypicality. §3.4 introduces the natural state model. §3.5 discusses an alternative approach, the field-guide conception.

§3.4 The Natural State Model

The issue under present scrutiny is how to reconcile the presupposition of a shared human nature with the observation that no general characterization captures all and only members of our species. There is a simple rejoinder. No definition of human nature worth its salt was ever intended to apply to all and only humans. Concepts such as universal anatomical architecture or shared human nature are only meant to frame *normality*. Individuals with a non-standard number of eyes, toes, kidneys, or chromosomes are deemed "abnormal" because of unusual genetic conditions or exposure to environmental disruption, such as trauma or developmental mishap. The expected follow-up is what exactly is meant by "(ab)normal" in this context.

Before we get going, a brief word of caution is advisable. As we'll see in later chapters, normality, naturalness, and various other cognate notions are slippery matters with a long history of abuse.[9] Non-white ethnicities have been marginalized as degenerate variants of Caucasians. Women have been taken to be incompletely or imperfectly formed men. Homosexuals have been classified as deviant heterosexuals. Some of these prejudices are fortunately a thing of the past. But others are still lurking in modern societies. With this warning in mind, the challenge is to find a scientifically kosher notion of (ab)normality, which vindicates the relevant conception of human nature without legitimizing pernicious, unfounded stereotypes.

There is an old strategy that purports to spell out the idea of normality underlying human nature and reconcile it with the existence of rampant variation within and across species. Simply put, the proposal is to conceive the nature of species as biological or psychological mechanisms that produce the defining phenotypes. Deviation from "normal" appearances is then accounted for as the result of causal interactions between these developmental mechanisms and

---

[9] Detailed discussion of "dehumanizing" uses and abuses of human nature can be found in Sahlins (2008), Smith (2011), Mikkola (2016), and Kronfeldner (2018).

76   THE QUEST FOR HUMAN NATURE

interfering forces. This explanatory strategy, examined in greater detail in the present section, is known as the *natural state model*.[10]

According to the natural state model—which has ancient roots, harking back to Aristotle—each member of a species possesses a causal mechanism, or set thereof, that produces the species' essential attributes, that is, its characteristic phenotype. Left to its own devices, the causal essence of a species invariably produces typical phenotypes. Yet, various factors may interfere with the process, resulting in individuals with abnormal features.

An example should help drive the point home. According to the natural state model, every human possesses a causal essence, a set of developmental mechanisms that in the absence of interfering forces will produce its defining phenotype. This phenotype will roughly correspond to the idealized depiction provided by textbooks such as *Gray's Anatomy*. Without perturbation, everybody would display this same architecture—or to be more precise, the defining blueprint for its appropriate subclass since, on this view, men and women have different phenotypes and correspondingly divergent features. More specifically, what would happen to organisms if we were all raised in the absence of interfering forces? On a radical reading of the natural state model, all members of the relevant class would be indistinguishable. On a more charitable gloss, we would only be identical with respect to defining features, that is, traits belonging to our nature. In what follows, I focus on this weaker, more plausible interpretation of the theory. Yet, clearly, no organism is raised in a vacuum. Minor tinkering will produce slight discrepancies, such as negligible differences in height, skin tags, or other subtle deviations. Occasionally, however, major disturbances will produce a more substantial departure from the ideal: unusual numbers of limbs or digits, missing parts, or severe physical or psychological dysfunctions. "Abnormal" individuals are members of the species, as they have the signature causal mechanisms, the capacity to develop "normally." Yet, the realization of their potentiality is thwarted by traumatic disruptions or interfering forces.

---

[10] My critical outline draws inspiration from Sober (1980)—who, to the best of my knowledge, was the first to introduce the expression "natural state model"—and Buller (2005).

The natural state model has a history of success in science. Consider Newton's first law of motion, the *principle of inertia*: in an inertial frame of reference, an object either remains at rest or continues to move at constant velocity unless acted upon by some force. Now, presumably, no one has ever witnessed an object moving indefinitely at constant speed without being propelled by some force. This is because Newton's law describes only entities in the absence of interference. And no object in the universe satisfies these idealized conditions; everything is affected by forces such as gravitation. Similar considerations apply to Galileo's study of the trajectory of projectiles, or the postulation of perfectly rational agents in neoclassical economics. All these models depict idealized scenarios, absent interfering variables. Can similar explanations be applied to the life sciences? Does the natural state model capture the normality underlying ascriptions of human nature? Unfortunately, squaring the intuition behind the natural state model with current biological wisdom proves trickier than expected.

For starters, the natural state model, in its traditional guise, presupposes a privileged path of development—or, more plausibly, a handful of paths—that results in the "normal" or "natural" state of the organism. All other ontogenetic paths are the result of disturbing forces and, in this sense, "abnormal." The underlying insight is crystal clear: there are natural vs. unnatural ways to be. Having two functioning eyes is natural for humans; having one eye is not. To turn this into a substantive claim, we need to specify what counts as the *natural state* or *normal phenotype* of an organism or species. As we move away from simplistic cases, the association of each genotype with a privileged phenotype becomes increasingly harder to defend. Crudely stated, there's no distinction between natural and unnatural states. What is found instead is developmental plasticity, framed by norms of reaction. Time to introduce these notions and motivate my skepticism.

Our home planet is inhabited by millions of species and billions or trillions of organisms. Each individual comes with myriad qualities: size, weight, color, structure, etc. To keep things manageable, let's focus on one characteristic in a single type: height in a variety of plant, call its species "*s*." What is the "natural height" of plant *s*? A little reflection should convince us that this question is meaningless. The phenotype exhibited by an organism is the result of a complex network of interactions between genes, current phenotypic makeup, and a range of environments. Depending on the selection of environments, the array of phenotypes will change, often quite drastically. This malleability displayed by organisms, called *developmental plasticity*, is captured by graphs known as *norms of reaction*.[11]

The norm of reaction of a genotype *g* is simply a graphic representation that plots the phenotypic variation in an organism *o* with genotype *g* as a function of a change in environments $e_1 \ldots e_n$ in which *o* might survive. To illustrate, visualize the graph (see figure), plotting how a phenotypic variable—height—associated with the genotype of plant *s* fares as we vary an environmental factor: altitude. The diagram shows that this genotype will reach roughly 10 cm of height if grown at 2,000 feet above sea level; 40 cm if grown at 6,000 feet; and over one meter in height above 10,000 feet.

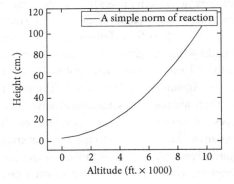

Norms of reaction are conceptually simple and quite informative. At the same time, it is important to emphasize that they are also extremely hard to obtain. Plants are among the more tractable cases, as they are relatively easy to clone: just clip and replant. Still, think about how

---

[11] The concept of *Reaktionsnorm* was first introduced by the German zoologist Richard Woltereck (1909). Since then, norms of reaction have been widely employed in both philosophical (Hull 1986; Kitcher [2001] 2003; Barker 2015) and scientific (Lewontin 1974, 2000) discussions of the relation between genotypes and phenotypes. For current overviews of developmental plasticity, see West-Eberhard (2003) and Gilbert and Epel (2009).

many other variables need to be held constant in order to effectively isolate the contribution of altitude to height: latitude, temperature, soil composition, precipitation, exposure to sunlight, etc. And this will only provide information about how one environmental variable (altitude) affects one phenotypic variable (height) in a single genotype. Things get exponentially more complex in the case of animals, which are much more challenging to control. Figuring out norms of reaction for humans is often the toughest case: for evident ethical reasons, cloning a person for experimental purposes is a hard pass. With this in mind, it should be clear why biologists know rather little about norms of reaction for most species, especially our very own.

Let's set these practical complications to the side, however, and ask whether norms of reaction could in principle supply the notion of normality underlying the natural state model, thereby providing an adequate account of human nature. Suppose that, with painstaking work, we are able to delineate the contours of the norm of reaction for a specific genotype. In other words, we select a certain genotype and meticulously figure out how its corresponding phenotype changes as a function of the environment. The next step is discovering how to read the normal state of such organisms off this information. Going back to our toy example, we have our plant s with its genotype g, and we now know how the phenotypic height of s varies across different environments, across different altitudes. What is the natural state—the normal height—of plant s?

One straightforward solution is to stipulate that normality should be understood statistically, taking as natural the more frequent phenotype produced by the genotype in question. Thus, if, say, 80% of plants of type s fall within the 40–60 cm range, that is the natural state of plant s. As intuitive as it is, this strategy is not especially popular, for obvious reasons. Suppose that a certain strand of corn is routinely grown in a specific region because of its especially high yield. This does not seem to make the abnormally high phenotype in question "natural." On the contrary, this is a paradigmatic case of artificial selection. More generally, statistical frequency does not capture the relevant notion of normality. Blue eyes are statistically abnormal, but they are functionally normal. Conversely, certain minor diseases such as tooth decay may be the statistical normality.

80   THE QUEST FOR HUMAN NATURE

There are two possible routes for refining this preliminary attempt. On the one hand, a more direct path consists in seeking some rationale for privileging some phenotypes as more "normal" or "natural" than others. On the other hand, a slightly more circuitous alternative attempts to provide some independent justification for selecting one or more of the environments listed in the norm of reaction as the "natural" ones. Next, we can specify the natural phenotype(s) for the genotype g at hand as the one that develop(s) in the natural environments(s). Let's address both strategies, in turn.

The obvious move for identifying some phenotypes as more "normal" than others is to cash out biological normality in terms of *functional* normality in the context of an *etiological theory*. Allow me to elaborate and anticipate some considerations that will be developed in greater detail in Chapter 8. According to a popular insight harking back to Wright (1973), the function of a trait x can be characterized in terms of the effects which explain the presence of x via its causal history. A couple illustrations should drive the point home. A spoiler on a race car does several things. It prevents the car from being lifted when traveling at high speed, it slows the car down, it provides a convenient—if dangerously fragile—step stool, it makes the car look slicker, and much else. Still, the function of the spoiler is to increase adherence to the asphalt, as opposed to all the other things it does, because that is the reason why engineers added the spoiler to the car. Once we move from artifacts to natural systems, we can no longer appeal to the intentions of designers. With biological organisms, the solution is to look at *natural selection*. To rehash a well-known example, the function of the heart is to pump blood, as opposed to, say, making noise. This is because pumping is the purpose for which the heart evolved—it is part of its causal history—whereas making noise is a byproduct. Pumping blood is the function of a "normal" human heart.

As we shall see in later chapters, etiological theories, popular as they are, are not universally accepted—they are rivaled by *causal-role* accounts. This is not the place to get bogged down in technical details. The important point for our present purposes is that selected effects, in and of themselves, do not salvage the notion of normality underlying the natural state model from the threat of developmental plasticity and ubiquitous variation. The reason is that etiological accounts, at best, tells us which functions evolved. As such, humans who lack the capacities specified in this causal story will suffer from functional failure. Yet, etiological accounts do not distinguish between more or less natural instantiations of these structures. To see this, consider the following examples. The etiological account will tell us that the function of a peacock's colorful tail is to attract peahens, as opposed to, say, scare predators. However, the notion of developmental plasticity, encapsulated in the relevant norms of reaction, will reveal that there are many phenotypes corresponding to this goal, which will develop in different environments. And none of these phenotypes counts as more "natural" than others, just like no specific height of plant s is more or less normal.

These considerations lead us straight to the second, roundabout strategy for determining the natural state of biological organisms. Suppose we were able to provide some independent justification for selecting one or more of the environments listed in the norm of reaction as the "natural" ones. We could then specify the natural phenotype for the genotype at hand as the one which develops in the natural environment(s). There is an influential route, popular among evolutionary psychologists, for picking out some environments as natural, namely, to identify them as the *environment of evolutionary adaptedness* (EEA), that is, the statistical composite of environments in which the species in question has evolved and to which it is adapted.[12]

Promising as this strategy may appear, it faces several substantial drawbacks. To be clear, the problem is not with the EEA per se. There is nothing inherently muddled or conceptually confused about attempting to learn more about the types of environments where a specific population or species evolved. But characterizing the EEA as more "natural" or "normal" for an associated phenotype feels arbitrary. The EEA is defined as a statistical composite. There is no principled reason for privileging the environment with the highest average fitness over, say, the environment with the higher overall fitness. Furthermore— and this is more generally a challenge for all etiological theories of function—there is no clear rationale for favoring explanations

---

[12] The concept of EEA was introduced by Bowlby (1969, 1973) and subsequently developed by Symons (1979). For critical discussions see Buller (2005) and Downes (2010).

82   THE QUEST FOR HUMAN NATURE

grounded in natural selection over other well-documented causes of evolution, from mutation to recombination to genetic drift.

Confronted with these objections, it may seem reasonable to shift our focus from phenotypes to genotypes or ontogeny. Instead of searching for the natural "state" of an organism or species, we could look for a normal genotype or some normal developmental pathway through which most organisms develop or would develop, if placed in the appropriate context. Cutting to the chase, unfortunately, this won't do either. Switching from phylogeny to ontogeny does not change the refrain. Inherent in norms of reaction is developmental plasticity, the idea of alternative ontogenetic pathways, which will consistently recur as the chapters unfold. To complicate things further, even finding a handful of "natural" genotypes or "normal" developmental pathways wouldn't be sufficient. The natural state model presupposes that, for *every* coding gene, there must be a natural genotype for organisms to have at that locus. This "natural" allele is, of course, the one that contributes to the production of the "normal" phenotype.

Let's start wrapping things up. This section examined an influential strategy for cashing out human nature as capturing the state of a normal human being: the natural state model. Nevertheless, the sheer amount of variation and developmental plasticity found in nature and crystallized in norms of reaction frustrated our initial attempts. Next, we explored the possibility of salvaging the natural state model by appealing to a common human evolved cognitive design. Specifically, the claim is that humans who lack the capacities specified in that design, in the sense developed in etiological functional models, are suffering from functional failure. However, etiological theories fail to provide a naturalized baseline of normality. Similarly, identifying the EEA as determining our natural state faced insurmountable objections. In short, providing a suitable rationale for separating normal from abnormal states appears to be an exercise in futility.

Despite all this, there remains an intuitive aura of "normal development," conceived as the developmental pathway with which we are more familiar in recent, locally prevalent environments. Hull (1986) notes that this has little biological significance. From an evolutionary standpoint, all the alleles a species now possesses were once rare, in fact unique. Developing Hull's insights, others have taken this to show that the natural state model, with its alleged distinction between "normal" and "abnormal" features, has no biological basis. Nothing justifies viewing certain phenotypes, genotypes, or environments as "normal." In Buller's words:

> Therefore, the Natural State Model, on which any distinction between "normal" and "abnormal" human characteristics must rely, has no basis in biology. Nothing in biology justifies viewing certain phenotypes, but not others, as the "normal" phenotypes for a genotype, and nothing in biology justifies viewing certain genotypes, but not others, as the "normal" genotypes for humans. There is substantial variation in human populations at both the phenotypic and genetic levels, and our best biological theories to date simply do not partition that variation into "normal" and "abnormal" variants. (Buller 2005, p. 438)

Echoing Hull, Buller concludes that "there is no such thing as human nature. . . . A truly *evolutionary* science of human psychology will not only abandon the quest for human nature, but, with it, the quest to be a science in the model of physics or chemistry" (p. 457). I'd suggest a more modest conclusion, one which does not pull the plug on human nature, at least not yet. The life sciences do not provide a principled naturalized distinction between normal and abnormal traits, which is precisely what we'd need in order to ground the natural state model.

§3.5 Field Guides

Quick pit stop to fill up our tank and catch our breath. This chapter set out to provide a general outline of various conceptions of human nature. §3.2 kicked off with a popular definition, according to which human nature boils down to a human essence, that is, a set of necessary and sufficient conditions governing membership into our species. Thus conceived, there is no human nature. No single explanatory trait, or cluster thereof, is shared by all and only humans. Nevertheless, the demise of traditional species essentialism does not bring our quest for human nature to a close.

84   THE QUEST FOR HUMAN NATURE

The concepts of human nature stemming from sociobiology and evolutionary psychology are not essentialist, at least they are not explicitly so. Wilson's endeavor is grounded in an application of the "modern synthesis" of genetics and evolution. To be sure, the proposal is hardly uncontroversial.[13] As we saw in Chapter 2, the tenet that our genes hold the key to our nature is in dire need of elucidation—we'll return to it in Chapter 5. Nevertheless, Wilson does not presuppose the existence of any human essence. As such, his view cannot be rejected solely on the grounds articulated by Hull. Similarly, the argument from Gray's Anatomy (§3.3) overtly assumes or supports no biological essentialism. Physiologists are perfectly aware that having the canonical structure is neither necessary nor sufficient for being human. Anatomy textbooks describe "normal" patients. The same goes for psychology books. The burning question is how to cash out a notion of normality that captures relevant commonalities without legitimizing dehumanization.

With this goal in mind, §3.4 described an influential explanatory strategy, the natural state model, which purports to naturalize the relevant concept of normality. Simply put, the idea is that a species' nature can be understood as a set of causal mechanisms, possessed by every member of the species. In the absence of interfering conditions, this causal structure invariably produces the defining phenotype—or, better, the set of defining phenotypes—associated with the species in question. Applied to the specific case of humans, this strategy yields a conception of human nature. Plausible and intuitive as this seems, the natural state model faces some devastating drawbacks making the presupposed notion of naturalized normality difficult to extrapolate. As noted by Hull's "On Human Nature," contemporary biology seems to eschew normality in favor of some form of developmental plasticity. The present section explores a different way of cashing out human nature, one that allegedly disposes altogether with the problematic

---

[13] As Richerson (2018, p. 157) recently observed, "The trouble is that this [Wilson's] picture doesn't offer a principled reason to restrict the operation of cultural processes to a very late phase of human evolution, when it is fairly clear that culture-driven gene–culture coevolutionary processes operated fairly deep into the history of *Homo*, if not throughout the whole history of the genus."

notion of normality. I refer to it as the "field guide" approach to human nature, for reasons that should become clear soon enough.

To appreciate what differentiates the field guide conception from its competitors, it is useful to follow Machery (2008, 2018) in drawing a distinction between two notions of human nature. On the first, *essentialist* conception, human nature is a set of properties that are individually necessary and jointly sufficient for being human. This corresponds to our definition from §3.2. The essentialist ideal is deeply rooted in folk biology: the intuitive body of knowledge about animals, plants, and various other properties and events that people spontaneously rely upon when reasoning about biological matters. Machery acknowledges that no plausible set of characteristics fits this bill. Yet, he continues, there is a second, more promising *nomological* conception of human nature according to which "human nature is the set of properties that humans tend to possess as a result of the evolution of their species" (2008, p. 323). As an illustration, Machery deems bipedalism to be part of human nature. The rationale, of course, is not that all members of our species walk on two legs. We all know that there are people born without legs, who have lost their legs, or who are otherwise unable to ambulate, without this affecting their affiliation to *Homo sapiens*. The claim is rather that

> being bipedal is part of human nature, because most humans are bipedal animals and because bipedalism is an outcome of the evolution of humans. The same is true of biparental investment in children, fear reactions to unexpected noise, or the capacity to speak. According to this construal, describing human nature is thus equivalent to what ornithologists do when they characterize the typical properties of birds in bird fieldguides. (Machery 2008, p. 323)

While Machery (2012) later disavows the analogy with field guides, in my opinion, the label captures quite well the distinctive feats of the general approach. Hence, I shall stick to it.

A few clarificatory points should promptly be emphasized. First, on the nomological conception, traits belonging to human nature are neither necessary nor sufficient for being human. All that matters is that they are possessed by most humans, in virtue of our

86   THE QUEST FOR HUMAN NATURE

evolutionary history. The "most" proviso, Machery notes, rules out bimodal properties, such as traits widely shared by females but not males (ovaries) or vice versa males but not females (facial hair). While it would also be possible to develop a bimodal notion of human nature—field guides, after all, often describe male and female birds separately—Machery opts to focus on psychological and behavioral similarities across all humans. Second, unlike the natural state model, the nomological approach is not a "normative" conception. There is nothing wrong or deficient about a human who lacks some or even all the properties belonging to their nature. Third, Machery claims that Hull's evolutionist arguments, which provide a devastating blow to the essentialist conception of human nature, leave its nomological counterpart unscathed.

Machery's nomological approach to human nature is hardly uncontested.[14] Yet, before discussing critiques and limitations, in the following section, let's first introduce some cognate accounts that, while differing in subtle respects, converge on some core aspects. For this reason, I subsume all these views under the overarching moniker of *field guide conceptions of human nature*. One related proposal has been developed by Ramsey (2013, 2018, 2023), who, like Machery, begins by distinguishing two accounts of human nature:

> One approach—the trait bin approach—holds that human traits fall into two mutually exclusive bins: the nature category and the other category (containing, say, cultural or learned traits). The second approach—the trait cluster approach—takes human nature to consist not in a bin of traits, but in patterns of trait expression. (Ramsey 2018, p. 42)

This should have a familiar ring to it. The essentialist views, considered in §3.2, are a paradigmatic exemplar of a "trait bin" account as they group in the nature bin traits essential to our species. Nonetheless, Ramsey maintains, not all trait bin approaches are essentialist. To wit, he considers Machery's nomological account, previously outlined, as

---

[14] For a critique, see Lewens (2015a, 2015b, 2016). Rejoinders are found in Machery (2012, 2018).

an attempt to rescue a trait bin approach from the pitfalls of essentialism. According to Machery, a trait falls into the human nature bin if and only if it is possessed by most humans and is a product of evolution. This, Ramsey argues, is unsatisfactory. It is the whole idea of a trait bin account that should be disposed of.[15]

What is Ramsey's alternative? It is dubbed the *trait cluster approach to human nature*. The guiding insight is that traits simpliciter fall neither within nor outside of human nature. Instead, human nature lies within the patterns of expressions of the properties. Ramsey first defines individual nature as the patterns of expression of an individual's features over its set of possible life histories. Thus construed, individual nature encompasses patterns within and across individual life histories, providing the foundation for human nature broadly construed:

> Consider the individual nature of each human. If we were to combine the possible life histories from each individual's nature, then we would have human nature as the patterns of trait expression over the totality of extant human possible life histories. (Ramsey 2018, p. 49)

I shall not belabor the differences between Machery's nomological conception, Ramsey's trait clusters, and related proposals in the current literature.[16] Similarly, I will not assess their relative merits and competing edges of one over the other. I want rather to focus on their overarching commonalities. Both accounts explicitly eschew any essentialist tendency. In addition, contrary to the natural state model, their approach does not provide a normative conception of human nature, in the sense that they do not purport to specify any evaluative notion of normality beyond mere statistical frequency. For this reason, I classify them both as *field guide* conceptions of human nature: definitions that, like field guides for naturalists, describe and

---

[15] "Machery's account was challenged on the basis of how it attempts to sort traits into the human nature bin. His approach has problems generated by including only majority traits, and by excluding traits that are clean of evolutionary influence. I suggest that it is not just Machery's rendering of the trait bin approach that is problematic, but the approach itself" (Ramsey 2018, pp. 44–45).

[16] As Ramsey (2018) notes, his "cluster conception" bears some analogies with other analyses of human nature, such as Griffiths (2009), Samuels (2012), and Cashdan (2013). Remarks going along the same limes can also be found in Godfrey-Smith (2014).

88   THE QUEST FOR HUMAN NATURE

explain evolutionary and, more generally, biologically salient features of human beings.

Before moving on, I briefly examine one more related account of human nature. In a recent monograph, Kronfeldner (2018) spells out

> a post-essentialist, pluralist, and interactive account of human nature. The account is post-essentialist since it eliminates the concept of an essence, which has traditionally been attached to the idea of a human nature; it is pluralist since it defends that there are in the world different things that correspond to three different kinds of post-essentialist concepts of a nature of humans; it is interactive since, first, nature and culture interact at the developmental, epigenetic, and evolutionary levels and, second, since humans repeatedly create parts of their nature via classificatory and explanatory looping effects. (p. xv)

This post-essentialist, pluralist, and interactive account, Kronfeldner maintains, captures and revises four traditional pillars of human nature—specificity, typicality, fixity, and normalcy—thereby addressing traditional challenges. Somewhat surprisingly, after devoting the better portion of the monograph attempting to clarifying what is left of human nature, Kronfeldner concludes that it may well be advisable to flat-out eliminate the expression "human nature" from our scientific vocabulary. All the pluralistic replacements for old, discredited, essentialist notions could abstain from the language of human nature without significant loss of meaning—a thesis that we shall explore in later chapters.[17]

Kronfeldner's study goes on to discuss three overarching hurdles for human nature—dubbed the "dehumanization," "Darwinian," and "developmentalist" challenges, respectively. The second portion of the work aims to craft a scientifically kosher, post-essentialist surrogate that successfully addresses these challenges, as well as discussing some normative implications. It should be clear, even from this cursory

---

[17] Other eliminativist proposals that suggest eschewing the term "human nature" altogether include Griffiths (2002), Lewens (2016), Laland and Brown (2018), and Sterelny (2018).

summary, that pigeonholing such rich discussion as a "field guide" approach would be unduly narrow. Nevertheless, Kronfeldner's proposal does overlap quite substantially with the accounts of Machery and Ramsey. Specifically, they all steer clear of dangerous "dehumanizing" uses pertaining to normative views of "normality" in favor of naturalized descriptions. For this reason, I classify all these approaches as field guide perspectives.

In conclusion, this section showed that it is possible—indeed advisable—to outline a scientific conception of human nature that steers clear of both the widespread albeit problematic essentialist characterizations and the normative undertones of the natural state model. I clustered these alternative definitions under the "field guide" moniker, as they all treat our nature as a general description of humans akin to the one provided by field guides. The field guide analyses discussed here are not immune from controversy. Critique includes both friendly fire, that is, objections from cognate proposals, and worries from authors who view the search for human nature as a bankrupt endeavor to be abandoned altogether. I opted not to discuss the pros and cons of specific proposals. Rather, in the next, concluding section, I focus on two general issues: what we want a notion of human nature to accomplish and whether any of the approaches discussed so far can attain all these feats.

§3.6 Through Thick and Thin

The notion of human nature is shrouded in mystery. Scholars from various fields vehemently argue over this hallowed concept and its momentous implications. Such controversies notably do not align neatly with disciplinary boundaries. The contours of the dispute do not trace conventional subdivisions, such as science vs. humanities, genetics vs. evolution, or natural vs. social sciences. This goes to show that disagreement about human nature is more complex, nuanced, and multifaceted than academic monoliths. With these considerations in mind, let's return to the issue that kindled our discussion throughout this chapter, namely, where there is a human nature. This question cannot be meaningfully posed, let alone addressed, without first settling

90   THE QUEST FOR HUMAN NATURE

two preliminary issues: what human nature is and how it should be characterized.

Providing a set of adequacy conditions for a theory of human nature is a thorny endeavor. For one thing, different authors are likely to disagree on what such a concept is intended to accomplish and if it even exists. Furthermore, no one has the authority to impose their own constraints, especially on a topic with a rich and diverse history like human nature. Hence, let's focus on what is expected of such a theory. As mentioned at the outset of §3.2, the notion of human nature has traditionally been used to refer to universally and distinctively human features. The further requirement that such traits be biological as opposed to only cultural is better replaced by the condition that properties belonging to human nature must be explanatory.

These preliminary considerations can be molded into three general desiderata for any theory of human nature. First, human nature should pick out a set of traits that is *universally* human, shared across the entire species. Second, these traits should be *distinctively* human, in the sense of providing a comparison and contrast between *Homo sapiens* and other species, capturing what makes us similar to and different from them. Third, a concept of human nature should be *normative*, in the sense that features classified as part of our nature should contribute to an explanation of our physiology, culture, ethical status, or other aspects of humanity that we deem valuable and worth emphasizing. Borrowing a distinction from ethics, let's call *thick* those concepts of human nature that purport to satisfy all three conditions, while reserving the label *thin* for those definitions that drop one or more of our three desiderata.[18]

It is crucial to emphasize that the three requirements of universality, distinctiveness, and normativity are conceptually independent, in the sense that whether a specific property satisfies one of them has no bearing on whether it satisfies the other two. Consider the following

---

[18] The distinction between "thick" evaluative concepts, which combine evaluative and non-evaluative descriptions, and "thin" purely evaluative concepts was introduced by Williams (1985). It should be evident that, by allowing "thin" concepts of human nature to be purely descriptive, completely dropping the evaluative dimension encapsulated in the third normativity requirement, I am departing slightly from Williams' original account.

examples. Synthesizing carbon is a human universal that is hardly diagnostic of humans, applying to all forms of life on this planet. Having human parents is both universal and distinctive. Linguistic ability is a distinctively human feature that is not universal. Whether any of these properties has normative value ultimately depends on whether we take carbon synthesis, human ancestry, or linguistic ability to have explanatory welter with respect to our ethical or biological status as humans. With these considerations under our belts, let's move on to ask how the three families of theories of human nature discussed throughout this chapter fare with respect to these core features.

First, we explored the widespread tenet that human nature coincides with a human essence, that is, a necessary and sufficient set of intrinsic conditions for being a specimen of *Homo sapiens*. Traditional essentialism provides a thick definition of human nature that satisfies all three of our desiderata. For starters, essences are, by definition, universal, since any organism that lacks said essence would thereby not count as human. By the same token, essences are distinctively human since any organism or AI system satisfying conditions essential for being human is thereby human. In addition, essences are meant to explain both our phenotypic appearance and normative status. In short, traditional essentialism provides a simple, straightforward, and clear-cut definition of human nature that satisfies all traditional desiderata. No wonder it is such a popular option.

Alas, such precision carries a burden. Amid the rampant disagreement surrounding human nature, one of the rare points of consensus that emerged over the past few decades is that there are no species essences. As Darwin and Wallace already observed, variation is ubiquitous across the biological kingdoms. This holds at all levels, from the hereditary to the behavioral, from the phenotypical to the genotypical. Hull echoed this in the 1980s: if any property is essential across all biological species, this may well be variability. To be sure, *which* particular variation we exhibit at any specific moment is largely a function of evolutionary happenstance. *That* we do, however, is hardly haphazard. These considerations undermine both stronger and weaker strands of essentialism. The former take essences to be sharply defined as sets of jointly necessary and sufficient non-relational conditions for belonging to a kind. Weaker forms of essentialism identify species membership

92 THE QUEST FOR HUMAN NATURE

with reasonably large multimodal clusters of these properties. In short, if human nature is identified with human essences, there is no human nature. Cut the pie any way you like, both biological and psychological essentialism are essentially dead and gone.

What implications does the demise of essentialism have for human nature? If human nature is inextricably tied to essentialism, it too follows suit and goes down the drain. This may not be such a terrible conclusion to draw. Perhaps organisms and species need not have a nature at all. Echoing Hull, many have come to view human nature as a legacy of a bygone age, an outdated chimera that has overstayed its welcome. Furthermore, as mentioned, it is a notion that is dangerously ripe for dehumanization and other forms of abuse. It can be used to entrench what, in fact, is very much amenable to change. There is a real risk that we generalize as part of human nature tout court what is typical of only a subset of us, and accidentally so. The presence and effects of such distortions have been experimentally validated. Psychologists are now aware of the biases triggered by the exclusive use of Western college students as experimental subjects when drawing conclusions about humanity in general.[19] All these considerations suggest that it may well be high time to put to rest our long-standing quest for human nature.[20]

At the same time, the outright rejection of human nature together with essentialism might be tantamount to throwing the baby out with the bath water. Authors such as Chomsky, Lewontin, and Pinker have pointed out that some notion of human nature is all but indispensable in the social sciences. In the second half of this book, we shall witness firsthand how difficult it is to talk about racial identity, human rights, gender equality, functional normality, and the boundaries of a quality human life without an underlying human nature, or some surrogate notion. Hence, pace Hull, it looks like we may need some viable account of human nature, after all, one that distances itself from the

---

[19] For an extensive discussion of this point, see Henrich et al. (2010); Henrich (2020).

[20] Or, as Lewens (2018, p. 9) puts it, more mildly: "These worries do not threaten the very idea of human nature, but they do remind us of the hurdles that need to be cleared before we can confidently make claims about what is typical of humanity in general."

strictures of traditional essentialism. With this possibility in sight, we moved on to consider two alternative conceptions of human nature.

One approach is embodied by the *natural state model*, which fuels the intuition that human nature captures the contours of *normality*. The underlying idea is that human nature—or, more generally, the nature of any species—consists of a set of causal mechanisms that, in the absence of interfering conditions, would invariably produce the defining phenotypes associated to the species at hand. The natural state model wisely acknowledges that finding a set of properties that is both universally and distinctively human is a hopeless endeavor. The clever rejoinder is to replace both desiderata with a condition of normality or *typicality*. Every organism is associated with a "natural state," a phenotype corresponding to the way the organism would develop if we idealized away all disturbances. The resulting conception of human nature remains a thick one, as the natural state model grounds qualified notions of universality and distinctiveness, as well as normative conclusions about what humanity ought to be and why it matters. The issue with this proposal is that the relevant notion of human nature cannot be straightforwardly naturalized. Finding a notion of normality that boils down to biological theory and practice is arduous, arguably impossible. Hopes of developing a science of human nature fade accordingly.

Third and finally, we explored a more modest "field guide" conception of human nature, which drops any pretense of normativity in favor of a descriptive account akin to an anatomy textbook or ornithology manual. The guiding thought here is to give up the anachronistic taxonomic project of formulating a catalogue of traits that are found in all and only humans or in "normal" people. This, nevertheless, is perfectly compatible with the assumption that some properties—psychological, physiological, or anatomical—are present in most of us and that evolutionary processes explain why those properties became and remain so prevalent within our species. From this standpoint, the claim that trichromatic vision is an element of human nature commits one to nothing more than an assertion of its widespread presence and an underlying evolutionary rationale.

Both the natural state model and the field-guide conception go hand in hand with the insight underlying the argument from Gray's Anatomy

94   THE QUEST FOR HUMAN NATURE

developed by evolutionary psychology. Anatomy textbooks do not purport to describe all and only human beings. Differences are idealized or abstracted away to generate a prototypical, "normal" human. This is useful, indeed indispensable, for pedagogical purposes. Similarly, generic depictions reproduced in ornithology manuals provide non-experts with an effective, ready-made tool to distinguish, say, blackbirds from starlings. The same approach could be applied to human beings to create a field guide which may turn useful to intelligent alien visitors checking us out. Despite the truism that all organisms, from starlings to humans, are unique, textbooks and field guides do their job and do so quite well. They wield diagnostic power in the face of rampant variability. Perhaps human nature should follow suit.

There is, however, a key difference between these two ways of cashing out the argument from Gray's Anatomy. The natural state model provides a thick account of human nature. Field guides, in contrast, settle for a "thin" conception: a perspective that is anti-essentialist, non-normative, and co-dependent with culture. This is their chief source of attraction. By adamantly disavowing essentialism, they bypass Hull's objections grounded in variability. By eschewing any normative overtone, they steer clear of the pitfalls of the natural state model, which fails to naturalize the relevant notion of normality. In addition, critics of normativity will point out that this is a point in their favor, as any discussion of functional normality and statistical typicality is a gateway to marginalization and other forms of discrimination. Now, to be sure, most advocates of the natural state model have no such discriminatory goals in mind. Yet, as the proverb goes, the road to hell is paved with good intentions.

At the same time, the field guide's main strength turns into its Achilles' heel. Trading in essentialism and normativity for evolutionary history sets the stage for a viable, scientifically kosher notion of human nature. But it may end up giving up too much. No field-guide conception can provide the foundation for all the important work prescribed by Chomsky. It remains doubtful that such a thin characterization can capture all the distinctive features of a bona fide concept of human nature, especially one intended to ground social science and social change.[21] To do so, we need a stronger normative underpinning.

---

[21] On this note, see also Lewens (2015a, Ch. 4) and Lewens (2015b, Chs. 4 and 5).

In conclusion, let's return to our guiding question: is there a human nature? The answer depends on how human nature is construed. Understood as a human essence, no, there is no human nature. Conceived as a field-guide-like cheat sheet summarizing the diagnostic features of humans, yes, there clearly is a human nature. However, this is unlikely to provide a solid foundation for normative and descriptive discussions in social science. For this, we are in dire need of a thicker, more robust characterization of human nature. No other suitable candidate is in sight. One charitable moral that can be drawn from our discussion is that the very concept of human nature is too broad, too vague, and too slippery to be addressed head-on. Is it possible to break the overarching theme down to more precise, tractable topics? This, I suggest, is where we should focus our attention. To this effect, the next stops in our joint venture, over the next two chapters, will be innateness and genetic determinism.

4

What Makes a Trait Innate?

> Accuse not nature: she hath done her part;
> Do thou but thine.
> —John Milton, *Paradise Lost*, 1667

§4.1 Hardwiring and Responsibility

Let's regroup. Our point of departure, back in Chapter 1, has been the methodological issue of how to investigate the notion of human nature, with its hallowed history. Chapter 2 introduced some modern research projects purporting to develop a science of human nature: sociobiology and its intellectual heirs, among which evolutionary psychology is the most vocal. Wilson and his followers maintain that the key to our nature lies in our genetic endowment, gradually shaped by natural selection throughout our phylogenetic history. We should all agree that human beings, like all other biological species, are the product of evolutionary forces such as natural selection—although the readiness of sociobiologists and evolutionary psychologists to embrace adaptationist paradigms and to draw socially relevant conclusions from them should raise a few eyebrows. Nevertheless, it remains unclear what these evolutionary stories purport to capture. What is the intended outcome of a "science of human nature"? The target of explanation was scrutinized in Chapter 3. The most clear-cut answer is that a science of human nature should pinpoint a human essence, that is, a set of universally and distinctively human properties. Unfortunately, thus construed, there appears to be no such thing as human nature, as a non-trivial set of intrinsic properties shared by all and only humans is nowhere to be found. A more promising rejoinder is that human nature purports to capture what it means to be a *normal* or *typical*

The Quest for Human Nature. Marco J. Nathan, Oxford University Press. © Oxford University Press 2024.
DOI: 10.1093/oso/9780197699249.003.0004

human, along the lines of an anatomy textbook or field manual. The natural state model provides an influential implementation of this strategy. Nevertheless, the notion of a natural state assumes a biologically kosher, naturalized notion of normality, which is much thornier to develop than it initially seems. As we shall see in later chapters, science does not explain normality; it presupposes it. Alternatively, we can conceive of human nature along the lines of a field guide, a manual for readily identifying members of our species based on evolutionarily salient traits. The drawback of such "thin" characterizations is that they are incapable of much normative heavy lifting.

The present chapter, in conjunction with the following one, explores a possible way out of this impasse. Skeptics and supporters alike agree that "thick" conceptions of human nature are broad, vague, and slippery. Tackling them head-on yielded mixed results. There seem to be just too many conflicting assumptions, intuitions, and expectations concerning who we are and what exactly the experimental studies should capture. This suggests breaking down human nature into more tractable topics, proxies better amenable to empirical inquiry. With these considerations in mind, Chapter 5 will set out to ask whether human nature could be identified with a set of genetically determined traits. Before doing so, the current chapter brings the concept of *innateness* onto the main stage. The presupposed connection between innateness and human nature should be intuitive. The traits constituting our nature coincide with innately human traits. But this notion of innateness calls for elucidation. Etymologically, "innate" simply means "inborn." Our query can thus be rephrased as asking on what basis we determine whether a feature is inborn or innate.

Before delving into the thick of things, let me spend a few preliminary words motivating why readers, including those without a vested interest in cognition, should be intrigued. Talk of innateness, much like genetic determinism, is hardly confined to technical scientific debates. Pop-science books and newspaper articles regularly advertise alleged discoveries that traits such as violence, racism, religion, and intelligence, are "innate," "genetically determined," or "hardwired." These terms are often treated as synonyms. But, in order to fully grasp the meaning of these claims and what exactly is at stake, we need to shed some light on these notions and their interrelations.

98 THE QUEST FOR HUMAN NATURE

Non-specialist audiences seem captivated by the alleged innateness of human characteristics, especially socially significant ones, such as greed, altruism, and violence. Why the obsession? The main reason, I surmise, has to do with *responsibility*. Dubbing a trait "innate" takes moral and sociopolitical responsibility away from the rest of us. Now, as we shall promptly see, labeling a property "innate" does not ipso facto entail that it is fixed or hard to change. Still, many find it enticing to infer from the premise that members of a particular community, ethnicity, or group are born violent, that there is little to nothing that we can do to stop them from expressing this tendency. In contrast, the argument runs, if these people have become aggressive because of the environment where they are raised—education, social status, or lack thereof—then we too could be blamed for failing to adequately curb such manifestations. One may even argue, heaven forbid, that society owes these groups an amelioration of their subpar conditions.

If these preliminary remarks are on the right track, it is not hard to envision why innateness plays such a pivotal role in human nature and cognate debates. Consider once again Wilson's characterization of human sociobiology. His original project was grounded in an attempt to establish how the core features of human nature are shaped by our biological endowment, in relative independence of culture. Yet, as we shall see in Chapter 5, cashing out the claim that a trait is "encoded in our DNA" is by no means trivial. The relation between genotype and phenotype is indirect and complex. Depending on how exactly it is construed, the claim that our nature is at root genetic may swing from being an obvious platitude to an overhyped exaggeration. Still, one could say, the crucial observation underlying Wilson's insight is not that who we are depends directly on our genetic inheritance. The core tenet rather is that our nature is something we do not acquire. It is part of us from the very beginning of our lives. This is the hypothesized link connecting innateness with human nature. The aim of this chapter is to sharpen this relation and develop it more systematically, an endeavor that will pose several conceptual challenges.

Here are some distinctions that should be kept on the back burner in the course of the ensuing discussion. First, there are *semantic* questions about the concept of innateness. What does it mean to claim that a specific trait is "innate"? Does the term have a univocal definition, or does it assume different hues in different contexts? Specialists from various fields talk about innateness, and so do many non-specialist readers. Are all these people talking about the same thing when they refer to innateness? Second, there are *methodological* issues. Is the notion of innateness scientifically acceptable or should it be rejected? In talking about innateness, are we asking about how the term is, in fact, used, or how it should be used? Is our discussion of innateness predominantly a descriptive one or a normative, prescriptive one? Third, and finally, there are challenges concerning the *scope* of the concept at hand. Which traits are innate? Are there many innate traits, or only a few? Are there any innate traits at all?

The current chapter is structured as follows. After some brief stage-setting remarks in §4.2, §4.3 delves into our main course: innateness. Rather than kicking off the discussion by proposing what innateness could be, I begin by considering what innateness is *not*. Specifically, we'll present some popular definitions and emphasize why, despite shedding light on the pesky and elusive concept of innateness, all of them fall short of a comprehensive and adequate analysis. Where does this leave us? §4.4 considers some influential arguments purporting to show that in the end we might be better off eschewing the concept of innateness altogether. §4.5 blazes a different trail. Instead of pursuing a definition of innateness, we shall provide an overview of contemporary empirical evidence about the innate human cognitive endowment, a feature often referred to in psychology as *core knowledge*. The mainstream view in cognitive developmental psychology—humans possess multiple psychological capacities and are born with a substantial amount of innate knowledge—leaves room for learning and cultural influence alike. §4.6 wraps up with an overarching summary connecting both innateness and core knowledge with human nature.

§4.2 Two Kinds of Scientific Questions

Hypotheses involving innateness play a pivotal role across various scientific fields. These presuppositions are especially prominent in the cognitive sciences, where innateness is introduced to explain a broad array of psychological phenomena, such as intelligence, facial

100 THE QUEST FOR HUMAN NATURE

recognition, language learning, mathematical skills, and folk-physical concepts of cause and effect.[1] Interestingly, despite their pervasiveness, it remains obscure and controversial how these theoretical assumptions, and especially their appeal to innateness, ought to be parsed.

Quibbles with innateness are hardly novel, going at least as far back as Plato's discussion of *anamnesis* (recollection) in the *Meno*. Still, the debate, in its current guise, was shaped in the seventeenth and eighteenth centuries. Oversimplifying a bit, early modern philosophy followed two different paths regarding the nature, extent, and justification of knowledge: empiricism and rationalism. The original dispute between these two epistemological stances concerned whether we have inborn knowledge about the world and its structure. Rationalists held that some of our knowledge is gained pre-birth. Empiricists, in contrast, held that all concepts are acquired postpartum, by a mind that comes into the world as a tabula rasa, a blank slate. Descartes championed innateness. Locke—who deemed the notion of innateness meaningless, teetering on incoherence—repudiated it. Over time, the debate shifted from a dispute about the *causes* of beliefs and knowledge to an epistemological feud regarding the *justification* of knowledge. Are all our beliefs accounted for by experience, or are some warranted by "pure reason" alone? According to rationalists, reason can be a route to true knowledge, independently of experience. In contrast, empiricists insisted that experience is the only source of finding out what the world is really like. In the nineteenth century, Francis Galton, a cousin of Darwin, reframed this debate in terms of the biological distinctions between nature vs. nurture, separating traits into innate vs. acquired.

Setting these historical roots aside, providing a satisfactory account of innateness has become all the more pressing in the twentieth and twenty-first centuries. One reason is that the emergence of novel experimental techniques, especially in the field of developmental neuroscience, has made it harder to determine what should count as evidence for or against innateness. In addition, as we shall see, the very

---

[1] For a discussion of the role of innateness in psychology, see Samuels (2004) and Khalidi (2016).

notion of innateness has frequently come under attack from scholars who view it as scientifically unnecessary, conceptually confused, and bordering on incoherence. Such considerations concern cognitive scientists, who aim to characterize our innate cognitive endowment with a strong motive to clarify the notion of innateness on which such inquiries build and depend.

Before moving on, I should address a preliminary methodological objection. Some frustrated readers may feel a bit befuddled by our stalemate. Why is our intellectual quest proving so darn thorny? It shouldn't be so difficult to figure out whether a trait is innate or part of our human nature. The point of approaching these questions experimentally was precisely to avoid getting bogged down in philosophical quagmires. What has gone south? To appreciate what's going on, it is helpful to draw a distinction between two different kinds of scientific questions: empirical vs. conceptual ones.

On the one hand, *empirical* questions are inquiries that can be addressed, more or less directly, by investigating the world around us. Here, we already have a well-formed question. What we lack is an answer or, perhaps, a strategy for figuring out the solution. A simple example should help drive the point home. Consider the aim of finding out which gene is responsible for the sickling of red blood cells in patients affected by Sickle Cell Anemia. Such a task presupposes a lot of biological theory. We need an operational definition of "gene," a characterization of pathologies with genetic triggers, techniques required to sequence DNA and individuate genes, and much else. With all of this under our belts, we then need to scrutinize the world and come up with a clear answer. Doing so may well be very difficult. It requires lots of tedious, painstaking experimental work, taking up much time, energy, and resources. But we know perfectly well what we are seeking. The real challenge is how to obtain a solution to the puzzle at hand.

On the other hand, there are scientific questions of a very different ilk. I like to call them *conceptual* because the theoretical framework required to address them cannot be presupposed, as we could in the case of "empirical" queries. It must be spelled out explicitly for the inquiry to even get off the ground. To illustrate, take a deceptively simple question that we shall discuss in greater detail in Chapter 5: what is a gene? Contrary to the previous empirical endeavor—the search for the

102   THE QUEST FOR HUMAN NATURE

gene responsible for the sickling of red blood cells—in the conceptual case, we cannot merely assume that we have a preliminary definition of "gene" guiding our research. We must spell out and defend a specific conception of what a gene is, without presupposing any preconceived answer. Otherwise, the conceptual question would make no sense. We are on the hunt for concepts which will then be employed in subsequent empirical projects.

I should emphasize that both sets of questions—empirical and conceptual—are *scientific*, in the sense that both kinds of inquiries are an integral component of the scientific enterprise. Sure, conceptual questions overlap with philosophical and more theoretical endeavors. But it would be a crass mistake to allow science to offload semantical issues to conceptual analysis, a crucial error that plagued logical positivism as it emerged early in the twentieth century. With all of this in mind, it should become clear that the issues presently under scrutiny—from human nature to innateness to genetic determination—are paradigmatic examples of conceptual questions: scientific, not empirical (in the above sense), and deeply theoretical. As such, we cannot provide a straightforward factual yes-no answer. We are knee-deep in philosophy.

§4.3 What Innateness Is Not

The previous section set the stage by outlining the historical origins of contemporary discussions of innateness, as well as drawing an explicit distinction between scientific questions of two ilks: empirical vs. conceptual. Our current task—providing a viable account of innateness—belongs to the latter category. The present section considers some influential strategies for analyzing innateness. As we shall soon discover, finding an adequate and informative definition is trickier than it may initially appear. Following the lead of Samuels (2004), I individuate three general strategies for characterizing innateness based, respectively, on common sense, biology, and psychology. Each of these families encompasses various proposals. Let's examine them, in turn.

The first set of definitions purports to make more rigorous the commonsensical notion of innateness implicit in our everyday usage of language in mundane non-technical settings. This can be done in various ways. One straightforward suggestion is to characterize innateness as *non-acquisition*. From this standpoint, innate traits are simply not acquired. For instance, I never learned how to breathe, making this capacity innate. The shortcoming of this suggestion is that, upon further scrutiny, it turns out to be vacuous. There are lots of different notions of acquisition, many of which are metaphorical or allusive, and it is far from clear which ones, if any, are relevant for capturing innateness. We are thus trading in one vague concept for another.

We need to make "acquisition" more perspicuous. But doing so is hardly trivial. To wit, consider the following proposal. A characteristic c is acquired by an individual i if and only if there is some period t_n when i has trait c, and a time t_{n-m} when i does not. Nice and clean-cut. The drawback is that, in this minimal sense, virtually all traits turn out to be acquired and none is innate. As Locke himself foresaw, it is easy to find some point in time, sufficiently early in development, when individuals lack any candidate for the trait c in question: language, limbs, breathing, and so forth. In short, this minimal notion is too minimal, trivializing the entire proposal. Something more is needed to characterize innate traits. What could this x-factor be?

The obvious rejoinder is to add temporal constraints. For instance, for a trait to be considered innate it must be present at birth, being literally "inborn." Plausible as this appears at first, presence at birth is strictly speaking neither necessary nor sufficient for innateness, at least based on pretheoretical intuitions. Growing evidence of various forms of prenatal learning—environmental influences on a baby in the womb—show that many traits typically not classified as innate may be present before birth. Instances include learning to distinguish the voice of the mother from other auditory signals or preferential engagement with face-like visual stimuli. Conversely, already Descartes anticipated, features widely considered "innate" may occur at later stages of development. Secondary sexual characteristics, such as the growth of pubic and facial hair, are prime examples. A more speculative illustration involves the canalization of emotions, which may not yet be complete at birth.[2] As a rejoinder we could always revise our

---

[2] For experimental data on prenatal learning, see Webb et al. (2015) and Reid et al. (2017). A discussion of the canalized emotions hypothesis can be found in Izard (1991).

104   THE QUEST FOR HUMAN NATURE

intuitions and decide to count traits learned in the womb as innate and the capacity to grow pubic hair as acquired. But this would lead to a radical departure from the standard meaning of innateness.

A different commonsensical intuition characterizes innate features as the product of causal interactions "internal" to the organism, as opposed to "external" or environmental ones. Innate traits are produced "internally." Thus stated, the definition is overly simplistic. As we shall discuss in Chapter 5, even the staunchest nativist—that is, advocate of innateness—must acknowledge that all traits, anatomical and cognitive, are jointly caused by a blend of internal and environmental factors. Still, many nativists ascribe a privileged role to internal processes in the development of innate traits, relegating environmental factors to triggers or background conditions. This privileged role calls for clarification. Unfortunately, common sense is of very limited help here.[3]

In conclusion, common sense does not offer any viable definition of innateness. This should not be surprising. Although innateness has become a prominent fixture in everyday parlance, it remains a predominantly technical concept. Hence, let's look at its role in the sciences. We'll address, in turn, two obvious candidate fields: biology and psychology.

Our second family of definitions draws inspiration from the life sciences. One enticing suggestion is to spell out innateness in terms of genetic determination. The guiding insight—which harks back to Lorenz—is that a certain feature c in a particular organism is innate just in case c is determined by genetic factors alone. But this presupposes a precise conception of genetic determination. While I defer a comprehensive discussion of this central issue to the following chapter, we can provisionally distinguish two traditional routes. On the one hand, *causal* accounts view a trait c as genetically determined if and only if c is caused, in some appropriate way, by genetic factors. On the other hand, *representational* strategies, favored by Lorenz himself and developed in greater detail by Maynard Smith, take a trait c to be genetically determined when c is encoded in the genome.

---

[3] A scientifically updated version of this view is Northcott and Piccinini (2018). I do not discuss in detail this revamped approach, as it is not directly connected to human nature.

WHAT MAKES A TRAIT INNATE? 105

As Chapter 5 will make clear, neither strategy is devoid of problems. The main issue undermining the causal approach is that virtually no trait is produced by genes alone. Phenotypic and behavioral traits alike depend on a complex interaction of genetic and non-genetic factors. No one, thus far, has been able to characterize precisely the causal relation between genes and phenotypes in a way that privileges certain traits as determined or innate. Similarly, Lorenz and Maynard Smith's thesis that innate features are those "represented by" or "encoded in" the genes equally calls for elucidation.[4] There is a pretheoretical and relatively unproblematic sense in which DNA inscribes a coded representation of proteins (§5.2). But, since the vast majority of traits causally covary with both genetic and environmental factors, specifying exactly how genes represent complex phenotypic traits and cognitive structures remains an arduous, wide-open challenge.

None of this should be all that shocking, especially given our discussion in previous chapters. The relation between genotype and phenotype is best captured not directly, but in terms of a norm of reaction (§3.4). As we shall see in §5.3, genetically determined traits too can be characterized as having a flattish norm of reaction. From a similar standpoint, it might be possible to construe innateness as a sort of *developmental invariance*—an alternative biological definition. While invariance-based accounts differ in detail, they all share the core insight that a phenotypic trait counts as innate for a given genotype if that phenotype will emerge in all—or, more plausibly, in an appropriate range of—environments, roughly, the "normal" environments for organisms with the genotype and phenotype in question.

Invariance accounts have significant virtues. They capture the intuition that innate traits must be developmentally stable, quasi-universal, and possessed by all "normal" members of a species. Still, they are not flawless.[5] For one thing, as noted in §3.4, cashing out a biologically kosher notion of normality—applying to genotypes, phenotypes, or environments—is quite the challenge. Furthermore, this proposal has the unpalatable consequence that the same trait can be both learned *and* innate. Consider traits that are highly invariant only because the

---

[4] For details, see Maynard Smith (2000), Griffiths (2001), and Godfrey-Smith (2007).
[5] These problems are discussed in Samuels (2004).

106 THE QUEST FOR HUMAN NATURE

environmental conditions required to learn them are ubiquitous. For instance, most human beings acquire the belief that the sky is blue. Quasi-universality and stability hardly make this mental state "innate."[6]

A third, related biological conception defines innateness in terms of *high heritability*. While the notion of heritability—with all its advantages, caveats, and limitations—will be covered in detail in §5.4, the guiding thought is that a trait c can be classified as innate if and only if variation with respect to c within a population of reference is disproportionately due to genetic differences, as opposed to environmental ones. The main attraction of this proposal is that it preserves the intuition that innate traits are in some way determined by the genes, while dodging the above problems with causation and representation. Still, high heritability does not seem necessary for innateness.[7] To wit, consider traits, such as opposable thumbs in humans, which are very near fixation. Heritability is standardly defined as the proportion of overall phenotypic variation that is due to genetic variation, that is, Vg/Vp (§5.4). It follows that, where there is no phenotypic variation at all, as in the case of opposable thumbs, the denominator Vp is zero, and the heritability of the trait is thus undefined.

In sum, sketching a satisfactory, uncontroversial account of innateness based on its explanatory role in biology is more difficult than

---

[6] An invariance-based definition of innateness is offered by Sober (1999). A variant employs *canalization*: a trait t of an organism with genotype g is dubbed "innate" to the extent that t's development is insensitive to the range of environmental conditions under which t emerges (Ariew 1996, 1999; Collins 2005; Garson 2015). By requiring that the development of innate traits is insensitive to environmental variation—as opposed to merely invariant across environments—this formulation avoids the previous objections. Yet, it threatens to trivialize the debate (Samuels 2004). The worry is that assessments of canalization depend on what sort of environmental variability one takes as relevant to the process at hand. This, in turn, depends on the explanatory interests of those who employ canalization in the first place. The concern, in other words, is that disputes over innateness reflect differences of explanatory emphasis. Similar accounts have been offered in terms of entrenchment (Wimsatt 1999), triggering (Khalidi 2007), and closed-process invariants (Mallon and Weinberg 2006). Finally, I should also acknowledge that, strictly speaking, Garson (2015) does not analyze innateness in terms of canalization. Rather, Garson proposes to replace innateness with canalization. Thus construed, this becomes an eliminativist proposal, along the lines discussed in §4.4.

[7] See, for instance, Ariew (1996), Sober (2000), and Garson (2015). In addition, as noted, heritability and norms of reaction are two sides of the same coin. The hurdles of defining innateness in terms of one concept will apply, *mutatis mutandis*, to the other.

WHAT MAKES A TRAIT INNATE? 107

expected. Before throwing in the towel, let's consider a third family of strategies which looks at the role of innateness in psychology and cognitive science.

An intuitive suggestion is to provide a scientific refinement of the commonsensical thesis, discussed earlier in this section, of innate traits as acquired, that is, "not learned." This strategy, which harks back to Plato, seems promising when applied to many psychological properties. The capacity to learn a language is a good candidate for an innate human feat, from this standpoint, as it is not something we learn, in any meaningful sense of the term. In contrast, the specific natural languages we apprehend—English, Japanese, or Suomi—depend on environmental exposure. Still, nagging concerns linger. For one thing, this proposal yields counterintuitive results when it is applied to traits outside of psychology. A sunburn on the skin is clearly not learned, except perhaps in a metaphorical sense. Yet, it is clearly not an innate trait either. More seriously, the term "learning" itself turns out to be almost as murky as "innateness," and cognitive science does not seem to have any clear-cut suggestion for refinement.[8]

A final proposal worth mentioning has been advanced by Samuels (2002, 2004), who develops some insights from Cowie (1999). Samuel's suggestion is that a set of mental structures is innate, roughly, if they are not acquired by cognitive or psychological processes. The insight underlying Samuel's *psychological primitivism* is that innate cognitive structures are the ones whose acquisition cannot be explained by psychology. To be sure, this does not mean that these traits cannot be explained tout court. They may be accounted for at a neuroscientific, anatomic, physiological, molecular, or some other lower level. The

---

[8] For modern applications of innateness to psychology, see Fodor (1981) and Cowie (1999). General problems with learning and acquisition are discussed by Mameli and Bateson (2011). In this psychological context, it is also worth mentioning the *triggering* approach to innateness, pioneered by Stich and developed further by Khalidi (2007). On the triggering account, innateness is construed in dispositional terms. An innate cognitive capacity is one that has a disposition or tendency to be triggered based on an environmental input that is impoverished by comparison to the resultant cognitive capacity. While connected to the "canalization" view mentioned in the context of biological approaches, Khalidi explicitly acknowledges that his view is not intended to apply more broadly than cognitive science. The main question confronting triggering accounts is whether triggering itself constitutes a robust scientific concept. This is an objection that will be addressed in §4.4.

108   THE QUEST FOR HUMAN NATURE

point is that if x is innate for psychology, then x's acquisition cannot be explained within the boundaries of psychology itself.

Samuel's account has notable advantages. For one thing, it handles well many difficulties that plague its main competitors. It does not tie innateness to pre-theoretic notions of not-acquired, inborn, or internal. It does not presuppose any loaded concept such as genetic determination, traits coded in the genes, invariance, or high heritability. It does not identify innate traits with cognitively not-learned ones. In addition, Samuel's proposal frames two central issues in psychology and cognitive science. First, it delimits the scope of psychological explanation. Once we know that a given structure is innate, we ipso facto know that our current psychology cannot be expected to explain how it was acquired and that we must instead look to biology or some other science for an explication. Second, discovering which structures are innate also furnishes us with the resources, the "building blocks," from which to construct developmental psychological theories.

At the same time, as Samuels himself openly admits, thus crudely stated, psychological primitivism will not quite do. One difficulty is that the account presupposes some appropriate distinction between psychological-cognitive levels and other levels of scientific explanation. Although it is often assumed in cognitive science that some such distinction exists, where exactly to draw it is far from straightforward. Even more seriously, in its present form, the proposal overgeneralizes by incorrectly characterizing some cognitive structures as innate—for instance, psychological effects resulting from environmentally induced brain lesions, such as the effects of a car accident.[9]

Samuels' (2004) rejoinder is to add a *normalcy* condition to his account: a cognitive structure is innate for a given organism only if the organism would acquire it in the "normal" course of events. Adding such a clause seems like the right strategy for addressing the overgeneralization problem, as the troublesome cases are clear instances of abnormal development. It does, however, come at a cost. As discussed in §3.4, providing a naturalized notion of normality is no simple matter. As Samuels himself acknowledges, the problem is not germane

---

[9]   Other issues with Samuel's view are surveyed by Khalidi (2007) and Linquist (2018).

to the cognitive sciences. The task of providing a precise definition of normality is no more pressing in psychology than it is in other areas of science, from genetics to evolution to economics. True that. But a widespread problem constitutes a problem, nonetheless. Hence, as it stands, Samuels' proposal remains subject to trivialization worries. In addition, and even more important from our standpoint, appealing to normality feels a bit like cheating. Presupposing a notion of normality would fix most problems with all other analyses presented above. We did not allow it earlier. Why would it suddenly become acceptable?

Taking stock, this section examined various proposals for defining innateness, grouping them in three categories depending on whether they are grounded in common sense, biology, or cognitive science. While all these analyses shed light on innateness and its connections to human nature, none seems to capture fully these concepts. Does this mean that there is no innateness? §4.4 presents an influential "eliminativist" view that purports to eschew innateness altogether. Next, §4.5 reviews some of what developmental psychology has revealed about the structure of the human mind and invites us to ask what role innateness plays in such explanations. Onward!

§4.4 Eschewing Innateness

§4.3 emphasized a shift in meaning among competing definitions of innateness spanning various fields. "Innateness" denotes features as diverse as traits present at birth, behavioral differences produced by genetic variation, adaptations shaped during the course of evolution, canalized developmental pathways, properties shared by most members of a species, non-acquired instincts, distinctively organized behavioral modules driven from within, or it could be a primitive concept unexplainable within the contours of a field. Each proposal sheds light on some aspect connected, more or less loosely, to innateness: a popular belief, a methodological research strategy, a classificatory scheme, or a preliminary intuition. Yet, none of these analyses appears broad and perspicuous enough to provide an adequate definition of innateness, fully capturing how this concept is applied across disciplines.

110   THE QUEST FOR HUMAN NATURE

There are several candidate explanations for this breadth. Perhaps innateness has different meanings in different contexts. Or an appropriate overarching definition may not yet have been found. This section examines an alternative "eliminativist" diagnosis, according to which innateness is a hybrid notion that ought to be purged from scientific and ordinary parlance alike. This idea has been spelled out by Griffiths (2002).[10] Let's take a gander.

Griffiths maintains that the concept of innateness is confusing because it conflates various independent properties. More specifically, innateness bundles together three core ideas. The first is the notion of a *species nature*. Innate traits are frequently taken to reflect what it means for an organism to belong to a certain species, with associations to universality or, better, typicality. Applying this insight to *Homo sapiens*, human nature is intended to capture what it means to be a human being and what is universal or typical for humans (§3.2). Second, innateness is associated with *intended outcome*. Innate traits, from this standpoint, capture how a normal organism is supposed to develop (§3.4). To lack these traits is to be malformed or dysfunctional. This normative dimension is often associated with natural selection. Innate traits are those that an organism is designed to possess, based on its genetic blueprint. The third and final notion standardly associated with innateness is *developmental fixity*. Innate traits are taken to be insensitive to environmental stimuli in development. In this sense, innate traits are "hard to change" because doing so would disrupt or impair the development of an organism. Griffiths claims that these three broad ideas—species-typicality, intended outcome *qua* product of adaptive evolution, and insensitivity to environmental factors—are empirically dissociated from and conceptually independent of each other. Is this true? If so, is a theoretical construct that covers them altogether useful or desirable? We now address both questions, in turn.

To appreciate why conflating these concepts may trigger confusion, let's focus on their interrelations. Consider, first, species nature, understood in terms of typicality. (Whereas Griffiths talks about

---

[10] Related proposals include Mameli (2008a), Keller (2010), Bateson and Gluckman (2011), Mameli and Bateson (2011), Shae (2013), Garson (2015), and Kronfeldner (2018). A response is provided by Khalidi (2016).

WHAT MAKES A TRAIT INNATE? 111

"universality," I switch to "typicality" since, as we saw, the former notion is overly demanding.) The standard notion of typicality conflates two distinct features: monomorphism and panculturalism. A trait t is *monomorphic* in species s if all—or, more plausibly, the vast majority of—members of s express the same phenotype for t. To illustrate, the inability to synthesize vitamin C is monomorphic in *Homo sapiens* because it is common to all of us. In case you were wondering, no, this characteristic does not constitute a plausible human essence, in the sense discussed in §3.2, as it is not distinctively human, being common to most *Haplorhini* primates. In contrast, a trait is *pancultural* just in case it is found in all cultures. For instance, Wilson's incest taboos discussed in §2.3 are allegedly pancultural. Importantly, while all monomorphic traits are pancultural, the converse does not hold.[11] Many pancultural traits are polymorphic, existing in multiple variants. Hair color, for instance, is pancultural, but comes in different hues: black, blond, ginger, and so on. In short, broad-brush appeals to generality or typicality fail to draw the distinction between traits that are monomorphic or pancultural.

Neither form of typicality—monomorphism or panculturalism—is tightly connected to adaptive evolution or intended outcome, the second core feature of innateness. Evolution by natural selection is perfectly capable of producing both polymorphisms and monomorphisms. Conversely, non-adaptive evolutionary mechanisms, such as developmental constraints, may also produce monomorphic traits. To wit, the reason why there is no land-dwelling animal the size of a blue whale is not that smaller size is necessarily adaptive. Rather, an organism that heavy living on land would be crushed under its own weight. Similarly, as any evolutionist worth their salt knows, evolved traits need not be pancultural. In short, innateness unduly conflates the distinct notions of species nature and intended outcome.

Along the same lines, Griffiths notes, both species nature and intended outcome should be kept distinct from developmental fixity, the

---

[11] Strictly speaking, the inference from monomorphic to pancultural depends on whether monomorphism is defined over a species, as I've done, or over a population. In the latter case, it is possible for the allele and corresponding phenotype to become fixed in one population but not another, making the trait in question polycultural. To keep things simple, I shall assume that monomorphism is defined over entire species.

112   THE QUEST FOR HUMAN NATURE

third remaining core feature of innateness. There is no intrinsic tendency for evolved adaptive traits to be buffered against variation in environmental inputs to development or to become typical, let alone universal, in species.

In sum, Griffiths maintains that the conceptual core of innateness conflates elements that are better kept separate. These considerations raise intriguing follow-ups. Wherefrom does the notion of innateness originate? Why did people start referring to certain characteristics as "innate"? Griffiths persuasively argues that the concept of innateness is an expression of *folk essentialism*—the intuitive, prescientific postulation of biological essences. Widespread and intuitive as it is, folk essentialism is false and inconsistent with Darwinism. It should thus be rejected. And yet, it is a widespread cognitive trait, likely pancultural, and possibly a canalized outcome of cognitive development. Thus, attempts to stipulate a new, restricted meaning of the term "innateness" are unlikely to be successful. The goal should be to formulate a more accurate understanding of living systems, not preserving folk-biological assumptions. The use of new, neutral terms for each of the three properties is preferable to the retention of the term "innate" for one or more of them. Let's explore this proposal in greater detail.

First and foremost, we need to clarify the meaning of *folk biology*, an expression which ambiguously refers both to pre-scientific thought about the animate realm and to the field which studies it. Folk biology is chiefly investigated by cognitive anthropologists, who set out to describe and explain allegedly pancultural patterns of reasoning about the living world transcending cultural specificity, and by cognitive psychologists who study the emergence of these patterns of reasoning in children as well as their manifestation in adults.

Research in folk biology has produced intriguing results. To wit, it has been discovered that children think in distinctive ways about the living world. Kindergarten-age kids believe that each organism possesses some unobservable property that explains its distinctive observable features, and which preserves its identity through change. For instance, youngsters in that age group will maintain that if a raccoon is made to look like a skunk, it will nevertheless retain its essential raccoon-nature. While the details of these psychological inferences remain to be determined, what is clear is the prominent essentialist explanatory strategy found in folk biology.[12]

Griffiths concludes that folk essentialism clutters several biological notions, such as the pre-Darwinian concept of species, the concept of innateness, and, more generally, the concept of human nature. Folk biology considers essences as shared by all and only members of a species. It presupposes a natural-state-like model of variation of the kind discussed in §3.4 where variants are viewed as deviations from an "ideal" type. From this standpoint, essences strive to realize themselves. A trait linked to an organism's essence will thus tend to reassert itself when the distorting interference preventing its development is removed. Suppose that having stripes is essential to tigers. Yet, because of a forced dietary change, Tigger the tiger loses its stripes. The striped pattern is expected to reappear as soon as the distorting influence, the nutritional interference, is relaxed and the tiger returns to its "normal" diet. Furthermore, essences have normative overtones so that variant individuals are not merely different but perceived as deviant. Organisms who stray away from their natural state are not as healthy and flourishing as their "normal" counterparts, and no good can come of such deviation from the "natural" course of things.

The essentialist conception of species is a central feature of folk biology. Yet, as a *scientific* theory, it has been refuted. This should not be overly shocking, given all the problems with essentialism surveyed and discussed in Chapter 3. Contemporary taxonomists, ecologists, and other evolutionists have developed various definitions of biological species. All these concepts emerged smoothly from the pre-scientific practice of categorizing organisms into folk species. But we have moved away from it. Folk-biological species are conceived in terms of underlying essences shared among all and only members of the species and which unequivocally determine the true nature of the individual. This is the typological perspective that Darwin had to displace in order to establish the gradual transformation of one species into another from a

---

[12] There is considerable controversy regarding the specifics of this essentialist pattern of inference (Carey 2009; Strevens 2019). Do young children have a full-blown "theory" of living things or a simple set of beliefs regarding species' essences? Is this inference specific to biological domains or is it broader? In the context of this work, we can set these technical debates aside.

114 THE QUEST FOR HUMAN NATURE

single or small set of common ancestries. While the debate on biological species continues, virtually all contemporary evolutionists agree that species are not types to which individual organisms more or less imperfectly conform, but abstractions from the pools of overlapping variation that constitute the actual populations of a species. This is the perspective that Mayr dubbed "population thinking."[13] In short, the simplistic taxonomies provided by folk biology provide fast-and-frugal heuristics. Non-specialists can use them to interact effectively with the plants and animals common in their region because, at most times and places, species are sharply separated from one another. Still, the scientific limitations of folk taxonomies emerge with clarity when working at larger geographical and temporal scales.

With all of this in mind, we are finally in a position to piece together Griffiths' critique of innateness and, derivatively, of human nature. As we saw, folk essentialism—the intuitive, prescientific conception of species—implies a belief in unobservable essences shared by all and only members of a species. These essences explain the normal characteristics of the species in question. They reassert themselves when these core features are tampered with or otherwise disrupted. Any deviation from them is viewed as "abnormal," not merely in the sense of being statistically atypical. Departure from normality marks an individual who is deficient, normatively wrong, lacking some core aspect. This cluster of interrelated ideas, applied to *Homo sapiens*, can be conveniently summarized and conveyed via the traditional essentialist concept of human nature, which also becomes synonymous or quasi-synonymous with the innate features that characterize our own species. As Griffiths (2002, pp. 80–81) himself puts it:

> The idea of human nature is, I suggest, the application of folk essentialism to our own case. Human nature is also a near synonym for the *innate* features of human beings. If you give [a] popular-science talk and assert that, for instance, addictive behaviour is part of human nature, you can count on your audience interpreting this to mean that addictive behaviour is innate. It is hard to change, found in all

---

[13] For a discussion of typological vs. population thinking, see Mayr (1959) and Sober (1980). A recent overview of the species debate in biology is Nathan and Cracraft (2020).

cultures, and so forth. Conversely, if something is innate, then it is at least reasonable to refer to it as a part of human nature. I think this is true even of diseases that are described as innate. We are "naturally" disposed to suffer from some diseases, such as those of old age. If innateness differs from human nature it is, perhaps, in having weaker normative overtones. I conclude, then, that the vernacular concept of innateness is also an expression of folk essentialism.

Given these considerations, should we continue employing the notion of innateness? Griffiths answers in the negative. He argues that the innateness concept has promoted and continues to foster a conflation of biological properties that, as animal behavior studies conclusively showed decades ago, should be kept distinct. Innateness allows writers, especially in more popular venues, to shift from the view that a trait has an adaptive history to the claim that said trait is insensitive to environmental influences in development. Discussions of rape and sexual jealousy, commonly found within the evolutionary psychology literature surveyed in Chapter 2, insinuate that we are forced to live with these aspects of "human nature" despite the clearest theoretical commitment by evolutionary psychologists to the dependence of evolved traits on the developmental environment. Similarly, developmental fixity is seen as a precondition of evolutionary explanation despite massive evidence to the contrary. Universality—in either of its senses: monomorphism or panculturalism—is taken to be the hallmark of adaptive evolution. Hence the efforts devoted by some evolutionary psychologists to documenting universality and by social constructionists to documenting cultural differences. The continuing use of theoretical concepts such as innateness and human nature, Griffiths goes on, are responsible for the conflation between all these distinct biological notions and illicit inferences from one to the other. For all these reasons, innateness should go, and human nature should follow suit as rapidly as possible.

Some readers will likely protest. The history of science, the objection runs, is replete with errors, blunders, and mistakes of all sorts. Sure, there are cases where a faulty concept has been eliminated from our ontology: phlogiston, caloric, celestial spheres, and ether are all well-known examples. But this is hardly the norm. To wit, the term "atom" literally means "indivisible," which is how the concept was defined, from its ancient Greek origins all the way through classical Newtonian mechanics. And yet, when physicists discovered that atoms can be broken down into smaller, more fundamental constituents, the reaction was not to discard the concept wholesale. Rather, the definition of atom was revised, such that nowadays atoms are no longer taken to be indivisible particles. Something similar could be done to salvage innateness, revising the concept as opposed to flatly eliminating it.

Griffiths preempts this objection with an interesting rejoinder. Of course, he notes, it is possible to redefine "innateness" to make use of only some limited portion of its connotation or restrict it to more specific contexts. Still, all three core features of innateness are biologically relevant. Hence, no matter how "innate" is redefined, different terms will be required to refer to the aspects of the concept excluded by such stipulation. Indeed, each of these three broad ideas needs to be further subdivided to mark critical conceptual distinctions. Furthermore, and even more significantly, innateness is a concept that has transcended the domain of science and has pervaded common parlance, constituting a highly intuitive way of thinking about living systems. This extant connotation acts as a catalyst that draws new, revamped technical definitions back toward its established meaning. Indeed, we already have terms expressing these ideas more precisely. If a trait is found in all healthy individuals or is pancultural, then say so. If it has an adaptive-historical explanation, write that. If it is developmentally canalized with respect to some set of inputs or is generatively entrenched, claim that it is so. If the best explanation of differences among a certain trait in a certain population is genetic, call this a genetic difference. If we mean that the trait is present early in development, we can simply state as much. These simple adjustments could prevent methodologically reflective colleagues from misusing the term "innate." Nonetheless, hardly anyone implements them. We keep talking about innateness and human nature, generating confusion as well as perpetuating pernicious stereotypes. We might then be better off pulling the plug. It's not clear—yet—what there is to lose.

Time to take stock. This section explored an influential argument suggesting that the concept of innateness should be discarded. Indirectly, this could also put an end to futile discussions of human nature. These, Griffiths argues, are hybrid concepts that only foster confusion and perpetuate mistakes. They have no place in science and should have no place in everyday parlance either. But not everyone is ready to heed Griffiths' call. After all, the widespread use of innateness and human nature in the biological and cognitive sciences may well mean that these concepts play a prominent role, a baby that we would not want to throw out with the bath water.[14] To address this concern, the following section presents some insights that contemporary psychology has shed on the structure of the human mind.

§4.5 Core Knowledge

§4.3 surveyed candidate definitions of innateness. Common sense identifies innateness with traits that are not acquired. From a biological perspective, innateness has been frequently connected with genetic determination, canalization, and high levels of heritability. In cognitive science, innateness is associated with traits that emerge independently of any active process of learning and with a notion of psychological primitiveness. While this sheds light on what it means for a specific trait to be innate, all these definitions fall short of an adequate and fully satisfactory account of innateness per se. Quilting these insights into a precise analysis remains an open challenge. Next, §4.4 explored a notable attempt to rid us of innateness altogether. Although it would be possible, in principle, to eliminate references to innateness in both scientific and common jargon, in practice this is unlikely to happen, at least for the foreseeable future. Innateness is too deeply rooted in our thinking for it to be set aside and replaced by more perspicuous expressions.

---

[14] A reaction to Griffiths along these lines is found in Khalidi (2016), who argues that when there is significant continuity between a scientific concept and a lay concept, retention should be privileged over elimination. As should become clear in later chapters, I am quite sympathetic to the idea that concepts such as innateness or human nature are too entrenched to be discarded. Nevertheless, I am also skeptical that these notions can be "naturalized" by providing a scientific explanation, in biological or psychological terms. Hence, I shall develop my own reaction to eliminativism in due course.

118 THE QUEST FOR HUMAN NATURE

We must now clarify how innateness is connected to human nature. What does embracing innateness entail? What would go missing by eliminating this notion? What concepts could replace it? This section argues that our current conception of the mind is best viewed as falling within the pitfalls of two extremes: radical nativism vs. blank-slate-like conceptions. Following psychological nomenclature, I dub this intermediate position a form of *core knowledge*.[15] Determining the respects in which core knowledge is analogous to and different from innateness and human nature will prove useful in assessing the role played by these concepts in contemporary theories of the mind.

Traditional cognitive science has been dominated by two conceptions of human nature. On one view, the human mind is a flexible and adaptable mechanism for discovering and predicting regularities in experience. This position traces back to British empiricists like Locke, who popularized the conception of the mind as a tabula rasa. To be sure, no scholar worth their salt takes this "blank slate" image literally. At best, it is a suggestive metaphor. Still, the strongly empiricist image of the human mind as a single learning system that copes with all the diversity of life remains vivid. Indeed, it has been invigorated by cognitive psychologists and neural network theorists. On a second, competing stance, our mind is a collection of myriad special-purpose mechanisms, independently shaped by evolution to perform a particular function. This latter model, inspired by the work of Darwin and subsequent developments in evolutionary biology, gained prominence and its clearest statement in sociobiology and, more recently, evolutionary psychology.

Before moving on, it is important to address a preliminary nagging concern. Does it matter which model of the mind one adopts? If so, why? The short answer is that the choice at stake deeply affects explanations of human behavior. As I have tried to emphasize throughout the book so far, the impact of these questions transcends purely academic disputes. Much public discussion has focused on the diverging ways in which these views account for human conduct. Does a certain portion of the population—say, a given gender or ethnic

---

[15] The label "core knowledge," as well as much else in this section, is borrowed from Spelke and Kinzler (2007).

subgroup—excel in the study and application of mathematics because its members have worked more diligently, because they have access to better schooling, or because they have inherited greater talent and aptitude? Do adolescents join violent gangs because they have learned aggressive behavior from their communities, perhaps exacerbated by unfair sociopolitical conditions, or because they possess a biological predisposition toward intergroup competition? Behind these specific questions lurks a more general concern. To what degree can human beings determine their fate and choose their own future? With enough training and cognitive effort, can every person develop their mathematical talents and control their aggression? Answering these questions presupposes a clear stance on the nature and structure of our mind. This is why these debates matter and do so crucially.

Once we agree on the significance of these questions, we can move on to ask which psychological model is the better one. Should we view our minds as single, general-purpose learning systems, or as a mosaic of myriad special-purpose predisposed modules? Over the past few years, prominent psychologists have persuasively suggested that the answer is neither. Both views are equally misguided. Rather, we are endowed with a small number of modular systems of core knowledge, which provide a solid foundation for flexible skills and systems of belief. This section presents this intermediate position and explores its implications for our understanding of innateness.

In an influential study, Spelke and Kinzler (2007) maintain that studies of human infants and non-human animals focused on the ontogenetic and phylogenetic origins of knowledge provide evidence for at least four core systems of knowledge. These systems represent inanimate objects and their mechanical interactions, agents and their goal-directed actions, sets and numerical relationships of ordering, addition and subtraction, and the geometry of spatial layout. Each system centers on specific principles that individuate entities in their domain and support inferences about their behavior. Each system, moreover, is characterized by signature limits that allow investigators to identify it across tasks, ages, species, and cultures. Let's explore these systems of core knowledge in greater detail.

The first core system, one of the most extensively studied, is the system of *object representation*. As the name suggests, this framework

120 THE QUEST FOR HUMAN NATURE

governs the way objects are represented by humans based on three fundamental spatiotemporal principles. First, *cohesion*: objects move as connected, bounded wholes. Second, *continuity*: objects move on continuous, unobstructed paths. Third, *contact*: objects do not interact at a distance. A simple example should help drive the point home. When we represent something as, say, a brick, we expect it to be cohesive, moving around as a unit, not as scattered parts. If a portion of the brick is hidden from our visual field, covered by a napkin, the invisible component is assumed to still be there. If we throw it, we anticipate it moving along a continuous trajectory, as opposed to disappearing and reappearing elsewhere. Finally, the brick may shatter a window, but only if it comes in contact with it, not from afar. Evidence from non-human primates, newly hatched chicks, human infants, and distant cultures, such as secluded Amazonian tribes, suggests that these principles constitute a homogeneous system, virtually universal within our species, present at birth—or shortly thereafter—and culture independent.

A second core system represents *agents* and their *actions*. Interestingly, when an entity is conceptualized as an agent, the expectations we project on said entity will be different compared to the ones we would have if that same entity were characterized as a mere object. An agent need not be cohesive, continuous in its path of motion, or subject to contact when interacting with other entities. The signature features of agential representation are *goal-directedness*, *efficiency*, *contingency*, *reciprocity*, and *gaze direction*. To illustrate, consider an infant engaging with a cartoon character, such as Mickey Mouse. Mickey can willfully intend to break a window and do so efficiently. In contrast, the behavior of the brick is neither goal-directed nor efficient. Furthermore, Mickey can decide whether to break the window, whereas the brick has no such choice. Mickey can reciprocate. He can break Minnie's window in response to Minnie insulting him. The brick can do no such thing. Finally, as an agent, Mickey can interact with things from afar. By tracing his gaze, he can follow his dog Pluto out on the run, point to it, or talk about it. An inanimate object, in contrast, has no such intentionality. The existence of an inborn homogeneous system for representing agents and their actions, with its signature features, has been corroborated by studies in non-human animals and in human infants. Newly hatched chicks, rhesus monkeys, and chimpanzees are sensitive to what their predators or competitors can and cannot see. Similar considerations apply to human babies. These studies accord well with the physiological signatures of "mirror neurons" in both monkeys and humans. Together, these findings provide evidence for a core system of agent representation that is evolutionarily ancient and that persists over human development.

A third core system is structured around principles that strikingly contrast with both object and agent systems, and which show their own distinctive signature marks. This is the system regulating *number representation*. It is governed by the following properties. First, number representations are *imprecise,* and their imprecision grows linearly with increasing cardinal value. Second, number representations are *abstract.* They apply to diverse entities encountered through multiple sensory modalities, including arrays of objects, sequences of sounds, and perceived or produced series of actions. Third, number representations can be *compared and combined by operations of addition and subtraction.* The second and third features are intuitive: the number two can be applied indistinctively to represent two apples or two cows, and these two representations can be combined to represent four animals. But what does it mean to say that number representations are "imprecise" and, furthermore, that this "scalar variability" produces a ratio limit to the discriminability of sets with different cardinal values? The basic insight is the following. Imagine representing numbers as dots. The number one corresponds to one dot, the number two to two dots, and so forth. We immediately "see" a single dot as one, two dots as two, three dots as three. We need not count, and we never confuse them. Now, try the same experiment with ten, eleven, and twelve dots. It's a lot harder, almost impossible. To be sure, we can easily count the dots. But we do not directly perceive eleven dots as eleven and as qualitatively different from ten or twelve dots. What this shows is that there is a limit to the discriminability of sets representing ciphers, which rises exponentially. Evidence for such a modular, distinctive, universal, and inborn system of number representation comes from human infants, adults, non-human primates, and cultures such as the Munduruku, a remote Amazonian tribe allegedly with no verbal counting routine, no words for exact numbers beyond "three," and little formal instruction.

122   THE QUEST FOR HUMAN NATURE

A fourth core system captures the *geometry of the environment*, that is, the distance, angle, and sense relations among extended surfaces in the surrounding layout. When young children and non-human animals are disoriented, they try to reorient themselves by focusing on the structure of the surrounding space. This search depends on two specific processes. First, a *reorientation* process that is sensitive only to general layout. Second, an *associative* process that links local regions of this layout to specific objects. Interestingly, these same organisms do not use the layout of objects. Human adults show much more extensive use of landmarks, but they too rely primarily on surface geometry when they are disoriented under conditions of verbal or spatial interference. Setting technicalities aside, the basic insight is simple. Human beings of all ages and exposed to all sorts of cultural influences orient themselves by focusing on the overall geometry of the environment (a mountain range in the landscape) and fail to represent non-geometric properties of the layout such as surface color or odor. Subjects also fail, under some conditions, to capture geometric properties of movable objects. As with the previous modular systems, evidence includes human children, non-human animals, and human adults from a range of cultures.

In sum, Spelke and Kinzler maintain, a substantial—and growing—body of evidence suggests that the human mind is not a single, general-purpose device that adapts itself to whatever structures and challenges the environment affords. Neither is our mind a "massively modular" collection of hundreds or thousands of special-purpose cognitive devices. The human mind appears to be built on a small number of core systems, such as the four ones previously presented: object representation, agent and action representation, number representation, and the geometry of the environment.

There may also be other systems of core knowledge, rooted in our evolutionary past, which emerge in infancy and serve as foundations for learning and reasoning by children and adults. At the time their 2007 paper was published, Spelke and Kinzler had begun investigating a fifth candidate system for identifying and reasoning about potential *social partners and social group members*. Evolutionary psychology allegedly shows that social interactions are a salient feature of every human community, whose adult members show *cooperation, reciprocity*, and *group cohesion*. Studies of infants further reveal that such

WHAT MAKES A TRAIT INNATE? 123

tendencies emerge at early stages of development. Some experiments also suggest that three-month-olds show a visual preference for members of their own ethnicity compared to other races. This preference is influenced by the infants' experience, for it depends both on the ethnicity of the baby's family members and the predominance of that race within their larger community. Infants also look preferentially at faces of the same gender as their primary caregiver. Still, this and other systems of core knowledge require further theoretical support and experimental confirmation.

What conclusions should we draw? What implications does the existence of these systems of core knowledge have for the human mind? On the one hand, these psychological systems are responsible for several cognitive errors and maladaptive actions. To illustrate, recall how the object representation system is based on the principles of cohesion, continuity, and contact. Now, many objects that we encounter and interact with during our everyday lives do, indeed, abide by these general guidelines. Nevertheless, we should be careful before generalizing such observations. At the smallest and largest scientific scales, for instance, objects are neither cohesive not continuous. Quantum physics reveals that matter is less solid than it appears, force fields elude any commonsensical notion of continuity, and the force of gravity is a perfect example of action at a distance. Similarly, physical space can be described in non-Euclidean multi-dimensional terms, mathematicians have discovered transfinite numbers well beyond the reach of core cognitive domains, and the social sciences have described many instances of human intentions which depart, deliberately or inadvertently, from overt, goal-directed actions. In short, gaps and inaccuracies in core representational systems pose hurdles. No wonder we are so prone to errors in reasoning about properties of object mechanics, non-Euclidean geometry, or numbers that violate their core principles. The most dangerous of all these errors may spring from the system for identifying and reasoning about the members of one's own social group. A predisposition for dividing the social world into "us vs. them" may have evolved for the adaptive purpose of detecting safe and trustworthy partners. But it can also be misemployed in modern, interconnected, and multicultural societies, leading to racism, violence, and warfare.

124 THE QUEST FOR HUMAN NATURE

Despite this bleak picture, not all news is bad. Spelke and Kinzler also draw positive morals from these same examples. First and foremost, although core conceptions are resilient, they can be overcome. The history of science and mathematics provides numerous examples of fundamental conceptual changes that occurred as thinkers became aware of the mismatches between the principles governing their reasoning and the outside world. If core conceptions of social partners lead to errors and harmful conflicts, they too should be open to change, because human cognitive development is malleable. For example, the alleged "preference" displayed by many three-month-old infants for faces of people who are phenotypically similar to their own and their immediate family's can be dampened by precocious exposure to faces of individuals belonging to different ethnicities. And biased attitudes toward members of other groups can be mellowed by certain types of inter-group contact. This shows that even the deepest-rooted biases aren't set in stone—good for us! Spelke and Kinzler (2007, p. 92) conclude their outline by stressing:

> Core systems for representing objects, actions, numbers, places, and social partners may provide some of the foundations for uniquely human cognitive achievements, including the acquisition of language and other symbol systems, the development of cognitive skills through formal instruction, and the emergence and growth of cooperative social networks.

The main question, from our standpoint, concerns how our brief excursus into cognitive psychology is tied to the notions of innateness and, more generally, human nature. Is core knowledge a surrogate for innateness? Does it provide a viable definition of innateness in psychology or even across the board? Spelke and Kinzler do not address these questions explicitly. Their systems of core knowledge are introduced as a better, more plausible conception of the human mind than either of the two extremes, that is, the hard-core empiricist view of the mind as highly pliable and the myriad hyper-specialized modules of evolutionary psychology. I concur. Still, it is unclear whether core knowledge provides an analysis of innateness and human nature, a representative instance, a replacement, an "eliminativist" proxy, or

WHAT MAKES A TRAIT INNATE?   125

something altogether different. Furthermore, evidence supporting the core knowledge hypothesis presupposes that this is a general feature of primate or even mammalian adaptive design. These broad modules are not distinctively human, which would make them an odd candidate as a foundation for a theory of human nature.

In short, much remains to be done to connect all these dots. What emerges from our discussion is that embracing innateness does not require the hyper-modular conception of the mind popular among evolutionary psychologists. And pace Pinker's suggestions to the contrary in *The Blank Slate*, rejecting innateness does not mean viewing the mind as a tabula rasa.

§4.6 A New Favorite

Time to wrap things up. The previous pages have focused on innateness, a concept hotly debated not only for its definition and implications but for its scientific status too. Prominent scholars across various fields have questioned the very soundness and plausibility of this notion. In molecular developmental biology, innateness is often dismissed as an antiquated term. In behavioral ecology, it is frequently considered confused and teetering on incoherence. In cognitive psychology, there is a fairly even split between advocates and detractors. In addition to this intriguing hodgepodge of scientific stances, talk of innateness has also permeated common parlance, where various traits—from sport talent to intelligence, from musical ability to mathematical aptitude—are routinely categorized as "innate" and treated accordingly.

Are they really? Authors such as Wilson maintain that the only plausible answer is a resounding yes. To wit, in the course of an influential discussion, he boldly proclaims that "Are human beings innately aggressive? This is a favorite question of college seminars and cocktail party conversations and one that raises emotion in political ideologues of all stripes. The answer to it is yes. . . . Only by redefining the words 'innateness' and 'aggression' to the point of uselessness might we correctly say that human aggressiveness is not innate" ([1978] 2004, p. 99). I've tried to show that things are not quite as black or white. Intuitively, a trait is innate when it is inborn, not acquired, present at birth, and

126   THE QUEST FOR HUMAN NATURE

produced "internally." Yet, we saw how difficult it is to cash out these truisms in a precise fashion. Without a clear analysis, it remains difficult to assess Wilson's contention.

This chapter tried to reframe the underlying dispute to determine what is really at stake. §4.2 set the stage by recounting the emergence of the question of innateness within the historical debate between rationalists and empiricists in the seventeenth and eighteenth centuries and clarifying the conceptual status of human nature and cognate notions. §4.3 examined an array of definitions—grounded, respectively, in common sense, biology, and psychology—which revealed how spelling out a general, informative analysis of innateness is trickier than may initially seem. §4.4 outlined an influential argument, cashed out by Griffiths, suggesting that innateness is the product of folk biology and as such has no place in science. Finally, §4.5 presented some contemporary research on systems of core knowledge, which appears tightly connected to traditional conceptions of innateness. The precise relation among core knowledge, innateness, and human nature remains murky. While these cognitive systems are not acquired and are present at birth, as we saw neither feature is necessary or sufficient for innateness. And there seems no non-question-begging way of classifying them as genetically determined or "internally produced." Setting intrinsic psychological interest aside, it remains indeterminate in what sense, if any, all these structures are "innate."

Despite much discussion and clarification, we are stuck with our original set of issues. What does it mean—and what should it mean—to claim that a specific trait is innate? Is there a univocal meaning or does it vary contextually? Is the notion of innateness scientifically acceptable? Which traits, if any, are innate? Do we need a definition of innateness? Could this definition shed light on human nature? These are questions whose interest transcends mere academic disputes. They are central for how to research, teach, and debate contemporary socially significant issues.

Try this thought experiment. Imagine being the editor in chief of the science pages of some major national newspaper or magazine. You need to find a way to present the results discussed here to the general public. You must repackage our conclusions about human nature, innateness, and core systems, as they pertain to violence, intelligence, racism, and other socially significant traits. How would you do it in such a way that you will get the public interested, while maintaining scientific respectability and intellectual honesty? This is an open challenge that deserves more of our attention. Pace Wilson, college seminars and cocktail party conversations may need a new favorite conversation topic.

Setting scientific journalism and social gatherings aside, the most pressing issue, from our present perspective, is the relation among innateness, genetic determinism, and human nature. At the end of Chapter 3, I surmised that thick conceptions of human nature may be too broad to be addressed head-on. Looking directly into human nature did not yield the expected fruits. The suggested alternative was to break the overarching notion of human nature into smaller, more specific, and more tractable proxies. With this objective in mind, we set out to explore the topics of innateness and genetic determinism. The tight connection between innateness, genetic determinism, and human nature is hard to overstate. Many traits traditionally associated to human nature are also routinely classified as innate or as genetically determined. Yet, without a clear analysis of these notions, which keeps eluding us, we are left without a viable conception of human nature too. Before crawling back to the drawing board, however, we still have an arrow in our quiver. Could genetic determinism itself be the key to human nature? This is the focus of our next chapter.

5

Are We Genetically Determined?

O gente umana, per volar sù nata,
Perché a poco vento così cadi?
O human creatures, born to soar aloft,
Why fall ye thus before a little wind?
—Dante, *Purgatorio* (XII, 95–96), translated by
H.W. Longfellow (1867)

§5.1 Genetics to the Rescue

Customary recap to get our juices flowing. Chapter 2 presented the first systematic attempts to develop a true science of human nature: sociobiology and its intellectual descendant, evolutionary psychology. The conception of human nature underlying both approaches is evident. Natural selection shaped human DNA for most of the evolutionary history of our species, in relative independence of any cultural interference. Gradually selected genes powerfully influence the development of both bodies and minds, our anatomy and behavior alike. Genetic traits are thus the key to grasping who we are.

No scholar worth their salt should question that natural selection has played a prominent role in molding our current state. What remains murky is the object of inquiry: what is a science of human nature intended to capture? What does it mean for traits to belong to our "nature"? Chapter 3 surveyed three answers. First, we explored the possibility that our nature comprises a set of necessary and sufficient conditions for being human. Intuitive as this may sound, there are no human essences, voiding the proposal. Second, the natural-state model purports to capture what it means to be a "normal" member of our species. The hurdle here is that reading the relevant notion of

The Quest for Human Nature. Marco J. Nathan, Oxford University Press. © Oxford University Press 2024.
DOI: 10.1093/oso/9780197699249.003.0005

normality from biological or psychological data is hardly straightforward. Third, "field guide" conceptions characterize human nature as a set of diagnostic features for our species. While we can surely pinpoint a cluster of traits that distinguish us from other animals, it is questionable whether this "thin" analysis of human nature can do all the normative heavy lifting demanded of it by authors such as Chomsky.

The previous chapter blazed a different trail. Human nature is a broad, overarching, and semantically loaded concept with a long-standing history. Instead of tackling human nature head-on, perhaps we could find a more tractable proxy, with less baggage and more amenable to scientific inquiry. Following this path, Chapter 4 considered whether it may be possible to identify human nature with a set of traits that are innate to us. The notion of innateness turned out to be no less fraught with controversy than human nature itself. Providing a clear definition is neither simple nor uncontroversial. Prominent scholars have suggested that innateness is a hybrid, heterogeneous notion that would be best eschewed and replaced by more precise scientific surrogates. Furthermore, the most promising extant accounts restrict the notion of innateness to some subfield or another. As such, they lack the generality to ground the notion of human nature tout court. In short, replacing human nature with innateness did not bear the desired fruits. We keep on marching.

The present chapter continues where the previous one left off, with a subtle twist. As noted, innateness has a history as long and loaded as human nature itself. Perhaps it would be advisable to approach both topics from a more contemporary standpoint. The obvious strategy is to look at genes and their properties. It is quite common to identify the features belonging to human nature with traits influenced by the genes, both within and outside of technical academic disputes. Indeed, the insight goes all the way back to Wilson's sociobiology. But what does it mean for a feature to be "genetically determined"? Regardless of its strong and evident connections to human nature, the underlying issue is provocative and controversial in its own right. As such, it deserves a self-standing, chapter-long discussion.

The core intuitions are simple enough. To label a certain trait as "genetically determined" is nothing more than to say that it is the consequence of a specific genotype. Great. But there is a predictable

130　THE QUEST FOR HUMAN NATURE

follow-up. How should one understand the tenet that a trait is produced or determined by a genotype or that it follows from it? Clearly, it would be overly demanding to presuppose that the feature in question is caused by genes and genes alone. As we shall shortly see, no phenotypic variant is produced by genes in isolation. At the same time, explicating determinism as stating that genes play *some* role in its production runs the risk of trivializing it, as genes contribute, in some form or another, to the formation of virtually every characteristic. So, what are we implying when we assert that, say, eye color or height are genetically determined whereas religious affiliation and sport allegiances are not? The goal of the ensuing pages is to clarify these heated disputes by surveying what is currently known about the relation between genotypes and phenotypes.

Here is the master plan. Before setting sail, we need to make sure that everyone is aboard. §5.2 provides a primer of basic theoretical foundations regarding genes, genomes, and their role in producing traits. Readers with a strong background in biology, in need of no refresher, are advised to skip this section and begin with the following one. §5.3 focuses on the main tenets underlying the views of both genetic determinists and their opponents, what each party is claiming and what they are objecting to. We shall then spell out a preliminary notion of genetic determinism according to which a trait is genetically determined if and only if it has a flat or mostly flat norm of reaction. §5.4 connects the idea of genetic determinism with *heritability*, a technical construct purporting to quantify the degree of variation that is due to genetic differences in a trait across a population of reference. We shall scrutinize claims by contemporary behavior geneticists who maintain that highly heritable traits include not only physical characteristics, like eye color and skin tone, but also behavioral ones, such as personality and social attitude. §5.5 explores some developmentalist challenges to genetic determinism. §5.6 outlines the prospects of cashing out an adequate interactionist model of how genes and environment jointly produce who we have come to be. Finally, §5.7 wraps things up by drawing some general conclusions.

§5.2 Genes, Genomes, and Genotypes

The science of genetics has come a long way since its nineteenth-century origins, rooted in Mendel's pioneering experiments crossing strands of pea plants and their "rediscovery" in the early 1900s. We now have a sizable—and steadily growing—body of knowledge, technology, and applications. Mention of genes and their properties has become widespread in common parlance. Talk of features "in the DNA" of athletes, teams, populations, or groups pervade discussions of sports, politics, economics, and much else.

It is certainly refreshing to see how a portion of the general public has finally mastered the rudiments of our biological endowment. Nevertheless, pitfalls are always round the corner. The nuances of genetic activity may lead to more or less subtle misunderstandings. A well-established fact can easily be bloated into a preposterous urban legend. Truisms quickly morph into pernicious falsehoods. Providing a comprehensive account of elementary genetics transcends the scope of this work. The modest aim of the present section is to provide some common background and get some basic facts straight. This will provide the backdrop for a meaningful discussion of how genes affect who we are and what we do. As noted earlier, readers with a strong background in contemporary biology are allowed to flip to §5.3.

Heeding sound advice from Maria von Trapp, let's start at the very beginning—a very good place to start. In almost every cell of the human body there's a "genetic instruction book," packed into a DNA double helix.[1] These instructions play a crucial role in building us, shaping our limbs, governing the arrangement of our internal organs, influencing the color of our eyes, and much else. Simply put, this blueprint guides our transformation from simple unicellular zygotes to complex multicellular organisms. The significance of genetic information becomes evident once we recognize that relatively minor tweaks in input may lead to major discrepancies in output.

---

[1] The qualifier "almost" is required because there are types of cells, such as mature red blood cells and mature hair cells, which do not contain any nuclear DNA. In what follows, we can safely set these exceptions to the side and focus on cells with DNA.

132   THE QUEST FOR HUMAN NATURE

Given the prominent role that genes play in shaping our body, it should be unsurprising that genetic differences also influence our psychology and behavior. None of this is remotely controversial. As the eminent biologist Theodosius Dobzhansky cautioned us back in 1962: "People vary in ability, energy, health, character, and other socially important traits, and there is good, though not absolutely conclusive, evidence that the variance of all these traits is in part genetically conditioned. Conditioned, mind you, not fixed or predestined" (p. 112). Even contemporary authors, such as Prinz (2012), who downplay the significance of genes in shaping our mind, are acutely aware of these facts. No biologist, philosopher, or other scholar worth their salt challenges any of this. Yet, these truisms are sometimes presented in deeply misleading ways, promoting the idea that human behavior is genetically controlled and that environment plays a negligible background role. These are quite separate and considerably more controversial tenets.

The first step to acquire the ability to identify and appreciate the difference between platitudes and absurdities is to pinpoint some nuts-and-bolts truths about genes and their products. For starters, the biological blueprint for many living creatures—and all multicellular organisms like us—is encoded in their DNA. Deoxyribonucleic acid is a molecule constituted by a very long sequence of four types of chemical bases: adenine (A), thymine (T), cytosine (C), and guanine (G). Each base is paired up with a complementary base, linked together by a backbone of sugars and phosphates. Together, these two strands constitute the famous "double helix."

We are now ready to introduce the very idea of a genetic code. Collections of three bases, called "codons," encode instructions for making amino acids. For instance, the sequence "AGT" codes for serine. Amino acids, such as serine, are organic compounds composed of nitrogen, carbon, hydrogen, and oxygen, which constitute the basic building blocks of proteins. Proteins, in turn, are among the main bricks of the cells making up organisms. Some stretches of DNA contain instructions for stringing together amino acids into sequences called polypeptide chains. Since there are twenty kinds of amino acids, attentive readers will surely note that there are many more codons than amino acids in the human body. This means that the DNA code is "degenerate," that is, redundant, in the sense that different codons code for the same amino acids. "AGT" stands for serine, but so does "AGC."

With all of this in mind, we can provide a preliminary molecular definition of *gene*. From a biochemical perspective, a gene is a stretch of DNA that carries information for building a polypeptide chain. To be sure, this is not a fully comprehensive analysis because it fails to cover regulatory genes: stretches of DNA that govern the behavior of other genes, for example, by indicating where a sequence starts and stops or by serving as landing sites for specific molecules that turn genes on and off. But the identification of genes with structural chains should suffice for our present purposes. I also stress that not just any stretch of DNA is a coding gene. According to recent estimates, roughly 98% of the human genome is neither structural nor regulatory. It's often dubbed "junk DNA" and its function is currently unknown, if hotly debated.

Given what we just said, it should be evident that genes influence organisms by governing the construction of proteins. But just as clearly, they do not do it alone. Other key components of protein production include mRNA, tRNA, and ribosomes. Oversimplifying a bit the key aspects, first mRNA latches on to DNA and makes copies of genes by a process of "transcription." Next, tRNA transfers mRNA in the cytoplasm to the ribosomes which, in turn, string amino acids together in a procedure called "translation." And this is just the beginning. Once polypeptide chains are born, molecules cause them to fold into three-dimensional structures: proteins, the key ingredient of cells. Some proteins are built up from several polypeptides. There are about thirty thousand proteins in the human body, an amount which may well exceed the total number of genes.

Most cells contain a complete copy of the genome. Still, cells endowed with identical DNA may vastly differ because, within any given cell type, some genes will be turned on and some will be switched off via a process of gene regulation. Human DNA consists of roughly 3 billion bases. Genes vary in size, from a few hundred bases to a few million. The current estimate is that humans have between 20,000 and 25,000 genes. This is a humbling discovery, since fruit flies have 13,600 genes and mustard grass has 25,300 known genes. We share 40% of the genes in worms, 50% of the genes in fruit flies, and an estimated 98.5% of genes in chimpanzees. This suggests that what matters is not

134   THE QUEST FOR HUMAN NATURE

how big or unique your genome is, but how you use it. Similar stocks of genes may lead to startling differences. Most variation in structural genes, such as the *homeobox*, has devastating effects. But there are also healthy variations, "alleles" governing traits like hair color or skin tone.

With all of this under our belts, let's get to the juicy core. Is it accurate to conclude that "genes code for traits"? The answer is yes, if coding is understood along the lines sketched above. Nevertheless, we need to be careful. While talk about genes "coding" for traits, especially psychological traits, can be quite seductive, it is also potentially misleading. It may give the false impression that human bodies and minds are under genetic control, just a small step from the pernicious hoax that "DNA is destiny." This is problematic enough when it comes to bodily features. In the case of psychology, things get even messier. Currently, there is no solid evidence directly linking specific genes to specific behaviors. The relation between genes and conduct is indirect and complex. Variations in certain genes correlate to some degree, usually negligible, with behavioral traits, and many other factors contribute as well. Further, and crucially, genes do not exert any influence on their own. Their activity ultimately depends on many other genes, extra-genomic biological material, and other factors outside the organism. But these qualifications are frequently forgotten, or mischievously set to the side.

How can these hypotheses be assessed? One popular method to search for genes affecting behavior, common among behavior geneticists, is to use *linkage studies* to correlate bits of DNA with phenotypic traits. Another, pre-genomic strategy involves *heritability studies*, whereby population geneticists estimate genetic contributions to behavior by measuring correlations between traits and degrees of familial relatedness. The assumption is that, if a trait runs throughout an entire family, it is much more likely to be genetic. Yet, as we shall see, the inference from "heritable" to "genetic" is strongly controversial. Given the high stakes, it is crucial to diagnose and correct any possible misconception regarding the relationship between genes and behaviors.

In sum, there is no real debate about whether genes can influence behavior. They can. Controversy concerns the precise nature of that connection. Genetic determinists argue that many human traits are strongly shaped by our genes. Developmentalists retort that genes provide only very broad and general capacities. Between these extremes lies a spectrum of stances. But, regardless of whether they fall more toward the "naturist" or the "nurturist" side of the continuum, any theorist worth reading must acknowledge the basic facts about genes, genomes, and genotypes recounted in this section. Genes matter, and so do environmental stimuli. The difference between these views, appropriately framed, must therefore be a matter of nuance. We are finally ready for our main course: genetic determinism.

§5.3 Genetic Determinism

Has it occurred to anyone how hard it is to have a non-question-begging political discussion with someone we vehemently disagree with? (Insert smirk emoji here.) Debates on capitalism, socialism, neoliberalism, communism, and virtually any other ideologically tainted "ism" are characterized by a sort of bait-and-switch, which is just as prominent on national television as it is at Thanksgiving dinners. Every time one of the discussants raises an argument meant to show some evident problem with position x, the opponent retorts, "This is not what I meant by x. . . . What I really mean is . . ." And just like that the cycle begins again. For this and many other reasons sociopolitical discussion can be frustrating—*et le mot est faible*.

A parallel situation characterizes discussions about genes and their effects on behavior. Genetic determinism is a position which is periodically proclaimed dead. Hardly anyone out there presents themselves as a card-carrying "genetic determinist." And yet, new forms and variants of genetic determinism constantly arise. As soon as one particular proposal is shot down, the typical rejoinder is that true intentions have been misunderstood. The *real* claim, properly construed, is such-and-such. And now we are back to square one, hopelessly striving to hit the bullseye on a moving target.[2]

---

[2] This point is borrowed from Kitcher ([2001] 2003), who, in turn, traces it back to Oyama (2000).

136   THE QUEST FOR HUMAN NATURE

A paradigmatic instance of this attitude can be found in the writings of E. O. Wilson. As discussed in §2.3, Wilson at times seems to be advancing a sober variety of interactionism, according to which "[e]ach person is molded by an interaction of his environment, especially his natural environment, with the genes that affect social behavior" ([1978] 2004, p. 18). But the tone swiftly changes when he writes on the following page: "The question of interest is no longer whether human social behavior is genetically determined; it is to what extent. The accumulated evidence for a large hereditary component is more detailed and compelling than most persons, including even geneticists, realize. I will go further: it already is decisive" (p. 19). So, which one is it? Is social behavior a consequence of genetic determination or does it stem from balanced interaction? Is there a difference between these stances? To answer, we first need to get clear on what precisely is the issue.

At the most general level, genetic determinism holds that all human characteristics—or, more charitably, a significant subset thereof— arise from our genetic makeup. But how should this claim be parsed? Note that, depending on how we read this proposition, its meaning may swing from obvious platitude to preposterous overstatement, with a whole spectrum of interpretations in between. To wit, if what we are claiming is that all traits emerge from the expression of genes during development, in the sense that our genetic endowment plays a role in the production of all our attributes, then no one should contest this. As we saw in §5.2, genes play a prominent role in the development of virtually anything. On the other hand, construed as the tenet that all variation is genetic—in the sense that to any phenotypic difference between human beings, physiological or behavioral, there invariably corresponds some quantifiable genetic difference—then, as Dobzhansky reminded us early on, the claim is false and demonstrably so. Now, consider an intermediate reading where differences at the genetic level provide the best explanation of phenotypic variation. This is a subtly controversial claim, albeit one that cannot be accepted or dismissed as obviously right or wrong without looking further into what is meant by "best explanation" and other background assumptions. In short, our preliminary genetic-determinist thesis is

ARE WE GENETICALLY DETERMINED? 137

subject to interpretations of varying epistemic status. Clarifying what's at stake is a precondition for fair assessment.

Unsurprisingly, the same sort of semantic ambiguity emerges if we try to ask what it means to reject genetic determinism. Intuitively, the most clear-cut way to oppose any form of genetic determination would be to endorse an extreme form of "environmental determinism" according to which genes play no role whatsoever in the production of human traits. While this position has the virtue or being crystal clear, it has a major drawback in being plainly false. Consequently, no serious scholar even comes close to it. A more nuanced—but still radical— critique of genetic determinism comes from "developmentalists," or "developmental systems theorists," who, as we shall see, argue that the role of genes in development is vastly overestimated (§5.5). The most widespread opposition to determinism is unquestionably a mild version of "interactionism," according to which human traits are produced by a balanced blend of genes and environment (§5.6).

Some caution is well advised here. As we have stressed repeatedly, any scientifically informed author duly acknowledges that a combination of genes and environment is necessary for the development of any trait. Consequently, some basic form of interactionism is accepted by virtually all biologists. This includes scholars with genetic-determinist inclinations, such as Wilson, who view interactionism and genetic determination as mutually compatible. On the other side of the spectrum, some bread-and-butter strand of interactionism is also the starting point of the aforementioned developmentalists who, at the same time, also contend that this biological baseline does not go far enough in rejecting the primacy attributed to genes.[3]

Hold on a second. If interactionism provides the middle-of-the-road alternative that everyone can agree with, then why is that not the end of the controversy? Why did I just present it as a way to oppose genetic determinism? The problem, succinctly put, is that interactionism—much like genetic determinism and developmentalism—can be construed in

---

[3] The observation that virtually everybody agrees on how both genes and environment influence phenotypic and behavioral outcomes is duly noted by Barker (2015, Ch. 3). Interestingly, Barker also suggests that the very image of a spectrum of positions is a serious oversimplification, which ignores the various ways in which these factors can interact.

138 THE QUEST FOR HUMAN NATURE

various incompatible ways. This makes it paramount to ask what exactly the underlying claim amounts to. Is it simply the truism that both genes and development do something? How should we apportion their causal contribution, in equal parts? And, just like that, we are straight back to square one. We still got chores to do.

Let's begin to refine the main tenets characterizing genetic determinism, keeping in mind all the basic biological facts discussed in the previous section. When is a trait "genetically determined"? Here is a crude sketch, inspired by Kitcher ([2001] 2003). A specific trait t in organism o belonging to species s is genetically determined if and only if there is some gene, or group of genes, g, such that any organism that is a member of s, developing from a zygote that possesses a certain form, or set of forms, of g, would come to have t whatever the other properties of the zygote and whatever the sequences of environments through which the developing organisms passed. Setting complications aside, the core insight is intuitive. A phenotypic trait t is genetically determined by a set of genes g if and only if *any* organism o possessing g will acquire t, regardless of the environment in which o develops or any kind of disturbance. This preliminary characterization has the virtues of being razor-sharp and precise. Let's see if it withholds serious examination.

As Kitcher promptly emphasizes, the definition under present scrutiny is quite demanding. The phrasing "any organism possessing g will display t" leaves no room for exceptions. Nice and clean-cut. But pinpoint precision comes at a cost as, thus conceived, hardly any trait will count as genetically determined. The motive is simple. Consider a trait that looks like a promising candidate to be genetically determined: eye color. Eye color was traditionally described as a single-gene trait, in the sense that it was once believed that the color of one's eyes depended on a single gene. Recent work has revealed that at least eight genes influence the final color of human eyes. Clearly, all genes require some environmental trigger, and the ones controlling the concentration of melanin in specialized cells are no exception. Yet, the intuition runs, specific alleles at the relevant loci make the key difference to the final product. Indeed, despite its contrastive status, eye color is standardly chosen to illustrate genetically determined traits:

To say that blue eyes are inherited is not meaningful without further clarification, because blue eyes are the product of an interaction between genes and the largely physiological environment that brought final coloration to the irises. But to say that the *difference* between blue and brown eyes is based wholly or partly on differences in genes is a meaningful statement because it can be tested and translated into the laws of genetics. (Wilson [1978] 2004, p. 19)

But now, consider whether eye color counts as "genetically determined" based on the preliminary definition proposed above. The answer is negative, and the reason is clear. In the environment in which I, in fact, was raised, it may well be true that my genotype was the cause that actually made a difference to the color of my eyes.[4] Yet, it is simply not true that my genotype will express the same phenotype, the same eye color in *all* possible environments. Make sufficient adjustments to my environmental trigger—my diet, exposure to various substances, and so forth—and the color of my eyes will change accordingly. Something must have gone south.

To see how deep this problem runs, consider a trait that is even more obviously genetically determined: Huntington's Disease (HD).[5] HD is a notoriously devastating neurodegenerative disorder caused by an unstable expansion of a "CAG" repeat within the coding region of a single gene, near the tip of chromosome 4. Whereas the sequence of both the wild type and the mutated alleles of the *huntingtin* gene and the structure of the encoded protein have been known since 1993, HD-related neurodegenerative disorders cannot yet be cured, prevented, or even effectively mitigated. Sadly, no environment has been found or engineered where the mutation in question does not produce the pathological phenotype when the patient reaches a critical age between thirty and fifty. And still, on the definition proposed above, not even a paradigmatically genetically based condition like HD will count as genetically determined. This is because there are environments where people with the Huntington genotype do not display the phenotype.

---

[4] For a discussion of genes as causes that "make a difference" see Waters (2007).

[5] The observation that, on the definition at hand, not even HD counts as determined, as well as the discussion of its implications, is borrowed from Kitcher ([2001] 2003).

140   THE QUEST FOR HUMAN NATURE

Consider, for instance, the extreme situation where a person carrying the pathological genotype dies before reaching the critical age or, less drastically, hypothetical contexts where the effects of the disorder can be cured or at least alleviated. So, strictly speaking, not even the pathological genotype of currently incurable genetic diseases such as HD are expressed in *all* environments. What morals should we draw?

The appropriate reaction, I maintain, is *not* to reject the genetic determination of these traits. Wilson is right that eye color is determined by the genes, and the same can be said for HD. As we shall see, there are more controversial examples. But these are not them. The point is rather that the proposed definition of genetic determination—any organism possessing g will display t—is inadequate. Perhaps, with ingenuity, we could discover traits "causally closed" to the immediate biochemistry of DNA which are genetically determined in this sense. But let's not beat around the bush. Any analysis that won't countenance HD as genetically determined ain't no definition of genetic determinism. It needs revision. But how, exactly?

Kitcher suggests an obvious strategy for softening our preliminary account, namely, to weaken the—unreasonable—"in all environments" proviso by replacing it with "in most environments," or something analogous. In addition, we could restrict our attention to complexes of causal factors that enable the organism to develop to the age at which the trait would "normally" first appear. This should rule out counterinstances to the genetic determination of HD involving environments where the patient passes away before reaching the critical age at which the disease typically kicks in. This already feels much better. Nevertheless, a nagging concern remains. As we saw in Chapter 3, cashing out a naturalized, biologically kosher notion of normality is no joke. Sure, an environment in which one drops dead at eighteen better not be "normal." But where exactly do we draw the line, and on what basis?

Setting these significant complications aside, Kitcher suggests the following general strategy for determining whether a trait is genetically determined. First, begin by identifying the phenotypic properties of organisms whose causal impact we set out to explore. As discussed ad nauseam, virtually every phenotypic trait is the product of both genetic and environmental factors. Hence, parsing the causal factors affecting the trait in question requires separating the contribution of particular kinds of DNA sequences, on the one hand, and everything else, on the other hand. Once this is done, we can inquire into how the phenotype varies as the genotype is held constant while other factors—the constitution of the zygote, the molecules passed across cell membranes, nutrition, and so forth—are allowed to change.

Once we strip away technicalities, the graphical representation of this interaction should have a familiar ring to it: it is the norm of reaction of the genotype, first encountered in §3.4. As Kitcher's discussion makes clear, our good ol' friend, the norm of reaction, provides a simple but effective strategy for visualizing genetic determinism. In its crudest form, genetic determinism claims that a certain trait has a flat norm of reaction: the phenotype remains constant no matter how the environment varies (see figure). As we anticipated, despite being clear-cut, this preliminary definition is problematic. Various refinements suggest themselves. The norm of reaction may be flat *almost* everywhere, restrict attention to *healthy* environments, focus on *slight* variation, and so forth. So, genetic determinism is a matter of degree, after all. At the same time, this malleability imposes a trade-off. Flexibility is inversely proportional to precision. Still, equipped with a better understanding of genetic determination, our next task is figuring out which traits have a flat or virtually flat norm of reaction.

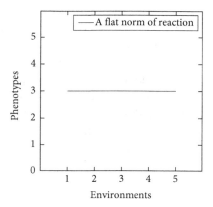

142 THE QUEST FOR HUMAN NATURE

§5.4 Heritability, Behavior, and Determinism

The previous section outlined a general definition of genetic determinism. Simply put, we can label a trait—phenotypic or behavioral—"genetically determined" just in case its associated genotype has a norm of reaction that is flat or virtually so. Setting vagueness aside, pathological conditions like Huntington's Disease and non-pathological states like brown eyes can now be plausibly treated as genetically determined. But how far can we take this? Does this strategy also apply to human conduct? Genetic determinism is often assumed to shed light on violence, intelligence, musical talent, and other psychological traits studied by behavior geneticists, evolutionary psychologists, and cognate researchers. The crucial issue is whether the distribution of these qualities across human populations is best explained in terms of genes, or if they are mostly the product of "external" factors such as schooling, training, or socio-economic status. It is paramount to emphasize that deepening our understanding of these issues does not have merely academic interest. It also has deep social import and momentous consequences.

Some contemporary scholars have gone as far as maintaining that all, or virtually all, mental traits are "heritable." Echoing Wilson, behavior geneticist Thomas Bouchard Jr. (2004, p. 148) begins an overview of the genetic influence on human psychological traits by proclaiming: "Among knowledgeable researchers, discussions regarding genetic influences on psychological traits are not about whether there is genetic influence, but rather about how much influence there is, and how genes work to shape the mind."[6] Bouchard's proposition calls for elucidation. Addressing two preliminary sets of questions is crucial to frame the main point within the appropriate context. First, how exactly should one parse the claim that genetic influence and determination are ubiquitous? We need to scrutinize

---

[6] Bouchard's endorsement of the quasi-universality of genetic influences on psychology, more recently revamped by Plomin (2018), is often presented and motivated as a radical reading of Turkheimer's (2000, p. 160) *first law of behavior genetics*: "All human behavioral traits are heritable." This is somewhat ironic as Turkheimer's law was originally advanced as a *critique* of behavior genetics, not as an endorsement of it. I am grateful to an anonymous reviewer for bringing this point to my attention.

the current evidence and what follows from it. Second, what is heritability and how is it connected to genetic determinism? This section addresses both issues, in turn.

For starters, as discussed in previous sections, there is a sense in which the claim that all behavioral traits are "influenced by the genes" and all that remains to be established is how much, is a platitude, an uncontroversial truism. Once again, having the appropriate set of genes is a precondition for being human and behaving as one. My ability—and limitations—in learning to speak Mandarin depend in no small part on the basic cognitive structure of my mind, shaped by my biological endowment. No matter how long we expose an earthworm, dolphin, or chimp to linguistic stimuli, they will not be able to process Mandarin or any other natural language in any substantive sense. At the same time, it seems clear that the target of scholars such as Bouchard is not merely this cliché. What they are maintaining is that differences in psychological traits among human beings depend to a large extent on our genes, which makes them heritable. To fully understand this view, we need to move to our second issue: heritability.

Simply put, *heritability*—denoted by h^2—is a descriptive statistic purporting to index the degree of population variation in a trait that is due to genetic differences. Accordingly, the complement of heritability, $1 - h^2$, indexes variation in a trait, relative to a population, which is contributed by the environment, broadly construed, plus error of measurement. The higher the heritability value of a trait, which ranges over the closed interval between 0 and 1, the greater the contribution of genetic variation to individual fluctuations in that trait. A toy example should help drive the point home. Consider a human population P composed of one hundred individuals. In this deme, there is a phenotypic trait t which comes in two variants: t_1 and t_2. $x\%$ of people have t_1 and the remaining $100 - x\%$ have t_2. To say that trait t has heritability 1 means that variation in the trait in question depends entirely on genetics. If t is a genetic condition, such as Huntington's Disease (§5.3), then its heritability will be 1 or very close to it. In contrast, if t captures whether members of P have watched the latest blockbuster movie, its heritability will likely approach 0. If t has a heritability of 0.5, it means that half of its variation is due to genetic factors while

144   THE QUEST FOR HUMAN NATURE

the other half is due to environmental factors. Basic as this surely is, it should be enough to get us going.

First and foremost, how is any of this related to our present concerns? Attentive readers will surely note the tight correspondence between many traits that are strongly heritable and features that are genetically determined. A trait with high heritability does not vary based on changes in the environment. This in turn can be captured by the property in question having a flattish norm of reaction, which is precisely how we defined a genetically determined trait in the previous section. But being able to numerically quantify the respective contribution of genes and environment has obvious attractions, making these concepts clear, testable, and precise.

So, how do we operationalize and evaluate heritability? An accurate measurement of the heritability of a phenotypic or behavioral trait requires a *behavior genetic study*: a methodological strategy that falls within the purview of behavior genetics.[7] While most traditional behavior genetic studies were essentially comparative analyses of human twins vs. adoptees, in the current post-genomic era, the use of twin studies to estimate heritability is typically paired with genome-wide association studies, or GWAS.

The core insight underlying these genetic studies should be intuitive. Kids raised within the same household can be assumed to share roughly the same environment, whereas children in different households allegedly have distinctive environmental exposures. From a genetic standpoint, identical twins have very similar genotypes. Heterozygous twins share roughly 50% of their genetic endowment, whereas adopted siblings are genetically no closer than two random strangers. With these considerations in mind, the observation that a property is shared by genetic unrelated siblings, like adoptees, suggests that the property in question is environmental. In contrast, a trait shared by young homozygous twins living in different households seems to imply a higher degree of heritability. As we shall shortly see, things are substantially

---

[7] As Bouchard (2004) notes, the label "behavioral genetic studies" is a misnomer, as it suggests a focus on genetic traits alone. In truth, whether psychological traits under scrutiny are heritable or environmental is an open empirical question. For a comprehensive meta-analysis of twin studies, see Polderman et al. (2015) and Harden (2021a, 2021b).

more complicated. Nevertheless, this simplified reconstruction is meant to capture the structure and rationale underlying human behavior genetic studies.

To envision what's going on, let's inquire into differences in genetic heritability among organisms and, specifically, whether the magnitude of h^2 varies across individuals and species. First, note that the high heritability of certain traits is hardly breaking news. We have long known that, say, eye color, hair color, and height are highly heritable in the technical sense just discussed. No one should be surprised to hear that taller parents tend to have taller offspring, and that your chance of having blue eyes is greater if both your parents are blue-eyed. The high heritability of these traits was never under dispute, although providing exact values is no simple matter. Yet, some behavior geneticists put forth more controversial views. Bouchard, for one, claims that we now have decisive evidence for the substantial heritability of personality traits, such as neuroticism (0.48) and extraversion (0.54), intelligence, which ranges from 0.22 at age five to 0.85 at age fifty, psychological interests, such as being artistic (0.39), social (0.37), or enterprising (0.37), psychiatric illnesses like schizophrenia (0.80) and phobias (0.20–0.40), and social attitudes like conservatism (0.45–0.65 over age twenty) and right-wing authoritarianism (0.50–0.64 in adults).[8] Now, this is actually shocking!

Even if this data can be taken at face value—and, as we'll promptly discuss, this should not be assumed uncritically—this is hardly the end of the story. As Bouchard himself acknowledges, we now face a series of new questions regarding the source and mode of population variance across these traits. First, what kind of gene action is involved: is it an additive, linear influence or is such interaction more complex? Second, are the effects of a gene, or set thereof, more pronounced in certain members of the population? For instance, is the genetic effect stronger in, say, women vs. men, or older vs. younger individuals? Third, are

---

[8] Bouchard (2004) addresses only *univariate* analyses of traits taken one at a time. *Multivariate* analyses tell us the degree to which genetic effects on one score ("trait measure") are correlated with genetic effects on a second score, at many points in time. As discussed by Harden (2021), in the post-genomic era twin studies are typically complemented with GWAS. It should be noted that Harden's conclusions are more nuanced, qualified, and cautious than the boisterous statements of Bouchard or Plomin.

146   THE QUEST FOR HUMAN NATURE

there meaningful gene-environment interactions? Some genes may lead people to live a more stressful life which, in turn, could have an effect on their own psyche. Are folks with specific genotypes more prone to look for certain environments? Could sensation-seeking individuals be disposed to actively pursue more dangerous settings?

In sum, researchers assumed that phenotypic traits like height and eye color are significantly influenced by genetic factors, whereas social attitudes are largely environmental. Over the past few decades, some behavior geneticists have rejoined that virtually every reliably measured psychological phenotype, normal or abnormal, is strongly driven by genetic properties. Heritability, the argument runs, varies less than we dared to imagine. Shared environmental influences often—but not invariably—matter less than genetic factors, and frequently decrease to zero, or close to zero, after adolescence.

What conclusions should we draw? Bouchard boldly suggests that a psychology worth its salt must focus on the molecular mechanisms by which genes transact with the environment to produce behavior. To be sure, while the rudiments of such accounts are in place, examples are few, details are sparse, and major mysteries linger. How are behavioral traits influenced by non-additive genetic processes? Why are most psychological traits moderately vs. highly heritable? Does heritability vary across species? Why are some traits determined by genes vs. environment? All these questions still await a clear answer. Nevertheless, Bouchard concludes, we now know enough to proclaim: "Genetic influence on psychological traits is ubiquitous, and psychological researchers must incorporate this fact into their research programs else their theories will be 'scientifically unimpressive and technologically worthless'" (2004, p. 151). Just how decisive this evidence is, is worth discussing.

As seductive as it surely is, the project of quantifying the relative contribution of genes and environment conceals some obvious caveats and pitfalls. Following Bateson (2001), I briefly present and examine three of them.[9]

---

[9] Related considerations are developed in Block (1995) and Garson (2015, Ch. 4).

First and foremost, it is important to stress that the heritability of a trait is not a fixed and absolute property of the trait itself or of the organisms that possess it. The specific value that we attach to a property is relative to the underlying population of reference. Allow me to elaborate. As discussed above, h^2 distinguishes the proportion of variation in a trait that is due to genetic differences from that which is dependent on environmental changes. But note how the very quantity that we are trying to operationalize—variation—depends heavily on the contrast class. To wit, imagine comparing variation in skin tone in a population of a thousand native Icelanders. Now, add to the sample size an equinumerous group of sub-Saharan Africans. The trait in question will now vary a lot more. Yet, clearly, this is not because of any novel physiological process. What has changed is rather the population of interest. In short, attempts to quantify heritability are heavily dependent on *who* we are measuring and *under what conditions*. To be sure, we can—and should—always strive to control for irrelevant influences. But the obtained measure of heritability is never an absolute value. It is invariably a function of the selection of the class or classes being examined.

A second noteworthy observation is that low heritability does not entail that the trait is unaffected by the genes. Vice versa, high heritability hardly signifies that the environment has a comparatively minor role in the production of the trait in question. A simple example should help visualize the main point. Recall that heritability is intended to be a measure of variation. Now, what happens to traits that do not vary, or which vary to an insignificant degree? For instance, most human populations are bipedal, that is, walk on two legs, and have opposable thumbs.[10] Because of relative lack of variation, the heritability of these traits is very low, indeed close to zero. But this is not because genes have no role in producing the phenotypes in question. Quite the contrary, genes play a prominent part in the explanation of these features that distinguish humans from species, such as chimps, gorillas, and

---

[10] Why do I say "most" as opposed to "all" human populations? The reason is that, if we allow populations to be identified on a fine-grained scale, then it becomes possible to find groups of humans most of whom lack these features. A detailed discussion of statistical normality for human populations will be postponed until Chapter 8.

148   THE QUEST FOR HUMAN NATURE

other apes, which that are close to us from an evolutionary perspective. Analogously, if a trait t_1 has a higher heritability than trait t_2, we ought not infer that genes play a more significant role in the production of t_1 than t_2.

A third and even more serious shortcoming of heritability estimates is that they presuppose that genetic and environmental influences are statistically independent of each other and do not interact. Once again, the rationale is straightforward. The main idea underlying heritability is that we can take the overall variation of a trait in a population and break it down to the contribution of genes vs. environment. Nevertheless, in many cases, the effects of genes and environment do not simply add together to produce the combined result. The effect of genes may crucially depend on the environmental backdrop against which they are placed—athletically more gifted children often receive better coaching, for instance. Such complex interchange is expressed well by norms of reaction. This effectively shows that, while estimates of heritability are captured by norms of reaction, norms of reactions provide a lot more information and are therefore difficult to obtain, a point that will become central in the ensuing discussion.

Meanwhile, what interim conclusions should we draw? None of these drawbacks is news to the specialists. Professionals should be perfectly aware of the limitations of heritability just rehearsed—which, note, hold regardless of whether the values of h^2 at hand are gathered via twin studies, GWAS, or altogether different techniques. Still, despite these shortcomings, behavior geneticists maintain that heritability remains a meaningful and useful metric.[11] We just need to use it wisely. Detractors have a different and less charitable take on it. Consider, for instance, the following quote from Evelyn Fox Keller (2010, p. 5)

> The casting of the debate as an effort to determine 'how much of our behavior is driven by our genes versus the environments in which we grow up and live' poses a question that is not only unanswerable but . . . is actually meaningless. Indeed, we scarcely need the new sciences of genomics and epigenetics to teach us this lesson.

---

[11]   A perspective along these lines is defended by Harden (2021a, 2021b).

Or think about Bateson's (2001, p. 155) comments:

> From an adaptationist standpoint, the development of a phenotype appropriate to the circumstances in which the animal finds itself makes a great deal of sense. Nevertheless, the striking ways in which environmental factors can trigger one of a set of alternative responses pose serious difficulties for those behavior geneticists who seek to partition variation into genetic and environmental components. And worse is to come.

The core issue becomes whether we can do better and—if heritability and behavior genetic studies are overly simplistic, prone to misinterpretation, or otherwise problematic—what to put in their place. With this concern in mind, §5.5 explores a "developmentalist" strategy that has emerged in recent decades and considers whether it constitutes an improvement over more reductive approaches.

§5.5 The Developmentalist Alternative

Providing a precise and informative characterization of genetic determinism turns out to be thornier than it appears at first blush. The view cannot be the preposterous suggestion that genes and genes alone are responsible for the production of prominent physical and behavioral traits. Similarly, it would be overly demanding to cash it out as the requirement that an organism with a specific genotype will invariably produce the associated phenotype. Following Kitcher, §5.3 construed a genetically determined trait as one with a flattish norm of reaction, that is, a trait whose covariation with "normal" environmental changes is negligible, or virtually so. §5.4 introduced *heritability*. This concept, which lies at the heart of contemporary behavior genetics, purports to quantify, in precise mathematical terms, the contribution of genes vs. environments in the variation of traits. Despite well-known limitations, behavior geneticists are fond of the explanatory power of heritability studies. Critics are less impressed, finding the notion of heritability murky, misleading, teetering on incoherence.

150   THE QUEST FOR HUMAN NATURE

The question becomes whether there is a better alternative and, if so, what it might be.

This section explores *Developmental Systems Theory*, DST for short, an approach—or, better, a family of approaches with a shared theoretical outlook—that has emerged over the past few decades.[12] DS theorists, like everyone else, begin with the truism that all traits are influenced by both genetic and non-genetic factors. But, from a general DST perspective, this "interactionist consensus," in and of itself, is a marginal improvement over the nature-or-nurture stance it is intended to supplant. DST purports to move beyond the basic interactionist tenet that all biological organisms are the product of a combination of nature and nurture, genes and environment. As three leading proponents present it, "Developmental systems theory...is an attempt to do biology without these dichotomies" (Oyama et al. 2001b, p. 1). On the following page, they go on to elaborate by explaining:

> There are many kinds of influences on development, and there are many ways to group these interactants together. DST does not claim that all these sources of causal influence play the same role, nor that all are equally important (whatever that might mean). Rather, different groupings of developmental factors are valuable when addressing different questions. The distinction between genes and every other causal factor in development ("environment") is just one more grouping, possibly helpful for some purposes, much less so for many others. Many developmentally constructive interactions do not fit traditional categories, and for this reason have largely been overlooked or marginalized. Oppositions between genes (or biology) and learning, or between genes (or biology) and culture, are endemic to many fields but are miserably inadequate for capturing the multitude of causal factors needed for any reasonable treatment of ontogeny or phylogeny. (2001b, p. 2)

This calls for elucidation. Once we move past slogans, what exactly does it mean to get rid of these allegedly false dichotomies? A complete

---

[12] Various versions of DST have been articulated by Griffiths and Gray (1994), Lewontin (2000), Oyama (2000), Oyama et al. (2001a), and West-Eberhard (2003).

presentation, let alone discussion, of DST lies beyond the scope of this work. As noted, the movement encompasses various authors with distinctive and subtly nuanced positions. In what follows, I restrict my attention to the proposal that our entire view of the genotype-phenotype interface is in dire need of a makeover. Specifically, I consider some influential objections against the very notion of norm of reaction advanced, most decisively, by Lewontin, one of the main inspirations and driving forces behind DST.

Lewontin has been a key player in pinpointing and developing the skeptical remarks undermining heritability and naïve genetic determinism discussed at the end of §5.4. His seminal work, spanning multiple decades, has been instrumental in shaking the foundations of the interactionist credo.[13] As Kitcher ([2001] 2003) notes, many of Lewontin's insightful critiques unveil how determinists have overlooked various kinds of complex interactions between genetic and non-genetic factors. And yet, Lewontin maintains, these conclusions do not quite go far enough. The blade must cut deeper. We need to free ourselves from the grip of the old mechanistic picture of the universe as a complex clock-like machine, famously popularized by Descartes. We should recognize the interdependence of organism and environment, thus formulating what Lewontin in collaboration with Levins (Levins and Lewontin 1985a) has labeled *dialectical biology*. From this standpoint, there is a fundamental error behind interactionism, one which can only be rectified by reconceptualizing the field. Let's look at what such a reconstruction might look like.

A first concern voiced by Lewontin revolves around the observation that environments cannot be identified prior to and independently of the organisms inhabiting them and their distinctive forms of behavior. The mistake lurking behind norms of reaction, from this standpoint, involves conceiving of organisms as adapting to independently specified environments, which gradually mold the underlying genotype. A simple example should help clarify the main point. As we saw in §3.4, a norm of reaction presupposes the specification of a series of environments making no reference to organisms. One

---

[13] See especially Lewontin (1974, 1991, 2000) and Lewontin et al. (1984).

152 THE QUEST FOR HUMAN NATURE

subsequently examines how an organism fares in the contexts in question. Yet, Lewontin invites us to ask how we determine with precision what counts as a component of a specific environment and on what basis something is included or excluded:

> Are the stones and the grass in my garden part of the environment of a bird? The grass is certainly part of the environment of a phoebe that gathers dry grass to make a nest. But the stone around which the grass is growing means nothing to the phoebe. On the other hand, the stone is part of the environment of a thrush that may come along with a garden snail and break the shell of the snail against the stone. Neither the grass nor the stone are part of the environment of a woodpecker that is living in a hole in a tree. That is, bits and pieces of the world outside these organisms are made relevant to them by their own life activities. (Lewontin 1991, pp. 109–10)

In the end, Lewontin notes, norms of reaction presuppose that we have a clear understanding of how to order relevant environments along the x axis of the graph depicting the norm of reaction. This, it turns out, is less obvious than is typically assumed.[14]

A second rejoinder against plain interactionism concerns *developmental noise*. Lewontin maintains that, even if we had complete knowledge of both genes and sequences of environments, this would not be enough to accurately predict the development of a phenotype. His illustration involves an asymmetry in the distribution and number of bristles on the left-right axis of fruit flies, which can be strikingly dishomogeneous. Such difference cannot be explained by discrepancies in either environment or genotype, as these are the same on both sides of such tiny organisms. Rather, Lewontin argues, this must be a product of developmental noise: stochastic occurrences of random events. None of this is captured by standard norms of reaction.

A third concern central to the DST critique involves the concept of *causal parity*. No interactionist—indeed, no genetic determinist

---

[14] This insight has inspired *niche construction*, the process by which organisms— and humans are a prime and extreme example—alter environmental states, thereby modifying the conditions and the sources of natural selection (Odling-Smee et al. 2003).

worth their salt—denies that many factors are involved in development. The whole point of a norm of reaction is to isolate some causes and investigate how the effect varies when other variables are altered. But note that genes have a privileged role within norms of reaction, which partitions all causes involved in the production of a phenotype as genetic vs. non-genetic. This, developmentalists insist, is a mistake as there is no reason for preferring representations that foreground the role of genes. To be sure, there is nothing inherent in the notion of norm of reaction that requires partition along this specific axis. In principle, one could create a norm of reaction that keeps the environment constant and varies the genotype. Then why do we always end up discussing whether genotypes are all-powerful? Why does democracy-in-theory invariably turn into elitism-in-practice?

A fourth and final objection against interactionism and norms of reaction alleges that the widespread practice of talking about genes "for" traits is muddled. The idea of genes coding for green eyes, tallness, or aggression is part of a tradition in biology—the "gene-eye view" (§2.3)—that emerged in the 1960s. To be sure, trained biologists know perfectly well that talking about a gene "for" eye color does not mean that a single allele, or set thereof, is solely responsible for producing the trait in question. Wilson, for one, is adamant on this score.[15] Still, developmentalists have two concerns regarding this common parlance. For one thing, it fuels pernicious misinterpretations. Readers without the experience of a professional geneticist may lack the background to interpret these claims in the appropriate light. Hearing that there is a gene "for" blue eyes, they could be led to believe that this is an inevitable, unchangeable property, although this is a non sequitur. This may not be a big deal, as this assumption is not altogether unreasonable. But now consider analogous claims regarding behavioral or psychological traits. Here the—erroneous—assumption that someone has a gene "for" violence or lacks the gene "for" intelligence harbors potentially devastating implications. We thus need to tread carefully.

---

[15] A classic discussion of the "gene-for" locution can be found in Dawkins (1982). Specifically, Dawkins draws a distinction between the *evolutionary context*—where a gene-for-*x* is selectable just in case it has a positive effect on the appearance of *x*-phenotypes in actual genetic and physical environments—and the *developmental context*, where the blending effects of genes on ontogeny become of paramount importance.

154 THE QUEST FOR HUMAN NATURE

A second concern with genes "for" traits is that this way of talking violates the kind of causal parity introduced in the previous paragraph. Griffiths and Gray (1994) argue that, just like we talk about genes for traits, we could also single out cytoplasmic or landscape features for traits. And yet, we seldom do so. In short, the primacy traditionally accorded to genes in biology can and has been questioned.[16] While this debate remains open, developmentalists argue, the importance of genes has been vastly exaggerated. This is reflected and crystallized in norms of reaction. Hence, they too must go.

In sum, DST does not merely eschew crude genetic determinism. It also jabs at the mild interactionism embodied in norms of reaction. From a DST standpoint, organism and environment are interdependent, there is developmental noise in the production of phenotypes, the notion of genes "for" traits cannot be legitimated, and genes play no privileged role in the causal network. To be clear, this causal parity thesis should not be cashed out as the suggestion that there is no difference between the particular causal roles of genes and other developmental factors, such as endosymbionts or imprinting events. The key issue at stake is that such differences do not justify building entire theories of development and evolution around a distinction between what genes do and what every other factor does.[17]

Still, not everyone is on board. Some authors rejoin that these charges go too far. Countering the extremes of genetic determinism by discarding the very gene-environment interface, or expunging nature vs. nurture, throws the baby out with the bath water. It leads biology toward obscure forms of holism which view the specific contribution of parts of a complex system as inextricably tied to the contribution of the whole. A better solution is to work toward the development of true interactionism that avoids relapsing into determinism. The following section explores what such an interactionist stance could look like.

---

[16] For philosophical discussions about the privileged role of genes in molecular-biological explanations, see Weber (2005), Waters (2007), Woodward (2010), and Nathan (2012).

[17] This point is developed, in detail, by Griffiths and Knight (1998).

§5.6 Toward Tried 'n' True Interactionism

Our current issue is how to characterize the relation between genotype and phenotype in an accurate and informative fashion while avoiding the seductive deceptions—and perilous implications—of crude forms of genetic determinism. §5.5 traced the developmentalist route, according to which interactionism doesn't go quite far enough in countering the excesses of determinism. DST recognizes the interdependence between organism and environment and formulates a "dialectical" biology that does not single out the contributions of genetic over non-genetic factors. We need to distance ourselves from genes-environment, nature-nurture, and other false dichotomies. Some feel that this takes it too far. Despite all the acknowledged limitations, the study of genes and their effects on phenotypes has a long history of staggering success. Classical Mendelian genetics first, and molecular biology later, have substantially advanced our understanding of organisms, humans included. Going back to square one, the argument runs, is uncalled for. Now, it may well be that DST will turn into a much more powerful explanatory framework than anything genetics or genomics currently have to offer. And if that day ever arrives, a complete overhaul of the molecular sciences will not only be welcome but recommended. Until then, however, no radical reconceptualization is needed. Better stick with approaches that have withstood the test of time.

A view along these lines has been offered by Philip Kitcher, who maintains that Lewontin's constructive proposal—and more generally DST—lapses into the obscurity of biological holism. Genetic determinism keeps cropping up, Kitcher quips, not because of some subtle misconception about the general character of biological causation, but because biologists are prone to misapply generally correct views:

> One moral we might draw [from Lewontin's arguments] is that we have a defective instrument, but that, I have been urging, is incorrect. There is nothing the matter with the type of model that has been applied. Rather, the trouble lies in the difficulty of the task and the tendency for the impetuous to bungle. (Kitcher [2001] 2003, p. 294)

156 THE QUEST FOR HUMAN NATURE

Of course, Kitcher continues, we might do better if we had different tools. So maybe there is a case for moving beyond interactionism after all—not dismissed as a false or incoherent doctrine but as a source of models too primitive for the important task of fathoming human ontogeny. A different set of theories for development, such as dialectical biology or developmental systems theory, would be welcome if they provided us with new insights. Unfortunately, however, neither dialectical biology nor DST currently offers anything that can be put to work; they are mostly negative, critical paradigms. A better solution, Kitcher suggests, is to develop an improved form of interactionism. What would an interactionism that steers clear of both genetic determinism and obscurantist holism look like? Is there a safe passage through the Scylla of naïve determinism and the Charybdis of radical developmentalism?

The first step is to identify where exactly crude genetic determinism goes astray. Here, Kitcher stresses, Lewontin's powerful critique examined in §5.5 is perfectly on point. The real issue with genetic determinism, according to Lewontin, is straightforward. Contemporary estimates of heritability do not even get close to revealing the contours of norms of reaction. Therefore, the suggested conclusions are not as much false as unfounded, premature.

Since this is a crucial point, for our present purposes, allow me to briefly elaborate. As we've repeatedly emphasized, even the staunchest defender of determinism is—or at least should be—perfectly aware that genes alone do little to nothing. The production of all phenotypic traits, including the apparently simpler ones like eye color, require a complex interaction between genes, other cytological and developmental machineries, and environmental factors. Having said this, it is perfectly possible, in principle at least, to break down this causal thicket and distinguish the contribution of genetic causes from the import of other environmental factors. This is precisely the guiding insight underlying behavior genetic studies. The notion of heritability is intended to provide a reasonably precise quantification of the contribution of genetic factors to the variability existing in a population vis-à-vis the role of the environment. Furthermore, we've introduced a conceptual tool that proves very useful in capturing and visualizing this variation: the norm of reaction. Once again, norms of reaction provide a graphic depiction of how the phenotypic expression of a specific genotype covaries with changes in the environment. The less variation we have as environments shift, the more genetically driven a trait is, which will be captured by the flat or relatively flat shape of the curve.

Now, here's the rub. As discussed in §3.4, simple and intuitive as they are, complete norms of reaction are extremely difficult to compile. Recall our toy example where we were trying to determine how the height of a plant is affected by changes in altitude. In many respects, this appears like an ideal setup. Obtaining clones—copies of the organism with the same genotype—is easy enough in the case of many plants: just clip and re-soil. Both the height of the organism and the altitude of the environment are relatively precise properties which are easy to operationalize and measure, at least at the scale we're working with here. And the conditions that affect the growth of plants are relatively well-known and easy to control. In short, we are set for success, or so it seems. And yet, pitfalls are lurking behind every turn. There are myriad potential interfering factors and confounding variables to control for. The growth and resulting height of a plant is affected not just by elevation but also by soil composition, availability of water, exposure to sunlight, seasonal shifts, meteorological conditions like wind and hail, and many other determinants. In short, discerning with sufficient precision the impact of elevation on the height of a plant turns out to be much more complex than we initially surmised.

With this in mind, imagine plotting a simple phenotypic human trait: how nutrition affects height. Here we have all the same confounding variables we had with plants, and then some. Height is affected by a complex cluster of factors. In addition, a lot of controlling experiments available with vegetables are not applicable to human beings. It would be morally outrageous to clone two genetically identical individuals, raise them on a coerced controlled diet, and see how this affects their height. Having said this, the study of height in humans is far from a worst-case scenario. Height is a relatively well-defined, easily measurable trait, and much is known about what may or may not influence it. Now try playing the same trick with psychological traits. How do we operationalize and measure them? How much do we really know about what has an impact on what? Note that this is precisely what behavior geneticists like Bouchard and Plomin are purporting

158   THE QUEST FOR HUMAN NATURE

to accomplish. With all these complications in mind, how confident should we be in numerical quantifications of religious aptitude or political inclination being "0.4 or 0.57 heritable"?

In conclusion, while the quantification of genetic influence on physical and psychological traits makes perfect sense in theory, it faces an astounding range of practical challenges. Cross-cultural surveys tend to do better if the entire space of non-genetic causal variables is covered. This is hard enough with plants. Humans? Fuhgeddaboudit! Striking gaps in knowledge and inaccuracies emerge clearly in attempts to determine IQ and other mistakes of early popular human sociobiology and, subsequently, of evolutionary psychology.[18] The besetting sin is the tendency to draw conclusions based on woefully inadequate evidence. Norms of reaction are just too hard to obtain. The problem is not the quality of the tool, but its prohibitive cost.

Some readers may be left with a sense of discouragement. They may feel that any hope of shedding light on the phylogeny of our species, physical or psychological, is irremediably lost. Are we condemned to perpetual oblivion? Of course not. Scientific discoveries are costly and hard-won. Refusing to jump to premature conclusions, especially in the case of socially sensitive issues, is hardly tantamount to throwing in the towel. We know something about the role of genes in producing phenotypes. Hopefully, in the future we'll discover a lot more. We're just not there yet. And there is no reason to be ashamed or apologetic about our ignorance, as scientists such as Stuart Firestein (2012) have pointed out.

An important, albeit oft neglected question is *why* behavior geneticists, evolutionists, and other biologists focus so often on genes. Confident biologists, Kitcher notes, believe that new molecular techniques will enhance socially important facets of human behavior. Sophisticated researchers typically begin with genes not because they are convinced of their predominance over other factors, but because they are interested in sketching a neurochemical story. The main rationale is pragmatic. Genes promise to deliver effective explanations. In some instances, this strategy has paid dividends. Research on opioid

---

[18] On this point, see Lewontin et al. (1984), Kitcher (1985b), Gould (1996), and Barker (2015).

ARE WE GENETICALLY DETERMINED? 159

addiction and alcoholism, for instance, has provided illuminating insights on these dangerous and sadly widespread conditions. Other times, the reasons for entering such a research program are more questionable, as in the case of intelligence or aggressive behavior. In these latter cases, there are good reasons for suspecting that there are complex and varied environmental causes, thus rendering the hypothesized norms of reaction highly fallible.[19] We'd do better by focusing on environmental triggers. Sometimes it's just easier to "blame" it on the genes. But this is an urge we ought to resist.

Following Kitcher, let's pose two pressing questions regarding attempts to unearth genes "for" complex human traits. First, is the investigation informed by a commitment to explore the impact of some factors, while others vary, in a way that recognizes our ignorance about environmental causes and that pragmatically deploys the genetic techniques to remedy that ignorance? Second, does the information to be acquired lead to a social policy that is both applicable and morally defensible? By keeping these issues in mind, interactionism has the potential to truly straddle the middle lane, incorporating the insights of both genetic determinism and developmentalism, while eschewing respective excesses. As Kitcher puts it:

Unless we have a scientifically informed and ethically sophisticated public discourse about possible programs of genetic research, we are likely either to lose important benefits or, more likely, by accepting the most extravagant promises at face value, mix in significant social harms with the improvements we seek. Because he sees the latter possibility so clearly, Lewontin has come to advocate a "dialectical biology" that will move beyond interactionism. I have tried to argue that critiques of interactionism are flawed, that they do not respond

---

[19] An interesting illustration of both the causal relevance of genes and the modulating effects of environments is the *Dunedin Multidisciplinary Health and Development Study*: an ongoing, longitudinal study of the health, development, and well-being of a general sample of New Zealanders. Data from this study—which began when patients were born in 1972–73, has followed them through midlife, and which will hopefully continue further—suggests how specific genetic profiles can interact with social and other environmental stressors to produce anti-social outcomes. Yet, the effects of that same genetic makeup are indistinguishable from "normal" alleles when the subjects live in a less stressful milieu. I am grateful to a reviewer for bringing this to my attention.

160   THE QUEST FOR HUMAN NATURE

to the genuine problems of using biology to promote human good, and that there is no substitute for a detailed examination of the merits of individual cases. ([2001] 2003, pp. 297–98)

In conclusion, the previous two sections explored two alternative reactions to genetic determinism. Interactionism purports to retain a gene-environment interface, albeit one that does not encourage illicit inferences. From the unassailable premise that genes causally contribute to the production of traits hardly follows the conclusion that "DNA is destiny" or similar absurdities. Developmentalism takes this a step further, suggesting that the traditional genes vs. environment dichotomy needs to be overhauled by a more "dialectical" biology. Personally, I am inclined to follow Kitcher's responsible "tried 'n' true" interactionism, at least until DST starts delivering on its promises. Be that as it may, the remaining pressing issue, for our present concerns, is where this leaves us with respect to human nature. To this we turn in our final section.

§5.7 Deep Answers to Deep Questions

Time to wrap things up. This chapter focused on genetic determinism. What's that? At the most general level, genetic determinism holds that prominent features of all biological organisms, humans included, arise from their genetic makeup. The problem with this formulation is that it is too vague to be adequately assessed. Depending on how we parse it, its meaning may shift from obvious platitude to a boisterous overstatement, turning the thesis under scrutiny into a moving target. To wit, in the space of a couple pages, Wilson switches from acknowledging that people are molded by an interaction of genes and environment to stating that the evidence for genetic determinism was "already decisive" back in the late 1970s, at the time he was writing. How exactly to parse such pronouncements remains murky.

In an attempt to sharpen the dispute, §5.2 introduced some basic facts regarding the relation between genotypes and phenotypes. These considerations emphasize how genes play a key role in the production of virtually any trait, physical or mental. But they don't do it alone. The challenge is reframing the core debate between friends and foes of determinism against a shared interactionist backdrop that acknowledges the indispensability of both genetic and environmental factors in shaping who we are.

With this goal in mind, §5.3 reframed the central thesis of genetic determinism in terms of norms of reaction. From this standpoint, a trait is deemed genetically determined whenever it has a flat or virtually flat norm of reaction, that is, if the expression of the trait is invariant to changes in "normal" environments—a notion first encountered in Chapter 3, and which still resists any attempt at naturalization. Modulo this caveat, we now have a clear and testable candidate hypothesis.

So, which traits are genetically determined in virtue of having a flattish norm of reaction? Behavior genetic studies employ the concept of *heritability* to quantify the amount of variation in a population of reference due to genetic vs. non-genetic factors, respectively. A high heritability value in phenotypic traits such as height, eye color, and skin tone may not be all too shocking. But, in addition—and much more controversially—some behavior geneticists have maintained that even psychological, cognitive traits such as personality, mental ability, psychiatric illness, and social attitudes are heritable, up to a striking degree. This form of genetic determinism should be taken with more than just a grain of salt, especially in the face of inherent limitations in the concept of heritability rehearsed in §5.4.

If heritability studies are deeply problematic, how should genetic determinism be countered? §5.5 presented the "developmental alternative," which tries to dispose altogether of nature vs. nurture, genes vs. environments, and other traditional dichotomies. The concern is that this may be taking it a step too far, throwing the baby out with the bath water. Classical Mendelian genetics and molecular biology are highly successful research programs. Neither "dialectical biology" nor DST can boast remotely comparable achievements, at least thus far. We therefore sought a different path.

§5.6 outlined a middle-of-the-road interactionist stance, moving away from the excesses of genetic determinism without completely overhauling current methodology. From this perspective, what is perplexing about heritability studies is not that genes have a crucial role to play in the production of psychological traits or that their

162   THE QUEST FOR HUMAN NATURE

contribution can be contrasted to that of environmental or other factors. What should raise eyebrows is the confidence with which behavior geneticists quantify the causal influences on these traits. Recall the arduous challenges in defining the contours of norms of reaction in the case of plants, which are much easier to manipulate and raise fewer ethical quibbles. We can hardly be so sure that all alternative explanations have been ruled out when it comes to cognitively nuanced and complex organisms such as humans. Thus construed, the issue with genetic determinism is not much its falsity as the lack of robust corroborating evidence.

Before moving on, two brief closing remarks. First, in the end, are we genetically determined or are we not? This question, it seems to me, is ill-posed as it conflates two distinct and independent senses of "determinism."

On the one hand, whether we are genetically determined may be interpreted as asking whether DNA is destiny, that is, whether we are the hapless product of genetic or evolutionary happenstance. The answer is clear. We are not. Our life is no more canalized by our biological endowment than it is by our surrounding environment. Now, surely, there are vexing puzzles about whether free will and moral responsibility can be reconciled with our best physical theories. But this is an altogether different problem, independent of genes and genomes, which I set aside for another occasion.

On the other hand, the question of whether we are determined by our genes or environment may be conceived as asking whether it is possible to predict the complete development of a trait, given accurate and exhaustive knowledge concerning genetic and environmental influences. This is a much subtler and more intriguing issue. Radical genetic determinism seems committed to answering in the positive. Not only would it be possible, in principle, to compute the development of any trait from genetic and environmental data. In addition, assessments of heritability are already contributing, in practice, to partitioning the range of these influences. More modestly, sophisticated interactionists could respond that while such derivation may be theoretically feasible, it remains a de facto impossibility. We still lack both the detailed information and the computational power to make any informed guess and we should therefore tread carefully.

ARE WE GENETICALLY DETERMINED?   163

Developmentalists take this a step further, claiming that such derivation is an in-principle impracticality. The partitioning of causes into genetic vs. environmental is hopelessly muddled. As such, we should not expect it to shed much light on our signature traits.

Are we genetically determined in this latter, more nuanced sense? This is a tough question. While the strong genetic determinist position strikes me as unreasonably optimistic, it is difficult to choose between the other two stances. Whether or not human development could theoretically be predicted, given enough biological and ecological information, is not a puzzle that can presently be solved. Nevertheless, it should be emphasized that neither option gives any currency to the first sense of genetic determination, the pernicious dogma that DNA is destiny.

Moving on to the second and final remark, is genetic determinism or something close to it useful in science or society? Does it promote a socially dangerous agenda? Does it shed new light on the notion of human nature? I am inclined to offer a negative answer to all these queries. The reason is that, when faced with complicated questions, people demand simple answers. This is certainly true in politics and economics. What caused the 2008 recession? What started World War II? The same happens with biological and social events. How did Mozart become a musical genius? How effective is education in eradicating violence? Everyone is well aware that numerous factors contribute to complicated events such as a war, a downturn in the economic market, the ability to produce a musical masterpiece, or a spike in violent crime. But people want to cut to the chase: what *really* made a difference? And this is the first step on the road to confusion. We should not seek a simplistic solution to a sophisticated query.

The very idea of genetic determination encourages this pernicious tendency. As Bateson (2001, p. 149) aptly notes: "Explanations in terms of combinations of conditions is [sic] perceived as wooly, obscurantist, and running counter to the successful analytical programs of science." And yet, dreadfully oversimplified notions, as seductive as they may be, often end up corrupting true understanding. The assumption of DNA constituting a "blueprint" or a "set of instructions" for producing phenotypes constitutes a case in point. Sophisticated biologists are perfectly aware that even a relatively simple phenotypic trait, such

164 THE QUEST FOR HUMAN NATURE

as the color of your eyes, requires a subtle blend of genetic, developmental, and ecological ingredients. Still, the general public may misinterpret this gene-centric talk as proving that such characters depend solely, or mostly, on our genotype. Heritability studies that purport to provide more or less exact quantifications of the relative apportionment of causal responsibility of genes and environment—often based on dreadfully inadequate evidence—certainly do not help. Deep questions call for deep answers. We better come to terms with this.

In conclusion, the notion of genetic determinism is too murky to shed any substantial light on the concept of human nature. Presently, the set of traits that have a flattish norm of reaction will, at best, capture highly heritable bodily features, such as eye color, which are stubbornly resilient to environmental changes. None of them are likely to provide any groundbreaking insight on who we really are and ought to be. We better keep moving. But where to next?

* * *

Brief interlude. At this point in our journey, more than a few frustrated readers may feel inclined to pull the plug on the entire project. Motivated by Chomsky's remarks, we initially set out to provide a systematic study of human nature because this appeared to be the foundation of any serious social science or theory of social change. But we do not seem to have all that much to show for all the effort we put in. Five long and hefty chapters into our discussion, clear-cut answers continue to elude us. Something is going on. Could it be that the very notion of human nature is a chimera? Perhaps, contra Chomsky, Pinker, and Lewontin, we do not need a precise characterization of human nature to ground the social sciences. The second half of this book explores this possibility. Rather than striving to define human nature so that we can approach it empirically, we'll focus on the implications—scientific, sociopolitical, and philosophical—of the very notion of human nature. First stop, in the following chapter, is a normatively loaded notion that continues to have momentous implications for our lives: the concept of human race.

6
Oppression or Emancipation? Part (i)
Human Races

I believe in pride of race and lineage and self
—W. E. B. Du Bois, *Credo*, 1904

§6.1 From Human Nature to Human Races

Where do we stand with respect to our quest for human nature? Chapter 1 kicked off with Chomsky's dictum: there is no serious social science without an underlying conception of human nature. Chapter 2 revealed that developing a true science of human nature is less straightforward than it initially appeared. Chapter 3 sought a viable definition but reached the conclusion that human nature may be too broad a concept to be analyzed directly. We therefore followed a different path, breaking human nature down into more tractable proxies: innateness (Chapter 4) and genetic determinism (Chapter 5). Both surrogates turned out to be just as thorny and elusive as human nature itself. What conclusions should we draw?

A cautious, preliminary moral is that the solution to the mystery of human nature cannot simply be inferred from empirical data alone. Laboratory toil, invaluable as it surely is, falls short of conclusive force. Philosophical reflection and conceptual analysis are also necessary to sharpen our inquiries. Still, a deeper concern lingers. What's missing is not merely answers to our queries. We lack a clear sense of how our guiding questions should be raised. Something has gone south.

One possibility is that we've set up the wrong target. Do we need a human nature? Is our nature really presupposed in theoretical discussions of who we are and ought to be? The second half of this book

The Quest for Human Nature. Marco J. Nathan, Oxford University Press. © Oxford University Press 2024.
DOI: 10.1093/oso/9780197699249.003.0006

166   THE QUEST FOR HUMAN NATURE

addresses these nagging concerns. We'll leave definitions of human nature and cognate concepts behind and focus on their scientific and sociopolitical implications.

Our point of departure is whether human nature is inherently oppressive or may also play an emancipatory role. My long answer will keep us busy for two hefty chapters. First, we shall discuss a normatively tainted concept that has had and continues to have profound implications for our lives: the notion of human races. Next, Chapter 7 will focus the discussion on sex and gender equality and other important items on the feminist agenda.

Here is the master plan for oppression vs. emancipation, part (i). §6.2 will get us going by sketching a brief overview of the dire history of racialism. §6.3 sets the tone by presenting some basic facts about human genetic diversity which are often misrepresented. The following three sections will outline three different answers to the question of whether human races exist: naturalism (§6.4), constructionism (§6.5), and eliminativism (§6.6). Finally, §6.7 wraps up by discussing more directly whether talk of races presupposes a human nature.

Before getting started, I must address a preliminary concern. I doubt that anyone will second-guess my decision to delve into such a timely and pressing topic as race. But how do races fit into our theme? What's the connection between human races and human nature? Here're two answers.

First, races constitute a microcosm in our macrocosm. Given the hurdles encountered in the previous five chapters, it may be tempting to shift our focus from our entire species to smaller, more cohesive units. Races are an obvious candidate. Next, by quilting together independent analyses of specific races, one may hope to obtain an overarching depiction of humanity. Alas, this strategy is doomed to failure. Human races, we shall promptly see, are no less fraught with controversy than human nature itself. This is not to say, of course, that studying races yields nothing of value. Quite the contrary. The point is that it's challenging enough to draw a sharp line between us and other animals. Partitioning our species will not be any easier.

A second reason for focusing on the relation between human races and human nature seems more compelling. Races provide an effective case study to assess the scientific and sociopolitical significance of human nature. Allow me to briefly elaborate. With the emergence of racial skepticism in the aftermath of the horrors of World War II, many started to view the subdivision of humans into distinct races as a pernicious mistake. All people are equal in rights, dignity, and potential. Still, how exactly this claim is to be parsed and justified—were the need ever to arise again—is hardly obvious. A straightforward strategy appeals to a shared human nature that grounds our common humanity. This raises the pressing concern of whether human nature is part of the problem or part of the solution. Is our common nature a portal to dehumanization or the key to emancipation from the pitfalls of oppressive racism? If the former, we better find some adequate surrogates.

§6.2 A Brief History of Racialism

As far back as we can gaze, societies have grappled with human diversity by partitioning people into distinct groups believed to be significantly separate from one another. Yet, the use of "race" as a categorization of human beings is relatively recent, first found in the English language in the late sixteenth century, imported from the French *rasse* and the Italian *razza*. Initially, the term had a meaning similar to other classificatory terms such as "type," "sort," or "kind." Its modern connotation was established in the 1700s, when systematic travel and exploration across the globe became more common, and "race" became widely employed for grouping people in the colonies.

The practice of dividing humans into separate races can be discerned in the work of natural scientists and Enlightenment thinkers—including Cuvier, Buffon, Blumenbach, Voltaire, and Kant—and remained prominent through the nineteenth century. Races were identified roughly based on superficial phenotypic properties, like skin tone, hairstyle, and facial features. These races were believed to share prominent psychological and behavioral properties in virtue of common ancestry. In addition, races were often, though not invariably, ranked. Unsurprisingly, in the Western tradition, white Europeans were viewed as free men and the pinnacle of humanity, superior to Amerindians, who were gradually being conquered, and Africans brought in as slave labor. This pseudo-scientific attitude persisted

168   THE QUEST FOR HUMAN NATURE

through the early twentieth century. Prior to World War II, *Homo sapiens* was perceived as a polytypic species with biologically distinct subgroups or races. This biological differentiation was taken to be the result of long periods of independent evolution, when races were largely isolated from each other.

No one should be shocked to hear that classical *racialism*—the view that superficial phenotypic properties signal deep biological and psychological differences, with some races being superior to others—led to notorious abominations, from slavery to genocide. Yet, traditional anthropological ideas about human diversity shifted decisively only in the twentieth century. Shortly after World War II, partly as a response to the horrors of Nazism, the United Nations Educational Scientific and Cultural Organization (UNESCO) released a statement, drafted by leading sociologists and anthropologists, criticizing the folk notion of race, long assumed to be self-evident. Challenging the consensus of their time, they insisted that all humans are equal and alike. It is habit that drags us apart. The notion of race must be treated as a social myth, a position which came to be known as *racial skepticism*.

The dismantling of race continued in the second half of the twentieth century, as anthropologists and biologists piled on evidence supporting racial skepticism over racialism and other kinds of typological thinking. New genetic data undermined the old credo. It was found that there is significantly more genetic diversity within racial groups than between them. Consequently, the narrative unfolded, humans cannot be meaningfully divided into a few discrete races. Studies of human biological diversity began to focus less on classification and more on variation patterns among populations and evolutionary processes shaping them. Controversial research persisting in looking for cognitive or behavioral differences between races was harshly criticized.[1]

Then the proverbial pendulum started swinging back. Molecular data collected over the past four decades thinned the fragile consensus underwriting racial skepticism. New research in genetics and molecular biology divides humans into distinct groups based on genetic

---

[1] Examples of projects that have been frowned upon include Jensen (1969), Herrnstein and Murray (1994), and Rushton and Jensen (2005).

properties. Some geneticists have further claimed that their findings support or vindicate the folk concept of race. These considerations raise pressing concerns. Do these discoveries legitimize traditional views which divided humans into discrete demes? What does modern science tell us about human races?

We can distinguish three general stances concerning human races. First, *naturalism* purports to justify the biological "reality" of race. From this standpoint, humans can legitimately be divided into natural groups, which have sociopolitical significance. Second, *constructionism* conceives of races as real but social as opposed to natural kinds. Third, *eliminativism* treats races as fictions to be abandoned, much like the discarded concepts of witches and ghosts. After discussing human genetic variation, the bulk of this chapter outlines these three stances. Yet, before getting down to business, let's pose some preliminary questions. Should we care about the ontology of race? Does the choice between these three stances really matter? If so, why? If not, why not?

Setting sociopolitical implications and connections to human nature aside until §6.7, the study of race has opened business opportunities. Corporations sell kits to determine "ethnic backgrounds" and reconstruct family histories. Pharmaceutical companies target drugs to specific racial groups. A well-known example is *BiDil*, a prescription medicine marketed in the United States to treat heart failure in patients of African descent. One could wonder about the appropriate response to these commercial moves. A naturalist could welcome these developments providing meaningful information about our ancestry and allowing more precise, targeted medical treatments. Race is an important biological factor, the argument runs, not to be ignored on pain of injustice. Eliminativists, in turn, would presumably treat these products as commercial scams, and potentially harmful ones. If races are fictions, a drug targeting a specific race has the same physiological significance as marketing a product for goblins or wizards. Constructionists might agree with eliminativists that there is no need for differential medical treatment. Yet, they may add, social differences must be considered in deciding a course of treatment or the approval of a drug. If the choice between these stances matters, then how should we adjudicate them? What kind of evidence is decisive? To answer these questions, we first must get clear on genetic diversity.

170   THE QUEST FOR HUMAN NATURE

§6.3 Human Genetic Diversity

The study of human variation has intriguing applications. Genetic variation—the focus of the present section—has proven quite useful to forensic scientists and indirectly to Hollywood producers. At certain loci on our genome there is so much individual difference that a person can be reliably picked out from a genetic test performed on a blood sample. This data can be used to identify DNA left on a crime scene and narrow a pool of suspects. Despite their intrinsic interest, we'll set forensic applications of genetics aside as such molecular information does not reveal much of consequence about the nature of our species or race.[2]

More pertinent to our current exploration, specific patterns in genetic variation provide evidence concerning individual ancestry, roughly defined as the geographical regions where one's biological ancestors dwelled.[3] As anticipated in §6.2, knowing an individual's history may have biomedical applications if it turns out that ancestry influences disease-susceptibility and drug response. In addition, many people nowadays seem interested in learning more about their own personal and familial genealogy. For all these reasons, it is worth asking what genetics can tell us about our identity and history, as species, races, or individuals. This section surveys the ongoing dispute over the measurement of human variation and its implications for understanding who we are and what our true "nature" may turn out to be.

Let's kick off by establishing three basic facts. First, nobody disputes that people diverge at multiple levels: phenotypic, cognitive, behavioral, etc. All organisms vary. Pervasive variation across the biological world was already evident to pre-evolutionary typologists, who viewed individual idiosyncrasies as distortion from ideal types (§3.4). It was equally apparent to Darwin and his followers, for whom variation is a core tenet of evolutionary dynamics (§2.2). Second, variation is nodal. Individuals fall into clusters in phenotypic space. Third, these clusters—demes, races, or species—are the product of evolutionary processes acting on individual differences. None of these

---

[2] For a detailed discussion of these forensic applications, see McSwiggan et al. (2017).
[3] A classic study is Cavalli-Sforza et al. (1994). An updated overview is Reich (2018).

preliminary points is controversial and has not been for a very long time. What has been, and continues to be, heavily disputed is the biological significance of variation. For the better part of the twentieth century, there was a considerable spectrum of opinion regarding the relative amount and weight of *intra-group* variation—variation within a specific population of organisms—as opposed to *inter-group* variation, that is, variation between groups of biological individuals. These debates were partly a consequence of uncovering new scientific facts and partly reflected general sociopolitical biases derived from our social experience.

How are these disputes to be settled? Until an objective method of quantification of genetic diversity became widely available, assessments of the degree of variation within and between groups inevitably remained subjective. Unsurprisingly, it was biased in the direction of attaching greater significance to variation *between* groups, likely reflecting a widespread classificatory tendency in human psychology. None of this, of course, is to deny that pre-molecular biological groupings into the major clades of life was quite successful, even by modern standards. Many species were identified long before the advent of genetics or even of the evolutionary framework. Ethnobiology has indeed confirmed that foragers are strikingly effective at dividing organisms into bona fide species and recognizing similarities among them. Nevertheless, there is always a risk that classifications based on phenotypic traits reflect superficial as opposed to deep biological differences. Such cognitive biases emerge vividly with non-human animals and become more pronounced the further we move away on the evolutionary spectrum. To wit, imagine being saddled with the sorting of mice into types. Most people tend to focus on basic phenotypic differences, such as size and fur coat hue. But it is hardly obvious that superficial alterations reflect deep differences among complex organisms. It may well be that grouping mice into, say, black, brown, and white fails to capture significant biological factors while obliterating subtler discrepancies. And the task becomes even more arduous once we switch to species phylogenetically more distant from us, such as insects or bacteria. But, even if we do not place much trust in our classificatory strategy, for a long time we lacked a viable alternative.

172 THE QUEST FOR HUMAN NATURE

Molecular biology to the rescue! The 1960s brought about a revolution in the assessment of inherited variation, fueled by innovative molecular techniques. Protein electrophoresis and immunological interventions enabled a locus-by-locus direct and objective assessment of genetic variation among individuals. Oversimplifying a bit, the idea was to identify a random handful of genetic loci where humans are known to vary. This data could then be used to estimate the degree of variation within and between human populations on a firmer quantitative basis. Specific patterns in genetic variation provide evidence of whether a gene is currently under selection. If genes are being acted upon by evolution, there may be differences in those genes and associated traits across geographic regions or populations. If variation in certain genes is widespread and knows no ethnic or geographic boundary, that variation is not a useful guide for dividing us into racial groups.

This now sounds like prehistory. Modern-day researchers can decode entire genomes, sequence DNAs of organisms, and compare them base-by-base. And the cost of doing so is steadily decreasing, while the speed and efficiency are increasing. Thanks to all these developments, the original question of how much variation there is between groups can now be addressed experimentally. Unlike old subjective judgments, molecular techniques do not require any a priori intuition about the existence and significance of variation among individuals or populations. So, how much genetic variation is there?

Not so fast. Despite staggering technological advancements, methodological hurdles still stand in our way. In his groundbreaking paper, "The Apportionment of Genetic Diversity," Lewontin (1972) examines three issues which over half a century later remain both pressing and worthy of discussion.

First, there is the question of how to pick the samples. The goal is to study genetic diversity across our entire species. Who should we test? Ideally, we would collect DNA from every human. In practice, that ain't gonna happen. There's just too many of us. We must select a representative sample. Yet, a little reflection will reveal some pitfalls. Suppose that we have the resources to examine one thousand units. Clearly, we shouldn't gather all of them from the same city as that would not represent humanity as a whole. Let's pick them from across the planet. Given that there are 195 countries in the world, we could pick five members per country and still have a handful to spare. But something isn't quite right. Five samples from China's population of almost 1.4 billion, and five samples from San Marino's fewer than forty thousand? That would hardly be proportionate, under-sampling the former and overestimating the latter. Perhaps we could weight nations by overall population. Then, tiny European countries like Luxembourg and Andorra would not be included at all. Same with Amazonian tribes whose presence on the map would be washed out by the welter of over 200 million Brazilians.

Setting technicalities aside, the central issue should now be evident. By focusing on larger, more populous countries, the contribution of small, isolated, and usually more genetically distinct demes is effectively reduced to zero. And so is the amount of diversity calculated to exist between populations. The moral is that, while we should always strive to avoid bias, there is no such thing as *the* "correct" sampling. Tough, consequential choices cannot be avoided. Lewontin (1972, p. 385) is adamant on this score:

> In this paper I have chosen to count each population included as being of equal value and to include, as much as possible, equal numbers of African peoples, European nationalities, Oceanian populations, Asian peoples, and American Indian tribes. Both of these choices will maximize both the total human diversity and the proportion of it that is calculated between populations as opposed to within populations. This bias should be borne in mind when interpreting the results.

A second methodological problem concerns racial classification. Wait, how did races enter the picture? Aren't we assessing genetic diversity across *individuals*? Yes. Yet, given that every person has a unique genome (§3.2), the question becomes whether we can cluster genotypes based on similarity. Ethnicity provides candidate groupings. In other words, races supply classificatory hypotheses for clustering genomes together in virtue of closeness.

The standard method of classification into races begins with geography. Setting aside concerns involving timescale—which shall be addressed in §6.6—we can start by separating human populations

174 THE QUEST FOR HUMAN NATURE

based on where they live or, better, where their ancestors lived. The inhabitants of Europe speaking Indo-European languages, the indigenes of sub-Saharan Africa, the Aborigines of North and South America, and the people of mainland East and Southeast Asia become the modal groups that, at the time when Lewontin was writing, used to be called "Caucasian," "Negroid," "Amerind," and "Mongoloid." Next, all those not yet included are sorted by affinity or set up as separate races or sub-races using linguistic, morphological, historical, and cultural information. For instance, are Australian Aborigines part of Southeast Asia or are they racially separate?

Intuitive as this may seem, once again pitfalls await round the corner. Despite the unassailable existence of nodes in the distribution of human morphological and cultural traits, populations are sprinkled between the nodes so that boundary lines must be arbitrary.[4] While it is relatively easy to categorize Papuan Aborigines and South American natives as belonging to different races, how should we establish an objective criterion, a dividing line drawn in the continuum from South American Indians through Polynesians, Micronesians, Melanesians, to Papuans and Native Americans? In short, some populations always create difficulties of classification. Are Lapps Caucasians or Asian? Linguistically they are Asians, morphologically they are ambiguous; their MNS blood group is clearly non-Asian but also a poor fit for European frequencies. Analogous difficulties affect Hindi-speaking Indians, Urdu-speaking Pakistanis, and many other peoples.

Lewontin's classification yields seven "races," adding South Asian Aborigines and Oceanians to the usual four races, while also segregating Australian Aborigines together with Papuan natives:

> I have chosen a conservative path and have used mostly the classical racial groupings with a few switches based on obvious total genetic divergence. Thus, the question I am asking is, "How much of human diversity between populations is accounted for by more or less conventional racial classification?" (Lewontin 1972, p. 386)

---

[4] As we saw in Chapter 3, rampant and continuous variation makes it extremely difficult to divide people into normal vs. abnormal, a point that will be reinforced in Chapter 8. Similar considerations affect any classification based on phenotypic traits.

OPPRESSION OR EMANCIPATION? PART (I)   175

The bottom line is that there is no absolute way of partitioning humans into candidate similarity classes. Overwhelmed? Great, you should be!

Once both problems—sample picking and racial classification—have been addressed, we are confronted by a third methodological issue of different ilk. The basic data obtained in the genetic samples are frequencies of alternative alleles at various loci, or "supergenes," in different populations. The challenge is to use this data to operationalize diversity. Any measure of diversity, Lewontin notes, ought to have the following four characteristics. First, it should be at a minimum—for the sake of convenience, we can use the value 0—when there is only a single allele present, so that the locus in question shows no variation. Second, for a fixed number of alleles, variation should be maximum when all are equal in frequency. The diversity value is much less when one of the alternative kinds is very rare. Third, diversity ought to somehow increase as the number of different alleles in the population grows. Specifically, if all alleles are equally frequent, then a population with several alleles is obviously more diverse than a population with just two of them. Fourth and finally, the diversity measure ought to be a convex function of frequencies of alleles. A collection of individuals constructed by pooling two populations is always more diverse than their average, unless the populations are identical in composition. There are two measures that fit all four requirements.[5] One is the "proportion of heterozygotes" (h) that would be produced in a random mating population or assemblage. A second option is the "Shannon information measure" (H), widely used to characterize species diversity in community ecology. In his study, Lewontin (1972) opts for H, which, without introducing unnecessary technicalities, can be viewed as quantifying the level of "surprise" of a particular outcome, closely related to the physical notion of entropy.

We are finally ready for the results we've been waiting for. Lewontin analyzed data from seventeen polymorphic loci, including the major

---

[5] One ordinarily thinks of some sort of analysis of variance (ANOVA) for this purpose, as an analysis that would break down genetic variation into a component within a population, between populations, and between races. ANOVA, however, is an inappropriate technique for dealing with allelic frequencies since, when there are more than two alleles at one locus, there is no single well-ordered variable whose variance will be calculated.

176   THE QUEST FOR HUMAN NATURE

blood groups. Gene frequencies are given for the seven standard "races." Less than 15% of all human genetic diversity is accounted for by differences between human groups. Differences between populations within a race account for an additional 8.3%, so that only 6.3% is captured by racial classification.[6] Lewontin (1972, p. 397) concludes that no justification can be offered for the continuance of racial classification, which has virtually no genetic or taxonomic significance:

> It is clear that our perception of relatively large differences between human races and subgroups, as compared to the variation within these groups, is indeed a biased perception and that, based on randomly chosen genetic differences, human races and populations are remarkably similar to each other, with the largest part by far of human variation being accounted for by the differences between individuals. Human racial classification is of no social value and is positively destructive of social and human relations. Since such racial classification is now seen to be of virtually no genetic or taxonomic significance either, no justification can be offered for its continuance.

Lewontin's results—about 85% of total genetic variation is due to individual differences within populations and only 15% to differences between populations or ethnic groups—and his related suggestion that the division of *Homo sapiens* into these groups is not justified by genetic data, have been quite influential. Despite the over half a century that has gone by since its publication, Lewontin's study has passed the muster of time and is still quoted approvingly to this day. To be sure, as we shall see, some geneticists question the implications that Lewontin draws. Yet, the moral is that, despite the technology that provides precise genetic assessments, issues about human diversity are not straightforwardly empirical. They depend on substantive background assumptions. We discussed three methodological hurdles. First, how do we pick out representative samples of humans across

---

[6] This allocation of 85% of human genetic diversity to individual variation within populations is still inflated because of the overweighting of these small groups, which tend to have large gene frequencies that deviate from the larger races. These points are further developed in *The Genetic Basis of Evolutionary Change* (Lewontin 1974).

the globe? Second, how do we cluster individuals into races? Where should boundaries be drawn? Third, how do we operationalize diversity? With these results and corresponding caveats under our belts, let's move on to ask in what sense, if any, races exist and whether this sheds light on our main course: human nature.

§6.4 Race Naturalism

The previous section surveyed some evidence concerning the amount of genetic variation across human populations. Lewontin interpreted these results as flat-out undermining the biological significance of human races. He concludes his classic 1972 study by suggesting that no justification can be offered for the continuing practice of classifying humans into separate races. Lewontin's proposal has not been heeded. Half a century later, people are still routinely clustered according to race. Is this a mistake? To answer this question, it is crucial to keep the issues of race and genetic variation separate. None of the points raised in the previous section are especially controversial. What calls for immediate attention are their racial implications.

We can identify three overarching stances regarding the ontological status of race. First, naturalism views race as a real, genuine, objective biological category. Second, constructionism takes races to be social constructions, as opposed to natural kinds. Third, eliminativism sees races as fictional entities in dire need of displacement. The present section focuses on naturalism. The other two approaches will be addressed in due course.

Many readers will find it tempting to view the ontological debate on human races as a straight-up empirical issue. A simple analogy may help drive the point home. Over the centuries, science has confirmed the existence of certain entities while eschewing others. The idea that physical matter is made up of indivisible microscopic units called "atoms" harks back to Democritus, in the fifth century BCE. Subsequent developments have vindicated this speculative hypothesis. Physicists still believe—with excellent reason—that matter can be broken down into atoms, although these particles are different in significant respects from the ones originally envisioned. For one thing, atoms are no longer

178 THE QUEST FOR HUMAN NATURE

taken to be indivisible. Yet, this is not the fate of all scientific posits. To wit, roughly a century after Democritus, Aristotle explained the motion of the planets and other astral bodies by positing a set of celestial crystal spheres revolving around the Earth, which sat still at the center of the universe. Modern astronomy realized that there are no crystal spheres framing the astral vault. Hence, these entities have been eliminated from our ontology, the catalogue of things believed to exist. The main question concerning the status of human races, from this perspective, is simple. Are races like atoms or like celestial spheres? Do they exist or do they not? Thus construed, the dispute can be usefully phrased as whether races are natural kinds.

What exactly does it mean to ask whether races are natural kinds? How should this issue be settled? What evidence are we supposed to look for? Following a long-standing tradition whose roots dig all the way down to Aristotle, a kind purports to capture the classification of objects in terms of essences. From this standpoint, every kind is associated with a set of properties that are necessary and sufficient for an object to belong to the kind, and which explain membership therein. This is precisely the essentialism discussed in §3.2. As we saw, the property of being platinum is governed by the essential property *having atomic number 79*, which is a feature shared by all and only platinum atoms, and which explains membership into said kind. Are human races kinds in the same sense as platinum? This would require a racial essence, that is, a set of necessary and sufficient conditions for belonging to a particular race. No one should be shocked that no such essence is to be found. The basic facts about genetic diversity outlined in §6.3 conclusively reveal that there is no specific genetic sequence shared by all and only members of a race. And a little reflection will generalize this conclusion to biological essences of any other sort. If there is no intrinsic property shared by all and only humans, the chances of finding a non-trivial property shared by, say, all and only Caucasians or East Asians are basically null. In brief, if human races are construed as Aristotelian kinds—that is, kinds defined by essences—then there are no human races. Case closed.

Does this mean that races are not a biological category? No. Concluding that races are not natural kinds tout court would be overly rash. With essences off the table, there remain alternative conceptions

OPPRESSION OR EMANCIPATION? PART (I)   179

of kinds that seem more congenial to racial classification. For instance, according to a tradition pioneered by Locke, kinds are unified not by essences but by shared overlapping properties. These properties play a pivotal role in the causal structure of the world and, accordingly, in our explanations. From this viewpoint, concepts have essences, individuals do not. Could races be "Lockean" kinds? This requires finding some property that characterizes all and only members of a race without being essential. Even better, what is needed is a set of properties that is shared, to varying degrees, by all members of a race. According to a *homeostatic property cluster* (HPC) conception, kinds can be construed as sets of co-occurring properties underpinned by homeostatic mechanisms causing and sustaining such features.[7] Thus conceived, species and races may be characterized as natural kinds. Nevertheless, as we shall now see, the dispute is hardly settled.

Studies of human genetic structure conducted over the past few decades witness the consistent emergence of two broad patterns.[8] First, African populations exhibit greater diversity and less linkage disequilibrium than non-African populations.[9] This makes intuitive sense. African populations are older—*Homo sapiens* originally evolved in Africa before dispersing— and have thus had more time to accumulate random genetic mutations. Hence, non-Africans are less diverse, from a genetic standpoint, compared to native Africans. Second, human variation is "clinal," that is, continuously distributed. Allele frequencies change gradually across geographic space with few sharp discontinuities, so that nearby populations are genetically closer, and similarity is inversely correlated with geographic distance. Once again, this is hardly shocking news. Since proximity constrains migration routes, individuals tend to mate with those who live nearby, and neighboring populations obviously tend to exchange more genes than distant ones.

Because of these patterns of variation, many anthropologists argue that classic racial classifications misrepresent the biological diversity

---

[7] This HPC conception of natural kinds has been developed by Boyd (1991, 1999).

[8] Discussion in the remainder of this section borrows heavily from Bolnick (2008).

[9] *Linkage distribution*—the non-random association of alleles at two or more loci descending from single, ancestral chromosomes—is a measure of proximal genomic space. Hence, less linkage disequilibrium in a population signifies increased genetic diversity.

180   THE QUEST FOR HUMAN NATURE

and evolutionary history of our species. Most traditional notions of race describe racial groups as equivalent, biologically distinct units. The basic facts just rehearsed suggest otherwise. From a genetic standpoint, non-Africans are effectively a subset of Africans since our entire species originated there.[10] No discrete boundaries separate humans into a few genetically isolated clusters and the members of each racial group are highly variable (§6.3). Consequently, human races do not appear to reflect distinct genetic groups. All of this is consistent with—and indeed vindicates—the results outlined in the previous section. To the best of my knowledge, Lewontin's stance on human genetic variation has withstood the test of time. What have been questioned, and remain under fire, are the critical implications that Lewontin himself has drawn concerning human races, or lack thereof. Let's look at some of these dissenting voices.

Some critics allege that, while Lewontin makes no mistake in his estimate of genetic differences among in-group and between-group variation, he does err in concluding that studies of DNA variation have no relevance to racial classification. For one, Edwards suggests that Lewontin's conclusions are based on the assumption that the analyzed data contains no information beyond that revealed by a locus-by-locus analysis and then drawing inferences solely based on the results obtained. In contrast, the taxonomic significance of genetic data often arises from correlations among different loci, since it is these that may contain the information enabling a stable classification. Edwards thus argues that "[a] proper analysis of human data reveals a substantial amount of information about genetic differences. What use, if any, one makes of it is quite another matter. But it is a dangerous mistake to premise the moral equality of human beings on biological similarity because dissimilarity, once revealed, then becomes an argument for moral inequality" (2003, p. 801). A similar perspective is advanced by Rosenberg and colleagues (2002), who maintain that, Lewontin notwithstanding, genetics does distinguish human groups, races included.

Crucially, none of these scholars appeals to a "genetic essence." All agree that no DNA sequence is shared among all and only members of

---

[10] As discussed by Niezen (2003), these migratory patterns raise interesting questions for who exactly counts as "native" and corresponding definitions of "indigenism."

OPPRESSION OR EMANCIPATION? PART (I)   181

a specific race. Still, race naturalists rejoin, the genetic endowment of humans can be clustered in similarity groups that seemingly support racial divisions based on rough continental ancestry. These studies are widely cited as vindicating traditional ideas about race and the patterns of our biological diversity. We now briefly look into how these studies work and why they are so controversial. While I shall attempt to set unnecessary details to the side, a general understanding of these results is crucial for contextualizing race naturalism as well as its general implications for human nature.

Many modern genetic studies of race are based on a Bayesian computer program called *Structure*. Simply put, *Structure* supplies a model-based clustering method that infers population structure from multi-locus genotypes, allocating individual samples into populations. The software takes as input genetic data from various individuals. Then, based on this data, it searches for the most effective way to divide such samples into K clusters, for any given value of K. Thus, assume that we feed the software genetic samples from one hundred individuals. We can then tell the software to break these hundred samples into two, three, four, or fifty clusters, according to how the value of K is set.[11]

Focus on what *Structure*-based studies purport to show. Some of these articles report that humans can be broken down into genetic clusters that roughly correspond to traditional racial subdivisions (Rosenberg et al. 2002). In addition, *Structure* can be used to predict the continent of origin of individuals based on genetic information and can do so with an accuracy of approximately 99% (Bamshad et al. 2003).[12]

[11] In assessing the results obtained with this software, it is important to keep a few limitations in mind. First, *Structure* only provides a rough approximation. Therefore, running the same data set different times may yield conflicting results. Second, the model is not appropriate for all data sets. Third and finally, I shall not discuss here the considerations that led a group of scientists to select a certain set of loci or alternative ones. This would require a technical detour that transcends our present concerns.

[12] In an influential study, Rosenberg and colleagues (2002) analyzed variation at 377 autosomal microsatellite loci in 1,056 individuals from around the world. In the abstract of their article, they claim to have identified six main genetic clusters: Africa, Eurasia, East Asia, Oceania, America, and the Kalash of Pakistan. Yet, in the body of the paper, they actually present results for various values: $K(2-6)$. Data for $K > 6$ was also analyzed, but not published because *Structure* identified multiple ways to divide individuals into K clusters for $K > 6$. Another well-known study, illustrating a more ambitious stance, was conducted by Bamshad and colleagues (2003), who analyzed 100 *Alu* insertion

182   THE QUEST FOR HUMAN NATURE

Now, what do these results reveal? At a minimum, they confirm that significant genetic differentiation exists among sampled populations. But the authors take them a step further, as demonstrating—or, more modestly, strongly suggesting—the existence of substantial genetic differentiation among continental groupings, effectively vindicating "ordinary" conceptions of human races. Does this follow? Here we must tread carefully.

Consider, first, the study by Rosenberg and colleagues. The observation that *Structure* sorted samples into six genetic clusters, in and of itself, is not all that significant. It did this because it was instructed to do so. The software also divided that same data into two, five, ten, and twenty genetic clusters, depending on the specific input value of K. What is noteworthy is that five out of six clusters obtained with $K = 6$ roughly correspond to major geographic regions. Nevertheless, this grouping does not necessarily provide a better representation of human genetic differentiation than alternative ones, especially since the authors do not report the most likely number of clusters, nor did they publish the probabilities of the observed data given each value of K.

Moving on to the study by Bamshad and collaborators, it is indeed remarkable that *Structure* was able to correctly predict the continent of origin for 99% of sampled genomes. Yet, skeptics like Bolnick (2008) rejoin, these analyses included only data from widely separated regions of Africa, Asia, and Europe. The observed modularization may thus reflect geographic distances between sampled populations more than continental divisions per se. Indeed, when samples from India were included in a data set with Europeans and East Asians, *Structure* identified the optimal number of clusters as one. In other words, when more inclusive geographic samples are analyzed, continental groupings no longer appear so genetically distinct.

polymorphisms in 565 individuals from sub-Saharan Africa, East Asia, Europe, and India, as well as 60 microsatellites in 206 of the individuals from Sub-Saharan Africa, Europe, and East Asia. They used *Structure* to determine the number of genetic clusters present in their data set. When analyzing samples from Sub-Saharan Africa, East Asia, and Europe, they found that $K = 4$ maximized the probability of observing that set of data. They used *Structure* to assign individuals to genetic clusters and to estimate the proportion of individual ancestry from each genetic cluster. Strikingly, *Structure* was able to accurately identify the correct continent of origin for 99% of individuals.

OPPRESSION OR EMANCIPATION? PART (I)   183

In sum, these studies are often cited as showing that groups defined by continental ancestry or race are genetically differentiated, providing support for various forms of race naturalism or biological realism.[13] Critics retort that these bold conclusions reflect the way the authors presented the results rather than the results themselves. Rosenberg and colleagues offer no evidence that $K = 6$ represent the most likely number of genetic clusters in their data set. Yet, virtually all references to this study mention the identification of either five or six genetic clusters. Why all the hype?

Bolnick (2008, p. 77) suggests that "these particular results have been emphasized simply because they fit the general notion in our society that continental groupings are biologically significant. This notion is a legacy of a traditional racial thought and seems to persist even when not clearly supported by biological data." Similarly, Bamshad's team emphasizes three continental groupings, although *Structure* found *four* genetic clusters in the complete data set of sub-Saharan Africans, East Asians, and Europeans. Could it be that, when the authors recognized that including samples from India demonstrated continuous distributions of genetic variations in Eurasia, these samples were excluded from most analyses, implying fake discontinuities? The mode of presentation, Bolnick concludes, reinforces traditional racial views of human variation, unsupported by data:

> Recent studies of individual ancestry have been cited as verifying traditional ideas about race, but these studies do not present new data suggesting that racial groups are genetically distinct. Rather, the data and *structure* analyses reported in [these] studies are consistent with our current understanding of human genetic structure. However, the results of these studies have been described and interpreted in ways that both reflect and reinforce traditional racial views of human biological diversity and the evolutionary history of our species. The disconnect between the results and the interpretations of these results is unfortunate since they are playing an important role in the reification of race as a biological phenomenon. (2008, pp. 81–82)

---

[13] A current defense of race naturalism can be found in Spencer (2004, 2019).

184 THE QUEST FOR HUMAN NATURE

It is important to emphasize that race naturalism is not inherently tied to genes and genomes, or variations therein. A different strategy for vindicating racial naturalism views races from a *cladistic* standpoint. In the field of cladistics—a method of classification of organisms according to the proportion of shared measurable characteristics—a "clade" is defined as a group of organisms believed to have evolved from a common ancestor. Accordingly, races can be taken as reproductively isolated populations, where biological relations are depicted as phylogenetic trees. Each branch, that is each clade, corresponds to an individual race: a taxonomic class, a monophyletic unit, a group composed of an ancestor and all its descendants. From this standpoint, genetic diversity merely provides evidence for constructing the tree in question. It is worth noting that human races, thus construed, could no longer exist. Because of increased travel and integration, reproductively isolated human populations may well be disappearing or have already disappeared.[14] With all this in mind, let's tie up some loose ends.

In the light of all the open issues surveyed in this section, the plausibility of race naturalism is still widely disputed. Assessing whether data from human genetic diversity supports the biological reality of race remains an open question kindling heated debate. The important take-home message, for our present purposes, is that a great deal of care is required when interpreting empirical work. Experimental results alone do not settle the issue one way or the other. Even when this data is acquired and processed with the utmost care, it can be twisted, more or less deliberately, to support diametrically different conclusions. So, the jury is still out on this this one. Meanwhile, let's set race naturalism aside and explore some alternative options. §6.5 focuses on a family of questions that can be grouped under the aegis of race constructionism. §6.6 discusses an eliminativist proposal.

---

[14] A cladistic analysis of races along these lines is developed by Andreasen (1998).

§6.5 Race Constructionism

The previous section spelled out race naturalism, a stance according to which races are natural kinds: real, objective biological categories. Our point of departure was the observation that, just like there are no human essences, there are no racial essences either. Nevertheless, this well-established truth, by itself, does not imply that races are not natural kinds. The obvious rejoinder is to weaken the "Aristotelian" conception of kinds unified by essences into a "Lockean" view according to which kind membership is governed by entities satisfying defining conditions. From this standpoint, essences are properties not of entities but of definitions. Alternatively, on the HPC conception, kind membership is governed by a cluster of properties—genetic, phylogenetic, or otherwise—none of which is essential for membership. These proposals are neither uncontroversial nor problem-free. Yet, they open the door for human races to be natural kinds.

An altogether different strategy for analyzing race is to maintain that races are indeed kinds. However, they are not natural, but *social* kinds. Allow me to briefly elaborate this intuition, which is the foundation of *race constructionism*, the focus of the present section. Natural kinds are unified by properties that play a role in sustaining the causal structure of the world and, accordingly, in explaining it. For instance, electrons constitute a natural kind because the properties that govern membership into this category play an important role in producing and explaining a variety of phenomena, such as electricity. Nevertheless, a kind can also play an important role in producing and explaining social phenomena. To illustrate, citizenship, religious affiliation, and school certificates are not natural kinds. No one in their right mind thinks that there is something biologically or psychologically unique about Dutch citizens, Buddhists, or JD graduates. Still, these are significant social categories that play a prominent role in our society. In this sense, these are social as opposed to natural kinds.

Two preliminary clarifications. First, characterizing precisely the distinction between natural and social properties is a notoriously thorny endeavor. In what follows, we shall dodge some bullets by simply taking natural properties to be studied by "natural" sciences like physics, chemistry, and biology. Accordingly, social properties are

186   THE QUEST FOR HUMAN NATURE

addressed by "social" sciences, such as economics, sociology, or anthropology. Second, from this perspective, the reality and objectivity of a kind are rather undemanding. All it takes for a category to be "real" is for it to pick out a set whose members are loosely connected, and which plays some relevant role in our society. The property *Being a Lakers fan* designates a real, objective property and so does *Having a Disney+ subscription*.

Let's see if human races can be aptly characterized as social kinds. The intuition is that the folk concept of race is neither a genetic kind nor a natural kind at all. At the same time, the reality and objectivity of races are retained by grounding them in their sociopolitical significance. How should this position be cashed out? What does it entail? If races are social constructs, should human nature be conceived as a social construct too? Race constructionism comes in two general strands: *sociopolitical* and *cultural*. The remainder of this section outlines and discusses both variants, in turn.

An influential version of sociopolitical race constructionism has been developed by Haslanger, who begins a recent essay by developing the relevant sense in which these social kinds are "dependent on us":[15]

> [I]nsofar as philosophical kinds such as *justice* and *personhood* "depend on us," it is not in the sense that we stipulate what they are (like *sheriff*), or in the sense that they serve in explanations of social phenomena (like *urban pioneers*). Rather, it is something along these lines: the adequacy of our theory is not to be judged simply by reference to "the facts," but also by its responsiveness to our prior understandings. (Haslanger 2019, p. 6)

Thus construed, "[a] social constructionist account . . . proposes that the conditions for being a member of a racial group are to be given in social terms, rather than in physical, biological, or other non-social terms" (2019, p. 22).

---

[15] Other notable strands of social constructionism include Omi and Winant (1994), Mills (1997, 1998), Hacking (1999), Sundstrom (2002), Mallon (2003), Taylor (2004), Alcoff (2005), and Ásta (2018).

OPPRESSION OR EMANCIPATION? PART (I)   187

This social dependence is the trademark of race constructionism. But various proponents differ in nuance. According to Haslanger's own sociopolitical account, a group G is "racialized," relative to a context C, just in case all and only members of G meet the following three conditions. First, they are observed or imagined having specific bodily features presumed in C to be evidence of an ancestral link to a certain geographic region, or regions. Haslanger groups all these bodily features as "color."[16] Second, against the backdrop of context C, these physical features—color, broadly defined—mark members of G as occupying certain kinds of social positions that are either subordinate or privileged, and having these traits is supposed to justify their social status. Third, the first two considerations play, or would play, a role in members of G having some social position of subordination or privilege. In short, the idea is that races, at least in the present social context in the United States, "are racialized groups, that is, those groups demarcated by the geographical associations accompanying perceived body types, when those associations take on evaluative significance (or social meaning) concerning how members of the group should be viewed and treated, and the treatment situated the groups on a social hierarchy" (Haslanger 2019, p. 26). To illustrate, to say that a person x is "Black" is to say that x is marked in the United States—recall that the definition is context-sensitive—as having relatively recent ancestry from Africa, and this situates x as subordinate in the social hierarchy in the United States. Similarly, in the United States whites have higher educational achievement than Latinx. This can be paraphrased as saying that a group marked by European ancestry is privileged and, as a result, has higher educational achievement than the group of people marked as having recent ancestry in Latin America, who are disadvantaged as a result.

In other words, races are groups demarcated by geographical associations linked to perceived body type when such associations take

---

[16] Drawing an analogy from traditional feminism, where sex is a marker of gender, Haslanger (2012) uses "color" as a contextually variable physical marker of race. Importantly, "color" here is broader than skin tone. It includes eyes, nose, and lip shape, hair texture, physique, and much else. Like early feminists viewed the social category of gender as the social meaning of the biological category of sex, Haslanger sees race as the social meaning of "colored."

188 THE QUEST FOR HUMAN NATURE

on evaluative significance concerning how group members should be viewed and treated. Hence, whether and how individuals and groups are racialized will depend on context. In the United States, Blacks, whites, Native Americans, and Asians are currently racialized; Italians, Germans, and Irish no longer are.

As Haslanger (2019) stresses, both strands of constructionism—cultural and sociopolitical—converge on various aspects. First, currently dominant races emerged in specific historical contexts. Second, physical marks of appearance, Haslanger's "color," is evidence of geographical ancestry. Third, races are hierarchically structured in current sociopolitical fabrics. At the same time, there are two chief differences between these variants. First, cultural accounts require that races as a group share a culture; sociopolitical accounts do not. Second, sociopolitical accounts take sociopolitical hierarchy to be a defining feature of race; cultural accounts do not. Thus, as Jeffers presents his "cultural" strand of race constructionism, explicitly inspired by Du Bois:

> Race is fundamentally social, in my view, but I do not take either politics or culture to be more fundamental in the sense of being what is essential for the social reality of race. Culture cannot be essential in this way if, as I hold, race is political at its origin. Politics cannot be essential if, as I believe, a future in which race is merely cultural is possible. (Jeffers 2019, p. 58)

Let's cut to the chase. Social constructionism is a rich and complex stance, developed in subtly distinct ways by different authors. This is not the place to discuss hues and nuances. Nor shall I attempt a comprehensive assessment of its advantages and limitations. Yet, since constructionism is a seductive position, I conclude our critical overview by noting two counterintuitive implications. While these observations fall short of knockout punches, they do emphasize that constructionist positions do not come free of charge.

First, many consider racial identity to be a defining constituent of who they are. For these persons, it may be misplaced—perhaps even offensive—to regard race merely as a response to subordination or privilege. Haslanger anticipates this objection and strives to mitigate its consequences: "As I see it, a racial identity is a kind of know-how for navigating one's position in a racialized social space. . . . The apt content for a racial identity, then, may be positive, affirmative, and empowering, even if the racialized social position one occupies is oppressive" (2019, p. 30). This may well be true. But it remains the case that our racial identity inherently depends on the embedded cultural milieu. Many do not stomach this, viewing race as more deeply connected to human nature than human nurture.

A second unpalatable consequence of race constructionism emerges in connection to religion. Religion is clearly a social construct. To be sure, many religions allow blood factors. Every child born of a Jewish mother is considered Jewish. Still, most (all?) religions allow forms of conversion. By following a designated path—which often requires years of learning, dedication, and sacrifice—one may eventually become Christian, Muslim, Buddhist, Jewish, Hindu, or Confucian. Are we open to say the same about race? Now, surely someone who is white cannot decide to become East Asian, Hispanic, or Native American overnight. But what if, after embracing a non-native culture for years, even decades, someone originally belonging to race x self-identifies as a member of race y? Could one "convert" or switch race? Replying that they would be lacking the appropriate phenotype, pedigree, or origin brings constructionism suspiciously close to forms of naturalism. Actually, naturalism may have the edge here, as it purports to reduce race to "deeper" biological feats, such as genotype or ancestry. In contrast, by focusing on phenotypic traits, constructionism runs the risk of excluding people who belong to a group but lack the typical "look." Individuals of mixed ancestry seem especially susceptible to this problem. This raises the issue of whether forms of constructionism could be developed without piggybacking on biological or phenotypic considerations.

While these remarks are admittedly not decisive, they do raise concerns. Race is an important constituent of our identity and, as such, it is deeply connected to our nature. Now, it would be a mistake to flatly identify human races with human nature. Nevertheless, as we shall see in §6.7, these concepts play structurally analogous normative roles. If constructionism fails to capture aspects of race that are deemed central to who we are, it might be worth exploring other options. One route is a resurgence of naturalism, along the lines outlined in §6.4. Many

190 THE QUEST FOR HUMAN NATURE

find this arduous to reconcile with biological knowledge and socio-politically perilous. Another path leads to the other extreme. If race does more harm than good, why not get rid of it? This eliminativist proposal is the next item on our menu.

§6.6 Race Eliminativism

§6.4 introduced naturalism as the identification of races with natural kinds, that is, biological groups. On a traditional Aristotelian account of kinds, there are no human races. Like there is no essence shared by all and only humans, there is no essence shared by all and only race members. This is not the demise of naturalism. On less demanding conceptions of kinds, races can be viewed as groups held together by non-essential properties, or clusters thereof. Nevertheless, things are more complicated than they appear at first blush. It is surely striking that a trained classifier software can reliably identify continental ancestry from a DNA sample. Still, this does not necessarily imply that people grouped together are members of distinct, genetically isolated races. §6.5 explored a different strategy, which characterizes human races as social kinds: groups whose significance is cultural or political. While constructionism is an attractive stance, it faces a dilemma. On one horn, a pure constructionism disentangles race from biology, an implication that many find unpalatable. On the other horn, re-introducing phenotypic features brings constructionism dangerously close to a pre-scientific naturalism. Neither option seems especially desirable. In the end, we are still confronted by our central questions. Are there human races? What could settle the issue?

One of the most attractive features of naturalism is the intuition that the reality of race can be treated as a straight-up empirical question. Either there are races "out there" or there are not. But such an appeal to objectivity could be a red herring. The discussion in the previous pages suggested that the dispute over the reality of race cannot be solved by looking at facts alone. One difficulty is that we can determine whether races exist only if the term "race" has a specific, determinable meaning. Is this assumption tenable? Is race a precise, univocal notion? If so, what is its connotation?

First and foremost, race is used both in ordinary parlance and in more specialized settings: political, economic, evolutionary, genetic, and so forth. It would be great if all these meanings converged. Unfortunately, it seems unlikely that when, say, a population geneticist talks about race, they have exactly the same concept in mind as a layperson who self-identifies as a member of a given ethnicity. Indeed, studies support the claim that Americans do not share a common understanding of race and related terms, when discussing the meaning of race currently adopted by the Office of Management and Budget. White participants, for instance, expressed confusion regarding why Arabs are included in the "White" category and why "Hispanic" is not a race.[17]

The general problem is hardly restricted to races. Parallel concerns emerged in our discussion of innateness in §4.3, where we saw that commonsensical judgments need not—and typically do not—coincide with technical definitions advanced by biologists or psychologists. Still, a disanalogy lingers. In the case of innateness, there seems to be a tacit consensus that technical definitions trump ordinary intuitions. When naturalists determined that whales are not fish but mammals, the general public eventually came to accept this conclusion and corrected its usage accordingly. Similarly, were we to learn that pediatricians stop classifying the capacity of growing facial hair as "innate" because it heavily depends on nutrition during the first year of age, we would presumably accept this discovery and move along. It is less evident that we would respond along these same lines when it comes to race. Indeed, Lewontin's results in human genetic diversity, surveyed in §6.3, have been extremely impactful since the 1970s. And yet classifications of people into races did not stop. The general public merely accepted that the main meaning of race may not be genetic. Perhaps speakers just need more time to metabolize these discoveries. This diagnosis strikes me as partial, at best. Race is not taken to be fully or even primarily scientific. People may defer to cognitive scientists and geneticists when it comes to what traits are "innate" or "genetically determined," respectively. But race feels different. There seems to be a *folk* concept of race

---

[17] For a discussion of these results, see Compton et al. (2013) and Spencer (2019).

192 THE QUEST FOR HUMAN NATURE

with a life of its own, separate from and independent of technical specialized meanings.[18] It is this "folk" notion that many contemporary scholars are after. The reason is not that the folk concept necessarily captures the true, deep meaning of "race." Rather, it is because it helps when communication is fraught. If there is a socially dominant conception of race, insulated from scientific discoveries, we must grasp it to recognize it, change it, preserve it, or discard it.

So, what is this folk concept of race? This is an arduous question, confronted by an array of challenges. First, it seems highly unlikely that there is a single, univocal, mundane concept of race across the globe or even a dominant one. Overwhelming evidence suggests that non-specialists in Europe, the United States, Russia, or Japan do not have exactly the same idea in mind when they talk about race. Hence, it is common for authors to restrict their discussion of race to specific countries or regions.[19] While this seems like a wise strategy, it does raise the challenge of how to apply these notions across various contexts. In short, what is the public meaning of "race"? Is there currently a single or dominant folk concept of race? If so, what is it or what are the main contenders? Much remains to be uncovered.

A second issue concerns who has semantic authority over folk definitions of race. Most contemporary philosophers of language accept some more or less radical form of semantic externalism, according to which the majority of speakers defers semantic authority to a subset of experts, adhering to a linguistic division of labor.[20] This is plausible. I may well leave it up to my butcher to determine the difference between "prime," "choice," and "select" grades of beef. But who should tell me what races really are? Biologists? Sociologists? Politicians? Lawyers? Presumably geneticists should define race in genetics,

[18] For instance, Hardimon (2003) summarizes the "logical core" of the ordinary concept of race as the notion of a group of human beings that is (i) distinguished from other conspecifics by visible features of the relevant kind; (ii) linked by common ancestry; and (iii) originating from a distinctive geographical location.
[19] From this standpoint, it is understandable that American writers such as Haslanger (2012, 2019) and Spencer (2019) focus on the meaning of race in the United States, where the topic is hotly debated. The present discussion may well suffer from analogous biases. However, a comprehensive discussion of race across the globe lies beyond our present concerns.
[20] Classic essays on the division of linguistic labor are Putnam (1975) and Burge (1979).

evolutionists must explain its phylogenetic meaning, and so forth. Setting aside local—albeit significant—disagreements within these epistemic communities, the question is who oversees the *folk* meaning of race. Should we conduct a nation-wide or world-wide survey and accept the democratic results, no matter how counterintuitive they are, or how much they run against what we, and others, take race to be?

A third family of concerns pertains to the sociopolitical implications of our definitions. I am confident that readers will agree that social justice is a noble endeavor. Still, open questions abound. Does the quest for social justice require race? If so, which concept and why? Do we need a "folk" concept of race, or a specialized one, or maybe a hybrid notion? If folk race is not an adequate tool to help the achievement of social justice, or it is even a barrier, how should we proceed? Once again, the underlying issue is who is in charge of making these impactful decisions.

At this point, frustrated readers will accuse me of "philosophizing," that is, unnecessarily complicating the issue. At root, the problem is a matter of reaching agreement. All definitions have a stipulative component. This is certainly true. Still, it would be foolhardy to believe that any stipulation would do equally well in fixing, once and for all, the meaning of race. Consider the following analogies. What percentage of China is tall? The answer depends in part on the height of Chinese people. This is an empirical question that is relatively easy to assess: go out and measure. Yet, the answer also depends on what is meant by "tall." If we define "tall for a human" as being over 7.2 feet and classify anyone who is not tall as "short"—another simplification—then most of China is short. But this is hardly enlightening. What percentage of the world is poor? Even if we had precise, reliable data on the wealth of each and every individual on the planet, we must converge on a definition of "poverty." If everyone with less than \$100M in the bank is poor, there will be lots of poverty. Conversely, by redefining poverty as having less than \$100, we could take masses out of destitution without actually ameliorating their predicament. A similar point applies to racial issues. No one doubts that being blond is a biological trait. But identifying "Caucasian" with "blond" would be misleading, triggering all sorts of socially disconcerting issues—just think of affirmative action. This point is captured well by Haslanger (2012, p. 303): "Truth

194   THE QUEST FOR HUMAN NATURE

alone does not set us free; there are too many irrelevant or misleading truths. The choice of truth must—at the very least—be insightful and judicious."

In sum, neither facts nor stipulations by themselves resolve the issue—a recurring theme throughout this book. Facts matter. But definitions are no less significant. Complex scientific issues require a blend of empirical and conceptual tools. But how are we going to find a satisfactory definition of a concept as polarizing, loaded, and elusive as human races? Some scholars have considered the possibility of throwing in the towel. The shortcomings of race naturalism, coupled with the difficulty of capturing the folk definition of race, have led some to suggest that races are fictions, they do not exist. As Glasgow (2019, p. 117) starkly puts it:

> [T]he overall balance of considerations pressures us to conclude that races are neither biologically nor socially real. And from this a pretty compelling argument for elimination follows: if races are neither biologically nor socially real, then race is an illusion. This is *racial antirealism*, and it is a stark claim. . . . Race does not exist.

What does it mean to claim that races don't exist, that they are neither biologically nor socially real? As we saw, astronomers once followed Aristotle in postulating crystal celestial spheres. Similarly, it was once common to believe in witches and ghosts, and some people still do. These concepts haven't been redefined, except maybe metaphorically—"my aunt is a witch; the player drafted last year has been a ghost!" They have been abandoned, discarded. Perhaps race should follow suit treating human races as nothing more than a fiction.

At first blush, eliminativism seems like a painless solution to the thorny issue of race and, especially, the pernicious plague of racism. If there are no races, then discriminating based on race becomes a nonfactor. When's the last time you've seen a goblin or a hobbit viciously harassed? Now, some readers may retort that this analogy completely misses the mark. Goblins or hobbits are not harassed because they do not exist. Racial minorities, in contrast, are very much real—and routinely discriminated against. This is a sad truth, of course. But the eliminativist could follow up with a rejoinder. Witches are not real but

OPPRESSION OR EMANCIPATION? PART (I)   195

real women are classified as witches and suffer for it. Horror occurred not that long ago. The infamous Salem witch trials took place in 1662–63 and that was far from the end of it. In some societies witchcraft is still perceived as a thing. In many affluent countries real women stopped suffering from being falsely accused as soon as witchcraft was recognized for what it is: the product of paranoia. Racial discrimination could follow suit, hopefully sooner rather than later.

Despite its noble intentions, critics view racial antirealism, especially in its eliminative variant, as overly radical, as throwing the baby out with the bath water. The problem, anticipated in §6.5, is that many people are not quite ready and willing to give up racial identity cold turkey. Some have strong feelings of legacy, belonging, and cultural heritage. These attitudes do not appear vacuous. And racial identity could also become precious ammunition in our fight *against* racial marginalization. Many people are not prepared to forgo prominent constituents of their lives as discredited tales, and it is not hard to see why.

Before moving on, I'd like to touch upon a different strategy that, although it is typically not categorized as "antirealist" or "eliminativist," fits in well with the spirit, if not the substance, of the stance under present scrutiny. In recent years, the notion of *ancestry* has been widely promoted as a better, more scientific alternative to race.[21] Although the term is often used without clear definition, "ancestry" generally refers to the geographic regions where one's biological ancestors lived. Because of its focus, ancestry is perceived as more specific and objective than race, which is highly charged and encompasses geographic origins, political history, socioeconomic status, skin color, and other perceived physical, behavioral, and genetic features. An individual can have ancestry from multiple geographic regions and the concept of ancestry is flexible enough that those regions could be local or broader. While this can be viewed as a "naturalization" of race, it seems to fit equally well the view that race be eschewed and replaced by better, more apt proxies.

---

[21] A development of this view is found in Collins (2004) and Jorde and Wooding (2004). Some of the shortcomings addressed in what follows are discussed in Bolnick (2008).

196   THE QUEST FOR HUMAN NATURE

As promising as this may appear, "ancestry" turns out to be no less problematic than "race." First, there has been little discussion of the size of ancestral geographic regions. Individuals of European descent may not have the same ancestry if we focus on French or Parisian origins. Second, the appropriate time frame for determining ancestry is equally context dependent. If one's grandparents lived in Canada, great-grandparents are from Russia, and distant ancestors grew up in Africa, how should their ancestry be determined? Third, in practice ancestry may not be all that different from race, as both are often established politically or culturally. Ancestry studies almost invariably pick continents as ancestral regions. Anthropologists and human geneticists use "ancestry" much as the general public uses "race." Indeed, some researchers explicitly define ancestry as an individual's racial group or the race of their ancestors. Further, just like a person may have ancestry from multiple geographic regions, contemporary notions of race also depart from the one-drop rule, accepting mixed races, as witnessed by the "other" category in the U.S. census. In short, while it is often claimed that ancestry, unlike race, is compatible with a clinal account of genetic variation, such advantages may well be merely illusory. Whether a loaded term should be traded in for a fresher one, or both should be shed, partly depends on the roles they play. This is the issue to which we finally turn.

§6.7   One Vision

Time to take stock. This chapter has pointed the spotlight on human races. After a brief history of racialism (§6.2), we outlined some basic facts about human genetic diversity (§6.3). These well-known observations provided the relevant backdrop to discuss three general stances on human races. First, naturalism defends the biological dimension of race (§6.4). To be sure, conceived as a brute form of essentialism, race naturalism is all but discredited. There is no essence that captures what all and only members of a particular race have in common. Hence, more sophisticated forms of naturalism view races as genetic similarity clusters or phylogenetic units. Second, constructionism views races not as natural but social kinds (§6.5). Third, eliminativism purports to pursue our scientific and sociopolitical agendas by eschewing races altogether and replacing them with more perspicuous categorizations (§6.6). What's the bottom line? What position should we adopt? Allow me two brief remarks on both issues, in reverse order.

All three frameworks—naturalism, constructionism, and eliminativism—are alive and well.[22] If prompted to lay my own cards on the table, I would opt for moving away from naturalism and developing a position along the constructionism-eliminativism axis. All we have discovered regarding human genetic variation and the evolutionary history of our species suggests to me that race is not a natural category. Sure, striking software predictions regarding the ancestry of individuals provide information of dubious relevance to tickle our curiosity. Yet, such "thin" genetic classification hardly resembles any bona fide biological categorization of people into races.

So, should races be eliminated? In my humble opinion, yes, they should. Still, as our discussion has made clear, some shared meaning is required for getting the conversation started. What exactly is it that we are trying to discard? This basic characterization of race is best pitched as a sociopolitical phenomenon.[23] Some people will resist the elimination of races, because of cultural ties and personal identity. Others will retort that racial classification is the outcome of deep cognitive biases, a system of core knowledge that encourages viewing social groups as "us vs. them" (cf. §4.5) All this suggests that getting rid of races will require much more than a tweak to the rules of political correctness. Still, based on the abysmal track record of racialism, my hope is that we—or more likely future generations—will learn how to live and cherish culture and diversity without any racial categorizations.

Turning to the former issue, what conclusions should we draw? The topic of human races clearly has self-standing value and interest. Yet, as noted at the outset, it also has strong connections to human nature. Early on in our journey, we realized that inquiring into the nature of

---

[22] For a recent survey and discussion, see Glasgow et al. (2019).

[23] An interesting and subtle blend of eliminativism and social constructionism applied to human races, along the lines I favor, has been developed by Appiah (2007, 2013), who has seemingly moved away from his earlier, more explicitly racial-eliminativist tendencies.

198   THE QUEST FOR HUMAN NATURE

our entire species may well be biting off more than we can chew. By selecting more tractable units of study, we attempted a "divide and conquer" approach. However, establishing the reality of race is no less fraught with controversy than the quest for human nature itself. These are not straight-up empirical issues that can be settled experimentally. To be clear, we do need to get some basic facts right to have meaningful debates about race. But facts are not nearly enough. Contemporary discussions of race involve a bunch of intermingled strands. First, we have ontological questions about the reality and existence of race. Second, there are semantic issues about the meaning of race and how folk and scientific definitions relate to each other. Third, race raises a host of moral and political questions regarding how societies should address racial injustice, what goals to prioritize and how best to achieve them. Is racial discrimination ideally addressed as a global issue or at more local levels? What level: national, regional, state, county, municipal, or smaller? What is the role of non-governmental institutions, sports teams, corporations, and individuals? Following Kitcher (2007) we could pose the fundamental issue by quipping: does race have a future? Recognizing that the answers cannot be found simply by "looking at the facts" but will require values is one step in a long stride—but a step in the right direction, nonetheless.

These considerations reveal why the debates on races and human nature are inextricably tied. The point is not merely that races do not provide a proxy for studying human nature. This is true, albeit unsurprising: §6.1 made it clear that trying to define human nature by focusing on human races would be an exercise in futility. The deeper and more intriguing observation is that the noble fight against racial inequality *presupposes* some notion of human nature that grounds our shared humanity. Allow me to elaborate. No matter which stance on races one decides to adopt—naturalism, constructionism, eliminativism, or something else—we should all agree that members of all races, whatever these races turn out to be, have equal dignity. And, as Lewontin observed long ago, there is no hope of grounding this lofty ideal in genetics or in any other biological facts. Our best bet is to explain our equal rights in terms of our shared humanity, our human nature, a concept that unfortunately has eluded us thus far.

Is human nature an inherently oppressive or emancipatory concept? Is human nature the cause of what Kronfeldner (2018) calls the "dehumanization" challenge? Or is it part of the solution? So far, we've focused on races. The following chapter brings sex and gender into the equation. "One flesh, one bone, one true religion. One race, one hope, one real decision." What's missing from Queen's 1986 hit "One Vision"—truthfully, inspired by Martin Luther King Jr.'s seminal speech—is *one human nature*. And "gimme fried chicken." But, fried chicken, while always appreciated, is hardly enough.

7

Oppression or Emancipation?
Part (ii)

Sex and Gender

Virtue can only flourish among equals.
— Mary Wollstonecraft,
A Vindication of the Rights of Women ([1792] 1975)

§7.1 Discrimination, Marginalization, Emancipation

The first five chapters of this book embarked on a quest for a scientific understanding of human nature. Despite all our efforts, we fell short of a clear-cut conception of who we are and what we strive to be. Humbled by these shortcomings, we started wondering whether a robust notion of human nature is truly necessary to pursue our sociopolitical agenda. Chapter 6 raised the issue of whether human nature plays an oppressive or emancipatory role. We began our exploration by focusing on a prominent notion that persists in deeply impacting our lives: the concept of human races.

The track record of racialism—the long-standing practice of partitioning human beings into separate races—is nothing worth bragging about. Its history is a tale of oppression, discrimination, and suffering. In the aftermath of World War II, a consensus was forged converging on racial skepticism, the thesis that race is a chimera. Over time, unanimity has eroded, paving the way for three general stances concerning the status of races. Eliminativism continues the trail blazed by racial skepticism, eschewing race as fiction. The other

The Quest for Human Nature. Marco J. Nathan, Oxford University Press. © Oxford University Press 2024.
DOI: 10.1093/oso/9780197699249.003.0007

two approaches purport to resurrect the legitimacy of race and find it a more respectable place in today's scientific and sociopolitical map. Naturalism views race as a biological category. Constructionism, in turn, defines races as constructed kinds of social or cultural ilk.

Which stance is the correct one? I suggest that this is an ill-posed question as it assumes that the existence of race is a straight-up empirical issue. Determining whether races are "real" is akin to asking which people are "poor" or "tall." The query itself presupposes a blend of facts and clear definition. A more fruitful approach invites us to ponder what concept of race, if any, is needed in order to realize a specific scientific and sociopolitical vision. From this standpoint, race is not so much discovered as it is posited. And to the extent that our anti-racist agenda assumes the fundamental moral and political equality of human beings regardless of ancestry—however this is conceived—it posits a human nature too. So, is human nature inherently oppressive or emancipatory? As it pertains to races, the answer is neither. Human nature is a precondition for meaningful discussion about races and cognate debates. And race can be used either to emancipate or to oppress. Human nature is a conceptual tool. It is up to us where and how we decide to apply it.

Still, worries about human nature and its discriminatory history are not confined to races. Similar concerns apply to marginalization of all sorts. This chapter focuses on sex and gender. The ensuing pages are structured as follows. Traditional theories of human nature seem to appeal to a blatant double standard (§7.2). They can surely divide us. But can they also play a unificatory role? One response, unraveled in §7.3, is to claim that human nature is a crucial player in all liberatory movements, no one excluded. The assumption of a human nature was instrumental to early waves of feminism. The mistake lies in the incorrect application of virtuous ideas. Some contemporary feminists reject this line of thought, viewing the very notion of human nature as conceptually bankrupt and pernicious from both a practical and a theoretical standpoint. The project of delineating a human nature should not be refurbished; it should be eschewed. These critiques are outlined in §7.4. At the same time, the resurgence of a "new feminist humanism" considers a universal human nature paramount to articulating and rectifying the damage done to women under patriarchy and to ground

202   THE QUEST FOR HUMAN NATURE

its positive vision of equitable and sustainable human relations. §7.5 considers the thesis that feminism, like any other social agenda, presupposes—indeed, requires—the guiding framework afforded by an adequate conception of human nature. §7.6 returns to our guiding question: is human nature inherently oppressive or can it play important emancipatory functions?

§7.2   A Tale of Two Standards

Welcome the elephant in the room. Historically, the idea of human nature has been used—dare we say abused?—to rationalize the oppression of social groups, from ethnic minorities to women, from the poor to the disabled. This kind of discrimination can take two equally pernicious forms. One strategy is to deem certain behaviors or characteristics statistically "abnormal" or otherwise deviant. Now, abnormality per se does not imply inferiority. But, as we'll see in Chapter 8, the step from atypicality to marginalization is a dangerously short one. For a long time, homosexuality has been treated as a distorted variant of heterosexuality. As such, homosexuals were—and occasionally still are—subjected to coerced forms of correction. An alternative strategy treats certain groups as "lesser by nature." Well into the twentieth century it was commonplace for Europeans to view ethnic minorities as inherently inferior to white males, justifying slavery, colonization, and other oppressive policies (§6.2). Fortunately, some of these discriminations are mistakes of the past, at least in affluent countries. Yet, there still are portions of the world where homosexuals are persecuted, and women are stripped of basic rights. Sadly, systemic racism, sexism, and homophobia are very much tangible even in the enlightened democracies of North America and Western Europe. It is not altogether uncommon to overhear odious statements such as "Women are inadequate to occupy positions of power," "Ethnic minorities are intellectually inferior," or "Homosexuality goes against human nature." What is their source and rationalization?

To answer this question, it is useful to track the conception of human nature in the normative theories of influential Western philosophers. The ethical and political systems of prominent thinkers such as

Aristotle, Rousseau, and Kant—briefly surveyed in Chapter 1—were grounded in substantive assumptions about core capacities and dispositions of our conspecifics. Many of these tenets purported to capture the inherent moral value and essential equality of *all* people. Unsurprisingly, some of these views have inspired emancipatory movements, such as feminism and the ideal of universal human rights. These are clearly noble and ecumenical endeavors. One may thus be tempted to conclude that human nature itself isn't oppressive after all.

Unfortunately, things are less straightforward than they initially appear. Upon further scrutiny, traditional conceptions of human nature conceal puzzlingly contrasting implications. On the one hand, talk about a "nature common to all humans" conveys a heartfelt message of universal equality. On the other hand, none of the aforementioned authors intended the natural entitlements of "man" to apply, for instance, to women.[1] Now, to be sure, neither Aristotle nor Rousseau nor Kant went as far as classifying men and women as distinct kinds. Aristotle, for one, viewed man as a "rational animal" and saw women as not fully devoid of reason. Hence, men and women do share some common nature. Yet, women were taken to differ from men in significant respects, with substantive moral and sociopolitical implications. These seemingly incompatible theses call for reconciliation.

A straightforward solution is to maintain that, while men and women partake in the same ideal, men and women realize this shared human nature differently. Aristotle, Rousseau, and Kant all outlined a predicament along these lines, where men and women are "separate but equal" with different albeit complementary roles, virtues, and ways of flourishing. Women and men have the same normative characteristics. But, in earnest, it is always man's nature alone, not a combination of both sexes' natures, that is canonized as "human nature." The virtues of women have traditionally been treated as inferior. While deemed capable of rational thought, women's full potential for physical and intellectual achievement compared to their male counterparts was limited, lesser. From this standpoint, men set the standard; they are the

---

[1] Many of the considerations discussed in this section are developed in Antony (1998).

204　THE QUEST FOR HUMAN NATURE

paradigmatic exemplars of humankind.[2] This goes to show how the two discriminatory strategies converge. Abnormality and inferiority are ultimately two sides of the same dangerous coin.

These philosophical stances have had—and continue to have—a powerful influence on the lives of women by providing theoretical rationalizations for their subjugation. Women have been denied access to serious education, political and commercial activities, and opportunities to develop their physical strength, while being confined to the domestic sphere because of who they are. As Antony (1998, p. 65) bluntly puts it: "*because of their natures*, women's entire lives are to be oriented towards pleasing and serving men." Analogous remarks apply to virtually all other marginalized groups.

These considerations raise a puzzling issue. How did theories that promised and predicated a grounding for universal equality become an effective rationalization for the exploitation of women as well as other groups? Antony (1998) sketches a plausible story. Appealing to differences among the natures of oppressors and oppressed is part of a prominent historical strategy for explaining and justifying oppressive social hierarchies. The first step is to represent the status quo as morally optimal. Nature, as Rousseau theorizes, invariably gives us the right guidance. In case anyone dares to question the course of nature, the second step emphasizes the futility of any attempt to breach strict natural laws. From this perspective, trying to educate women could be brushed off as a waste of time, as women are not naturally prone to learning. What if anyone were to point out that these laws have in fact been breached? Historically, in those rare cases where women were given an opportunity to learn, they were quite successful. In 1678, Elena Lucrezia Cornaro Piscopia, at the age of thirty-two, received a doctorate in philosophy from the University of Padua, becoming the first woman in the world to receive a doctoral degree. How could that ever happen? In response, the third and final step of the strategy under scrutiny argues that success in such "unnatural" pursuits jeopardizes well-being and, in more extreme cases, personal identity. Some of Kant's remarks can be viewed in this light. Even if women could

---

[2] For a discussion of various ways of implementing this strategy, see Mahowald (1994).

succeed at learning, he concludes, this would have the consequence of destroying the natural merits of their sex.

This three-pronged strategy—strikingly reminiscent of the arguments of sociobiologists and some evolutionary psychologists surveyed in Chapter 2—is ridden with tensions. If nature is viewed as deterministic, in the sense that the status quo is simply the unfolding of laws of nature, why do we even need prescriptions not to perturb it? After all, we do not warn people not to suspend the force of gravity. If women are hopeless at certain endeavors, why let them even try? If the current state is contingent, then how do we know that it is due to nature and not to social circumstances?

The views of authors such as Aristotle, Rousseau, and Kant should be contextualized as the product of a bygone time. It would be simplistic and ahistorical to dismiss them as symptoms of overt misogyny. And fault here hardly lies within philosophy alone. Science could and should be a powerful ally in the struggle for equality. Unfortunately, it has all too often been part of the problem instead of the solution. Throughout history, biology and psychology have pontificated that women are cognitively inferior to men. In the 1600s, the brain of women was deemed too "cold" or "soft" to sustain rigorous thought. In the late 1700s, the female cranium was taken to be too small for a powerful brain. By the end of the nineteenth century, the exercise of brain power became damaging for women's reproductive health. The twentieth century saw women as lesser than men in terms of visuospatial and mathematical skills. These allegations continue to date—from smaller brain size to fewer axonal "white" matter to less focused cortical activity—rationalizing pernicious conclusions about intellectual potential. Analogous misconceptions are fueled by the social and historical sciences.

All this is deeply troubling. The historical track record of human nature applied to women is a grim tale of marginalization which has been recounted numerous times.[3] Our present concern is whether human nature is *inherently* oppressive. Are discriminatory hues distortions

---

[3] These considerations are developed by Kourany (2010). For related discussions, see Schiebinger (1989), Marecek (1995), Wilkinson (1997), and Fausto-Sterling (1992, 2000).

206   THE QUEST FOR HUMAN NATURE

and abuses? Or is there something more fundamental that fosters the rationalization of injustice? To explore this issue, let's delve into the role of human nature within the feminist tradition.

§7.3 Human Nature in Classical Feminism

The role of human nature in feminist critique is more complex, multifaceted, and subtly controversial than many readers may expect. Pioneers of the movement presupposed that men and women are intrinsically on a par. Contrastive assessment of the status quo and normative policy recommendations are intimately connected to particular conceptions of our common state. Over time, many feminist authors have come to reject the tenet of a universal human nature or, more modestly, to deny its relevance for the feminist stance. Recent years have also seen a turn in the tide, which takes human nature as central to feminist theory and politics. So, is human nature a key component of the emancipation of women or a callous legacy of a bygone age? To approach this issue, it is instructive to examine more closely, first, how classical feminism approaches the topic of human nature and, second, how recent scholarship has come to reject or embrace these positions. Skeptical and supporting contemporary voices will be examined in §7.4 and §7.5, respectively. Meanwhile, the present section sets the stage by sketching four paradigms originally outlined in Jaggar's classic *Feminist Politics and Human Nature* (1983): liberal feminism, traditional Marxist feminism, radical feminism, and social feminism. These broad frameworks shed light on how some of the most influential feminist voices from the past approached the hallowed issue of human nature.

Jaggar's first framework, *liberal feminism*, digs its roots into the liberal philosophy that emerged with the development of capitalism and its rising demand for democracy, liberty, and the inherent equality of all citizens. Liberal feminists, simply put, demand that these very same ideals be extended to all human beings, women included. Understanding liberal feminism, thus construed, presupposes zooming in on the liberal conception of human nature, the philosophical foundation of liberal political theory.

Liberal political philosophy is grounded in a depiction of humans as rational agents. This assumption, in and of itself, is not especially original. Rationality has been a cornerstone of the Western canon at least since Plato and Aristotle. Yet, liberal theorists such as Locke and Smith had a rather specific characterization of rationality in mind. First, they assumed that rationality is at heart a mental as opposed to a physical capacity, leading to a "normative dualism" inspired by Descartes' philosophy of mind. Second, on the liberal conception, rationality is a property of individuals, not groups. This "abstract individualism" conceives of human beings in isolation from social or environmental circumstances. Human agents seek to maximize their self-interests, which are assumed to be relatively constant and universal across the species. A third assumption of the liberal conception of human nature is that rationality is possessed in approximately the same measure by everyone. The fourth and final staple is that rationality is normative, as well as descriptive. This entails that individuals who fail to develop their capacity for reason are not merely different but deficient, in that they fall short of their distinctively human potential. In sum, liberal political philosophy is grounded in a conception of human nature according to which all agents have equal potential for rationality, leading to a radical form of political egalitarianism. The central task of liberalism is thus to devise social institutions which safeguard individual rights while maximizing opportunity for autonomy and self-accomplishment.

The liberal strand of feminism was pioneered by Wollstonecraft's *A Vindication of the Rights of Women* ([1792] 1975), which influenced another classic: J. S. Mill's *The Subjection of Women* ([1869] 1989). At the heart of liberal feminism lies a systematic attempt to apply liberal principles to women as well as men. This involves showing that women are perfectly capable of full rationality, an assumption that, as self-evident as it now appears, has been repeatedly questioned in the history of philosophy, from the Greeks to the Middle Ages, from Hume to Rousseau, from Kant to Hegel. From the liberal standpoint, *reason*—or, to use a more contemporary term, *rationality*—is the essential human nature. All other qualities are accidental.

Hang on a second! How should Wollstonecraft's and Mill's essentialism be parsed? If human essence is a set of necessary and sufficient

208   THE QUEST FOR HUMAN NATURE

conditions for belonging to our species, their view falls prey to all the objections encountered in Chapter 3. There is no obvious way to characterize rationality to exclude all non-human organisms while including infants, cognitively disabled people, and comatose individuals. Providing a historically adequate reconstruction of Wollstonecraft's and Mill's account of essences lies beyond the scope of this work. All that matters, from our standpoint, is *that* liberalism considers rationality as the defining human quality, setting us apart from other species. *How* exactly it purports to do so is a different matter altogether.

Moving on, liberal feminism acknowledges that women and men display different attributes, biological as well as psychological. Still, observed differences between the sexes are not innate; they are the result of sex-role conditioning. Women's upbringing discourages them from developing their full capacity to reason. Hence, what is sometimes called the "nature of women," pitched in contrast to the nature of men, is nothing but an artificial construction. Does this mean that men and women are truly equal? Although they sometimes profess agnosticism, Wollstonecraft and Mill ultimately provide a positive answer. On the liberal stance, all "normal" human beings share the essential capacity to reason and the desire to be free, if these have not been extinguished by repression. These facts, Wollstonecraft concludes, are the basis of natural rights, which are inconsistent with rigid sex roles. In short, for liberals, the moral and political equality of women and men depends on their shared human nature understood in terms of overall rationality.

Liberal feminism undermines essentialist justifications of sexual relations, the tenet that women and men cannot be equal because of fundamental differences. An equally uncompromising reaction comes from *Marxist feminism*, Jaggar's second framework. As the name itself suggests, this approach is grounded in Marx's work, our obvious point of departure. At the heart of Marxism lies a scathing critique of capitalism originally formulated in the mid-1800s. At this time, the liberal-democratic transformation was coming to completion across Europe and the negative effects of the industrial revolution were becoming all too palpable. Marxist analysis rebukes the liberal principles underlying the bourgeois system as mere egalitarian rhetoric, disguising the deep inequalities marking all societies divided by class. The notion of class provides the key to the Marxist interpretation of all socioeconomic phenomena—the oppression of women included.

This approach is grounded in a conception of human nature explicitly at odds with the metaphysical and normative dualism of traditional liberalism. For Marxists, the trademark of humanity is not any abstract capacity for rationality. Classical Marxism begins with the assumption that humans are material beings with basic needs and aspirations. We must all get nourishment, seek shelter, find solace, and rest. And we must toil to satisfy such bare necessities. In this respect we are no different from other organisms. Yet, human beings are also the only species that engages in free conscious activity and can satisfy brute animal needs in distinctive ways. In a nutshell, this conscious, purposeful, and creative activity—which Marx dubs *praxis*—is what constitutes the core of his conception of human nature. Reason is not some universal or transcultural standard of thought. Rationality is rather expressed in action and fully developed by social organization. It is always and inevitably instantiated in specific socio-historical forms.

From this standpoint, we can appreciate the Marxist account of feminism and the oppression of women, which follows linearly his historical materialism. Like human nature, the nature of women cannot be discovered a priori. It requires rigorous empirical inquiry, focusing on productive activity and social relations. Women's nature must be formed via the dialectical interrelation of praxis, biological constitution, and environment. Marx himself never undertook a systematic investigation, filtered through the lens of an analysis of class, of the predicament of women in a capitalist society. This tab was picked up by Friedrich Engels ([1884] 1902), Marx's friend and collaborator. Engels stressed how, far from being "natural" in the sense of inevitable, the subordination of women is a form of oppression, resulting from the institution of a class society and sustained because it serves the interest of capital. In primitive societies, Engels maintains, where the work of both men and women was vital to survival, each sex was dominant in its own sphere, leading to a community where the status of women was equal to men. Indeed, Engels also suggests that early on women may even have been dominant because of the structure of the household, where all the women belong to one and the same gens, while men come from various gentes. This egalitarian state was

210   THE QUEST FOR HUMAN NATURE

destroyed by developments in the male sphere of production, starting with the introduction of agriculture and the domestication of animals. Early forms of egalitarian pairing marriages were eventually replaced by monogamy, which Engels understands primarily as an economic as opposed to a social or sexual institution. It is monogamy, Engels concludes, that keeps women subjugated in modern capitalist societies.[4]

So, what notion of human nature emerges from this critique, and how does it contribute to the feminist agenda? Jaggar stresses the ambiguity and inconsistency of the traditional Marxist stance. On the one hand, Marxism distances itself from liberalism in viewing human nature as biologically sexed, as necessarily male or female. On the other hand, despite their belief that biological differences between women and men are ontologically basic, Marx and Engel's decisive rejection of the "naturalness" of women's subjugation often leads them to minimize the social and political significance of such differences. "They emphasize continually that women's subordination results not from biology, but from the social phenomenon of class, that women in pre-class society were not a subordinate gender, nor are women among the contemporary working class" (Jaggar 1983, p. 67).[5]

In conclusion, traditional Marxism does not take a clear stance on the nature of men and women. Nevertheless, it should be emphasized how, from a Marxist perspective, biological facts do not dictate invariably fixed gender roles. Women and men are understood as partaking in the same core nature, grounding their equal status and rights. Human nature, characterized thusly from a dialectical-materialist perspective, is crucial for depicting humans, men and women alike, as well as our characteristic relations.

The third paradigm, *radical feminism*, is rooted in the women's liberation movement of the 1960s, sparked by the experience of a relatively small and uniform group of American women, predominantly white, middle-class, and college educated. The general approach of radical

---

[4] For a modern decolonial feminist perspective that argues for the existence of a patriarchal political order in communal societies before colonization, see Segato and Monque (2021).

[5] A classic feminist work presenting the distinctive perspective of working-class women of color is Davis (1981).

OPPRESSION OR EMANCIPATION? PART (II)   211

feminism is encapsulated by the opening remark of de Beauvoir's *The Second Sex* ([1949] 2009), one of the most iconic statements in modern feminist literature: "One is not born, but rather becomes, a woman." To be sure, the thesis that women are made rather than born is hardly a twentieth-century novelty. The contribution of radical feminists was wielding this insight as a conceptual tool in constructing a systematic critique of the condition of contemporary women. As Jaggar (1983, p. 85) puts it: "Radical feminism argues that gender is not only the way in which women are differentiated socially from men; they see it also as the way women are subordinated to men. The genders are not "different but equal." Instead, gender is an elaborate system of male domination. The theoretical task of radical feminism is to understand that system; its political task is to end it."[6]

Unlike liberalism and Marxism, radical feminism has not explicitly provided a unified paradigm of human nature. Still, patches of agreement emerge from the underlying hodgepodge. For instance, radical feminism joins forces with Marxism in replacing metaphysical dualism, dear to liberalism, with a view of humans as embodied beings. On the one hand, the radical feminist conception of human nature is less abstract than its Marxist counterpart, focusing specifically on human reproductive biology and its effects on sex and gender. On the other hand, in a different sense, radical feminism is more abstract than either the liberal or Marxist strands. This is because American radical feminists are often unaware of the need to employ historical as well as materialist methods in understanding human nature and human society. This failure to adopt a fully historical approach, Jaggar suggests, has flawed American radical feminist conceptions of human biology, human psychology, and social reality, falling prey to various forms of determinism, universalism, and social categorization—that is, the way people are (mis)classified by society.

---

[6] The radical feminist perspective has been developed by Firestone (1970). Some contemporary feminist thinkers find the claim, developed by radical feminism, that gender oppression consists exclusively or primarily in men oppressing women, unduly restrictive. Dembroff (forthcoming), for instance, argues that patriarchy elevates people who resemble culture's most powerful ideals of manhood—ideals that reflect men who are white, straight, wealthy, and not disabled.

212　THE QUEST FOR HUMAN NATURE

In sum, radical feminism is often taken as eschewing human nature tout court. This is a misconception. What is rejected is rather a static, predetermined conception of our nature. Metaphysical dualism is replaced by an embodied view of humans, grounded in the Marxist concept of radical freedom. Deeply influenced by Sartre's existentialism, de Beauvoir saw women's reproductive function as an obstacle to realizing the ideal of radical freedom required to determine our true human "essence." From this radical-feminist perspective, traditional female endeavors, such as giving birth and breastfeeding, are not activities at all, but "natural functions" involving no characteristically human project. Women's path toward freedom thus consists primarily in escaping the subordination assigned to them by their gender roles.

This leads us to Jaggar's fourth and final paradigm, *socialist feminism*—which incidentally is the one Jaggar herself favors.[7] Socialist feminism, in a nutshell, purports to synthesize core insights of both radical and Marxist feminism while avoiding the pitfalls of both traditions. Like its radical counterpart, socialist feminism also emerged from the women's liberation movement of the 1970s. Socialist feminists follow the lead of radical feminists in believing that old political analyses are incapable of explaining the oppression of women. New political and economic categories are required. Yet, unlike their radical precursors, socialist feminists shun universal and "biological" analyses in favor of a broadly Marxist-inspired historicist approach.

What is the notion of human nature that underlies the socialist-feminist agenda? At heart, socialist feminism is committed to a basic Marxist historicist conception of who we are, generated by the interrelation of biology, society, and environment. This complex interaction is mediated by human labor or praxis, which creates the distinctive physical and psychological human types characteristic of each society. At the same time, socialist feminists depart from traditional Marxism in significant ways. While Marxists focus predominantly on two specific human types—the capitalist and the proletariat—socialist feminism provides a more multidimensional depiction. In addition to being a part of an economic class, humans have a biological sex, we belong to

---

[7] In addition to Jaggar, central figures of the socialist feminist movement include Juliet Mitchell, Jane Flax, Gayle Rubin, Nancy Chodorow, and Dorothy Dinnerstein.

OPPRESSION OR EMANCIPATION? PART (II)   213

distinct age groups, and we have specific racial, ethnic, cultural, and national backgrounds.

In conclusion, the socialist feminist analysis is grounded in Marxist categories based on labor and economic structure. Yet, socialist feminists criticize traditional Marxism for overestimating the importance of waged labor outside the household. They stress the exploitation involving caregiving and homemaking endeavors, traditionally assigned to women by the sexual division of labor, which is indispensable, albeit unpaid and often unrecognized. They also decry the double duty that burdens most women who have children and who work outside the home, as well as the insecurity of stay-at-home mothers and the low salaries of child-care workers. But, like traditional Marxism, socialist feminism is based on a displacement of traditional conceptions of human nature by one that singles out and denounces the marginalization of women. In Jaggar's own words:

> Unlike liberalism and some aspects of traditional Marxism, socialist feminism does not view humans as "abstract, genderless" (and ageless and colorless) individuals with women essentially indistinguishable from men. Neither does it view women as irreducibly different from men, the same yesterday, today and forever. Instead, it views women as constituted essentially by the social relations they inhabit. (Jaggar 1983, p. 130)

Once again, the problem is not human nature per se but, its application. Some notion of human nature is all but indispensable for social critique.

To wrap things up, this section examined Jaggar's classical feminist paradigms. All four of them presuppose a substantial notion of human nature. Now, to be sure, liberal, traditional Marxist, radical, and socialist feminist frameworks posit distinctive conceptions of human nature to guide their agendas. Still, they all share the core assumption that *some* substantive notion of human nature is important—indeed, indispensable—for emancipating women and advancing a righteous call for gender equality. This presupposition has been questioned. Since the first waves of the movement for the liberation of women, challenges to the idea that feminism requires some underlying notion

214 THE QUEST FOR HUMAN NATURE

of human nature have come from various sides. These objections will be the focus of the following section.

§7.4 Friendly Fire

The previous section surveyed how the notion of human nature, often without being characterized in any substantial detail, plays a key role in the theorizing of intellectual pioneers of the feminist movement. But not everyone is on board. This section discusses friendly fire: an array of prominent critiques of human nature stemming from a variety of feminist rival perspectives.

Before getting down to business, a brief word of caution. Given its steady growth over the decades, feminist literature has become a rich, nuanced, and complex field of study. Doing justice to its multifaceted dimensions poses insurmountable challenges, especially trying to do so in the space of a few pages. My overview has no pretension of comprehensiveness. I present some influential feminist perspectives on human nature without assuming that these are the only or even the most important ones. Specifically, I focus here on three powerful arguments against human nature.

A first overarching concern stems from the a priori character of the standard philosophical method. Philosophy is traditionally pursued from the proverbial armchair, that is, based on reflection and introspection, as opposed to the empirically driven inquiries typical of the sciences.[8] This a priori methodology carries inherent risks. First, the selection of traits belonging to human nature may be biased depending on who is pursuing the analysis. As we saw in Chapter 2, determining whether traits like sexual division of labor or practicing sports are bona fide human universals is a substantive problem confronting even

---

[8] It is important to highlight the "standard" and "traditionally" qualifiers, as there are movements purporting to reform philosophy by making its methodology more empirical. Experimental philosophy, for instance, has been characterized as "the practice of systematically collecting and analyzing empirical data in attempting to answer philosophical questions or solve philosophical problems" (Systma and Livengood 2016, p. 19). While the methodological status of philosophy is now the subject of a lively discussion (Machery 2017; Strevens 2019; Kitcher 2023), these meta-philosophical debates transcend our present concerns.

careful researchers. Generalizing from firsthand experience or the limited circle of our own acquaintances surely will not help. Second, contingent properties may well be mistaken as essential. Let's say that playing sports is a universal across societies. We still need to determine whether sport is an essential, necessary human feature or merely a byproduct of environments we happen to inhabit and create. Third, whether or not candidate traits for human nature are universally human, such features may not truly be universally *valued*. Assume, for the sake of the argument, that rationality is indeed a human constant. Does the rest of the world value rationality as much as does the Western canon?

All three pitfalls—conflating universal vs. specific traits, essential vs. contingent features, universal vs. local values—become all the more pressing when scholars studying them form a socially homogeneous group. One hasty generalization will tend to confirm many others, giving a false sense of objectivity and epistemic security. Authors influenced by Marxist critiques have pointed out how the danger of distortion is especially prominent and pernicious when the homogeneous group of theorists comes from a position of privilege. People in dominant social ranks are often able to successfully limit the range of views brought to the public's attention. This occurs partly through their greater access to education and monopoly over effective means of publication, and partly because of their ability to coerce at least a veneer of agreement among subordinates. Since consensus is often taken as a sign of objectivity, lack of conflict is standardly viewed as a marker of confirmation. Some feminists see the traditional emphasis on reason and mentality, and accompanying devaluation of the physical, as reflecting both the values and the situation of privileged individuals. Lloyd (1984), for one, argues that mental activity can only be pursued by those who are relatively free of mundane cares and basic responsibilities.

None of this is especially novel or controversial. Charges of bias are a pivotal component of the feminist critique of traditional conceptions of human nature. Philosophers such as Aristotle, Kant, and Rousseau have been accused—justly, in my opinion—of providing a conception of humans that is skewed toward a subclass of our species: wealthy European white males. Feminists have explained the effects of this

216 THE QUEST FOR HUMAN NATURE

bias by suggesting that men and women think differently about social relations. Some authors characterize this as a discrepancy in perspective: men focus on justice and women on care. Others maintain that biological and social roles occupied by women provide a better theoretical normative standpoint than those occupied by men.[9] In short, the general critique, at least when applied to human nature tout court, is oldish news. What's remarkable is that analogous objections have also been raised *against feminist* conceptions of human nature. General feminist approaches have been accused of ignoring variation among women and being more or less implicitly biased in favor of the writer. Totalizing theories like Wollstonecraft's and Mill's liberalism or Marxism have been attacked, placing the stress on "particularity" and "location." De Beauvoir's existentialism has been saddled with extolling activities associated with men and denigrating those connected to women, such as childbirth and motherhood.

All this raises a red flag. Is there a viable path for the emancipation of all women, with no one left behind? We already saw how challenging it is to provide universal generalizations that range over humans. Capturing the predicament of women worldwide will likely be no easier. So, is it possible—in practice or in principle—to obtain an insightful, explanatory, and bias-free perspective on a significant subclass of people? And if the answer is negative, might we not be better off without human nature altogether?

A second feminist argument against human nature follows a different route. Human nature emphasizes commonalities among the sexes. But men and women may not be all that similar. Radical strands of *cultural feminism* view women's path toward freedom as consisting primarily in escaping the slavery assigned to them in virtue of their reproductive role. Some view this as misguided. Adrienne Rich (1976) argues that women need liberation not from motherhood, but from male domination of motherhood. Women's bodies are not an obstacle to realizing their potentialities. On the contrary, women's reproductive functions make them better able to realize uniquely human potentials, cognitive as well as physical. Some of these differences are now backed

---

[9] See, for instance, Gilligan (1982), Noddings (1984), Ruddick (1989), and Held (1990).

up by scientific evidence. Baron-Cohen's *The Essential Difference* (2003, p. 1) advances the thesis that "[t]he female brain is predominantly hard-wired for empathy. The male brain is predominantly hard-wired for understanding and building systems." The underlying thesis of course is one of "different but equal," neither sex being morally or physically superior.

Gynocentric writers such as Daly (1978) and Griffin (1978) take this a step further, advancing theories of essential differences between women's and men's cognitive and emotional attributes sufficiently prominent to be dubbed "sex-differentiated natures." Thus, for instance, according to such cultural feminism, women's bodies and sexuality make them closer to nature and therefore more intuitive and creative. Women's bodies should be emulated, not put down. These differences are to be viewed as the sign of moral and intellectual superiority over their male counterparts. Hence, women must free themselves not of their femaleness but of the artificial femaleness imposed by men. In short, if one disavows the shared physical or cognitive equality between sexes, human nature may become a hurdle.

Unsurprisingly, radical strands of cultural feminism are not especially popular. For one thing, it is not obvious how the position should be justified. On what basis should we reject the "separate-but-equal" stance? Do we have any evidence of an alleged "true self" beneath the socialized one? Is this position any better than the conservative, patriarchal, sociobiological, naturalized versions of human nature that feminists have long sought to overturn? In general, it seems to me that radical cultural feminism replaces one form of marginalization for another. The overarching goal is not to establish the moral or physical superiority of one sex or gender over another. The aim should always be equality. If human nature is responsible for this egalitarian ideal, then human nature should be re-invited to the party as quickly as possible.

A third strand of feminist critique of human nature is a radicalization of socio-constructionism.[10] This perspective—outlined in §6.5 in the context of human races—characterizes a group not as a natural

---

[10] A classic discussion of socio-constructionism applied to feminism is found in MacKinnon (1989). For more recent developments, see Haslanger (2012) and Ásta (2018), as well as other authors mentioned in §6.5.

218 THE QUEST FOR HUMAN NATURE

but as a social kind: a category not determined by nature and whose criteria for membership are sensitive to the viewpoints of intentional beings, which may shift over time. Many contemporary feminists adamantly oppose the sex-differentiated natures and cognate forms of biological determinism. "Man" and "woman," in the relevant normative sense, are better constructed as social categories.

The marriage of feminism and constructionism feels like a step in the right direction. Several theories of human nature are strongly influenced by sociopolitical factors and related prescriptive considerations. Various authors stress how the "biological" and the "social" cannot be neatly separated. Physiological needs and capacities influence social conditions, which feed back into biology. Indeed, the interpenetration of natural and cultural factors has been a *leitmotiv* throughout this entire book. Early on in our venture, we emphasized how nature should not be contrasted with culture. In this light, the prospects of analyzing categories such as *human being, female, woman, man*, and *male* as social kinds holds some promise.

A healthy dose of constructionism, administered in moderation, supports the existence of a human nature and its relevance to our normative agenda. Yet, more extreme forms of social constructionism have been turned into a sweeping critique of human nature. On a more radical reading, any concept understood to any degree whatsoever as a "biological concept" must be eschewed. This applies equally to nature and related categories, such as sex and gender. From this postmodernist standpoint, all traditional humanistic approaches suffer from a common defect. They posit "the dogmatic assumption that there is always some single thing—an essence, a definition, a nature—that can be found to underlie and explain observed diversity" (Antony 1998, p. 74).[11] Categories like "man" and "woman" are not fixed by nature or by anything at all. This assumption, they claim, reflects what Theodor Adorno diagnosed as a *logic of identity*, a mode of thought imposing a single static and abstract order onto the multiple and constantly shifting patterns of concrete events. Such thinking invariably

---

[11] On this point, see also Fraser and Nicholson (1990) and Young (1990).

OPPRESSION OR EMANCIPATION? PART (II)   219

leads to a pernicious projection and normalization of the thinker's own characteristics.

The postmodernist challenge to human nature has kindled enormous controversy. For one thing, many feminists have been starkly criticized on the grounds that they inappropriately universalize from the experiences of a small and homogeneous group of women. Second—and more central to our present concerns—this radical approach threatens not merely the possibility of a theory of human nature but a theory of gender as well, even socially constructed. And many feminists consider gender vital to their cause.

A rejoinder of this radical postmodernist critique has been offered by Holmstrom (2013), who rejects the tenet that nothing is a "given fact of nature" as overly extreme. Holmstrom stresses how social elements enter decision-making in all the sciences, natural sciences included. Whether women and men have distinct natures depends, first, on their characteristic properties and, second, on the importance of such features—where "importance" is to be evaluated relative to a specific theoretical context. Yet, the truism that there are different ways of representing reality, each yielding new discoveries and practical applications, does not prove that there is no reality that sets constraints on the ways of understanding differences between the sexes. As we saw in the previous chapter, social constructionism may require more realism and naturalism than many of its proponents like to admit. Moreover, Holmstrom continues, extreme social constructionism is also politically deficient. The normative importance of the supposed naturalness of race and gender is trivialized if everything turns out to be social. Furthermore, it is idealistic, neglecting the embodied state of humans.

Time to wrap things up. Human nature purportedly applies to all human beings, men and women alike. This is acknowledged by the traditional views of Aristotle, Rousseau, and Kant, all of whom identify, more or less explicitly, human nature with the nature of men. Historically, feminist critique takes issue with this asymmetry. Why is the nature of men routinely assumed to be the standard, while the predicament of women is viewed as bearing idiosyncratic features and sui generis problems? Such bias is unjustified. Inspired by these traditional shortcomings, feminist authors have attempted to do better. They have

220   THE QUEST FOR HUMAN NATURE

scrutinized the circumstances in which philosophers provide allegedly generic and objective theories of human nature, the methodology employed, and various background assumptions.

What morals should be drawn? One possible conclusion is that individuals in positions of advantage consistently theorize about some larger group in which they are the dominant members. This has led to the idea that human nature invariably reflects the position of the privileged, which is arguably true. Nevertheless, despite a concerted effort to overcome these limitations, analogous critiques have been raised within the feminist movement against "mainstream" feminism. White, heterosexual, middle-class feminists may end up canonizing their own conditions and circumstances. In a sense, none of this should be surprising. The root problem is a general issue that we've encountered multiple times throughout our joint venture. Like all biological species, *Homo sapiens* is characterized by extreme variation at multiple levels. Providing an objective, unbiased generalization of human beings is a daunting task, regardless of whether we focus on members of our species who are men or women, old or young, Guelphs or Ghibellines.

In the end, this section explored the possibility of flatly eschewing human nature from the feminist agenda. This may not be a desirable strategy. It is hard to see how egalitarian ideals can be pursued without an overarching notion of humanity to ground them. But what's the alternative? Does feminism require human nature to establish its claims? Where is this pesky conception of shared nature to be found? And the road goes on . . .

§7.5 Humanism Strikes Back

Quick pit stop to fill up our tank and catch a breather. §7.3 outlined four influential conceptions of human nature that underlie traditional feminist frameworks. §7.4 explored three potential rejoinders according to which feminism should steer clear of the very notion of human nature. First, given the difficulties in providing truly unbiased categorizations of some groups—natural or social—without marginalizing others, we might be better off doing without a theory of human nature altogether. Second, radical "cultural" feminists claimed that biological and psychological differences between men and women should be embraced, not downplayed. Third, authors inspired by post-modernism reject any endeavor which may "essentialize" individuals. None of these strategies comes free of charge. It is frustratingly hard to build a strong case for equality, justice, and emancipation without emphasizing that, despite personal differences and idiosyncrasies, we're all human. New feminist voices have recently surged defending the indispensability of conceptual organizers such as *sex*, *gender*, and *human nature*. This reemergence of a "new feminist humanism" is the subject of the present section.

December 10, 1948, Palais de Chaillot, Paris. The United Nations General Assembly proclaims the *International Declaration of Human Rights*. Its first article states: "All human beings are born free and equal in dignity and rights. They are endowed with reason and conscience and should act towards one another in a spirit of brotherhood." This document was premised on the commonality of needs, desires, and capabilities among all members of our species. Such an agreement may appear little more than a truism to contemporary readers. Yet, its sociopolitical significance is hard to overstate. It was a groundbreaking historical achievement. To wit, violations of women's rights could finally and unequivocally be condemned as violations of *human* rights. The idea of a common human nature, shared by women and men alike, replaced stereotypical sex-based differences. As a result, many kinds of domestic violence against women could no longer be justified on the grounds of "private business." Similarly, practices like female genitalia mutilation would not be concealed beneath the thin veil of "cultural practice." They came to be seen for what they are: a form of torture. In short, for over seventy years now infringements of women's rights have been viewed as violations of human rights. The issue that I wish to discuss is: do universal human rights presuppose a universal human nature? A positive answer entails a position that can be aptly dubbed *humanism*.

An influential call in support of a new humanism and its relevance for the feminist agenda comes from Martha Nussbaum (1995, 2000). Skillfully blending insights from Aristotle, Rawls, and Sen, Nussbaum argues that conceptions of human being and human functioning play a crucial role in any theory of justice. Furthermore, Nussbaum adds,

222 THE QUEST FOR HUMAN NATURE

they provide a powerful critical tool to evaluate the position of women around the world.[12] Let's elaborate.

To ground the thesis that human capabilities exert a moral claim calling to be developed, Nussbaum distinguishes two broad thresholds for human welfare. First, there is a level below which a life does not count as a human life at all. To wit, someone persistently held captive, starved, isolated, or tortured could not be living as a human—indeed, we would aptly describe such conditions as "inhumane." But there is also a second, higher threshold, which determines a *good* human life. Such conditions include good health, access to shelter, appropriate nourishment, opportunity for sexual satisfaction, choice in matters of reproduction, and the ability to cultivate an adequate education. Being deprived of these basic rights may not fully dehumanize an existence. But such an impoverished state is not worth pursuing, nor is it a worthy life. As a society, we have a duty to restore these capacities when they are missing, for instance because of an accident.

What about personal differences? As discussed at length, biological and psychological variation characterizes all human populations. Diversity must be acknowledged and indeed cherished. Nevertheless, when it comes to basic human rights, Nussbaum sees no ground to distinguish the functioning of men and women or to argue that they should be exercised differently. With all these considerations in mind, Nussbaum goes on to present specific legal rights and offer political policies to secure equal capabilities for all people. At the same time, respectful of the core value of autonomy, such norms must allow that not every woman and man may choose to exercise them.

Could Nussbaum's collection of capabilities underscoring a quality human life provide the analysis of human nature we've been longing for? To answer this question, it is illuminating to consider three objections that have been raised against the proposal on political and philosophical grounds.

---

[12] An Aristotelian conception of human nature, presupposed by Nussbaum, is articulated more explicitly with an ethical focus by Foot (2001) and Thompson (2008). A skeptical counter is offered by Lewens (2015a), who maintains that such *teleoessences* do not exist.

OPPRESSION OR EMANCIPATION? PART (II)   223

One concern is voiced by Jaggar (2006), who agrees that human nature plays an indispensable role in feminism (§7.3). Still, one may wonder whether Nussbaum's capabilities are superior to traditional human rights. Jaggar probes the strategic wisdom of denouncing marginalization and abuse as thwarting basic capacities as opposed to directly violating human rights with the complicity of governments, international economic policies, and institutions like the World Bank and the International Monetary Fund.

A second critique is raised by Antony (2000), who worries that no bona fide notion of human nature, whether grounded in capacities or in something else, can do this sort of normative work. Antony poses a dilemma-style argument. On one horn, interpreted empirically, claims about human nature can be presented as objective and independent of values. Yet, thus conceived, it is doubtful that they can support ethical conclusions. On the other horn, if human nature is merely a set of beliefs about what makes a human life worth living, this does not support hard moral and sociopolitical guidance. Nussbaum (2000) subsequently clarifies that the relevant theory of capabilities should be viewed as a substantive ethical framework. The issue then becomes whether and how this outlook is grounded in empirical facts.

A third objection to the capabilities model has been articulated by Holmstrom (2013). Holmstrom acknowledges that Nussbaum's approach may be strategically wise. Yet, they maintain that a feminist agenda requires a stronger stance on human nature and a more substantive foundation. Nussbaum, Holmstrom argues, purports to show that, in practice, women and other oppressed groups have all the distinctive human capacities and therefore have the corresponding rights. But it is this factual equality that must be established on solid grounds, not its sociopolitical significance. Men have lived in intimate contact with women throughout the history of our species and yet, until recently, they failed to acknowledge this equality of potential. Similar considerations can be applied to oppressed minorities that, as we saw in previous chapters, were denied equal status or even full-fledged humanity. What changed when the civil rights movement established greater equality for these groups? Holmstrom suggests that the shift was not one in ethical treatment. What morphed is not how people ought to be treated but the perception of relevant facts. The decisive

224 THE QUEST FOR HUMAN NATURE

realization was that women, ethnic minorities, homosexuals, and other marginalized groups have the same potential and humanity as groups in positions of power. Human nature, from this perspective, must establish and embrace these facts. Ethical consequences will inevitably follow, or so the story goes.

Let's take a step back. The significant point, for our present purposes, is not to criticize or defend Nussbaum's capabilities or any other feminist framework. Our guiding question is whether feminism or similar normative theories provide a viable analysis of human nature. And the verdict is patently negative, or so it seems to me. To be clear, this is not a shortcoming of these approaches. The issue is rather that prominent notions, such as human capabilities and human rights, do not explain human nature. They *presuppose* a robust notion of human nature. This observation is further reinforced by looking at Holmstrom's (2013) own constructive proposal.

Holmstrom's starting point should have a familiar ring to it. Variation at all levels is ubiquitous across our species. The guiding query—a problem that we have been grappling with throughout this book—is the alleged compatibility of rampant variation with the existence of a shared human nature. In other words, the issue is whether some principled rationale can be offered for crediting some features as more truly or fundamentally human than others. Holmstrom answers in the positive, reasoning that any theory of human nature worth its salt, feminist or otherwise, must encompass basic human biological needs. This presupposes values underlying the well-being of all people. Holmstrom suggests that humans universally avoid physical and mental pain, suffer from malnutrition and lack of clean water, and so forth. Harms that go beyond these basic physical needs are more difficult to pinpoint because of their greater complexity in the assessment of well-being. Nevertheless, both the existence and significance of all these core aspects of the human predicament are presupposed in most feminist critiques and—I personally would add—in any theory of justice, equality, and human rights.

Characterizing these basic needs sheds light on the all-important question of under what conditions a person could legitimately be considered oppressed. For starters, *feeling* oppressed is neither necessary nor sufficient for *being* oppressed. A cheerful slave is still a slave, whereas a powerful paranoid king who invariably feels trapped is likely not so. Maintaining that traditional gender roles are oppressive, Holmstrom argues, implies two facts. First, current social hierarchy must not be grounded in inherent abilities or inabilities. This condition rules out the possibility that women have intrinsic "natural" features that make them particularly suited to their subordinate social roles and lack the cognitive dispositions required for positions of greater power. While such allegations have repeatedly cropped up, they have now been conclusively disproven. The second condition for oppression is that people belonging to the marginalized group must not have deliberately chosen their role. Clearly, if someone willingly and genuinely decides to confine themselves to a subordinate role, they are not oppressed. But in many parts of the world women have little to no choice. They are forced into their subdued position simply because of their gender.

The challenge of course it to provide an illuminating analysis of what constitutes a "free choice." That a certain action is chosen does not entail that the resulting conduct is free. Prisoners routinely make decisions. Similarly, women sometimes acquiesce rather than choose, especially when options are limited and all outcomes are suboptimal. This, Holmstrom argues, may help explain why women sometimes make decisions that feminists find puzzling. For instance, some American women think that their desires for security and stability are best provided by traditional 1950s-style marriages. These are deliberations made by women in the context of male-dominated societies who accept subordination better than the alternative. At the same time, we must avoid paternalistic dismissals of any behavior that doesn't conform to our own credo. As we shall discuss in Chapter 8, it is overtly condescending to discount self-reports of well-being of individuals with disabilities on the grounds that they have a lower bar for what counts as a life worth living. By the same token, it seems to me, we should honor and respect the choice of women who willingly choose a "1950s-style marriage" without brushing off such decision as "not knowing any better."

Be that as it may, Holmstrom contends, if feminist scholars wish to claim the oppression of women who willingly make patriarchal bargains, they must also argue that in conditions of greater

226 THE QUEST FOR HUMAN NATURE

freedom fewer women would make that same choice. As noted, this presupposes two conditions for oppression. The sociopolitical position of women must neither be based on intrinsic (in)abilities nor must they be freely chosen. In the end this is the key to understanding who we are. Although human nature can take many shapes, the forms expressed in conditions of greater freedom, as opposed to those tied to subordinate positions within hierarchical power structures, are more expressive of a truly and genuinely human state. Only free of domination can everyone actively define their own personal variant of human nature, which is the ultimate goal of feminism as well as other liberatory movements challenging systems of power relations such as racism and class. Oppressive structures of all kinds lead to similar constraints, objective and internal, on people's abilities to make genuinely free choices about how to live. Yet—and this is the crucial point—if these inequalities are not rooted in our *nature*, how does one justify the power that a tiny minority has to determine so much in the lives of everyone else? Once again, positing some underlying notion of human nature is of paramount importance for actual liberation.

In conclusion, the notion of human nature has been vigorously attacked by authors who view this concept as a hinderance to their sociopolitical agenda. Many contemporary feminists have rejoined that overarching categories such as sex, gender, and human nature are not only important but indispensable for their movement and, more generally, for all forms of emancipation. Just as human nature is pivotal to capture what is common to all members of our species, sex and gender play a crucial role in determining the biological underpinnings and social conditions that are characteristic of females and women, distinguishing them from males and men. We can label this a *new feminist humanism*, since it is predicated on boiling down women's rights to overarching human rights. This is hardly the place for a comprehensive survey of theories of sex and gender. Nevertheless, our succinct excursus revealed that this new feminist humanism can be cashed out in various forms and degrees of strength. Nussbaum interprets human capabilities as an ethical framework, as opposed to a full-fledged empirical account. Holmstrom calls for a thicker, more robust notion of human nature, grounded in our biological and psychological needs. Both authors are among those who view an account of human nature as indispensable for feminism. With all these considerations in mind, we can wrap things up by returning to our guiding question. Is human nature at heart an emancipatory or oppressive concept? Is it poison or panacea?

§7.6 Poison or Panacea?

Assumptions about the degrees of overlap and variation in basic capacities underlie different theoretical frameworks of both socio-political and philosophical ilk. Are people inherently individualistic, as Hobbes maintained? If so the role of the government becomes protecting individual liberties from "natural" greed and envy. But were one to follow Rousseau instead in assuming that we are gentle and social creatures, this would provide a powerful argument for tempering the corrupting influence of the state. Smith motivates the need for a platform to exchange goods—an autonomous free market, a laissez-faire capitalist economy—by postulating a propensity to "truck and barter" at the center of our existence. Marx and the Franco-German Romantics turn this argument on its head, warning us that only social cooperation, as opposed to competition, enhances the full development of our true selves. The conflict fueled by capitalism only distorts our core values. Or consider the question: are human beings endowed with roughly the same set of abilities and talents or do individual differences run amok? Again, implications are momentous. If the human condition reflects the latter situation, a truly egalitarian society would be much more difficult to enforce and much less desirable for citizens compared to the former scenario. At the heart of all these debates lies one question: *what is our human nature?* Given these considerations, it is unsurprising how many authors have argued that assumptions about human nature play a prominent role in revealing unequal, unfair social arrangements and justifying policies geared toward rectification. Still, skeptics have two rejoinders worth addressing.

The first complaint is that such a line of thought is mere wishful thinking. Human nature and cognate categories—from races to sexes, from gender to disability, from health to normality—are not the solution to sociopolitical injustices but the cause. They are the disease, the objection runs, not the cure. Just look at the current global state. After three waves of feminism and centuries of activism, women are still not on a par with men. One need only pay attention to the news to realize that our society is imbued with racism. It is time to reshuffle the deck. Human nature, from this standpoint, is a social myth and a pernicious one too. We're better off without it.

It is admittedly hard to disagree that the current situation is far from ideal. At the same time, pulling the plug on the assumption of a shared human nature strikes me as throwing the baby out with the bath water. We have come a long way in the quest for securing equal rights to all members of our species. Pervasive stereotypes regarding race, gender, sexual orientation, and other marginalized groups are finally beginning to erode. Sure, we have a ways to go and much remains to be done. But this should not lead us to overlook the battles fought—and won— with much work and sacrifice. Furthermore, it is not clear what exactly the alternative is. Hull quipped that we do not need to be essentially the same to enjoy equal rights. This may well be true. But what are human rights themselves founded upon? Are they a primitive self-evident notion? We need some hook to anchor to when somebody challenges us to debunk the superiority of a certain sex, gender, race, or group. The significance of human nature for our broad sociopolitical agenda is captured well by Holmstrom (2013, pp. 553–54):

> So in conclusion . . . yes, human nature is important for feminists. Not just a *conception* of human nature, but the claim that this conception is in fact true. . . . This conviction can both help us envision a different and better society and also help motivate people to try and achieve it, thereby proving that it is true. This is especially true of feminists who do not just want equality with men in this unequal and unjust system, but who have a more radical emancipatory vision.

The normative role of human nature becomes even clearer once we tackle head-on the issue of *equality*. All humans, regardless of ancestry, gender, religious belief, and other differences, are on a par, in the sense of having the same rights, dignity, and moral status. But how should this ideal of equality be cashed out? As soon as we try to put some meat on these bare bones, thorny issues arise, many of which are framed by Amartya Sen's (1980) influential inquiry: *equality of what?* Should every individual be provided with the same starter kit? If so, many will undoubtedly rise above others because of superior talent, capacities, or mere luck. Or should everyone be granted an equal opportunity for success, at the cost of allocating resources in such a way that many will surely find inefficient and unfair? Must we sacrifice the excellence of a few talented individuals if this means elevating the predicament of the worse-off? How should the pressing issue of economic inequality be tackled? These thorny issues have been extensively discussed in political philosophy, spawning a hefty and growing literature that cannot be adequately addressed here.[13] The point is that, without some fundamental assumptions about human nature—what are basic rights, innate abilities, and naturally human states?—the debate does not even get off the ground. This was Chomsky's original insight.

The second skeptical remark against human nature is an old wraith that never ceases to haunt us. Let's grant that human nature is indeed a core item on our sociopolitical agenda. What reasons do we have for believing in the existence of a universal form of human nature awaiting to be revealed? Modern evolutionary theory teaches us that variation is not the exception but the norm. This is the root problem underlying any search for essences, natural states, thresholds for normality, objective groupings, and so forth. Do we have any convincing reasons for assuming that, once all individual idiosyncrasies have been abstracted away, there will be anything left? What are these motives and what justifies them? The writing has been on the wall all along, naysayers will maintain. We just got to face the dire facts.

Authors such as Holmstrom have replied that there is no inconsistency between the idea of a general human nature and the recognition of overarching rampant variation in our species, at both the physical and psychological levels. They take the critique of human nature to be methodologically ill-conceived. Humans evolved to have different physical properties in different physical environments. Similarly, it is the flexibility of the human brain that allows humans

---

[13] Some of the pillars of this discussion can be traced back to classic work in political philosophy, such as Rawls (1971); Nozick (1974); Raz (1986); and Dworkin (2000). An influential discussion of the social cost of economic inequality is Stiglitz (2012).

230   THE QUEST FOR HUMAN NATURE

to adapt psychologically to different social environments: "Differences amongst human beings exist *because, not in spite of,* a biologically based common human nature" (Holmstrom 2013, p. 547). Yet, as we saw in the first five chapters of this book, the existence of a shared structure along the lines of the argument from Gray's Anatomy is less evident and more difficult to establish than it initially appears.

Once again, it appears as though we have reached a stalemate. On the one hand, authors who deny the importance of a theory and conception of human nature for human rights struggle to find an adequate definition or surrogate replacements. Sure, we should all agree that we do, in fact, have the same basic rights, that we are morally on a par. No one ought to dispute such a truism. Still, it is only fair to ask *why* this is the case. Is this conviction of ours grounded in some deep truth about who we are or is it something that must be taken for granted? If this foundation is not some common notion of human nature, it is not clear what else it could be. The problem of bias—explicit and implicit bias— is indeed a real and important one at the heart of the feminist critique. But the challenges in providing a realistic description of who we are as women, men, and humans do not refute the existence of a common nature, at least not obviously so. On the other hand, scholars who believe that human nature is the foundation for our egalitarian theories, social and political, are saddled with the task of spelling out what this shared nature is. Liberalism hardly explains what makes rationality the core of humanity. Marx's *praxis* and radical freedom are powerful tools, but it is not clear in what sense are they part of us. All these issues remain unresolved.

Realists or naturalists about human nature will likely complain that all these normative approaches suffer from the same shortcoming: the lack of a solid scientific basis. Our political agenda requires an objective, value-free, fact-grounded foundation of the kind that only the natural sciences can offer. A value-laden, interest-relative, normative account will not do. In response, we may point out that this is precisely the route that we explored in the entire first half of this book. And begrudgingly we had to acknowledge that science alone could not deliver the conclusive answers we were seeking. As seen repeatedly over the chapters, attempts to naturalize human nature and cognate notions—from innateness to genetic determinism, to normality—have consistently fallen short. Furthermore, accepting that human nature is an irreducibly normative concept is not tantamount to forgoing objectivity in favor of a wishy-washy anything-goes stance. Natural science itself is much more value-laden than it appears at first blush. But this is a point that will be developed in further detail in Chapter 10. Meanwhile, how do we get out of our quagmire? I'm in agreement with the numerous and diverse scholars—including Chomsky, Holmstrom, Antony, and Lewontin—that serious sociopolitical critique cannot proceed without making substantive assumptions regarding our human, all too human nature. At the same time, we must come to accept that neither natural nor social science provides the necessary concepts and frameworks. And, one may add, getting the metaphysics right—whatever that may mean—is unlikely to constitute much progress either. We must blaze some new trail.

Over the past few years, questions of inclusion have risen to the foreground. Feminist authors, for instance, have begun to discuss whether traditional approaches to the metaphysics of gender are broad enough to include transgender individuals.[14] Similarly Kronfeldner (2018) maintains that traditional normative conceptions of human nature invariably lead to the "dehumanization" of some group or other. Issues of inclusion and dehumanization raise deep concerns and pressing challenges. Nevertheless, as we have seen throughout our previous two hefty chapters, I am skeptical that asking whether human nature is essentially oppressive or emancipatory is the appropriate question. It is neither. Human nature is a tool and as such it can be used in virtuous or vicious ways. The vexing problem is that this tool, as indispensable as it appears to be, remains elusive. Could it be that the mistake lies precisely in assuming that human nature is a scientific concept to

---

[14] While some of these ideas were pioneered by bell hooks, the contemporary discussion was sparked by Sandy Stone's "*The Empire* Strikes Back: A Posttransexual Manifesto" (1991), which attacked monolithic accounts of transsexuality, seeking to replace them with a multiplicity of narratives. Bettcher (2009) has subsequently examined this polyvocality via the principle that trans people have *first-person authority*. More recently, the claim that traditional mainstream feminism fails to adequately address the inclusion problem, leaving out trans* and genderqueer individuals, has been discussed by Jenkins (2016), Barnes (2020), and Dembroff (2020). Barnes (2022) and Gheaus (2023) consider one solution, which involves moving away from the claim that gender identity is the sole determinant of gender. It is worth mentioning that none of these works explicitly addresses or discusses human nature.

232   THE QUEST FOR HUMAN NATURE

begin with? Perhaps, as Jaggar (1983, p. 9) eloquently puts it, "a theory of human nature is at the core of both political philosophy and the life sciences.... [S]uch a theory is inevitably both normative and empirical and ... consequently, it is wrong to view political philosophy and the life sciences as separate and autonomous disciplines."

This is precisely the perspective that I intend to explore, develop, and defend in detail in the final chapter of this work. There I will suggest that human nature is indeed a scientific concept and an important one too. At the same time, it is not a construct that science can account for. Human nature is not an appropriate object of explanation or target of experimentation. It is not something awaiting discovery. The concept plays a different methodological role in empirical inquiries as an *epistemological indicator*. Yet, before wrapping up our joint venture with the limits and boundaries of scientific explanation we've still got a bit of work to do. The next two chapters discuss, respectively, two sets of social and bioethical questions. First, Chapter 8 will take a deeper look into the notion of *normality*. Is it grounded in facts or politics? Second, should the notion of human nature be enhanced? There are both grounds for optimism and excitement as well as reasons for concern. What is the conception of human nature underlying these pressing debates? These issues will be the subject of Chapter 9.

8

Normality

Facts or Politics?

Nature her custom holds,
Let shame say what it will.

—William Shakespeare, *Hamlet*,
between 1599 and 1601

§8.1 A Perilous Path

Customary recap. We set out on a quest for human nature (Chapter 1). Is there a science of who we are (Chapter 2)? What should it capture (Chapter 3)? Frustrated by failures to answer these questions directly, we tried breaking the slippery issue of human nature down to more tractable proxies: innateness (Chapter 4) and genetic determinism (Chapter 5). We explored strategies for elucidating what it means for a trait to be "inborn" or "coded in the genes." Neither provided an adequate surrogate for human nature. At that point, we shifted gear. Perhaps pursuing our sociopolitical agenda does not require any "thick" concept of human nature, after all. What if human nature does more harm than good, harboring oppression instead of emancipation? We split this discussion in two: races (Chapter 6) and sex and gender (Chapter 7). Controversies abound. Yet, what is clear is that a robust normative and descriptive ideal of equality across the species presupposes some shared humanity. Nevertheless, an illuminating analysis of human nature still eludes us. Where have we taken a wrong turn?

One hurdle that emerged early on and has lurked in the background ever since involves a characterization of *normality*. Recall

The Quest for Human Nature. Marco J. Nathan, Oxford University Press. © Oxford University Press 2024.
DOI: 10.1093/oso/9780197699249.003.0008

234 THE QUEST FOR HUMAN NATURE

that variability is the default state of all biological species and a necessary ingredient of Darwinian evolution by natural selection. Humans are no exception. The sheer amount of variation at all levels—genetic, phenotypic, and behavioral—forestalls any attempt to specify a nontrivial and explanatory essence that frames *Homo sapiens*. Most of us have similar bodily structures. Not everyone does. Many share a basic mental architecture, a set of cognitive capacities which can be cashed out in terms of "core knowledge." Not all of us do. The obvious rejoinder to these well-known observations is to emphasize that human nature does not—and was never meant to—capture all and only humans. It purports to describe and explain *normal* members of our species. This seems intuitive enough. At the same time, our initial ventures into normality, back in Chapter 3, were thwarted by two substantial problems. First, what is normality? It is commonly assumed that it is up to science to determine what counts as "normal." But, as we shall see, this is a misconception. The sciences *presuppose* a notion of normality, they don't discover it. So, where is the relevant notion of normality to be found? The second issue is that normality has often led to various forms of discrimination. It is difficult to single out a group of individuals as "normal" without ipso facto implying that the people in question are physically, morally, aesthetically, psychologically, or in some other way superior to any "abnormal" counterpart. The pressing question becomes whether we can find a conception of normality that fits the bill without wreaking yet more havoc in our society.

The present chapter points the spotlight on normality and its implications, descriptive and prescriptive. Given all the pitfalls encountered along the way so far, we'll set aside the project of determining which members of a species, deme, or social group count as "normal." Let's try a different strategy. We shall begin with people and their individual features before generalizing to larger units. For starters, we need to ask what it means to be a healthy person, both mentally and physically. This will quickly lead to a discussion of functional normality and disability. The reason is that disability is often viewed pretheoretically as a subclass of pathology, a dysfunctional impaired medical state of a person, which endures over time. Nonetheless, the apparent simplicity of these issues is deceptive. Making sense of the connections among health, normality, function, and disability will prove much harder than expected.

Here is our master plan. §8.2 kicks off with a seemingly straightforward problem: on what basis do we discriminate between healthy and pathological states of an individual? Next, §8.3 introduces a popular definition of health in terms of "normal function." §8.4 addresses some critical remarks, according to which normal function and cognate notions cannot be naturalized, that is, read off biological states, but are part of a normative agenda. Developing these insights, §8.5 brings disability into the picture, introducing three mainstream accounts and discussing their shortcomings. §8.6 draws some lessons from ecology to offer an original analysis of disabling conditions. §8.7 wraps up by bringing human nature back on stage and asking whether normality is the key to human nature or human nature is the key to normality.

§8.2 Health and Disease

Recall the thought experiment that got our juices flowing at the very outset of our joint venture back in §1.1. Imagine being an inquisitive alien from a distant galaxy quietly observing the people at a cocktail party, mall, stadium, theater, or other crowded event. You would likely be struck by the myriad properties and characteristics of humans. Tall vs. short folks. Long hair vs. short hair. Glasses vs. no glasses. Some features are uncommon, such as red hair, or even rare, like being taller than seven feet. Other traits are widespread, such as wearing clothes, or universal, like breathing oxygen or lacking the capacity to synthesize vitamin C. Some conditions are healthy variants, part of the evolutionary stock (§2.2). Others are pathological. Some illnesses—the common cold, bronchitis, or herpes—are relatively minor. Others are much more serious, potentially deadly, such as pancreatic cancer, AIDS, or Alzheimer's disease. This section discusses a family of deceptively simple questions. What is the difference between health and disease, between pathological and non-pathological variants? Why is our incapacity to synthesize vitamin C perfectly normal, whereas our incapacity to synthesize enough insulin is a disease, namely, type-I diabetes?

236   THE QUEST FOR HUMAN NATURE

Before getting started, I should preempt a skeptical complaint. Looking for a clear definition of disease may strike some readers as a pointless, "academic" pursuit. We know perfectly well which conditions are pathological and which are not. Why waste time searching for answers we don't need? The brief rejoinder is that the distinction between health and disease may be intuitive in clean-cut instances, such as cancer or diabetes. But a precise analysis is required to sort a range of gray cases, such as age-related markers, mild depression, obesity, and gigantism. The significance of asking whether these conditions are pathological is hardly scholastic. Health providers— private insurances and government plans alike—typically only cover documented diseases, leaving the treatment of other states to the patient, often with high out-of-pocket costs. In short, providing a viable characterization of disease is a socially pressing task. This issue needs to be settled. What distinguishes healthy variations from unhealthy ones?

Here is a relatively painless way out of our conundrum. In medical settings, *health* is routinely defined as *absence of disease*. This is accurate and informative enough. Yet, our puzzle is not quite solved. The hiccup arises as soon as we ask the related question of what disease is. If disease is explicated as absence of health, just like that we are stuck in a vicious circle. Our definitions of health and disease presuppose each other. Breaking out of this circle is one if not *the* central task of classic philosophy of medicine. Our target is an informative analysis explaining the truism that health is absence of disease. Before getting down to business, three preliminary clarifications.

First, for health to be understood as the absence of disease, the class of diseases must be much broader than is typically assumed. In addition to infection syndromes like malaria, spina bifida and other birth defects, disorders like cancer, and functional impairment such as limb paralysis, "disease" will also include obesity, exhaustion, and motion-sickness, as well as all injuries and causes of death, from broken bones to gunshot wounds, from bug bites to electrocution. This is because lack of health is broader than traditional illness, that is, an incapacitating condition supporting normative calls for treatment and responsibility. Not every disease makes its bearer ill. This oversimplification can be temporary. Equipped with a preliminary definition of illness, we can then provide a more perspicuous analysis, better applicable to medical practice. But let's begin by casting a wider net.

Second, an effective strategy to eradicate a disease is often to eliminate, block, or forestall its causes. But diseases should not be confused with their causes. Influenza the virus should not be conflated with influenza the condition triggered by the virus, which can be effectively cured by eliminating the infection. This basic point should become clearer by considering that, while smoking causes lung cancer, smoking is not the same as lung cancer. Similarly, while lack of exercise may cause diabetes, the two are not identical. And homozygous mutated sickled hemoglobin may cause respiratory crises, but the genetic trigger for the condition is not the pathology in question.

Third, and finally, it is useful to draw an explicit distinction between two notions of health: *theoretical vs. practical*. Practical health involves conditions that can actually be treated. In contrast, theoretical health pertains to a broader conception where it does not matter whether a specific condition is currently treatable or will be treatable in the future.

With these three caveats in mind, let's search for a non-circular analysis of health and disease. Following in the footsteps of the philosopher of medicine Chris Boorse (1977), we can begin by identifying six platitudes that ideally any working conception of health should capture and explain. The key issue is whether these intuitions can be molded into succinct, viable definitions. Spoiler alert: they cannot.

First, health is often associated with desirability and, conversely, disease with avoidance. It is generally true that we strive toward health and try to steer clear of disease. At the same time, undesirability falls short of a necessary and sufficient criterion for disease. There are many conditions that restrict well-being and are therefore avoided without being categorized as diseases. Lack of attractiveness, strength, speed, or endurance, shortness in height, poor coordination, and slow reflexes are prime candidates. Or consider universal human weaknesses, such as our need for sleep or dependence upon air, food, and water. None of these physical states is standardly conceived as a disease. Yet, all of them may affect quality of life, arguably more than minor diseases such as light allergies or mild viral infections. Further, some diseases may well be desirable under specific circumstances. Exposure to cowpox

238   THE QUEST FOR HUMAN NATURE

can save lives during a smallpox epidemic. Myopia could help a conscript dodge the draft and get out of fighting a grueling war. Becoming sterile might be a blessing in disguise for parents of already large families that refuse to make use of contraception. In short, while health is generally desirable, it cannot be undesirability alone that turns a certain condition into a disease.

A second, alternative strategy is to define disease via a form of medical positivism. From a positivist perspective, diseases are conditions that physicians happen to treat. In other words, what counts as a disease can be read off medical practice as opposed to being independently defined. While this stance can be often useful and handy, it falls short of a plausible general definition. Actual treatability—corresponding to the above notion of practical health—is overly demanding, as many bona fide diseases are currently untreatable: Huntington's and Alzheimer's, for instance. Conversely, MDs also treat conditions they do not regard as diseases. Consider practices such as circumcision, cosmetic surgery, abortion, prescription of contraceptives, or sex changes. In short, while looking at medical practice surely provides valuable insight, being treatable, in principle or in practice, is neither necessary nor sufficient for being categorized as a disease.

In clinical parlance, pathological conditions are often dubbed "abnormal." What does this mean? The obvious interpretation of normality is statistical, as a mean surrounded by some range of standard variation. In some instances, the precise boundaries may depend on population distribution, as in the case of height. Alternatively, the range of normality may reflect higher morbidity or mortality. As an example, the maximum normal diastolic blood pressure signals the threshold above which an individual incurs risk of deadly heart attack. This suggests a third definition of health as statistical normality. As we shall see, this route is pursued by many, including Boorse himself. Yet, taken at face value, statistical normality fails both as a necessary and as a sufficient condition for health. On the one hand, statistically unusual conditions may be perfectly healthy, such as AB-negative blood type, blue eyes, or red hair. On the other hand, unhealthy conditions may be typical, even widespread. Medical research suggests that disease processes are at work below the level of clinical detection in all of us. Some diseases, such as atherosclerosis, minor lung inflammation, and tooth decay, are commonly assumed to be universal, or virtually so, among humans.

Another commonplace observation contrasts health with the pain and discomfort associated with illness. Now, unfortunately, we cannot plainly identify disease with discomfort, as medical practice is replete with asymptomatic pathologies, such as tuberculosis, diabetes, liver cirrhosis, breast cancer, forms of heart disease, and severe internal lesions. Conversely, pain and discomfort may occur in perfectly normal and healthy processes, like teething, menstruation, and childbirth. Still, this may point to a subtler route, a fourth definition of disease *qua* disability. The underlying insight is that while not all diseases cause physical suffering, perhaps all diseases are disabling, covering pain as a special case. The concept of disability and its relation to physiology will be discussed in §8.5 and §8.6. In the meantime, consider three preliminary remarks. First, the notion of disability is no less murky and in need of elucidation than the concept of health itself. Second, a plausible analysis of disease via disability is hardly straightforward. It must be broad enough to include relatively minor conditions, like athlete's foot, eczema, warts, light myopia, and color blindness, while narrow enough to exclude inabilities to swim, speak Suomi, or see in pitch dark. It must relativize pathologies to contrast classes, since adults may be diseased if they cannot walk, but toddlers are not. Third, as we shall see, the flat-out identification of disabilities with diseases—the so-called "medical model"—raises concerns.

A fifth definition follows a growing movement which outright identifies health with a biological notion of fitness or adaptation. It should be evident that the fitness in question cannot be the classic Darwinian notion of pure reproductive success, that is, an individual's real or expected number of offspring (§2.2). Clearly, parents do not get healthier with every child and the healthiest traits are not those that promote large families. Fitness here is a synergy between organism and environment. This makes normality and health context-dependent. More importantly, adaptations—discussed in Chapter 2—are neither necessary nor sufficient for disease. A condition such as sickle-cell anemia can be adaptive in certain environments as it famously increases resistance to malaria. Conversely, lack of some advantageous ability, such as being able to throw a football, is alas not a pathology.

240 THE QUEST FOR HUMAN NATURE

Sixth, and finally, there is a tradition, going back to the nineteenth-century French physician Claude Bernard, which analyzes health as *homeostasis*. The guiding thought here is that health involves equilibrium, while disease disrupts this subtle balance. Many homeostatic regulating mechanisms are unquestionably important in physiology. Yet, other life functions, such as perception and growth, are not homeostatic. Reproduction is a disruption of homeostasis. Hence, crucial as it is, homeostasis cannot be flatly identified with health either.

In conclusion, this section introduced a core question in the philosophy of medicine: what are health and disease? We surveyed six influential themes. None of them yields a viable definition of these multifaceted states. The following section explores an analysis of health which, I suspect, many readers will find congenial. The idea is to identify health with normal function and, correspondingly, disease as dysfunction. In addition to the biomedical implications and intrinsic interest of health and disease, the hope is that normal function can provide a normative and descriptive baseline for human nature, the foundation for human rights that we've been seeking over the past two chapters.

§8.3 Health *qua* Normal Function

Providing a clear, principled, and informative demarcation between health and disease is trickier than we may have initially surmised. No one doubts that a line is to be drawn. What is hardly evident is on what basis to do so. An intuitive strategy is to treat health as normal function and conversely disease as dysfunction, that is, functional disruption. The guiding thought is compelling. Health coincides with normality, which in turn harks back to human nature. Accordingly, diseases, broadly construed, can be viewed as "abnormalities," deviations from normal parameters. The thesis that the normal and the natural go hand in hand has a long history. It traces its steps all the way back to Hippocrates' hypothesis, subsequently refined by Galen, that disease is disequilibrium between the four humors contained in the human body: black bile, yellow bile, phlegm, and blood. However, given our focus, we shall restrict our attention to contemporary implementations.

NORMALITY 241

A modern identification of the healthy with the normal and the natural has been offered by Boorse, whose biostatistical theory of health *qua* normal functional ability can be broken down into four core theses (1997, pp. 7–8):[1]

(i) The *reference class* is a natural class of organisms of uniform functional design, specifically, an age group or a sex of a species.

(ii) A *normal function* of a part or process within members of the reference class is a statistically typical contribution by it to their individual survival and reproduction.

(iii) A *disease* is a type of internal state that is either an impairment of normal functional ability, i.e., a reduction of one or more functional abilities below typical efficiency, or a limitation on functional ability caused by environmental agents.

(iv) *Health* is the absence of disease.

Let's discuss all four points, in reverse order. Thesis (iv) is simply a restatement of the platitude in need of explanation: health is the absence of disease. Thesis (iii) avoids circularity by providing a definition of disease that does not appeal to health. It focuses on normal function, captured by (ii). The idea is that a healthy organism is one that is able to perform all the standard functions for their reference class, as defined in (i). A disease is anything that impairs one or more of these processes. It should be evident that the cardinal thesis here is (iii): how are we to understand normal function? I shall not enter the long-standing philosophical dispute on the nature of functions, which has spawned a hefty literature. Nevertheless, to discuss the relation between function and normality—which lies at the heart of the debate on human nature—we'll need a brief detour into the old battlefield of functions.

As we anticipated in §3.4, talk of biological function is commonplace both in ordinary parlance and in more technical scientific discourse. Yet, providing an informative analysis of the concept of

---

[1] Boorse's (1977, 1997) biostatistical analysis of health as normal function has been developed by Daniels (1987) and Wakefield (1992). More recently, a revamped version of Boorse's insights has been offered by Schwartz (2007) and Garson and Piccinini (2014).

242   THE QUEST FOR HUMAN NATURE

function is no trivial endeavor. We can all agree that the function of the heart is to pump blood, as opposed to acting like a built-in metronome or burning glucose. But why? Normality adds a further layer of complexity. What is the *normal function* of a hand? Touching? Grabbing? Writing? Self-defense? Toolmaking? There is no one-to-one mapping between function and bodily structure. Most structures perform multiple functions, and one and the same function can be performed by several structures. Then what makes some uses "normal" and others "abnormal"?

Traditionally, there are two broad families of theories of functions. The first *etiological* analysis was pioneered by Wright (1973), who defined the function of an item *x* in terms of those effects which explain the presence of *x* via causal history. Commentators realized early on that, thus crudely stated, the proposal will not quite do. Not just any causal-historical story underwrites functional ascription. Consider a leaking hose in a lab emitting a noxious gas, which knocks out anyone who tries to get close to repair it. The leak in the hose is there partly because it persists in knocking out technicians. But that clearly is not its function. To dodge this and analogous counterexamples, subsequent developments required a specific kind of etiology, typically natural selection for biological organisms and designer intention for artifacts. Because of its restricted focus on evolution, critics such as Boorse maintain, "selected effects etiological theories" fail to provide a comprehensive and overarching account of functions. Natural selection is surely a prominent aspect of the causal history of biological organisms. But it may not be broad enough to cover all bona fide functions at all levels of organization. To wit, some functions may be due to developmental constraints or other physical features of biological systems.

This leads us to the second *causal-role* analysis kindled by Cummins (1975), who defines the function of *x* as *x*'s causal disposition to contribute to the output capacity of a complex containing system. Thus crudely put, the proposal won't cut it either. For instance, it is overly liberal in its functional ascriptions, it fails to recognize the function of defective organs, and it has trouble explaining the presence of functional items. Yet, like Wright, Cummins provided a key insight that can be and has been spelled out in various alternative ways. One such

NORMALITY 243

variant is Boorse's goal-contribution account, which underlies his bio-statistical definition of health, to which we now return.[2]

According to Boorse, the function of entity x can be understood simply as x's contribution to a goal. From this pure-use perspective, neither design nor selection is required for functional ascription. All that's needed is an entity's role in goal-directed activity. A couple illustrations should help drive the point home. Depending on the context, the function of a knife can be slicing through steak or becoming a paperweight. Similarly, a function of a peacock's colorful tail is to attract peahens because that is one of the goals it fulfills.

As these simple examples reveal, for Boorse all functional attributions are context dependent. Goals are determined, in no small part, by the researcher's interests, and different subfields of biology may privilege some aims over others. A pulmonologist may be primarily interested in how the COVID-19 virus produces respiratory crises. An immunologist, in contrast, may privilege how the infection tends to spread within the population. From the standpoint of health, Boorse claims, the relevant functions are physiological. More precisely, the physiological functions of a trait t are the causal contributions t makes to its bearer's survival and reproduction.

We are finally in a position to grasp Boorse's Thesis (iii). Ascriptions of normal physiological functions to a trait refer to the standard contribution of the trait in question in some population or reference class.

---

[2] Bibliographic chores are in order, a substantive endeavor given the hefty and growing literature on biological functions. The gas leak counterexample to Wright is spelled out by Boorse (1976). A discussion of the limitations of Cummins' original causal-role analysis can be found in Millikan (1989). *Selected-effect* etiological analyses are offered by Millikan (1984), Neander (1991), Griffiths (1993), and Godfrey-Smith (1994). A newer version is Garson's *generalized selected effects theory* (2016, 2019), which also provides updated surveys of the debate. Counterexamples are surveyed by Boorse (2002), who does not explicitly present his goal-contribution account as a refinement of Cummins. Still, such an interpretation seems hardly far-fetched. Indeed, while distancing their view from any etiological reading, Boorse (2002) doesn't openly decry a causal-role construction. While etiological and causal-role analyses of functions are the two traditional paradigms, they are not exclusive. A hybrid combination of both frameworks is explored by Kitcher (1993) and developed by Buller (1998), who introduces the distinction between "weak" and "strong" versions of the etiological theory. Other noteworthy accounts of functions include *value-centered* analyses (Bedau 1991), *system-theoretic* views (Schlosser 1998; McLaughlin 2001), and *modal* theories (Nanay 2010).

244 THE QUEST FOR HUMAN NATURE

Both qualifiers—"standard contribution" and "reference class"—call for further elucidation.

First, *standard contribution* addresses an issue that confronted us early on. The function of the lens in a human eye is to focus light on the retina. This does not apply to everyone. The lens does not increase the fitness of the visually impaired. This, Boorse argues, does not refute that the function of the lens in a human eye is to focus light on the retina. Such ascription remains true because it is overwhelmingly typical across populations for the retina to contribute to survival and reproduction thusly. Such conception of normality is purely statistical, as opposed to moral, aesthetic, or normative. It doesn't make "normal" individuals better or superior from any standpoint. It just signals that a phenotype is statistically prevalent.

Moving on to the second qualifier, a *reference class* is required to address another problem that we've encountered repeatedly. Traits that only apply to one sex or to a restricted age group may not generalize to entire species. It may be statistically abnormal for a ten-year-old kid not to be able to walk but it is perfectly in line with the expectations for a ten-week-old baby. Similarly, not being able to get pregnant may be unusual for a twenty-year-old female, but not for an eighty-year-old one, or for a male. The solution is to relativize normality to the relevant reference class, as per Thesis (i).

In sum, Boorse identifies the normal with the natural. Health is normal functional ability. Disease accordingly becomes any internal state that impairs health. This requires an appropriate relativization, not merely to a species but to a homogeneous reference class, that is, a set of organisms of uniform functional design. What is "normal" crucially depends on the class of individuals under scrutiny. Normal functioning in a member of the reference class is the performance by each internal part of all its statistically typical functions with at least statistically typical efficiency, that is, at levels within or above their population distribution. Diseases can be viewed from this standpoint as evolutionary failures to "catch up" with the rest of the species. Finally, Boorse replaces normal functioning with normal functional *ability* because many biological functions are only performed on appropriate occasions under the appropriate stimuli, not continuously.

NORMALITY   245

Is this an adequate account of health? It has quite a bit going for it. That health is normal functioning is considered by many a medical truism. Analyzing disease as disruption of normal function breaks the vicious circle, the circularity triggered by defining health as absence of disease while also defining disease as lack of health. Boorse mentions other virtues. His analysis keeps disease separate from treatability. It applies to traits with continuous distribution in the population, capturing extremal diseases. It makes health independent of asymptomatic diseases. It explains how to apply the notion of disease to animals and plants. Finally, it captures the general themes regarding health and disease discussed in §8.2. Not bad at all!

Virtues notwithstanding, problems and open issues linger. Some critics have pointed out that Boorse has trouble explaining *common diseases*—pathologies widespread among the population of reference—and *healthy populations* since, as long as a trait is normally distributed, the bottom 1% will count as diseased, regardless of negative effects or lack thereof.[3] A different difficulty is Kingma's (2010, p. 253) dilemma-style objection:

> The BST [Boorse's biostatistical theory] faces an inescapable dilemma: *without* situation-specific function it fails as an account of most of our dynamic physiological functions and cannot account for [certain] diseases. . . . Therefore, in order to make sense of dynamic physiological functions, the BST must adopt situation-specific statistics. But *with* situation-specific function it has trouble accounting for diseases that are the normal (i.e., species-typical) reaction to a certain environment, occasion or external factor.

Boorse considers these and related limitations not as refutations but as anomalies. Here, I shall not adjudicate the seriousness of such objections. The next section focuses on a more radical critique, which challenges the core of Boorse's proposal: the very idea of

---

[3] These problems are discussed by Schwartz (2007). The problem of common diseases, anticipated by Millikan (1989) and Neander (1991), is addressed in Boorse (2002).

246   THE QUEST FOR HUMAN NATURE

normality—and, derivatively, health and disease—as *value free*.[4] Note that this objection is central to our overarching discussion of human nature. In the first part of this book, we explored various influential attempts purporting to analyze human nature in terms of normality. If normality itself can be naturalized by the life sciences, as authors like Boorse argue, then this rekindles the possibility of developing a purely descriptive scientific account of human nature. Hence, a lot is at stake with the hypothesis that normality can be straightforwardly "read off" empirical data, untainted by personal biases, values, interests, and preconceptions. With that in mind, let's dig a little deeper.

§8.4 Normality under Fire

Normal function plays a pivotal role in discussions of healthcare, quality of life, and other sociopolitical and bioethical debates. At the same time, we know by now that normality is a slippery concept. Social critics view this as a crass understatement, pointing out that the term carries substantial ideological baggage. To describe people as "abnormal" is to marginalize them with a perniciously false aura of objectivity grounded in a misunderstanding of biomedical science.

Normality has thus come under fire, raising a host of pressing issues. Can a better, non-discriminatory notion of normality be vindicated by scientific research? Does current biology cash out an objective conception of functional normality and a clear-cut, factual distinction between normal vs. abnormal function? And can such a concept shed light on the notion of human nature? The previous section discussed an influential attempt to "naturalize" the concept of normal function. Boorse argues that diseases can be understood as impairments of normal function, where normal function is a straight-up empirical fact regarding an individual's reference class. This presupposition has been challenged. By drawing a distinction between the *level* and the *mode* of functional performance, Amundson (2000) maintains that the idea of

---

[4] For a normative conception of disease, see Cooper (2002). An analysis of health as secondary property, neither objective nor value laden, is articulated by Broadbent (2019).

biological normality is a myth. In addition, it is a dangerous myth as it fuels an already prevalent prejudice against certain functional modes. Amundson concludes that the disadvantages of "abnormal" people derive not from biology, but from implicit social judgments about the acceptability of certain kinds of biological variation. The present section explores this provocative thesis in greater detail.

Humans have numerous ways of categorizing themselves. Some groupings clearly have biological reality. To illustrate, the distinction between males and females is based on sexual differences. Other classifications have no such physiological grounding. No one seriously thinks that there is any psychophysical distinction among political affiliations, sports allegiances, or religious faith: *gauche* vs. *droite*, Cowboys vs. Eagles, Muslim vs. Hindu. Occasionally, some category once believed to be biological turns out to be not so or, more modestly, its "naturalness" is questioned. Consider, for instance, the partition of humans into distinct races. As we saw in Chapter 6, just a few decades ago races were widely assumed to reflect biological differences. Although certain scholars still defend some version of this naturalistic stance, it is no longer the only—or arguably the dominant—viewpoint. As we have seen, social constructionists and eliminativists offer a host of counterpoints against the biological reality of race. Could a similar argument be developed to debunk the notion of normality? Amundson believes so:

> I consider the concept of *normal function* to be similar to the traditional concept of race. Like the concept of race, the concept of biological normality is invoked to explain certain socially significant differences, such as unemployment and segregation. Like the concept of race, the concept of normality is a biological error. The partitioning of human variation into the normal versus the abnormal has no firmer biological footing than the partitioning into races. Diversity of function is a fact of biology. (Amundson 2000, p. 34)

While Amundson questions any "naturalistic" approach to normality, his primary target is Boorse's biostatistical theory. As discussed in the previous section, Boorse's analysis of health and disease is grounded in a notion of biological normality. The health of trait t within a reference

248   THE QUEST FOR HUMAN NATURE

class C is defined as t's statistically typical contribution to the survival and reproduction of individuals in C bearing t. Disease, in turn, is understood as disruption of normal function. Health and disease, readers will recall, are straightforward, non-evaluative, theoretical concepts within medicine and physiology. But this positivistic attitude is grounded in the naturalization of normal function. Variation of function among species members is sufficiently narrow to justify a dichotomy between "normality" and "abnormality" based on the distribution alone. The issue becomes whether human variation supports a functional determinism of this ilk.

Amundson's negative answer is grounded in a subtle distinction: level vs. mode of functional performance. The *mode* of a function corresponds to how the outcome is achieved. The *level*, in contrast, is the quantitative degree of performance that is obtained. To illustrate, consider two kids, Jill and Jack, racing to the nearest gas station. Jill wears rollerblades, Jack is riding a bike. Both kids cross the finish line simultaneously. Jill and Jack achieve an identical level of performance, in the sense that it takes them the same amount of time to complete the course. Yet, the mode of achieving such outcome is quite different: skating vs. biking. Similarly, when I run a marathon, my mode of performance is identical to a professional athlete's, namely, running. Nevertheless, our level of performance is remarkably different, as they can complete the course much faster than I ever could, can, or will. The same applies to biological functions at various organizational levels: genetic, physiological, behavioral, etc. The goal of obtaining food can be fulfilled at different levels, depending on the quality and amount gathered, and with different modalities: hunting, harvesting, or stealing.

With this in mind, we can frame Amundson's target more precisely. *Functional determinism* is the claim that biological functions take place in a uniform mode and at a relatively uniform performance level by a statistically significant portion of the population—the so-called "normals." Is such goal-directedness expressed in our species design? Can we legitimately talk of "human design" and read functional (ab) normality off physiology?

Amundson's negative argument is grounded in *developmental plasticity*, the variability in traits that an organism develops during its

NORMALITY   249

lifetime due to influences other than its genome (§3.4). Amundson provides four illustrations. The first involves a goat studied by the biologist E. J. Slipjer in the 1940s. Despite being born without forelegs, the goat learned how to walk bipedally. Second, consider hydrocephaly, a pathological condition where a backup of cerebrospinal fluid causes the brain ventricles to inflate well beyond their standard size. The pressure leads to enlargement of the cranium and corresponding reduction in the volume of brain tissue. In the most severe cases, ventricle expansion fills 95% of the cranium. While hydrocephalic people may be profoundly disabled, roughly half of them have typical IQs. One individual whose brain tissue was a mere 10% of the average person's was cognitively indistinguishable from their colleagues. Third, the skillset of wheelchair basketball players is typically appraised by comparing it to the model of non-wheelchair athletes. Yet, such theoretical assessments turn out to be poor predictors of on-the-field results. Mode of play farther from "standard" techniques may achieve a higher level of performance. Fourth and finally, while modern linguistic analyses of spoken languages are strongly tied to phonology, that is, spoken sounds, human language can manifest itself in radically distinct sensory and performance modalities, such as manual gesture, as evidenced by the existence of signed languages.

What do these examples show? Biological organisms—humans included—achieve objectives in various ways. One could legitimately expect a goat missing two legs not to be able to walk, substantial reduction in brain mass to significantly decrease cognitive performance, physical impairment to impact athletic skill, and aphasic humans should struggle with communicating. None of these theoretical intuitions is borne out. Prominent aims are reached through other means, displaying developmental plasticity in action. Amundson (2000, p. 43) concludes that these observations challenge functional determinism and species design: "In summary, the goal-directed processes of biological development are not finely tuned towards the production of functionally identical species members. Their inherent flexibility can be expected to generate a rich diversity of functional modes."[5]

---

[5] Analogous points concerning developmental plasticity are found in Bateson (2001).

250 THE QUEST FOR HUMAN NATURE

In sum, organisms fulfill goals in different ways. This is hardly specific to humans, as Slipjer's goat makes clear. Still, what is truly distinctive is the extent to which our own species can alter mode and level of function thanks to tools and technology. Sure, a few other species, such as primates and cetaceans, use tools as well. But the degree to which we do is unparalleled in nature. A motor vehicle allows the slowest person on the planet to move faster than any athlete. The weaker can easily overcome the stronger by using machinery. Weapons compensate for lack of brute strength. Computers provide anyone with a wealth of information and computational speed which dwarfs the brightest minds. From a biological perspective, tools can be viewed as integrations, extensions of our human functions. Amundson's point is that, even if we assume a fixed "normal" phenotype, the functional potential of any individual is unconstrained by such boundaries. What determines our limits is not phenotype per se, but what Dawkins (1982) dubs our *extended phenotype*, which encompasses our environment, natural as well as social.

One may be excused for surmising that the idea of species design with fixed functional potential is a discredited legacy of a bygone past—a new "natural state model" (§3.4)—revived by a handful of nostalgic essentialists. On the contrary, Amundson remarks, it continues to play a leading role in contemporary healthcare and cognate bioethical debates. Indeed, preservation and restoration of normal function are often viewed as primary goals of healthcare. To wit, Daniels (1987) describes three progressive layers of healthcare provision. The first is *prevention*. We must encourage people to pursue a healthy and risk-free lifestyle that minimizes their risk of debilitating conditions. The second level involves *cure* and *rehabilitation*. When some accident occurs, the default is to return people to species-normal functioning. When this strategy fails, and only then, should we offer a third level of *service* for those patients who cannot be "normalized."

Daniel's basic schema, Amundson argues, shows that mode is routinely ascribed higher priority than level of function. This hypothesis is backed by abundant social evidence. Atypical modes of function are often stigmatized, to the point that many people hide their diversity, typically disabilities, but occasionally superabilities too. Some refuse to use technology that would make their condition more apparent, even though such tools would greatly enhance their level of function. While the world record for completing a marathon is significantly faster for wheelchair users, many people are ashamed to race in a wheelchair. Similar points apply to white canes for the visually impaired, hearing aids, and analogous conditions. The observation that individuals try to hide disability is frequently interpreted patronizingly as a refusal to accept one's own limitations. In contrast, Amundson retorts, it's a sign of deep, systemic social prejudice against disabled individuals.

The existence of a species-specific state of normality—to be determined objectively, empirically—is often assumed as a truism. But the rationale for privileging mode over level of functional performance can also be explained via an alleged link between normality and opportunity, in the sense that people classified as "normal" tend to have more and better options for increasing their quality of life. These unfair edges enjoyed by the "normals" include better social, economic, and educational experiences. Although opportunity and well-being should not be conflated, opportunities provide effective options for increasing quality of life and should therefore be made more broadly available to all people. Quality of life, it is claimed, must always be measured against normal, primary functional human capacities. Since "abnormal" individuals have reduced opportunity, attempts to restore normality are therefore morally justified.[6] Does this assumption withstand scrutiny?

If the linkage between normality and opportunity were empirically accurate, functionally atypical individuals should report lower quality of life than functionally typical ones. Interestingly enough, this prediction is not borne out. Studies show that "disabled" people usually report a remarkable quality of life, as high as their "able" counterparts. Even people with serious impairments report a quality of life averaging only slightly lower than that reported by non-disabled people. Even physicians' estimates of the quality of the lives of disabled patients are much lower than the patients' themselves. Psychologists refer to this

---

[6] See, for instance, Daniels (1987) and Brock (1993). Another lucid critique of these accounts, along the lines of Amundson's sociopolitical perspective, is advanced by Silvers (1998).

252　THE QUEST FOR HUMAN NATURE

gap between what non-disabled people believe and what people with disabilities actually experience as the *disability paradox*.[7]

What morals should we draw? Intuitively, Amundson notes, if happiness does not correlate with normality, we should conclude that normality does not accurately measure quality of life. Some scholars turn this inference on its head. Since normality doesn't correlate with happiness, happiness must not track quality of life. To protect the link between normality and quality of life, Brock (1993) draws a distinction between *subjective* and *objective* assessments. Subjective aspects are the degree of happiness and satisfaction that a person experiences. Objective aspects include the person's own abnormality and the associated (mis)opportunity. From this standpoint, abnormal people who report a high quality of life are simply mistaken about their own wellness. Their subjectively high well-being is objectively low. What accounts for the mismatch between high subjective quality of life and low objective, normality-defined well-being? Brock's explanation is that functionally abnormal people who report a high quality of life have lower expectations than functionally normal people. Lowered expectations are more easily satisfied, and the easy satisfaction of low expectations yields a high subjective quality of life. This, to Brock, is not *real* welfare.

Amundson acknowledges that people labeled "abnormal" have a reduced range of opportunity and agrees that equality of opportunity is a prime moral objective. But Amundson finds Brock's approach shallow and patronizing, especially compared to the analogous perils of racism (Chapter 6) and sexism (Chapter 7). Here's his stark condemnation of the double standard:

> We are well past the time when academic discussion of race and sex was centered on rationalizations of how the disadvantages experienced by certain races and genders were caused by nature itself. But the normality discussions do just that. The abnormals are said to be disadvantaged by nature itself. If a black woman today considered herself to have a fulfilling life, would a moral philosopher be likely

---

[7] The disability paradox was first described and discussed by Albrecht and Devlieger (1999). For an updated survey, see Barker and Wilson (2019).

to suggest that her happiness only results from lowered expectations, and she is really getting *less* from life than a white male? I doubt it. But the abnormals can still receive this patronizing treatment. (Amundson 2000, p. 47)

In conclusion, Amundson questions the possibility of naturalizing normal function. Interestingly, the controversial aspect is not the pesky notion of function. It is *normality* that has come under fire. Departures from normality are straightforwardly characterized as either diseases or disabilities.[8] Diseases were examined in the first part of this chapter, in connection to health. The remainder of our discussion focuses on disability. What exactly is disability? What role does normality play in its identification? Where does human nature enter the picture? We now turn to these core issues.

§8.5 Three Models of Disability

The previous section discussed Amundson's attack on functional normality as it figures in Boorse's biostatistical theory. The point, of course, is not to downplay the impact of diseases. There is no denying that people suffer from, say, cancer or diabetes, that there are strategies to prevent these conditions, and that their effects can be cured or at least mitigated. The moral is that biology alone doesn't divide the population into healthy vs. sick, normal vs. abnormal, abled vs. disabled. These categorizations also depend crucially on how we classify and define diseases and which impairing conditions are prioritized. Disease was discussed in previous sections. The remainder of the chapter explores the connections between normality, (dis)ability, and human nature. To get the ball rolling, we need to take a closer look at what constitutes a disability.[9]

---

[8] As we shall see in the following section, the nature of disability and its relation to disease is a matter of heated controversy. However, it is crucial not to straight-up identify disability with disease, as most disability scholars insist that having a disability does not involve any departure from health.

[9] The discussion in §8.5 and §8.6 draws heavily from Nathan and Brown (2018).

254 THE QUEST FOR HUMAN NATURE

But, first, does this matter? Is this a pointless academic dispute? No. Across the globe—affluent countries included—people with disabilities suffer from striking inequalities compared to able-bodied individuals. To ensure equal opportunities and well-being for everyone, we must identify *who* exactly falls within the class of disabled individuals and *why* this is the case. Consequently, providing a working, plausible model of disability is of the utmost ethical, political, and practical significance.

Philosophical conceptualizations of disability typically display a two-tiered blueprint. First, the definition picks out some physiological characteristic that is identified as an impairment. An impairment is commonly conceived as a disruption in bodily function or alteration in physical structure. Second, this impairment is connected to social or personal limitation, broadly understood as a condition linked to some evident disadvantage. To illustrate, not being effectively able to walk, drive a car, or learn are examples of limitations linked to impairments. It is typically maintained that limitations associated with disabilities are connected to reductions of well-being and, as such, have significant social, political, and moral consequences. A viable model of disability must present some characterization of the relation between impairment and limitation. Three families of models can be identified in the relevant literature: the medical model, the social model, and the interactionist model. This section discusses all three of them, in turn.

The *medical* model is arguably the most intuitive one. Simply put, it depicts disability as a direct consequence of impairment, whose cause can be either an enduring "internal" biological dysfunction or an "external" accident, such as a traumatic impact or a bacterial infection. The medical model of disability has two main characteristics. First, the source of the disability is located within the body. Second, impairment is the primary cause of limitation.

Plausible as this may initially appear, the medical model is not popular among contemporary disability scholars because it allegedly mischaracterizes the relation between impairment and disability. The problem, succinctly stated, is that biological impairment in and of itself does not necessitate limitation, let alone any kind of disadvantage. The medical model is grounded in the assumption that the limitation faced by a certain group resides primarily in some intrinsic incapacity characterizing the class in question. Thus, to illustrate, the limitations faced by wheelchair users, relative to people who are able to walk, depend on their intrinsic bodily incapacity. But this assumption is more than dubious. Functional limitations seem neither necessary nor sufficient for disadvantages, which are often due at least in part to architectural barriers and other kinds of socio-environmental impediments. As critics promptly emphasize, if all buildings were wheelchair-accessible, wheelchair users would not be limited in any significant respect. Thus crudely put, the claim is too strong.[10] Architectural barriers may be eliminated in buildings and other constructions, but they cannot be fully removed in nature. Nevertheless, the main shortcoming of the medical model stands: it ignores the social dimension of impairment. We cannot understand a disability by focusing solely on an individual. We also need to consider the context or natural environment in which people are embedded.[11]

The second, *social* model of disability stems from a sociopolitical critique of the medical model. From this alternative point of view, disabilities are conceptualized as a limitation unfairly imposed on people with impairments. Oversimplifying a bit, there are two paths for fleshing out the underlying intuition, two—non-mutually-exclusive—strategies to capture distinct ways in which social and physical environments may lead to disadvantage. First, the "minority group model" identifies people with disabilities with historically oppressed minority groups subject to prejudice, stigma, and exclusion. Second, on the "human variation model," people with disabilities face limitations because of a mismatch between impairments and physical or social contexts. An impaired individual who finds themselves in a poor fit environment is more likely to encounter hardship and limitation.

Amundson's critique of normal function, outlined in §8.4, can be viewed along these social lines. From a medical standpoint, health, disease, and disability are straightforwardly read off our biological profile. There is a "normal" way of being a human, which is understood

---

[10] I am grateful to an anonymous reviewer for bringing this point to my attention.
[11] Objections to the medical model are discussed in Barnes (2016). A revamped articulation and defense of the medical model of disability against standard rejoinders can be found in Koon (2022).

256   THE QUEST FOR HUMAN NATURE

biostatistically. In contrast, Amundson observes, if we focus on the level of performance, as opposed to the mode, we see that there are many alternative paths for achieving the same end-goal. Incapacity to do so can be ascribed to lack of resources and social stigma as opposed to inherent individual limitations.

Despite its political accomplishments raising awareness of ongoing marginalization, the social model of disability has been criticized based on its metaphysical presuppositions. A first objection stresses how social models significantly underplay the role of impairments as a source of limitation. The concern—anticipated in our previous discussion of the medical model—is that even in a fully accessible and maximally inclusive environment, some individuals with disability will still face disadvantage. It is doubtful, the objection runs, that the inability to walk would pose absolutely no restrictions even in a fully wheelchair-accessible environment. No one should interfere with our attempts to make as many environments as possible wheelchair accessible. But this alone is unlikely to fully level the playing field. Hiking in nature, for one, would still be off-limits. Similarly, in a society where all text is available in braille, in audio, and in print, a blind person would have access to all sources and resources. It still doesn't follow that blindness would not pose any restrictions vis-à-vis reading. A second, related concern is that the welfare of disabled people may be less secure or robust than that of others. Even if everyone is given a chance to flourish, people with disabilities may require more effort or luck to do so or may be at greater risk in securing or maintaining the means to thrive. To wit, having more options may constitute an advantage, especially in case of an emergency or other situation where original plans are disrupted. Finally, the disabling implications of serious conditions, such as chronic pain or severe depression, are unlikely to be completely offset by any environmental intervention.

These counterintuitive features of the social model have led scholars to explore a third approach to disability, which is fundamentally an attempt to incorporate the insights of medical and social analyses while avoiding their respective drawbacks. *Interactionist models* hold that personal impairments and social factors are individually necessary and jointly sufficient for producing the limitations connected to the experience of disability. Interactionist models are popular, and it is not hard to see why. Interactionism arguably solves the major problems with medical and social accounts by recognizing that disabilities are triggered by a combination of biological and environmental conditions. Like the social approach, interactionism acknowledges the social dimension of disability. At the same time, interactionists incorporate the intuitive aspect of the medical model by attributing some role to impairment in the production of disability without committing to impairments being the sole, or even the primary disabling factor.

Alas, even this ecumenical effort leaves some stones unturned. Specifically, interactionism struggles to provide a principled distinction between conditions underlying genuine disabilities and conditions reflecting mere non-talents or lack of "superabilities." The following illustrations should help drive the point home. First, a student in a wheelchair schedules an appointment with a professor. Yet, since the department is not wheelchair-accessible, they are unable to reach the office. Second, a middle-aged individual would like to get to the top of a hill to enjoy the view, but they are too out of shape to hike all the way up. Third, an amateur mountain climber desires to reach the top of Mount Denali without using oxygen tanks but lacks the psychophysical means required for the quest. Note the structural similarity between these scenarios. In all three cases we have a person who is unable to reach a desired destination because of a combination of biological and environmental conditions. Yet, these examples vary in status. The first is a bona fide disability, with normative implications. Intuitively, the student has been wronged. Universities ought to provide equal access to all spaces. The second example is less clear-cut. Without further information—how steep is the hill? Why is the hiker out of shape?—it is hard to determine whether this is an instance of disability or non-talent. The third example is a clear case of lack of superability, not disability, which therefore warrants neither accommodation nor compensation.

How does one distinguish genuine disabilities from non-talents or lack of superabilities? Interactionism, in its traditional guise, struggles to provide a non-ad-hoc solution. The reason is that drawing a distinction between personal and environmental triggers in and of itself is insufficient. As our examples show, all three cases involve a limitation—not being able to reach a desired destination—produced

258   THE QUEST FOR HUMAN NATURE

by a blend of "external" and "internal" factors. The task becomes determining *which* personal and environmental traits yield true disabilities, thereby grounding claims for accommodation, and rationalizing which conditions seemingly do not warrant any normative intervention.

Should we conclude that interactionism ought to be abandoned? That would be overly hasty. Specialists are well aware that disabilities and non-talents lie on a spectrum. Providing a principled distinction between disability, non-talent, and lack of superability is an important endeavor that requires a painstaking combination of conceptual and empirical work on a case-by-case basis. Requiring a model to draw a line "from the armchair" would clearly be uncharitable. For this reason, the limitation discussed above in and of itself does not provide a rationale for eschewing interactionism. At the same time, we should obviously welcome a model that provides some general guidelines for how to demarcate disabling conditions like not being able to walk, which call for accommodation, from non-disabling conditions such as out-of-shape hikers or inexperienced climbers, where there is no obvious normative claim for intervention. Can this be obtained?

In a recent essay, Jeff Brown and I developed a strategy for addressing this problem. Extant proposals disagree on what produces a disability. Yet, all three models converge in either treating disabilities as features of individuals or not taking an explicit stance on this score. Advocates of the three mainstream models tend to focus on what *causes* disability. As a result, it becomes natural to conceive of disabilities themselves as *individual* properties. This might be a mistake. A clear rejection of this seemingly innocuous presupposition opens the path for a richer, more powerful analysis of disabling traits. The general insight is outlined in the following section.

§8.6 Lessons from Ecology

To appreciate the widespread tendency to conceive of disabilities as properties of individuals it is useful to draw an analogy between our three models and the debate concerning genetic determinism outlined in Chapter 5. Simple bodily features, such as having green eyes or black hair, are produced by a combination of two types of factors, which have received various labels: internal vs. external, biological vs. social, nature vs. nurture. It is now widely accepted that both kinds of influences are individually necessary and jointly sufficient for the development of such traits. The ongoing controversy concerns the relative contribution of each set of influences. Genetic determinists stress the causal prominence of genes and our biological endowment. Developmentalists question the meaningfulness of partitioning influence as genetic vs. environmental. Interactionists adopt a more balanced position, focusing on the decisive and irreducible contribution of both sets of factors in the production of phenotypes.

Note the correspondence with models of disability. Like genetic determinism, the medical model emphasizes the biological contribution to the experience of disability. Like developmentalism, the social model focuses on environmental triggers. Interactionists of both ilks adopt a middle-of-the-road perspective according to which phenotypes and disadvantages are the result of internal factors acting against an external backdrop. This analogy between disabilities and phenotypes is intuitive and illuminating. It reveals how advocates of medical and social models need not—and should not—endorse the untenable claim that impairments and environments, respectively, play *no* role in developing traits. Like sophisticated versions of both genetic determinism and developmentalism, they should stress the prominence, not the exclusivity, of these sets of bodily and social influences.

At the same time, the similarity between disabilities and phenotypes should not be stretched too far, as it may become potentially misleading. No one seriously disputes that traits are properties of individuals. Sure, environmental factors are partially responsible for Sam's green eyes and Pat's black hair. Still, once we set aside etiological questions—how these traits are produced—eyes and hair color are independent of environments. Sam has green eyes and Pat has black hair regardless of whether they live in New York or California, whether they like these traits or not, and whether these traits become a source of discrimination. These are features of their physical constitution. Disabilities are inherently different. Allow me to explain. The same impairment may well be a disability in one environment and not in a different one. As noted above, a wheelchair user may not suffer any disadvantage in a fully accessible city, while not being able to hike certain

260 THE QUEST FOR HUMAN NATURE

natural trails. This environment-dependent status makes disabilities closer to ecological niches than phenotypic properties. Follow-up question: what is a niche?

Oversimplifying a bit, one finds at least two concepts of niche in the ecological literature. The first corresponds to Elton's (1927) classic definition: a niche is a particular way of making a living in an ecological community. This characterization fits in well with the traditional view of environments posing selective pressures on organisms which, in turn, respond by adapting. "Eltonian" niches exist independently of the organisms that inhabit them. These entities are defined functionally, which means that the same niche can be occupied by different species in alternate environments, as long as the organisms in question play the same causal role. A "large carnivore niche" can be instantiated by lions in the African savannah and by tigers in the Indian subcontinent. On a second reading, niches can be viewed as volumes in multidimensional spaces, intended to capture the interactions between populations and their environments. On this view, first advanced by Hutchinson (1965) and subsequently developed by Lewontin (1978), the identification of the occupied region inherently depends on the population of reference. Setting subtleties aside, the dimensions of a niche are determined in part by the organisms that inhabit it. If lions and tigers interact with their ecosystems in a species-specific fashion, such variation will impact how exactly the large carnivore niche is implemented by each species. In short, on Hutchinson's view, a niche cannot be specified independently of its occupants. As Lewontin sharply puts it, niches are made, not found.

Subtleties aside, both definitions converge on one fundamental point: niches cannot be identified independently of the ecosystem in which they are embedded. This is not because the niche is created to a large extent by the surrounding environment. This is true, albeit irrelevant. The issue is that niches are *constituted*, wholly or partly, by reference to environments. A similar point applies to disabilities. Referring to a condition as a "disability," independently of the underlying context of reference, is elliptical and therefore strictly speaking meaningless. Disabilities cannot be reduced to an individual's experience, caused by biology, society, or a combination of both. Just like niches, disabilities are not properties of individuals alone. They are relational features of organisms embedded in environments. That disability cannot be causally explained without including environmental features is well-known. Yet, this is only part of the story. The remainder is that disabilities cannot even be identified independently of their context, implicitly or explicitly specified. To be sure, whether a certain individual, call them s, can hear certain sounds can be assessed independently of the environment where s lives. But the same cannot be said of whether such impairment constitutes a disability for s, which also hinges on the abilities of other members of the population, available technological interventions, and other environmental features. This neglected context-dependency makes disabilities relevantly analogous to ecological niches.

It may be useful to contrast this analysis with the three traditional accounts. Contra the medical model, from an ecological perspective, conditions can only be categorized as disabilities against the backdrop of a given environment. Even devastating states that are disabling across a multitude of contexts, such as Tay-Sachs disease—a genetic disorder that results in the destruction of nerve cells in the brain and spinal cord—may not count as disabilities in *all* conceivable contexts. Future biomedical advancements will hopefully forestall their debilitating effects, essentially providing less harmful "medical niches." At the same time, contrary to the social model, it does not follow that impairments never disable. Even in a fully accessible society, people with disabilities could still face disadvantages, and such conditions may interfere with performing potentially beneficial actions that enhance well-being. Finally, interactionists are correct that disabilities cannot be reduced exclusively to physical or environmental causes. Both sets of conditions play a necessary and jointly sufficient role. At the same time, this etiological insight is only part of the story. The ecological metaphor goes beyond interactionism, as it is traditionally presented, in emphasizing that disabilities are not only caused by biological and social factors. In addition, and crucially, disabilities are jointly *constituted* by both sets of conditions.

The "ecological" approach has significant implications for the conceptualization of disability. Here, I focus on an important consequence for normality and human nature.[12] Why do some disabilities matter

---

[12] For a broader and more comprehensive discussion, see Nathan and Brown (2018).

262 THE QUEST FOR HUMAN NATURE

for social policy whereas others are marginal? Why do I have an entitlement to read *Wuthering Heights* but not to climb them? We live in a society where reading, traveling, and being joyful happen to be desirable and achievable by most humans. In contrast, having perfect pitch, having a photographic memory, or being able to climb does not make a comparable difference to most of us. And living to be 180 years of age or telekinesis, as beautiful as they may sound, are not currently within our grasp. This is why the former conditions call for action, while the latter do not. These observations, humdrum as they may sound, have a momentous impact on Boorse's project of naturalizing a baseline for normality. If disabilities are heavily context-dependent, it will be impossible to determine whether a certain physiological state is a disabling condition without knowing which environments will count as relevant for its assessment. But such choice of ecosystem is definitely not something that can be naturalized, read off physiological data. It depends on an irreducibly normative choice.

In conclusion, the problem with naturalizing normal function lies with normality. Incidentally, I am also skeptical that the notion of function can be fully naturalized, whether this is done in terms of causal role, goal-contribution, etiology, or otherwise. But regardless, *normality* cannot be naturalized. This raises an intriguing question: is human nature the key to normality or is normality the key to human nature?

§8.7 Normality and Human Nature

This chapter covered a lot of ground: let's tie up some loose ends. Our discussion kicked off in §8.1 by noting how human nature is indissolubly tied to normality. There is no hope of capturing all human beings under the umbrella of human nature. There just is too much variation. At best, human nature can capture some prototypical notion of humanity. The question becomes how this baseline of normality should be understood. Chapter 3 examined a "top-down" approach, a natural state model that tried to explain variation in terms of deviations from an idealized state. Here we explored a different route, which consists in identifying the normal with the healthy and the natural. This led us straight to the distinction between health and disease. §8.2 set the stage by noting that providing adequate analyses of these concepts is not quite as trivial as many surmise. Traditional definitions of health as lack of disease and disease as absence of health work fine until we combine them, generating a vicious circle. Medical truisms—seek health and avoid disease, medics treats diseases, disease departs from the range of statistical normality, disease disables, health is adaptive, and health is organismic equilibrium—lay the terrain, but fall short of viable definitions. §8.3 advanced a more sophisticated account of disease as disruption of normal function. Medical practitioners adopt, more or less tacitly, a similar kind of conception when deciding if and how to intervene on a patient. But where does functional normality come from? Can the relevant notions be naturalized, that is, read off physiological data, as Boorse suggests?

The notion of function has been hotly debated in philosophy. Boorse's proposal has been challenged due to its failure to identify diseases with the right breakdown of functions. Be that as it may, §8.4 explored a different approach that identifies the problem with normal function not with function, but with normality. Amundson convincingly argues that what initially looks like a value-free assessment, upon further scrutiny turns out to be fueled by substantive normative presuppositions. From this standpoint, switching from a goal-contribution account of function to an etiological or causal-role analysis is not going to make much of a difference. Establishing that a specific trait has been selected for a particular function will not make the function in question "normal" in any prescriptively significant sense. If Amundson's critique is on the right track—as I believe it is—the task becomes identifying the disabling conditions that lead to unfair discrimination. But what is a disability? §8.5 outlined the three main extant frameworks for disability: the medical, social, and interactionist models, with their advantages and limitations. §8.6 drew some lessons from ecology to suggest that, like niches, disabilities are heavily context dependent. As such, it is impossible to characterize a true disability without a normative choice about which environments are relevant for its assessment.

What conclusions should we draw? As we anticipated in previous chapters, the notion of normality sets us on a perilous path.

264   THE QUEST FOR HUMAN NATURE

Its historical track record is one of brute discrimination. It is hard to single out some individuals as more "normal" without simultaneously marginalizing those who don't quite fit this bill. Yet, the moral, as I read it, is not to deny the existence of normality—a concept that, like human nature, is way too central to be swiftly set to the side. The point is rather that normality is not a natural state. It is the product of our attempts to theorize about nature. The natural sciences do not shed light on what it means to be normal. On the contrary, all relevant fields *presuppose* some notion of normality without being able to spell it out in any detail. Our understanding of disability, health, and disease cannot be separated from these normative background assumptions.

So, in conclusion, is normality the key to human nature or is human nature the key to normality? Normality plays a pivotal role in the natural and social sciences. It underscores the conception of health and disease underlying medical practice. It informs the classification of disability and efforts to overcome related injustices. As we saw, much biological and psychological practice presupposes some baseline of normality. And of course, there is no human nature without normality—these notions are effectively two sides of the same coin. Natural and social science would not exist without normality. So, eschewing the concept of normality tout court would be foolhardy.

At the same time, we should also recognize that normality is not something that can be inferred, more or less directly, just by looking at the relevant facts. It is a fundamentally normative notion and should be recognized as such. As normality cannot be naturalized, strictly speaking, there is no science thereof. There can only be a *politics* of normality, in the sense that what counts as "normal" for a human is not a straightforward empirical question. The issue of normality corresponds to what we called in §4.2 a *conceptual* scientific question, whose answer requires a subtle blend of description and prescription. It is in no small part a matter of what we value as a society and how we decide to pursue such goals. And, to the extent that the notion of human nature is inextricably tied to normality, the same conclusions should be extended to human nature as well.

This perspective was pioneered by Jaggar's groundbreaking work on feminism, surveyed in Chapter 7. It will be further developed in Chapter 10. Before getting there, however, we still have some chores to do. Is it possible to enhance our nature, transcending our very humanity? And should we be concerned about the prospect of doing so? These substantial issues are the focus of the following chapter.

9

Should We Be Concerned about Enhancing Our Nature?

> The different accidents of life are not so changeable
> as the feelings of human nature.
> —Mary Shelley, *Frankenstein*, 1818

§9.1 The Golden Age of Biotechnology

Reshuffle the deck and set aside human nature, just for a moment—we'll get back to it soon enough. We currently live in what has been aptly dubbed the "golden age of biotechnology." Over the past few decades, theoretical and technological advancements have progressed immensely, bestowing upon us powers that would have been unimaginable just a handful of years ago. What kind of powers? Broadly speaking, these involve the possibilities of deeply affecting the capacities and activities of the human body as well as the human mind at various stages of our lifespan. We have found the cure for devastating diseases. Since 1900, global life expectancy has more than doubled and is now well above seventy years. Several strategies have been discovered for ameliorating suffering, psychic no less than somatic. We can safely prevent fertility as well as boost it. Life can be initiated in the laboratory. The genetic endowment of a human fetus can be examined in the womb, screening for serious conditions and allowing informed decisions about whether to continue or terminate a pregnancy. We have the capability to transplant organs and replace parts of a human body with prosthetic surrogates. The selective increase of muscle mass and performance as well as the alteration of memory, mood, and attention by administering target drugs have become commonplace.

The Quest for Human Nature. Marco J. Nathan, Oxford University Press. © Oxford University Press 2024.
DOI: 10.1093/oso/9780197699249.003.0009

ENHANCING OUR NATURE   267

Procedures that a few decades ago would have been a wild dream are now routine practice, relatively cheap, and widely available to the general public. And at the rate at which technology and computing capacities are progressing, there is every reason to expect that the best is yet to come.[1] Brace yourself, you may be in for a real treat!

At the same time, these possibilities make some people anxious. Are there legitimate reasons for concern? What could such motives be? One obvious pushback is that powers unleashed by technology with good deeds in mind could be exploited for less than virtuous, even ignoble endeavors. Genetically engineered drug-resistant bacteria crafted for curative purposes may become instruments of bioterrorism were they to fall into the wrong hands. The capacity to alter people's mood, used properly, can help fight depression. But it could also be exploited by a dictatorship as an agent of social control. While these are real and pressing considerations, they transcend the scope of this work. Threats to national security, freedom, and social values are broader than biotechnological advancements. After all, extant inventions—from social media to nuclear power plants, from drones to high-resolution cameras—can also be twisted for less than virtuous goals.

In what follows, I restrict my attention to biotechnological issues that pertain directly to our overarching topic: human nature. In light of technological progress, genetic engineering, and other cutting-edge forms of pharmaceutical enhancement, one may speculate that it will soon be possible, if it isn't already, to enhance our human nature—whatever this turns out to be—and reject its shackles. How should we react to this possibility? In general, we can pinpoint two diametrically opposite responses to these biotech advancements and related concerns. These positions shape a heated debate that has unraveled over the past couple decades.

On the one hand, *bioliberalism*, also known as *transhumanism*, takes it that there are no decisive moral or prudential considerations against the use of human enhancement technologies and their broad availability.[2] Sure, there are hazards to be foreseen and avoided and it may

---

[1] An optimistic outline of the current human predicament is offered by Pinker (2018).

[2] Personally, neither label strikes me as optimal. The "bioliberalism vs. bioconservatism" opposition suggests that these bioethical positions neatly align to the corresponding political stances of liberals and conservatives. While there may well be

268 THE QUEST FOR HUMAN NATURE

well be advisable to treat some overly radical interventions as off-limits. Nevertheless, newly invented and improved techniques offer enormous potential. Whether and how to enhance who we are, bioliberals maintain, is ultimately a matter of personal choice. Individuals should have wide discretion over which of these technologies to apply to themselves and their families. Ideally, governments should interfere as little as possible with such decisions.

On the other hand, *bioconservatives* are worried about the prospects of modifying or transcending our nature by using pharmaceutical, genetic, synthetic-biological, and other technological means. The overarching concern is that enhancements may be "dehumanizing." They may undermine human dignity or something equally valuable about being human, as difficult as it may be to put our finger on what this means precisely. Rationale for prudence may be multifarious. It could derive from religious sentiment, such as the unwillingness to undo the work of a benevolent deity. Yet, uneasiness may also derive from secular considerations, from moral grounds to cautionary perspectives. But the core of all bioconservative stances is the assumption that technologies enhancing our nature should be banned or at least heavily scrutinized, regulated, and used sparingly.[3] The question is: *why*?

Issues revolving around the use of biotechnological powers to pursue perfection of body and mind and the anxieties this may or may

strong correlations, these two axes are strictly speaking independent and should be kept separate. "Transhumanism," in turn, implies that opening the door to enhancements goes hand in hand with the possibility of transcending species boundaries, which appears to be a non sequitur. Nevertheless, since I have no better alternative to offer, I stick to current nomenclature and use the labels "bioliberalism" and "transhumanism" interchangeably.

[3] Admittedly, my bioliberalism vs. bioconservatism dichotomy involves much idealization, as these positions come on a spectrum. As such, various alternative classifications would be equally justified. For instance, Giubilini and Sanyal (2016) divide positions regarding the morality of enhancements into *three* main categories. First, bioliberals, who believe that people should be free to enhance themselves. Second, a more moderate position which places considerable emphasis on the distinction between objectionable and non-objectionable forms of enhancements. Third, bioconservatives, who advance in-principle oppositions to human enhancements. Personally, I opt for a simpler two-tiered categorization chiefly because it seems to me that all bioliberals worth their salt draw *some* distinction between admissible and questionable improvements. Similarly, many bioconservatives will accept some minor forms of enhancements. Still, choices regarding how to break down the spectrum boil down to matters of classificatory convenience.

not cause have grown into an ongoing dispute which touches on some of the weightiest questions in bioethics, from the foundations of the life sciences to the means of human flourishing. In the words of one of the most outspoken supporters of transhumanism, the debate on enhancing our human nature "highlights a principal fault line in one of the great debates of our times: how we should look at the future of humankind and whether we should attempt to make ourselves 'more than human'" (Bostrom 2005, p. 204).

Providing a comprehensive overview of decades of discussion lies beyond my current interests. The more modest goal of this chapter is to explore the connections between the threat of dehumanization and the promise of super-humanization, on the one hand, and human nature, on the other. To determine whether we should be wary or excited about transcending the boundaries of our species, we need to ask the related question of what it means to be and act as a human being. To assess the states of being pre-human or post-human, and whether these should be feared or cherished, we need a firm grasp on what it is to be human, all too human. Thus conceived, human nature lies at the very core of this entire debate.

Here is the master plan. §9.2 kicks off by exploring an intuitive, albeit ultimately suspicious distinction between therapy and enhancement, which is often employed to draw the line between permissible and impermissible interventions. §9.3 zooms in on enhancement, as well as its uses and misuses. Why do many people find enhancements disquieting? If the distinction between enhancement and therapy does not hold water, on what basis should we separate acceptable manipulations from those that should be red-flagged? As we shall see—although none of this should be all that surprising at this point in our journey together—finding a clear-cut principle is much harder than many initially foresee. The following two sections discuss some influential arguments for and against human enhancements. §9.4 outlines a bioconservative stance that purports to defend the relevance and importance of *naturalness* in assessing our goals. §9.5 spells out a transhumanist defense of human dignity. §9.6 wraps things up by asking whether we can have a meaningful discussion of these positions without some substantive assumptions about human nature. Few readers should be shocked to hear that I will advance a negative

270 THE QUEST FOR HUMAN NATURE

answer. All these debates presuppose a substantive notion of human nature, albeit one that has eluded us so far. That will raise the questions of why human nature is so pesky, whether it is a scientific concept at all, and, if not, what kind of concept it turns out to be. But now I'm already getting ahead of myself.

Before getting down to business, I have a nagging preliminary concern to address. Some readers many worry that these are drastic overreactions. Are these issues worth discussing in detail at this point in time? Allow me to briefly elaborate the objection. Compared to other contemporary issues in bioethics, ethics, and sociopolitical philosophy, the prospects of transcending our own human nature via biotechnological enhancement may appear abstract, ethereal, remote, and all too academic to be a genuine concern calling for action. Why bother with science fiction, the argument runs, when the world is facing deeper, more pressing perils? On a planet confronted by perduring war, extreme poverty, pandemics, malnutrition, climate change, and local unemployment, should anyone lose sleep over threats of dehumanization or super-humanization? Perhaps our priorities should lie elsewhere.[4]

There is something deep and important about this line of thought. No one should deny that transhumanism hardly tops the list of present headaches and that the bulk of our energy and resources should be devoted to more pressing issues. At the same time, willfully ignoring less imminent threats and farther-fetched scenarios would be dangerously myopic. The undeniable observation that there are rapists and murderers "out there" is a sorry excuse not to thwart and prosecute petty crime. The existence of deadly diseases like cancer and ALS should not prevent pharmaceutical companies from developing better

---

[4] Some utilitarian concerns against enhancement, based on the worry that developing enhancers may drain resources from more urgent medical research, have been offered by Selgelid (2014). For utilitarian concerns in favor of enhancers, see Levy (2013). A more systematic response has been developed by Persson and Savulescu (2012), who, as their provocative title suggests, view our species, in its current form, as "unfit for the future." Consequently, they argue, a combination of moral and cognitive enhancement is necessary to make human beings better equipped for facing and addressing the pressing needs of the modern world.

antihistamines. Arguing that focusing on one problem precludes acknowledging others is posing a false dichotomy—"whataboutism" is a rhetorical strategy that is widespread and disturbingly effective, especially in the current political climate. A similar response applies to our present topic. The existence of other timely issues, even more significant ones, doesn't make less urgent matters unworthy of our care and attention.[5]

The push toward bioengineering perfection is the wave of the future, if not the present. Technology often advances in quantum shifts. Novelty may well sneak up on us before we even know it. If we are not careful, it may sweep over us and carry us under. As bioconservatives observe, recent gains in health and longevity have produced neither contentment nor satisfaction but an increased appetite for more and better. For all these reasons, it is important to discuss our future: what are we trying to achieve and how? On this note, it is instructive to look at analogous cases of intellectual neglect. For many years, ethical issues pertaining to cloning and genetic profiling have been swept to the side. Consequently, when suddenly the possibility of obtaining fast and cheap analyses of our genetic endowment made moral considerations more pressing, we saw legal, ethical, and bioethical discussions lagging dangerously behind. Something analogous may be going on these days with facial-recognition technology and other tracking devices, as well as Artificial Intelligence, whose normative implications have been swept under the rug for decades.

In conclusion, decisions we make today shape the world of tomorrow for us and generations to come. We must discuss and regulate human cloning, sex selection, embryo screening, whether we are comfortable prescribing psychotropic drugs to young children, and how vigorously to pursue research into the biology of senescence. We must begin immediately because, once the entire biotechnological machinery is in play, it will be arduous to halt it or even stall it. Hence, it is up to us to start thinking about these matters. And we should do it *now*, not wait until it's too late.

---

[5] For an insightful discussion of which agendas to prioritize, see Kitcher (2001, 2011).

§9.2 Therapy vs. Enhancement

The question of how the good become excellent is a hallowed one in the history of philosophy. It was famously raised and addressed by Plato in the *Meno*, where Socrates and Meno debate what human virtue is and whether it can be taught. We have also touched upon some of these issues in Chapters 4 and 5, in the context of our discussion of innateness and genetic determinism. Traditionally, the issue of excellency has been framed by distinguishing two kinds of improvements. Some sources of bettering lie within our grasp. Through learning, training, and hard practice, I can transcend what I am currently able to achieve physically and mentally. Following a grueling schedule, I can train to finish a marathon and learn to speak some Mandarin. Similarly, I could acquire the rudiments of playing the piano. In contrast, other objectives seemingly lie beyond my reach. I could not grow over seven feet tall and, despite all my efforts at training, completing a marathon under two hours is not and likely was never in my cards. Regardless of whether we view athletic abilities as natural or divine gifts, some goals transcend my limits. Similarly, many people will never be able to sing opera, become piano virtuosos, or write literary masterpieces, no matter how hard they try.

This was the situation until recently in the course of our history. Things may well be in transition. Biotechnology promises to bridge this gap between reachable and off-limits achievements, blurring a seemingly clear and timeworn distinction among improvements. Perhaps, by taking sufficient chemical substances and with mechanical replacements, I could have—or even still can—become an Olympic athlete. Suppose there were a neural surgical procedure which instantly turned anyone into a professionally trained classical pianist. Could we get to a point where teaching, learning, and practice are no longer necessary, leaving time for more enjoyable endeavors? And, if so, should we? The previous section outlined the ongoing debate between bioliberals and bioconservatives. Simply put, the former camp welcomes the chances of transcending the boundaries of our nature whereas their adversaries advance various cautionary warnings. This chapter considers both stances. For starters, let's look into whether transhumanist prospects are disquieting and what might make them so.

An intuitive answer is to contrast the "naturalness" of learning, training, and practice with the "unnaturalness" of pills, silicon chips, mechanical enhancements, and other artifacts. Yet, upon further scrutiny it becomes evident that this can hardly be the main source of concern. Aspirin, cardiac pacemakers, and prosthetic limbs are all human-made, and the excision of a tumor mass requires deviating the course of nature. Still—setting certain religious prescriptions aside—no one would consider the fabrication and installation of these entities, or the underlying acts of restoration themselves, morally dodgy. The opposition between natural and artificial cannot be the decisive factor. The headsprings of anxiety must lie elsewhere.

There is a popular strategy for determining which interventions should be allowed, indeed encouraged, and which must be carefully monitored. This involves drawing a distinction between two different kinds of interventions: *therapy vs. enhancement.* Therapy, simply put, is the treatment of documented diseases and disabilities. Thus, administering a painkiller to the suffering, restoring sight to the visually impaired, and healing fractured bones are therapeutic measures because they heal known pathological conditions. Compare this with enhancements: interventions aimed at altering the normal workings of the human body and psyche, such as bestowing upon an individual Herculean strength, the capacity to fly, or the ability to memorize the content of hefty books in seconds. Intuitively, the argument runs, therapy is ethically permissible, arguably even normatively required. Enhancement instead is, at least prima facie, morally suspicious. From this standpoint, the principal prescriptive norm becomes clear. Gene therapy aimed at curing cystic fibrosis is morally allowed and so is prescription of antidepressant drugs such as Prozac. In contrast, the insertion or modification of genes to enhance intelligence or the use of steroids by professional athletes to boost their performance is *streng verboten.*[6]

---

[6] An influential version of this distinction between therapy and enhancement is found in Sandel (2007). For a critique of Sandel from a social-model perspective, see Barclay (2016). A general rebuke of his "giftedness of nature" is found in Harris (2007) and Lewens (2015a). For a thorough discussion of different types of enhancements—cognitive, mood, physical, lifespan, and moral—see the essays collected in Savulescu et al. (2011).

274 THE QUEST FOR HUMAN NATURE

Is distinguishing between therapy and enhancement a plausible strategy to draw the line between morally acceptable and questionable uses of biotechnology? To address this question, a few clarifications are in order.

First, the same mode of intervention may be classified as therapy or enhancement, depending on its target. A couple examples should help drive the point home. The installation of prostheses, typically viewed as therapeutic, need not be so. Some may recall Oscar Pistorius, the South African sprinter who had both feet amputated when he was eleven months old due to a congenital defect. Whereas Pistorius petitioned to compete with "normal" athletes, many feared that his mechanical legs could bestow upon him an unfair advantage, drawing international attention to the case. For the record—pun intended—Pistorius' stint was relatively unsuccessful. Still, he rose to further notoriety in 2013 after being convicted of the murder of his girlfriend, Reeva Steenkamp. Conversely, while many consider genetic therapy as a paradigmatic case of enhancement, it also has therapeutic applications, for instance, in curing cystic fibrosis. In short, whether an intervention counts as therapy or enhancement depends on its ends, not its means.

Second, the therapy–enhancement divide is not merely academic. Health providers and insurance companies have bought into it. Treatment of disease and disability is typically funded. Most enhancers in contrast must be paid out of pocket. Thus, therapeutic eye surgery is often covered by insurance, whereas any plea to get reimbursed for increasing eyesight above 20/20—foresight and hindsight alike—would likely fall on deaf ears.

Third, the therapy vs. enhancement distinction is directly connected to the concepts of normal function and disability discussed in Chapter 8. Specifically, if we could follow Boorse in presupposing a naturalized notion of normal function, then we would thereby have a perfectly objective way of distinguishing therapy from enhancement. Unfortunately, persuasive arguments against normal function and related objections challenge the possibility of drawing the relevant distinction in straight-up empirical terms. As we shall see, similar concerns undermine our present analysis.

ENHANCING OUR NATURE   275

Leon Kass (2003), the former chairman of President G. W. Bush's Council on Bioethics and one of the most authoritative bioconservative voices, acknowledges that the distinction between therapy and enhancement is both intuitive and useful for calling attention to pressing bioethical issues. At the same time, Kass emphasizes, such distinction fails to ground any substantive moral analysis. What exactly counts as "enhancement"? Does the term mean more, better, or both? Better by what standards? At what point does improved sight become an enhancement? What about selective erasure of memory? Problems become especially acute for psychological characteristics, which, as we saw in Chapter 3, are even more difficult to operationalize. Restoring mental health is presumably therapeutic. But precisely how is psychic well-being to be distinguished from mere cheerfulness or contentment? In the many human qualities that follow a "normal" distribution, such as height, does the average spell out a norm or is the norm itself subject to alteration? Consider two individuals, α and β, who are the same height but are members of different populations, P_1 and P_2 respectively. Suppose that the average height of population P_1 is significantly lower than P_2. Does that mean that β is entitled to growth hormones in virtue of falling below the "norm," whereas α is not? After all, they are the same height. What if α is unhappier about their height than is β? If we help the short grow to average, thereby making previously average people short, that seems unlikely to provide new therapeutic entitlements.

In short—last pun, I promise—drawing a principled distinction between therapy and enhancement without presupposing normal function seems hopeless. Is that the right direction to explore? Many answer in the negative. Kass (2003, p. 13) is a prominent bioconservative voice among the naysayers: "Needless arguments about whether or not something is or is not an 'enhancement' get in the way of the proper question: What are the good and bad uses of biotechnical power? What makes a use 'good,' or even just 'acceptable'? . . . The human meaning and moral assessment are unlikely to be settled by the term 'enhancement,' any more than they are settled by the nature of the technological intervention itself." Given our own troubles with providing an adequate analysis of human nature, I'm inclined to agree. It would be wise to look elsewhere.

§9.3 'Sup with Enhancers?

The previous section raised the issue of enhancers and what feels so disconcerting about them. We sketched a preliminary answer by drawing a contrast with therapy. Intuitive as it may initially appear, the distinction at stake turns out to be suspicious.[7] Unless we appeal to an independent notion of biological normality—which, as discussed at length, should not be taken for granted—it's not clear where therapy ends and enhancement begins. It looks like we've taken a wrong turn. Perhaps the core issue is something *intrinsically* troublesome with enhancements, regardless of their connections with therapy. Follow-up: what might this "x factor" be?

One proposal is to stress how enhancements are inherently dangerous. Our safety-obsessed culture, the suggestion runs, sanctions practices that could turn out to be perilous.[8] This platitude seems to capture, for instance, what many find problematic about taking massive doses of antidepressants or other kinds of drugs, medical and recreational alike. Biological agents used for the purposes of self-perfection cannot possibly be entirely harmless. That could be what's wrong with them: they just ain't good for you! This is hard to dispute. At the same time, upon further scrutiny, this line of argument becomes difficult to justify. Life is replete with risk: from car racing to ice climbing, from sedentary lifestyles to smoking. Why don't we ban all these activities and products? The reason is that, as long as people are given access to information about downsides and advantages and deliberately choose to partake in them, they have a right to decide for themselves. Enhancers seem no different. After pondering all pros and cons, one can deliberate to use them despite potential inherent perils.

A second objection to enhancers is that they bestow unfair advantages upon the people who take them.[9] Consider for instance

---

[7] Providing a clear-cut definition of enhancement is a notoriously thorny endeavor. For a systematic discussion, see Savulescu et al. (2011) and Gyngell and Selgelid (2016).

[8] While authors such as Kass (2003) focus on inherent dangers, others have emphasized the related point that enhancers may have unintended consequences (Hirschman 1991; Fukuyama 2002). For responses, see Buchanan (2013) and Powell and Buchanan (2011).

[9] Egalitarian concerns with enhancers are raised by Mehlman and Botkin (1998), Glannon (2001), McKibben (2003), and Mehlman (2003). For rejoinders, see Buchanan (2013).

ENHANCING OUR NATURE   277

the use of blood thinners and steroids among professional athletes or mental stimulants in students taking a standardized test such as the SAT. Why do many people find them illegal, or at least immoral? Presumably, it is because they give an edge to their users. The athlete who won the race would not have triumphed had they not received the blood thinner. A student may not get into their dream college because someone else took their spot in virtue of their enhanced performance. But how persuasive is this line of argument, in general? And how far are we willing to follow down its path?

One problem lies in the very notion of unfair advantage, which is strikingly broad. To illustrate, in 1960, twenty-eight-year-old Ethiopian Abebe Bikila amazed the world by winning the Olympic marathon in Rome. For one thing, he was virtually unknown and un-heralded as an athlete. Second, he became the first East African to win an Olympic medal. Third, he completed the entire course running barefoot. It is unlikely that anyone could ever repeat this. Running has become even more competitive and modern shoes bestow too big an advantage upon athletes, as evidenced by the recent controversy on the potential benefits conferred by *Vaporfly* shoe technology, which is helping athletes break record after record. This is arguably not fair. A poor competitor who lacks the financial means to buy new shoes on a regular basis may well feel discriminated against. Are there differences between doping and shoes? One answer is cost: few competitors could afford the latest forms of doping. But we could always make steroids cheap, even free, and widely accessible. Would that level the playing field? If the rejoinder is that doping is dangerous, we are now back to our previous objection that, as noted, is shaky. In short, it's not clear why the use of enhancers is unfair. At least, it's no more unfair than other equipment available mainly to athletes from richer communities in affluent countries.

The overarching concern may be placed in a broader context. Many object to the use of doping and other enhancers in competitive settings because it is a form of *cheating*. But what does "cheating" mean here? On the reading assumed so far, cheating consists in winning in virtue of some unfair advantage that other competitors don't have access to. The problem is that enhancers are hardly the only form of cheating, thus construed. Access to training facilities, high-quality coaching,

278 THE QUEST FOR HUMAN NATURE

expensive equipment, and other resources may "un-level" the playing field along analogous lines.

There is, however, a different conception of cheating, one which lacks any competitive dimension. The underlying idea is intuitive. There are many areas of human life in which traditionally excellence could only be achieved with much discipline, sacrifice, and effort. Anyone can learn how to play a musical instrument or build athletic stamina, if they so desire. But fulfilling these goals requires a substantial amount of energy, practice, and training.[10] Obtaining the same results by means of drugs, genetic engineering, and implanted devices may feel "cheap." People should work hard for their achievements and building character is not merely the source of our deeds, but also their product. Learning to play the piano or acquiring the ability to complete a marathon in under three hours by merely swallowing a pill is not only unfair to other competitors. It is first and foremost unfair to ourselves. In this sense, it counts as cheating: it violates the spirit of a quintessentially human activity. This is the line that should not be crossed.

Once again, there is much to agree with. The hiccup is that things are not quite that simple. Where exactly should this boundary be drawn and on what grounds? For one thing, not all biotechnological interventions make excellence cheap. Steroids are not sufficient to make anyone a world-class athlete. They still require hard work. Sure, they help, but so do good shoes and upbeat music. And we don't condemn the latter. Doped athletes must work just as hard as non-doped ones—sometimes more, as in the infamous case of professional cyclists illicitly increasing the hemoglobin in their blood. In addition to their grueling races, these athletes had to secretly exercise at night to avoid blood-clotting causing heart attacks. Furthermore, not all biotechnological interventions make excellence cheap. Many of life's pinnacles have nothing to do with competition or adversity. Technology could help individuals who have been dealt a meager

---

[10] Malcolm Gladwell (2008) has popularized the so-called "10,000 hours rule," famously stating that this is the minimum amount of time required to become an expert or master performer in a given field. As catchy and easy to remember as this is, its validity has been questioned. Nevertheless, the underlying point stands: practice does make perfect!

ENHANCING OUR NATURE   279

hand. Why should we not accept it? What's wrong with restoring some fairness in life?

A third, related objection to enhancers has to do with reasons for acting.[11] The core matter, the objection runs, is neither fairness nor equality of access but rather "goodness of state." Suppose that someone invented a pill that mimics exactly the sensation of deep love. If I were to take the pill and suddenly fall for a random stranger, am I truly enamored? Consider a gas released at a rock concert causing everyone to have the best time of their lives. Is the audience really enjoying the show? Or imagine that you are appreciating a (this?) book because it has been sprayed with a chemical substance that enhances one's reading experience. In all these cases, people are acting appropriately. But they may not be acting for the right reasons. Similar intuitions could account for the wrongness of enhancement.

Focusing on the motives underlying action may appear like a promising strategy to analyze enhancement. Yet, as soon as we try to apply it, several difficulties arise. The main issue—which we've encountered repeatedly—concerns who determines which reasons are the "right" ones and on what grounds. If I only wanted to regain sight because I feel more attractive without glasses, does that delegitimize my request? What about someone who is seriously depressed about not being taller? Beliefs, desires, and other varieties of intentional states get us into a thorny thicket from which it will be difficult to escape with only minor scratches.

A fourth rejoinder to the use—and abuse—of enhancers centers around broad issues of freedom and coercion of both an overt and a more covert kind. The underlying insight is that enhancers wrongly limit personal choice. As discussed in Chapter 7, this can happen at either social or individual levels. Beginning with the former scenario, consider a tyrannical regime which discovers a chemical substance that mitigates in citizens the tendency to rebel. Such curbing of freedom can also occur within smaller social groups such as individual families when parents impose their personal aspirations and desires on their children, flatly disregarding the child's independence

---

[11] These third and fourth sets of considerations are advanced by Kass (2003).

280 THE QUEST FOR HUMAN NATURE

or real needs. Imagine that it would be possible to genetically engineer a strong human predisposition for, say, athleticism, musical talent, or mathematical genius. That looks like a disquieting prevarication of individual freedom, projecting the parents' aspirations upon their actual or potential offspring.

These are important considerations. Nevertheless, two nagging concerns remain. First, these troubling implications seem completely independent of enhancers per se. Sure, a despotic tyrant or totalitarian government could set out to control citizens by forcibly or secretively administering a drug. But very similar effects could be achieved through different means, such as propaganda, repression of the free press, and other forms of brainwashing. Personally, I worry a lot more about social media and its echo chamber effects, which is already tangibly wreaking havoc on our social texture, affecting especially the younger and more vulnerable portions, than potential and more or less dubious forms of genetic control. Similar reflections apply at the familial level. Genetic engineering would arguably constitute a restriction of individual freedom and a form of coercion. But the same could be said about peer pressure, social conformity, choices of schooling, and other parental decisions that may strongly affect the future of a young child. Once again, genetic engineering may eventually turn into another means for obtaining what is already being achieved through the environment. Before stressing about the future, we should take a closer look at the present and worry about what we may find right here.

A second concern with this analysis of enhancement as breaching personal freedom is that it fails to capture the problem with individual use. What's wrong with me, a consenting adult, making a thoughtful and conscious decision to enhance my own body or mind? If we are still not on board with this possibility, it means something else must be going on.

In conclusion, we've been inquiring into what makes enhancers so disquieting. If the present considerations are on target, the answer cannot be their danger, unfairness, wrong motives, or infringement of liberty. As Kass (2003) notes, putting uncomfortable gut feelings into words is not easy. We may feel a deep sense of repugnance with drugs that make us fall in love, erase painful memories, or drastically change our personality. But, as long as these enhancements are taken willingly, freely, and in full understanding, moral disgust hardly translates into sound argument. Is there something wrong with seventy-year-olds playing professional sports or kids instantly memorizing knowledge contained in entire dictionaries and encyclopedias? Is there wisdom in feeling repugnance? Bioconservatives answer in the positive. Bioliberals beg to disagree. The following pages examine arguments for both positions, drawing connections to human nature.

§9.4 Natural Goals

Let's take a breather. The question under present scrutiny is not whether we should seek to improve human life. There is no dispute here: we should. The issue is whether there is a boundary that must not be crossed. In other words, need our pursuit of "ageless bodies and happy souls"—to borrow Kass' felicitous phrase—be harnessed? And if so, on what grounds? §9.2 purported to capture the difference between "good" and "bad" interventions along the therapy vs. enhancement dimension. The insight is that therapeutic manipulation, which restores some "normal" or "natural" state, is permissible. Enhancement in contrast must be carefully monitored as it transcends our true selves. The challenge is determining on what basis to carve this distinction. Sure, there is an intuitively big gap between curing an infection and enabling someone to sprint one hundred meters under nine seconds. But without a clear notion of human nature or normal function it is difficult to picture where the line should be drawn and how. §9.3 blazed a different trail. The problem with enhancers, the argument runs, is not their departure from therapy. The issue is that they are intrinsically troublesome. But what precisely makes them disconcerting isn't obvious. We examined various candidate properties to the effect that they are dangerous and unfair, they rest on the wrong motives, and they infringe on personal liberties. While all these considerations capture something important about enhancers, none seems to get to the heart of the matter.

One option is to throw in the towel and embrace the bioliberal tenet that there is *nothing* wrong with enhancers. We shall blaze this trail in §9.5. Before doing so, the present section follows a different line of

282 THE QUEST FOR HUMAN NATURE

thought. So far, we have tacitly assumed that therapy and enhancement are different means for achieving the same end: making people happy, maximizing well-being without infringing the rights, liberty, and security of others. Given this noble endeavor, therapy is an appropriate strategy; enhancement is not. This could be a mistake. Could it be that what is problematic about enhancing nature is that it sets up the wrong goals? Is there something deeply troubling with the very pursuit of "ageless bodies and happy souls"? Let's fathom this issue based on an influential argument originally developed by Kass.[12]

At first glance, the case for ageless bodies seems unassailable. Prevention of decay, decline, disability, and debility. Eliminating feebleness, frailty, and fatigue. What could possibly be wrong with that? Why not let human beings live fully at the top of their powers and enjoy the best quality of life achievable, from the cradle to the grave? Even if we do not long for this personally or for our beloved, others should be allowed to decide for themselves. In short, if we truly had the possibility to spare human bodies from suffering the ravages of time, it would seem perverse not to do so or at least allow it as a possibility for those who so desire.

Kass deems this issue less clear-cut than it appears at first blush. Many human goods, its is argued, are inseparable from the temporal dimension of the human life cycle. Would it be desirable for everyone to go through life with a body that looks and functions like that of a teenager? Do we truly want to turn into light bulbs burning as brightly from beginning to end and popping off without a warning, leaving those around us suddenly in the dark? There seems to be something valuable about life having a shape, where everything is due in its season, our bodies reflecting this structure. What would intragenerational relations become, Kass asks, if there never came a point where children surpassed parents in vigor? Perhaps it would take away

---

[12] Kass' argument, grounded in the claim that intuitions and emotions, such as repugnance, offer reliable moral guidance in the field of bioethics, unravels across several publications spanning decades (Kass 1985, 1997, 2003, 2008). This presupposition has been scrutinized and criticized from both a philosophical and a moral-psychological perspective (Coady 2016; May 2016; McConnell and Kennett 2016). Incidentally, Buchanan (2009) and Briggle (2010) read Kass as a neo-Aristotelian, although Kass himself disavows this interpretation.

ENHANCING OUR NATURE   283

any incentive for the old to step aside and make space for younger generations. Indeed, the great increase in average and maximal life expectancy experienced over the past century has led to a prolongation of functional immaturity in the young. Is this a worthy trajectory to be prolonged and promoted? In short, one cannot think of enhancing the vitality of the old without retarding the maturation of the young. As Kass eloquently puts it:

> Those who propose adding years to the human lifespan regard time abstractly, as physicists do, as a homogeneous and continuous dimension, each part exactly like any other, and the whole lacking shape or pattern. Yet, the "lived time" of our natural lives has a trajectory and a shape, its meaning derived in part from the fact that we live as links in the chain of generations. For this reason, our flourishing as individuals might depend, in large measure, on the goodness of the natural human life cycle, roughly three multiples of a generation: a time of coming of age; a time of flourishing, ruling, and replacing of self; and a time of savoring and understanding, but still sufficiently and intimately linked to one's descendants to care about their future and to take a guiding, supporting, and cheering role. (2003, p. 26)

The point extends from ageless bodies to happy souls. True, painful and shameful memories are disquieting. So are guilty consciences, low self-esteem, melancholy, and depression. Yet, Kass suggests, there is something deeply troubling about the effortless pursuit of psychic tranquility, the attempt to eliminate negativity from our mental life. Trauma, shame, remorse, and depression are painful, sometimes crippling. But they can also be helpful and fitting. They often embody the appropriate human response to horror, disgraceful conduct, and sin. As such, they can be a guide for us in the future. There may be a connection between the feeling of deep unhappiness and the prospects of achieving genuine psychological bliss.

In conclusion, Kass purports to "make a case for finitude and even graceful decline of bodily powers" as well as "genuine human happiness, with satisfaction as the bloom that graces unimpeded, soul-exercising activity" (Kass 2003, p. 27). From this standpoint, a

284 THE QUEST FOR HUMAN NATURE

flourishing human life needs not an ageless body and untroubled soul. It needs *rhythm*:

> Fine aspiration acted upon *is itself* the core of happiness. Not the agelessness of the body, nor the contentment of the soul, nor even the list of external achievement and accomplishments of life, but the engaged and energetic being-at-work of what nature uniquely gave to us is what we need to treasure and defend. All other perfection is at best a passing illusion, at worst a Faustian bargain that will cost us our full and flourishing humanity. (Kass 2003, p. 28)

Kass' perspective—aim for rhythm, not for ageless bodies and happy souls—lacks one basic ingredient to be fully persuasive: *human nature*. Allow me to elaborate. Compare current life in the United States with life in the mid-nineteenth century. Welfare has improved along many dimensions: life expectancy, eradication of pain and disease, peace, technology, social justice, civil rights, wealth distribution, freedom, education, and much else. To be clear, I'm not suggesting that the current state is ideal. Far from it. Similarly, life has clearly not improved in all respects. And there may well be aspects that have deteriorated in the past century-and-change. One may bemoan, for instance, loss of biodiversity, environmental degradation, or extreme urbanization. But, all things considered, it is hard to deny that overall quality of life has improved. I highly doubt that anyone would seriously want to go back to the "good ole days" if offered an earnest choice.

Now, consider the current situation from an 1800s perspective. Could the nineteenth-century philosopher "Kass*" look to their future—our present—and decry a loss in meaning of life? People live longer, work longer, retire later, and family values have shifted substantially. In many respects we have become lazier, weaker, and more spoiled. The journey immortalized in the "Oregon Trail" game was extremely taxing in terms of risk, health, financial resources, and energy. That same itinerary can now be completed in relative safety, cruising along fully stocked highways or comfortably sitting on a jet plane. Have we lost some spirit of adventure? For sure. But would anyone, in all honesty, volunteer to return for good to the ways of the past? From this standpoint, Kass' argument starts looking a bit parochial, a conservation of the status quo. Now, if we had a biologically kosher notion of human nature, we could easily address this concern. We could cherish all the ameliorations to our human life while decrying those interventions, if any, that have dehumanized our *ley de vida*. We could also compare lives in the 1800s with the 2000s from that same perspective: what we have lost and what we have gained. But since any robust notion of human nature still eludes us, what exactly we are measuring or tracking remains rather murky.

§9.5 Nature's Gifts

Let's take stock. The previous sections have focused on the notion of enhancement and what exactly makes enhancers so disquieting. Specifically, §9.2 first attempted to capture the distinction between "good" and "bad" interventions by drawing a principled albeit elusive distinction between therapy and enhancement. Next, §9.3 considered whether there is something intrinsically disturbing about enhancement. Again, we came out empty-handed. §9.4 shifted gear, from focusing on the means that we may use to achieve a certain goal to assessing the "goodness" of the goals themselves. I like to believe that we've learned quite a lot along the way. Nevertheless, it is only fair to acknowledge that we have not been able to put our finger on what's so troubling about the prospects of enhancing who we are. Why not?

There is a further potential concern that we have brushed to the side. One could worry about the false promises of enhancements. Plastic surgery, especially in young individuals, perpetuates a false image as opposed to fixing insecurity. While this is a deep and important concern, its connection to human nature is loose. Analogous problems arise with respect to riches, fame, and social status. The problem hardly lies with enhancement per se. With all this in mind, it might be time to consider the possibility that there is nothing wrong with enhancements at all.[13] The goal of this section is to present and discuss the transhumanist stance, according to which the prospects of a

---

[13] A position along these lines is developed by Harris (2007). For a comprehensive discussion of enhancement, see the essays collected in Savulescu and Bostrom (2009).

286   THE QUEST FOR HUMAN NATURE

post-human future are something to openly cherish, not fear. To kick things off, let's reshuffle our deck. Instead of asking what is wrong with enhancement in and of itself, let's look into what, if anything, makes it so scary.

In an influential article, philosopher and bioethicist Nick Bostrom (2005) argues that the prospect of post-humanity is feared for at least two reasons. First, some expect the state of being post-human to be degrading and as such harmful to humans. Second, the very existence of post-humans might pose a threat to ordinary humans. There is also a widespread third worry, namely, that the emergence of post-humanism might offend some supernatural being. The concern is heightened if we further follow the monotheistic tradition in assuming that such a deity has deliberately created humankind in its own image as the pinnacle of the *scala naturae*. Bostrom sets this third objection aside and I shall follow suit. For one thing, the religious significance of human nature lies beyond my professional competence. Also, it does not directly pertain to the topic under present scrutiny, namely, the possibility of providing a scientific explanation of who we are. So, let's focus on the first two rationales. Bostrom believes that both fears are misplaced. What grounds can be offered? Let's take a look at some general arguments.

The concern that any post-human existence would be degrading to humanity has been forcefully advanced by Kass (2002, 2003) who, as previously noted, has long been an authoritative voice in support of bioconservative values. Kass' central point is that each species has its own nature, human beings included. Changing our nature into something else would be by definition "dehumanizing" and—less tautologically—disconcerting. Some bioliberals beg to disagree with the assumption that transcending our own nature is necessarily a perilous and immoral endeavor. Sure, some of nature's gifts are valuable and we rightly hold them in high consideration. Friendship, love, joy, compassion, and empathy are prime examples. At the same time, people hardly need be reminded that not all that is natural is ipso facto good and desirable. As we discussed in Chapters 6, 7, and 8, our own species is subject to or responsible for various well-documented horrors, from maiming disease to neonatal death, from murder to rape, from genocide to torture, not to speak of racism, sexism, ablism, and other forms of marginalization. It would thus be a mistake, Bostrom maintains, to flatly identify what is natural with what is righteous. Indeed, rather than blindly deferring to some "natural order of things," we would be better off reforming ourselves in accordance with our values and personal aspirations. Now, to be sure, as we already saw in the previous section, not all change constitutes progress. Still, Kass goes beyond this truism in claiming that technical mastery over our own nature will inevitably lead to utter dehumanization.[14]

What seems to be driving Kass' fears, and related concerns expressed by fellow bioconservatives, Bostrom continues, is that any deep and radical effort to ameliorate who we are will inevitably lead to some "Brave New World" scenario. Clearly, Huxley's celebrated fictional dystopia is not something we should aspire to. It is a static, totalitarian, caste-bound transformation of human society into a cultural waste-land whose members are indeed dehumanized and undignified. But the belief that this is the fate of any technology-enhanced humanity is at least questionable. As a futuristic prediction, it seems pessimistic. As metaphysical necessity, it is false. Furthermore, brave-new-worlders are not obviously post-humans. In many respects they are the same as us or even inferior. In brief, Bostrom (2005, p. 206) concludes, "*Brave New World* is not a tale of human enhancement gone amok, but it is rather a tragedy of technology and social engineering being deliberately used to cripple moral and intellectual capacities—the exact antithesis of the transhumanist proposal." Properly understood, transhumanism acknowledges that we must defend morphological and reproductive rights against wannabe world controllers. Government should not curtail these freedoms. What we need is liberty and debate, not constraint.

With this in mind, let's move on to the second reason to fear a post-human world. Annas and colleagues (2002) have denounced human

---

[14] Bostrom's argument is developed by Buchanan (2009) and Briggle (2010). It is interesting to note how claims of dehumanization cross-cut various positions pertaining to human nature. In Chapter 3 we considered Hull and Kronfeldner's warnings that appeals to human nature may turn out to be "dehumanizing," a concern that was echoed in subsequent chapters. Kass' argument brings emphasis to the possibility that trying to dispose of human nature altogether may equally trigger analogous dehumanizing effects.

288   THE QUEST FOR HUMAN NATURE

cloning and inheritable genetic modifications as "crimes against humanity." The emergence of a post-human species, from their perspective, would pose an existential threat to us original humans. It would open us to the perils of marginalization, discrimination, and, worse, genocide and bioterrorism. Bostrom's reply begins by acknowledging that these issues do pose significant concerns. At the same time, the argument continues, using the rhetoric of bioterrorism and weapons of mass destruction to cast aspersions on therapeutic uses of biotechnology to improve human states and capacities seems unhelpful—and, one may add, counterproductive. Slavery and discrimination are real, tangible human perils. We address them by setting up institutions to prevent them. Such measures do not require or presuppose equal abilities. Just like there are swarms of people with diminished physical and mental capacities, adding people with technologically enhanced potentiality need not rip society apart, triggering genocide or enslavement.[15]

One could rejoin by pointing out that, as we saw in Chapter 7, securing equal rights for all human beings, at least at a theoretical level, requires some universal, shared human nature. Some of this footing may be lost if post-humanity were to constitute an altogether different species. Bostrom preemptively addresses this kind of objection by casting doubt on the assumption that human enhancements would lead to an entirely separate species. It is more likely, it is claimed, that there will be a continuum. More generally, the idea of transhumanists joining forces and attacking humans is undoubtedly a logical possibility. But it is not a likely one. After all, it is equally conceivable that taller people join forces against shorter ones. Few—if any—citizens lose sleep over this potential threat.

In conclusion, inequity, discrimination, and stigmatization are serious issues and may well become all the more pressing in a post-human scenario. Transhumanism acknowledges this and calls for social remedies. Society has a duty not to enact a situation where a super-intelligent small group of people take over the planet. Yet, we're still quite far from this far-fetched scenario. In the final portion of his

---

[15] For a different reaction and response to Annas and colleagues, see Douglas (2013).

essay, Bostrom (2005) considers two further objections against transhumanism and cognate sources of anxiety.

First, is human dignity incompatible with post-human dignity? To answer this question, we need to clarify what is meant by "dignity" here, a notion often left unclarified. Bostrom considers two different senses. On the one hand, one can interpret dignity as moral status, in particular as the inalienable right to be treated with a basic level of respect. On the other hand, dignity can be understood as the qualities of being worthy, honorable, noble, and excellent. Fukuyama (2002) has argued that dignity is something that only a human can possess. Denying this, Fukuyama says, is dangerous, as it may cause some individuals—infants, cognitively disabled, or "normal" un-enhanced humans—to lose their dignity. The principle of equal dignity for all would thus be destroyed. Bostrom rejoins that, on both definitions, dignity is something a post-human can very well possess. It is noted—correctly in my humble opinion—how unsound it is to suppose that to warrant dignity to some people requires taking it away from others.

Second, and finally, Jonas (1985) attacks the assumption that parents should have broad discretion in deciding on genetic and other enhancements for their children. Such reproductive freedom, Jonas argues, would constitute a form of "parental tyranny" undermining the child's dignity and capacity for autonomous choice. Bostrom replies by questioning the premise that future generations would be defenseless against any machination to expand their capacities. Future humans could be less intelligent, less healthy, and could lead shorter lives if they really wanted to—but why would they? In general, if the alternative to parental choice is entrusting the child's welfare to nature's blind chance, that decision should be easy. Habermas (2003) echoes Jonas in suggesting that the mere knowledge of having been intentionally made could have ruinous consequences. The practice of morality, Habermas maintains, is based on the presupposition that every individual is responsible for shaping their own life. To the extent that social influence molds us, it mitigates our responsibility, ultimately reducing autonomy. The relevant reference point, Habermas notes, is the moment of birth where a wedge is drawn between "natural fate" and "socialized fate."

290   THE QUEST FOR HUMAN NATURE

Bostrom responds that it would be a mistake for someone to believe that they have no choice over their own life just because some— or even all—of their genes were selected by their parents. The choice is the same as if genetic constitution had been selected by chance. Actually, being smarter, healthier, and having better capacities may give the child increased freedom and choice. To be sure, one could worry about what could happen if things do not go according to plan. What if we shoot for smarter individuals and we end up with more depressed people? The concern here is real. But the situation might not be all that different from what we currently have. Parents may decide to sign up their children for music lessons to open a new universe while triggering frustration instead. In a way, that is just the way the cookie crumbles.

Bostrom concludes that the widespread anxiety revolving around post-humanity is unwarranted. Similarly flavored ominous forecasts cropped up in the 1970s concerning the psychological damage that would affect humans born from in vitro fertilization. Such predictions turned out predominantly false. Many objections are the result of prejudice. If listening to Mozart during pregnancy really made kids smarter—another colorful, albeit disproven urban legend—there would be no ban against listening to Mozart in the womb on the grounds that discovering this pre-programming would trigger psychological woe. Then, Bostrom asks, why raise this very same objection against genetic programming? Incidentally, I surmise that part of the problem has to do with the seductive appeal of genetic determinism and its related tendency to be misunderstood along the lines discussed in Chapter 5. From this standpoint, the issue with programming is that it is doubtful that any traits of choice are genetically determined in any meaningful sense.

Bostrom lastly moves on a different issue. Bioconservatives deny post-human dignity and view it as a threat to human dignity. Unless they're explicit on this, their argument looks like a double standard. This premise is denied by transhumanists. As Bostrom puts it:

> From the transhumanist standpoint, there is no need to behave as if there were a deep moral difference between technological and other means of enhancing human lives. By defending posthuman dignity

we promote a more inclusive and human ethics, one that will embrace future technologically modified people as well as humans of the contemporary kind. We also remove a distortive double standard from the field of our moral vision, allowing us to perceive more clearly the opportunities that exist for further human progress. (Bostrom 2005, pp. 213–14)

But what exactly do we mean by "human dignity" in this context? Bioconservatives such as Fukuyama (2002) and Kass (2008) recognize that providing a single, univocal definition of such an abstract and elusive concept is impossible. To be sure, one could provide a general characterization, such as: "The dignity of a person is that whereby a person excels other beings, especially other animals, and merits respect and consideration from other persons" (Lee and George 2008, p. 410). And now, suddenly, the debate on human dignity starts looking suspiciously like the debate on human nature. Just like that we are back to square one.[16]

In the end, the main question boils down to whether worries about the development of some sort of post-humanity are legitimate or misplaced. Rhetorically, authors with bioconservative leanings come up with various reasons for being wary of transcending our nature. These range from precautionary measures to defending human dignity, to concerns about promoting warfare, from the protection of young children to issues of marginalization. Bioliberals and transhumanists reject them, for a variety of motives. Who is correct? Should we be excited or concerned about the future of biotechnology as it pertains to our very own species? Answering this question lies beyond the scope of this work. The important point, for our present purposes, is that the substantiveness of the debate presupposes some robust notion of human nature. Otherwise, what exactly are we talking about? This is the point to which we now turn to wrap up our discussion.

---

[16] Alternatively, one could also consider the possibility that dignity is morally irrelevant or outright "stupid," a line of response put forth by Pinker (2008).

292 THE QUEST FOR HUMAN NATURE

§9.6 Promethean Predicaments

Time to tie up some loose ends. This chapter began by observing that we currently live in a golden age of biotechnology. We now have the theoretical and technological capacity to alter human bodies and minds in ways that would have been unimaginable just a handful of years ago. The intended purpose of these powers was never to produce perfect or post-human beings. The majority of such achievements has been conceived and developed with much more pressing and noble purposes in mind: easing suffering, preventing illness, curing ailment, overcoming disability, and the like. Yet, once people get a taste for them, these advancements produce new desires and aspirations, whetting our appetite for more. Things often take unintended and surprising trajectories. After all, when electricity was first discovered, people wondered what on earth could be done with it. Some of these goals are social. We may want to produce more peaceful and cooperative societies. Other objectives are more personal, geared toward self-improvement and various efforts to preserve and augment the vitality of the body and to boost the happiness of the soul. These aims are arguably the least controversial, the most continuous with the goals of modern medicine and psychiatry: from bettering health to ensuring peace of mind. As such, they are the most attractive to potential consumers and thereby easier to market. No one should question that there is much to celebrate. But are there also reasons for concern? If so, on what grounds?

A widespread reaction to the prospects of enhancing or over-enhancing our nature is encapsulated in the expression "playing God." This can be understood as the arrogance, the *hubris* of acting with insufficient wisdom. This cautionary principle has a relatively straightforward rationale. Like all biological organisms, the human body is a highly complex and delicately balanced system produced via evolution by natural selection over myriad generations. As the eminent biologist François Jacob (1977) argued decades ago, evolution is a "tinkering" process. Any attempt, natural or artificial, at improving these finely tuned systems is more likely to wreak havoc than it is to succeed. Geneticists know perfectly well that random mutations have much higher chances of producing negative as opposed to positive outcomes.

In the absence of deep knowledge, the effects of any such tinkering are likely to be unpredictable and nefarious. Care is well advised.

An influential version of this "hubris" objection has been advanced by Michael Sandel (2007).[17] Sandel describes our biotechnological efforts toward enhancement as re-inventing ourselves, a form of "hyper-agency," that is, a Promethean aspiration to remake nature, including our own nature, to serve our purposes and to satisfy our desires. The root of the difficulty is equally cognitive and moral: the failure to properly appreciate and respect the "giftedness" of the world, regardless of whether its origin is natural or divine. There surely is much to agree with this sobering critique of modern human societies as lacking modesty, humility, and restraint. At the same time, as we have repeatedly seen, not all of nature's gifts are welcome. We've been given beauty, love, and affection. But also war, cancer, and malaria. Consequently, not all manipulations are on a par. Some interventions are obviously legitimate, perhaps even normatively mandatory. Think about surgically fixing a broken limb. Others are clearly inappropriate or, more modestly, they raise no call for society to engage in reparation or restoration. My latent desire to have Tony Stark–like powers, as portrayed in the *Iron Man* movie series, is a case in point: I have no entitlement to it. The basic hiccup, once again, is where exactly to draw the line and on what basis one should decide.

Could this idea of mastery of nature give us some guidance in our complex relation with the world we live in? It is tempting to draw a distinction between biotechnological attempts to alter our "nature"— whatever that may mean—and nurturing or restorative practices such as healing the sick, educating the illiterate, or raising our kids right. Education and medicine are not a form of mastery of the universe. They enable or restore the "true" state of an organism. It is mother nature expressing itself, bringing our natural ability to fruition. But how exactly does one distinguish therapy from enhancement? And what precisely is wrong, dangerous, or disquieting about the idea of enhancement? As we have seen, these are frustratingly thorny issues. Bioconservatives have suggested various strategies for drawing the line, none of which is

---

[17] For related discussions of "playing God," see Peters (2002) and Weckert (2016).

294 THE QUEST FOR HUMAN NATURE

unproblematic or uncontroversial. Transhumanists retort that there is no line to be drawn in the first place. Prometheus gave fire to humans and the gods punished him for doing so. But in the end, we are all glad that we got something to cook our food, keep us warm, and brighten our nights. Whether the myth of Prometheus, courtesy of Aeschylus. is best interpreted as a tale of success or caution remains to be determined.

Once again, assessing this long-standing debate transcends the scope of this work. The important observation, for our present purposes, is that human nature plays a prominent role across the debate. Regardless of where you lie on the bioconservative vs. bioliberal spectrum, it is hard to even state and explain your position without presupposing some notion of human nature or some cognate concept like natural state or normal function. After all, to decide whether to enhance human nature, we need a human nature to enhance or protect to begin with.[18] Now we are right back to all the problems encountered throughout the book. All these discussions seem to presuppose a robust notion of human nature, which neither the sciences—natural or social—nor the humanities seem capable of delivering. How do we get out of this quagmire?

The overarching problem is hardly specific to the discussion under present scrutiny, which hinges on therapy, enhancement, and related concepts. The general situation should now be clear. Each of the topics discussed in the second half of this book vindicates Chomsky's dictum: human nature is important, indeed indispensable. The topics of races, sex and gender, health, disability, normality, and transhumanism presuppose some substantive concept of human nature. At the same time, the first five chapters revealed how hard it is to read the relevant notion of human nature off biological, psychological, or other data from the natural and social sciences. Throughout our voyage, I've been gesturing toward a possible resolution to this dilemma. Is it possible that the relevant notion of human nature is a scientific concept but not a concept that science is in a position to explain? What does this mean? What would such a concept even look like? It is high time to cash out my promissory note. This will be the final leg of our long journey together.

---

[18] The claim that some concept of human nature is presupposed in and inextricably tied to extant debates about enhancement is also advanced by Nielsen (2011).

10

Can Science Explain Human Nature?

> Really I don't like human nature
> unless all candied over with art.
> —Virginia Woolf, *Diary*, Vol. IV, 1931–35

§10.1 Retracing Our Steps

We've finally reached our last chapter: home stretch! This feels like an appropriate time to look back and retrace our steps throughout our journey. Our adventure began by asking some deceptively simple questions. What is it that makes us truly human? What do we share that separates us from the remainder of the animal kingdom? What, if anything, gives us distinctive moral and socio-political status? These hallowed issues have troubled philosophers since the dawn of the discipline. But we now know a lot more compared to, say, Plato, Aristotle, Hume, Rousseau, Wollstonecraft, Kant, Smith, Du Bois, Marx, or Freud. The sciences—both natural and social—have made strides. So, what have we learned about ourselves? Short answer: quite a bit! Our current body of empirical knowledge regarding human beings is way too substantial to be synthesized in a single book. Yet, despite this wealth of information, we have admittedly failed to provide a clear, exhaustive, and informative answer to our queries. We have not been able to spell out a viable account of human nature. Where have we gone astray? Despite the best of intentions, have we taken a wrong turn? To diagnose the outcome, let's briefly recap our voyage. Simply put, our overview of human nature can be broken down into two general phases.

The initial stage, spanning the entire first half of the book, focused on whether there is a human nature and what this human nature

The Quest for Human Nature. Marco J. Nathan, Oxford University Press. © Oxford University Press 2024.
DOI: 10.1093/oso/9780197699249.003.0010

296 THE QUEST FOR HUMAN NATURE

could turn out to be. Our springboard, in Chapter 2, was sociobiology: E. O. Wilson's uncompromising attempt to take human nature out of philosophers' hands and to approach it scientifically. Sociobiology and its intellectual descendant, evolutionary psychology, often present themselves as the "new science of human nature." We've surveyed various reactions to Wilson's agenda: some sympathetic, others critical. Chapter 3 sharpened our explanatory target. We explored three approaches. First, on an intuitive characterization human nature is identified with human essence, that is, a set of necessary and sufficient intrinsic conditions for belonging to the human species, conceived as a natural kind. Unfortunately, since there are no human essences, human nature *qua* human essence doesn't exist either. Next, we took up a suggestive analogy, originally introduced by evolutionary psychologists to motivate the existence of a shared human nature. This is the argument from Gray's Anatomy, which may be cashed out in two alternative ways. On the one hand, construed as a natural state model, our second approach to human nature captures what it means to be a "normal" person. On the other hand, a third option is to view human nature as a field guide, that is, a set of diagnostic features for identifying humans. The problem with the former strategy is that neither biology nor psychology nor any other branch of science provides us with a baseline for naturalizing the relevant notion of normality. The field guide conception is less controversial. But it remains questionable whether field guides spell out a thick notion of human nature robust enough to ground sociopolitical and other normative theories. At this point we shifted gears. Instead of targeting human nature in its entirety, we broke it down into more tractable proxies. Chapter 4 fathomed the hypothesis that some traits are innate. Chapter 5 examined various strands of genetic determinism. While these are intriguing topics in their own right, we had to acknowledge that an adequate overarching analysis of human nature remains nowhere to be found. It cannot be explicated either directly or indirectly, by identifying it with innate or genetically determined traits. Should we thus conclude that human nature is a chimera? Such a verdict may be unduly harsh.

The second stage, spanning the latter half of the book, took on a different angle. Chapter 6 explored various ontological stances on race and their implications for human nature. Chapter 7 brought sex and gender into the spotlight. We concluded that, despite human nature's brutal history of oppression, it is hard for racial and gender emancipation to eschew the assumption that we all partake in a common state. Chapter 8 reinforced the point that health, disease, and (dis)ability do not explain the underlying notion of normality; they rather *presuppose* a baseline of normal function. Chapter 9 outlined the bioliberalism vs. bioconservatism debate over the prospects of transcending our species' boundaries, and related concerns. Nonetheless, this dispute assumes that some line is there to be drawn.

The short of it is that human nature plays an important role across the natural and social sciences, which is precisely what ignited our discussion to begin with. Influential arguments, advocating equality regardless of race, gender, psychophysical abilities, or social status are founded upon some notion of pan-human rights. And *pace* Hull it is hardly obvious what could ground these human rights other than some notion of human nature. Analyses of health vs. disease or functional ability vs. disability require a threshold of normality, which is tantamount to outlining the contours of human nature. Finally, it is hard to see if and why we should temper radical enhancements, unless we presuppose an ultimate baseline of naturalness, which likewise rests on some conception of human nature. In short, human nature pervades all aspects of science, as well as the arts and humanities.

In a nutshell, we're stuck in a quagmire. While human nature plays an indispensable role across the board, an insightful analysis of this pesky concept is nowhere to be found. Importantly, the issue is not merely lack of a precise definition. Philosophers have long learned Socrates' lesson that clear explications are often hard to come by— try asking a political scientist to define "democracy," a legal scholar to define "justice," or a biologist to define "gene." The problem cuts deeper than vagueness. Nothing we have discovered about our species provides a conception of human nature robust enough to do all the theoretical heavy lifting we require of it. What's going on? Throughout our discussion we looked at science to answer our queries. This was an obvious move, especially given the track record of the humanities, not exactly worth bragging about either. Maybe it's time to revisit our core assumptions. Can science explain human nature? If so, where have we gone astray? If not, where else are we supposed to look?

298   THE QUEST FOR HUMAN NATURE

Here is the master plan for the last leg of our joint venture. We begin by placing our spark plug—the dictum according to which there is no social science *sans* human nature—within its broader context: Chomsky's seminal 1971 debate with Michel Foucault. Specifically, §10.2 spells out Chomsky's conception of human nature. §10.3 examines Foucault's rejoinder, namely, the suggestion that human nature is not a standard scientific concept but an *epistemological indicator*. What exactly does this mean? §10.4 develops Foucault's insights by arguing that epistemological indicators are bona fide scientific concepts whose role, however, is not to set up an object of explanation. §10.5 applies these insights to our main course: human nature is a central scientific concept that, paradoxically, science does not and cannot explain. §10.6 wraps up and bids farewell by revisiting one final time the ten general questions tracing our philosophical adventure.

§10.2   Quicksand

Back in Chapter 1, our intellectual journey kicked off with an influential quote from Chomsky's interviews with Ronat. To refresh our minds, Chomsky proclaimed: "Any serious social science or theory of social change must be founded on some concept of human nature. . . . There is always some conception of human nature, implicit or explicit, underlying a doctrine of social order or social change" ([1976] 2006, p. 126). This dictum was reinforced by our discussion over the previous four chapters. Indeed, human nature plays a prominent role framing various sociopolitical issues, from races to disability, from feminism to transhumanism. At the same time, the first half of this book pushed the conclusion that, despite all we've discovered, we still lack a conception of human nature robust enough to provide the normative substrate for these key debates. In light of this impasse, some readers may wonder what Chomsky himself took human nature to be. To appreciate Chomsky's own perspective, it is enlightening to go back to his celebrated 1971 debate with the French philosopher Michel Foucault.

At the very outset, Chomsky is asked by the moderator: "Which arguments can you derive from linguistics to give such a central position to this concept of human nature?" (Chomsky and Foucault [1971]

CAN SCIENCE EXPLAIN HUMAN NATURE? 299

2006, p. 2). Chomsky begins his response by pointing out that a rigorous study of human language confronts researchers with peculiar empirical challenges. Over the course of their lifetime, typical adults acquire a "language," that is, a rich, nuanced, and organized collection of linguistic abilities. These verbal dispositions are triggered by interactions within a community. Such a body of linguistic data to which people are exposed can—and should—be examined experimentally. When we do, Chomsky notes, puzzling phenomena begin to emerge.

First, Chomsky maintains, there is a striking information gap between stimulus and response. The data to which children are exposed is modest in quantity and degenerate in quality. It does not measure up to the articulate, systematic, and organized knowledge that kids eventually grow from this bare-bones trigger. Second, individual speakers subject to idiosyncratic personal experiences will come to develop remarkably congruent bodies of linguistic knowledge. Consider a native Irish and a native Australian who meet as adults after moving to Canada. These people will have lived unique lives. They had conversations on different topics using partially overlapping vocabulary and slang. They've read different books, picked their favorite movies, and listened to their music of choice. Still, they've developed a linguistic capacity which allows them to communicate rather effortlessly and efficiently with each other and within their communities. What one says, others understand. Third and finally, there are various structural limitations on the linguistic systems that emerge from this diverse range of experiences: natural languages, such as Suomi, Spanish, Mandarin, or Hindi. Sure, non-specialists, especially those who have tried mastering a second idiom later in life, are often struck by phonetic and grammatical discrepancies between these interfaces. Yet, many contemporary linguists follow Chomsky in positing the existence of general patterns of organization that at some level unify and constrain all human natural languages.[1] The scientific puzzle Chomsky alludes to involves explaining these three phenomena. How can such a rich and diverse but systematic linguistic body consistently emerge

---

[1] To be sure, the existence and significance of the language universals that characterize Chomsky's *deep structure*—a universal grammar beyond the first superficial layer

300 THE QUEST FOR HUMAN NATURE

from the limited input to which human children are exposed? This has come to be known as the *poverty of stimulus argument*.

Chomsky suggests that there is only one plausible explanation for the observations just rehearsed. In his own words, this is "the assumption that the individual himself contributes a good deal, an overwhelming part in fact, of the general schematic structure and perhaps even of the specific content of the knowledge that he ultimately derives from this very scattered and limited experience" (Chomsky and Foucault [1971] 2006, p. 3). The underlying intuition is clear. A child must begin with *some* knowledge. Clearly, such knowledge cannot be specific to any particular language, say, French or Dutch, as not every human being will grow up speaking these idioms. What newborns bring to the table prior to any verbal exposure is knowledge pertaining to *human* language in general, a system of a very narrow and specific kind which permits a relatively constrained range of variation. And, Chomsky's story goes, it is precisely because the child begins with this structured and restrictive schematism that they are able to bridge the wide conceptual wedge between an input constituted by scattered and degenerate data and an output of highly organized knowledge. This mass of innate organizing principles, Chomsky concludes, is among the core constituents of human nature:

> I would claim then that this instinctive knowledge, if you like, this schematism that makes it possible to derive complex and intricate knowledge on the basis of very partial data, is one of the fundamental constituents of human nature. . . . Well, this collection, this mass of schematisms, innate organizing principles, which guides our social and intellectual and individual behavior, that's what I mean to refer to by the concept of human nature. (Chomsky and Foucault [1971] 2006, pp. 4–5)

---

of verbal variants which unifies and constrains all human languages—remains debated (Evans and Levinson 2009; Piantadosi 2023). Nevertheless, the existence of *some* systematic patterns of organization in need of explanation is, for the most part, uncontroversial. What's hotly disputed is the extent of linguistic diversity and how best to account for underlying commonalities.

At first blush, Chomsky's proposed conception of human nature seems both promising and plausible. Human nature is the collection of innate organizing principles that guide social, intellectual, and individual behavior. How come I didn't bring this up back in Chapter 1, sparing readers much tedious work? Of course, this option has been on our plate. The problem is that, as it stands, it just won't do. The concerns are the very same ones that haunted us throughout this book. In what sense does such an innate schematism constitute our "human nature"? Surely it cannot be conceived as a human essence. Clearly not all humans develop a language or have the potential to do so. Cognitively impaired individuals, such as people in a vegetative state, unfortunately lack the necessary psychological skills. Others tragically die before they have an opportunity to acquire any linguistic knowledge. The obvious rejoinder is to rephrase the proposal as stating that "normal" or "typical" members of our species have these skills. Yet, how should normality and typicality be parsed in this context? It is hard to deny that statistically most humans grow up to learn some natural language. Similarly, an alien visitor could easily employ language as a diagnostic feature to pick out human from non-human animals. But is that really all there is to it? If so, there are more evident superficial properties that we could include in a field guide. Why delve into complex cognitive abilities when we could focus on our distinctive habit of wearing clothes instead?

Frustrated by these nagging concerns, one might shift focus on the innate component of the definition. Indeed, Chomsky's linguistic dispositions are analogous, in various relevant respects, to Spelke and Kinzler's core knowledge outlined in §4.5. This parallel may turn out to be a double-edged sword. The precise relationship between core knowledge, innateness, and human nature is murky. To wit, in what sense, if any, can systems of core knowledge be defined as "innate" or identified as part of our "nature"? Similar problems plague any attempt to cash out in detail the insight that Chomsky's innate schemata guide various forms of human behavior. What does "guide" stand for here? Could it simply entail that our verbal behavior is genetically determined, in the sense discussed in Chapter 5? We now have robust evidence that the structure of language is strongly constrained by specific intrinsic parameters. But as we noted ad nauseam, it is a long and

302   THE QUEST FOR HUMAN NATURE

dangerous jump from this platitude to the conclusion that human behavior, linguistic or otherwise, is regulated by genes in any substantive fashion.

In conclusion, it remains questionable whether Chomsky's proposal in and of itself can overcome the pitfalls that plagued our quest for human nature throughout the first part of this book. I should make it very clear that I am *not* questioning Chomsky's approach to the study of language. The phenomena elegantly presented are well-defined and the proposal is plausible—if controversial, as any substantive scientific hypothesis worth its salt should be. My rejoinder is that in Chomsky's research program a general concept of human nature is all but *presupposed*, in the sense that it is neither precisely defined nor explained. It is a state posited as existing without being precisely characterized. If you are still skeptical, try asking once again in what precise sense linguistic competence is a constituent of human nature. This brings us back to square one. In fairness, Chomsky is hardly alone in this regard. A similar attitude can be found in Hobbes, Smith, Marx, sociobiologists, evolutionary psychologists, and many others. Great company, for sure. Still, as a deep analysis of human nature, Chomsky's proposal remains as unpersuasive as all the other candidates discussed in detail. Have we made any progress? Or are we quietly being swallowed by quicksand?

§10.3 Epistemological Indicators

As we've seen, Chomsky presents human nature as a body of schematisms, that is, innate organizing principles guiding our behavior. Such use of schemata to explain the poverty of stimulus argument is intriguing and—in my opinion—quite plausible. The issue is whether we can make sense of Chomsky's further claim that these organizing principles are part of human nature. To answer this question, let's see what the other discussant brings to the table.

In overt contrast to Chomsky, Foucault is openly suspicious of human nature. The rationale is worth quoting and discussing: "I believe that of the concepts or notions which a science can use, not all have the same degree of elaboration, and that in general they have neither the same function nor the same type of possible use in scientific discourse" (Chomsky and Foucault [1971] 2006, p. 5). Foucault goes on to elaborate how in biology there are concepts with a classificatory function, a differentiating function, and an analytical function. To wit, the term "tissue" characterizes a certain body part; "hereditary feature" isolates certain elements; and "reflex" fixes relations. We need not enter the specifics of such—vague—distinctions. Taken at face value, the general observation that there are different types of scientific concepts, playing an array of roles, appears utterly uncontroversial. But let's keep moving.

Foucault goes on to draw a further distinction between *internal* and *peripheral* concepts. On the one hand, he quips, there are "elements which play a role in the discourse and in the internal rules of the reasoning practice. But there also exist 'peripheral' notions, those by which scientific practice designates itself, differentiates itself in relation to other practices, delimits its domain of objects, and designates what it considers to be the totality of its future tasks" (Chomsky and Foucault [1971] 2006, pp. 5–6). Internal notions don't appear all that mysterious. While Foucault is not fully explicit on this score, they appear to be standard terms posited in the context of a scientific theory— concepts such as *neutrino, cistron,* or *risk aversion,* I suggest. Less obvious are what are dubbed "peripheral" notions. What exactly is this pointing to?

Foucault illustrates peripheral notions as follows. In the seventeenth and eighteenth centuries, he argues, the concept of *life* was hardly employed in the study of nature. Its epistemological role, its scientific purpose, was fixing the position of natural beings indisputably, once and for all. By the end of the 1700s, the analysis and description of natural beings, biological organisms, showed an entire field of relations and processes, which have enabled researchers to define the specificity of biology in the knowledge of nature. With such considerations in mind, Foucault moves on to ask: "Can one say that research into life has finally constituted itself into biological science? Has the concept of life been responsible for the organization of biological knowledge?" (Chomsky and Foucault [1971] 2006, p. 6). His answer is thought-provoking:

304   THE QUEST FOR HUMAN NATURE

I don't think so. It seems to me more likely that the transformations of biological knowledge at the end of the eighteenth century were demonstrated on one hand by a whole series of new concepts for use in scientific discourse and on the other hand gave rise to a notion like that of life which has enabled us to designate, to delimit, and to situate a new type of scientific discourse, among other things. I would say that the notion of life is not a *scientific concept*; it has been an *epistemological indicator* of which the classifying, delimiting, and other functions had an effect on scientific discussions, and not on what they were talking about. (Chomsky and Foucault [1971] 2006, p. 6)

Foucault's proposal is not simple to unravel. Let me attempt a paraphrase. *Life*, as characterized in the 1600s–1700s, served a specific purpose. It hardly explained anything. But it drew a distinction between living and non-living beings, such that they could subsequently be studied. Classifying, say, redwood trees as "living" and stalagmites as "non-living," in and of itself, shed no light on them. It elucidates neither the entities themselves nor the rationale behind the classification at stake. It sets up a target of explanation without accounting for it. Now, fast-forward to the present day. As biology advanced, it made headway into the concept of *life*. To wit, much has now been discovered about the origin, constitution, and behavior of organic and inorganic compounds (Nurse 2020). But here's the rub. Have we finally *explained* life? Foucault answers in the negative. The reason, I take it, is that life was not in need of explanation to begin with. It was never put forth as something to be explained. The inferential role of life was to pinpoint a specific field of study. Life is meant to circumscribe a set of phenomena requiring explanation, without itself being a precise object of explanation.[2]

---

[2] I am here departing from Foucault's exact choice of words and helping myself to jargon that is standard in contemporary philosophy of science. The notion of "explanation" is potentially ambiguous as it may refer either to the phenomenon to be accounted for or to whatever provides the explanatory information. To avoid any confusion, philosophers of science refer to the object of the explanation as the *explanandum* (plural: *explananda*) and to whatever accounts for the explanandum as the *explanans* (plural: *explanantia*).

Now, some readers may retort that my endorsement of Foucault's point conflates two notions that ought to be kept distinct: *explanation* and *explication*. Fine, the objection runs, the natural sciences may not as yet provide a precise analytic definition of life. But this hardly entails that the general phenomenon of life lacks an overarching explanation. For instance, contemporary biology explains the distinction between living and non-living systems in terms of homeostatic metabolic processes coupled with mechanisms of development, heredity, and reproduction.[3] I agree, of course, that the life sciences have made strides in accounting for the mechanistic structure of living and non-living systems. Still, there is a subtle, albeit crucial difference between explaining the constitution of a system classified as "living" and providing a definition of life tout court. Accounting for the processes that keep me alive falls short of an explanation of life. This is because life in general encompasses many other living systems that are physically, chemically, biologically, and psychologically quite different from myself. As I will make clear in the course of my discussion, life is too broad and vague a concept to offer a precise target of scientific explanation.

Meanwhile, my reading of Foucault should now be evident. "Internal" or "scientific" concepts figure in scientific explanations as explanantia or explananda. In contrast, "peripheral" concepts delineate a set of explananda without any pretense of explaining them. Foucault calls this latter category of concepts *epistemological indicators*. His only illustration is *life*. Yet, similar remarks can be applied to other notions such as *disease, matter,* and *force*. Contemporary medicine neither provides any clear, general definition of disease, nor does it explain it in any substantive sense. Rather, it classifies conditions such as AIDS or Alzheimer's *as* diseases, which determines how to explain them. Similarly, physical theory measures, analyzes, distinguishes, and operationalizes various types of forces and matter. Still informative overarching explanations or non-circular definitions of force and matter are nowhere to be found in the relevant literature. With this distinction between scientific concepts and epistemological indicators firmly in place, we are finally in a position to better comprehend

---

[3] I am grateful to an anonymous reviewer for bringing this objection to my attention.

306   THE QUEST FOR HUMAN NATURE

Foucault's stance concerning human nature and its role in scientific inquiry:

> Well, it seems to me that the notion of human nature is of the same type [as the concept of *life*]. It was not by studying human nature that linguists discovered the laws of consonant mutation, or Freud the principles of the analysis of dreams, or cultural anthropologists the structure of myths. In the history of knowledge, the notion of human nature seems to me mainly to have played the role of an epistemological indicator to designate certain kinds of discourse in relation to or in opposition to theology or biology or history. I would find it difficult to see in this a scientific concept. (Chomsky and Foucault [1971] 2006, pp. 6–7)

Human nature, Foucault maintains, is not a scientific concept. It is an epistemological indicator—an indicator, for short. Thus construed, we begin to grasp why scientific explanations of human nature have consistently proven so elusive. To get there, a few clarifications are in order. We must clarify the scope of the impossibility of explaining indicators, that is, whether such a claim should be understood in practice or in principle. My argument begins in the remainder of this section and continues through §10.4 and §10.5.

For starters, why should science be unable to account for human nature? As research advances full steam ahead, can indicators not be gradually turned into full-fledged scientific concepts? At first, this seems exactly Chomsky's rejoinder to Foucault. Recall how Chomsky identified as part of human nature the substantial body of innate knowledge and psychological dispositions that enable children to develop complex linguistic competences based on degenerate, incomplete data. Thus defined, why couldn't human nature be explainable, if not now, then at some point in the future? Here is how Chomsky articulates his point:

> [I]f we were able to specify in terms of, let's say, neural networks the properties of human cognitive structure that make it possible for the child to acquire these complicated systems, then I at least would have no hesitation in describing those properties as being a constituent

CAN SCIENCE EXPLAIN HUMAN NATURE? 307

element of human nature. That is, there is something biologically given, unchangeable, a foundation for whatever it is that we do with our mental capacities in this case. (Chomsky and Foucault [1971] 2006, p. 7)

This is where things take an unexpected turn. Human nature, Chomsky continues, may well be the next peak that science should attempt to scale. One may wonder whether we are or will ever be in a position to fully explain, in biophysical terms, the acquisition and usage of human language. That such an explanation can eventually be given is, Chomsky says, an article of faith. Science has explained other things; it will explain this too.[4] But what reasons do we have for believing that science will eventually develop the appropriate concepts? Could anything possibly stand in our way?

Chomsky here draws a provocative analogy with the mind-body problem, the task of characterizing the relation between the mental and the physical which lies at the core of the philosophy of mind. The advancement of science, in the past, has often required expanding the domain of the physical. Consider Newtonian gravitational forces. To Cartesians, the very idea of action at a distance was rather mystical. Indeed, to Newton himself, it was an occult quality, a mysterious entity which hardly belonged in a truly scientific theory—an attitude crystallized by his own laconic stance, *hypotheses non fingo*, "I feign no hypotheses." Nevertheless, to the common sense of a generation later, action at a distance has been incorporated within science. What justifies this abrupt transition? What happened is that the notion of body, the very paradigm of the physical, had radically shifted. An uncompromising mechanist would be baffled by contemporary physical explanations. Any appeal to, say, electromagnetic forces, by strict Cartesian standards, should be off the table *qua* action at a distance. And yet, we now accept them without batting an eye. The reason is that physics has expanded, incorporating entirely new concepts and

---

[4] This dissonance in Chomsky's reply to Foucault has hardly gone unnoticed: "Chomsky's response seems to be more an endorsement of Foucault's original point than a counterclaim. His rather confusing comments hardly show that the sciences are in possession of a meaty, or restrictive, account of 'human nature'" (Lewens 2015b, p. 84).

308   THE QUEST FOR HUMAN NATURE

ideas capturing a broader range of phenomena. These are now familiar notions: force fields, gravitation, quantum entanglement, and the like. In short, Cartesian mechanics would be unable to explain the behavior of elementary physical particles just as it is in no position to analyze life and human nature.[5]

The debate between Chomsky and Foucault moves on in different directions. Both agree that there is no explanation for human nature within the purview of current science. Chomsky maintains that the question of human nature is fundamentally the scientific one of how we acquire and employ cognitive capacities. Nevertheless, this question cannot be answered with our current scientific toolkit. Foucault's stance is stronger. He seems to suggest that human nature cannot be studied scientifically because human nature is not a scientific concept at all. It is rather what he calls an *epistemological indicator* systematizing a body of scientific knowledge without shedding any real light on it. Let's look deeper into concepts of this ilk.

§10.4 Scientific Concepts *sans* Explanation

The previous section alluded to Foucault's suggestion that human nature is no standard scientific concept. It cannot be explained empirically and was never intended to be. As an epistemological indicator, its role is to circumscribe a specific inquiry without accounting for it. How should this claim be parsed? What is its proper modality? Is the contention merely that indicators cannot at present be broken down and analyzed further? Or is it the much stronger tenet that indicators are in principle screened off from scientific explanation tout court? Drawing this distinction appears to be Chomsky's initial rejoinder.

---

[5] More elegantly, in Chomsky's own words: "[O]ne might ask the question whether physical science as known today, including biology, incorporates within itself the principles and the concepts that will enable it to give an account of innate human intellectual capacities and, even more profoundly, of the ability to make use of those capacities under conditions of freedom in the way which humans do. I see no particular reason to believe that biology or physics now contain those concepts, and it may be that to scale the next peak, to make the next step, they will have to focus on this organizing concept, and may very well have to broaden their scope in order to come to grips with it" (Chomsky and Foucault [1971] 2006, p. 9).

Even if human nature cannot be explained as of now, it will hopefully be captured in the future near or far. In the course of his debate with Chomsky, Foucault never fully clarifies his position.[6] The discussion veers toward issues of freedom, creativity, and rationality. I wish to develop Foucault's insight. I argue that epistemological indicators—such as life or human nature—cannot be explained scientifically, neither in practice nor in principle. The reason is that when one tries to sharpen them, they end up dissolving and losing their original purpose. It is the goal of the present section and the following one to elucidate this claim.

To develop my proposal, let's begin by focusing on the nature of theoretical hypotheses. Science provides broad statements which capture and systematize patterns of events. Most of these initial generalizations can be made more perspicuous if need be. In some instances, the hypothesis can be improved in terms of accuracy by adding provisos and conditions expressed in the same vocabulary as the original statement. Other times, sharpening the preliminary generalization will require switching to the technical nomenclature of a different theory or domain of research.

While the underlying insight is intuitive enough, a few examples should help drive the point home. The observation that LeBron James is tall is a vague one. We could make it more precise by noting that LeBron is almost seven feet, or even sharper by asserting that LeBron is 6 feet 9 inches. We can keep going, providing more and more accurate measurements if necessary. Similarly, my car is heavy. But I can be even more specific by saying that my car weighs over three thousand pounds, my car weighs 3,325 pounds, and so forth. As a third and final example, my preliminary assessment that my coffee mug is hot can be refined by saying that my coffee is between 160°F and 180°F. Or I can be even more exact: my coffee is currently 182.7°F. In all these mundane cases, what I am doing is taking a simple predicate—"tall," "heavy," or "hot,"—and restating it in more precise terms within the same language, vocabulary, or jargon, broadly construed.

---

[6] Indeed, in his extensive body of work, Foucault never provides a systematic account of human nature. The most developed remarks are arguably found in "The Perverse Implantation," Chapter 2 of the first volume (1976) of his monumental *History of Sexuality*.

310 THE QUEST FOR HUMAN NATURE

At the same time, the following example illustrates a different way to sharpen a hypothesis. On a common reading, attributions of fitness in evolutionary biology capture the propensity of organisms to survive and reproduce. Now, consider a simple scenario inspired by Sober (2000): a population of organisms come in two variants, type-*a* and type-*b*. Over time, the relative ratio of *a*-types to *b*-types increases, suggesting that *a*-variants are "fitter" than *b*-variants. This accounts for the frequency shift in question. But one could also provide a more detailed and precise description of the population at hand, further capturing *why* type-*a* organisms are fitter than *b*-variants. For instance, one might note that *a*-variants have a lighter structure, making them more agile. This may further depend on a lower bone density due to a genetic mutation. Note, however, that by providing more and more precise depictions we'll eventually abandon the vocabulary of evolutionary theory and start using the language of physiology, molecular biology, biochemistry and, eventually, physics. Indeed, as Sober aptly notes, deeper explanations will no longer mention "fitness" at all. I should make it very clear that none of this is to say that once we move away from coarser descriptions, general terms will be eliminated tout court. In certain cases, we may want to eschew lower-level depictions—what Sober calls *consequence laws*—and revert to *source laws* mentioning fitness. My point is rather that sometimes the refinement of a coarse-grained generalization requires abandoning the original language and reframing the hypothesis in finer-grained terminology belonging to an altogether different theoretical domain. Once again, the process is perfectly reversible, if we ever need to drop a more realistic, circumscribed model in favor of a more abstract yet more broadly applicable one.[7]

---

[7] The point I am developing here is admittedly inspired by a well-known distinction originally drawn by the philosopher Donald Davidson in his classic 1970 paper "Mental Events." In presenting his own theory of mind—*anomalous monism*—and the related theses of the *supervenience* of the physical on the mental, *nomological irreducibility*, and the *normativity of rationality*, Davidson splits scientific generalizations into two broad families. On the one hand, *homomonic* generalizations can be sharpened within the same language of the original hypothesis. On the other hand, *heteronomic* generalizations can only be made more perspicuous by shifting to the vocabulary of another theory. I have opted to retain Davidson's key insight while dropping his terminology for three reasons. First, the labels "homomonic" and "heteronomic" are neither catchy nor intuitive. Hence, unsurprisingly, they are seldom employed. Second, my present argument is independent

CAN SCIENCE EXPLAIN HUMAN NATURE? 311

These considerations apply to virtually any domain outside of fundamental physics. Borrowing a piece of contemporary philosophical jargon, every time we have a property S that *supervenes* on physical properties P—in the sense that any change in S will necessitate a corresponding change in P but a change in P does not entail a change in S—we can always redescribe S at the level of P. The point is perfectly general. It literally spans the entire board, from mundane disposition ascriptions like the fragility of glass or the solubility of salt to explanations in the special sciences. Consider the observation that risk-averse subjects need to be offered a bigger incentive in order to buy a lottery ticket. This psychological disposition can be accounted for in terms of other cognitive capacities or by looking at the underlying neural mechanisms that implement it in the brain.

Setting details aside, my contention is simply that in some cases providing an adequate scientific explanation requires shifting to a different theory, a switch in vocabulary. This basic observation, however, is crucial to appreciate the sense in which, once the phenomenon under scrutiny has been identified and explained, an epistemological indicator may become disposable. At a macro-level of description, we can continue to classify plants as "living beings" much like we keep referring to basketball players as "tall." But, when we switch to a more detailed theory containing finer terms where such preliminary ascriptions are spelled out in greater detail, these coarse labels disappear. In phytology there is no longer a need for a general classification of plants as living beings. It is supplanted by a discussion of the physiological processes sustaining them. Similarly, precise data for comparing NBA players' stats has little use for the label "tall." These broad categorizations are not permanently eliminated, as in other contexts we may still want to refer to flowers as living and power forwards as tall. But it should also be

---

of anomalous monism and indeed of any stance with respect to the mind-body problem. Borrowing Davidson's labels could have suggested otherwise. Third and most important, Davidson seems to view the state of being homomonic and heteronomic as properties of the generalizations themselves. This strikes me as problematic. One and the same hypothesis can often be sharpened in different ways. Some of these refinements will use the same jargon. Others will switch to a different vocabulary. But the key point is that it is not a generalization per se that is "homomonic" or "heteronomic." Rather, these should be viewed as capturing how the generalization is sharpened. To avoid this subtle confusion, I have decided to adopt an altogether different terminology.

312   THE QUEST FOR HUMAN NATURE

clear that micro-depictions do not explain these coarse terms. Rather, they explain them away. The following section will apply these insights to human nature. Before doing so, the remainder of the present section briefly addresses three potential confusions.

First, some readers may legitimately wonder whether we'll ever hit epistemic bedrock. Can additional details be added ad infinitum or is there a non-fundamental layer where the explanatory buck stops? Experimental physics teaches us that, when working at the smallest scales, measuring becomes dangerously imprecise. Dig deep enough and no two liquids have exactly the same temperature. No two particles have identical mass or length. Actually, repeated measures of the same quantity will yield different readings. Now, is this uncertainty a limitation of current technological means or does it reflect an inherent feature of the world? This is an intriguing question, albeit one that fortunately we need not address here. Let's restrict our attention to levels where sufficiently exact data can be obtained.

A second clarification concerns the individuation of levels of explanation and their respective terminology. My simple array of examples could suggest that correctly mapping a concept to the appropriate theory or level is a straightforward matter. "Height," "weight," and "heat" belong to folk physics. "Fitness," in contrast, is part of the vocabulary of evolutionary biology. Simplicity here is deceptive. Once we move away from toy examples, subdivisions quickly become a lot messier. Is "ionic bond" part of the theoretical language of physics, chemistry, physical chemistry, or chemical physics? Should these fields be broken down further? Evolutionary biologists and molecular biologists frequently talk about genes. So, it looks like *gene* belongs to the languages of both theories. But is it the same concept? As many scholars have noted, "gene" and cognate expressions are theory-laden and often used differently across diverse contexts and with varying intentions.[8] In short, we must acknowledge that the subdivision of reality into explanatory layers should not be taken for granted. It is an oversimplification that presupposes several idealizations and stipulations.

---

[8] An overview of alternative usages of "gene" in biology is Griffiths and Stotz (2013).

Third and finally, readers with some background in the philosophy of science will surely recognize the connection between my discussion of levels of explanation and the traditional debate between reductionists and antireductionists. Simply put, reductionists contend that providing lower-level descriptions of a system invariably increases our explanatory power. Antireductionists disagree. They maintain that we eventually reach a threshold past which adding further detail will not increase the explanatory power of our depictions. In what follows, I shall remain agnostic between these two epistemic stances. Indeed, as I have argued extensively elsewhere, the way this debate is traditionally framed poses a false dichotomy (Nathan 2021).

In conclusion, many explanations transcend the boundaries of a field or theory. How is this related to the notion of indicator and its explanation, or lack thereof? An indicator is a concept that is introduced at a specific level of explanation. Let's call the level in question L_n. The role of the indicator is, as Foucault aptly puts it, to circumscribe a specific range of phenomena. For instance, living organisms have something in common that separates them from non-living entities. All forces share features that distinguish them from other physical quantities. Can this x factor be analyzed? Can it be pinpointed, made more specific? The answer is yes. Yet—and here is the rub—this explanation cannot be provided at level L_n. We need to shift to a different level, typically, a "lower" level L_{n-k}, although it may be possible for certain complex systems to be explainable only at a coarser level L_{n+k}. Now, what happens at these other levels? Has the indicator itself been explained? Well, not quite. What has been explained is why a certain specific phenomenon was originally classified as such. We began with a general concept of life. Next, we applied it to why redwood trees are classified as "living." Looking into these magnificent organisms has lots to say about why they are alive. So, we've made much progress. Nonetheless, as we descend levels all the way to L_{n-k}, we shift from life, to living redwoods, to their metabolism, to the biochemistry, and so forth. Meanwhile, our original indicator, the overarching concept of *life*, has not been explained. It remains at level L_n where it calls for no explanation. Its role—a very important one indeed—is to identify other phenomena that can be given analogous explanations, by shifting to other epistemic levels. With all of this in mind, the issue

314   THE QUEST FOR HUMAN NATURE

becomes what any of this has to do with human nature. The following section will attempt to connect the dots.

§10.5 Human Nature *qua* Epistemological Indicator

§10.3 introduced the notion of epistemological indicator. Indicators pinpoint something to be accounted for: they set up an explanandum without themselves being explainable. But *why* can an indicator not be explained? §10.4 sketched an answer. An indicator, I proposed, is a preliminary scaffolding, a placeholder for a concept that is introduced at a specific level of description but can only be explained at a different level. As such, the indicator can be explained, in the sense that we can account for whatever it points to. But explaining it is tantamount to explaining it away. Once described, the indicator becomes disposable and dissolves because we have shifted to a more fine-grained level of depiction where it is no longer present or needed.

What's the connection to human nature? In brief, Foucault was right in classifying human nature as an indicator, although he was wrong to contrast indicators—"peripheral" notions—with bona fide scientific concepts. Foucault's terminological choice is misleading because it suggests that indicators have no business in science. *Au contraire*, indicators play a crucial methodological role. This same insight can be applied to human nature. Somewhat paradoxically, at least at first blush, human nature performs a central job in science while not being explainable by science. From this perspective, there can be no science of human nature because such an endeavor would be self-defeating. The previous section developed my general suggestion that not all concepts are meant to be explained without this making them any less scientific. The present section applies these insights to human nature, spelling out my proposal and contrasting it with extant frameworks.

Let's get started by revisiting an issue that should be familiar by now. What does it mean to identify a certain trait or cluster of properties as belonging to "human nature"? What kind of information does it convey? Are we saying that it is an essence? An innate or genetically determined property? A target for an evolutionary explanation? All the above? Or perhaps something altogether different? A clear answer is

CAN SCIENCE EXPLAIN HUMAN NATURE? 315

still wanting. Foucault's insight suggests that the role of human nature *qua* epistemological indicator is to designate certain kinds of discourse in relation or in opposition to a certain field. So, if human nature is an indicator, what kind of discourse does it circumscribe and what are the relevant contrast classes? A general informative answer to this question cannot be provided. This observation was lucidly anticipated by Alison Jaggar:

> No single issue, of course, can be identified as "the" problem of human nature. Rather, there is a cluster of interrelated questions, many of which have been perennial objects of study for philosophy. These questions include ontological issues, such as whether human beings can be thought of as existing prior to or independent of society; and metaphysical and methodological issues, such as whether human beings are irreducibly different from the rest of nature or whether their activities can be understood in principle by the concepts and methods of natural sciences. Other questions include the basis, scope, and limits of human knowledge, and the nature of human fulfillment and self-realization. In modern times, a skeptical issue has been raised: is it possible to identify any human characteristics of human nature which all human beings have in common and which distinguish them from animals, or are persons living at different places and times, in different social contexts, so diverse that the only characteristics they may safely be assumed to share are biological? An attempt to provide a comprehensive and systematic answer to these and other questions may be called a theory of human nature. (Jaggar 1983, p. 19)

This perspective, four decades later, remains strikingly fresh, up-to-date, and accurate. Jaggar goes on to note—correctly, in my opinion—how "research in each of these disciplines also *presupposes* a certain model of human nature" (1983, p. 19). The only point of substance where I respectfully disagree is with the suggestion that a systematic answer to these and related questions may be called a "theory of human nature" in the singular. One thing that has hopefully emerged throughout our journey is that no perspicuous theory can undertake such a gargantuan endeavor. These diverse issues can only be

316   THE QUEST FOR HUMAN NATURE

addressed on a case-by-case basis, without this undermining the need for an overarching concept of human nature. Allow me to elaborate.

Different inquiries call for different methodologies. When Wilson proclaims that aggressive behavior belongs to human nature, as we saw in Chapter 4, his point is that such conduct is, in some sense screaming to be further specified, innate or encoded in the genes. The proposal is obviously not the preposterous contention that aggression is uniquely human. In contrast, when Chomsky identifies linguistic dispositions as belonging to human nature, he is conveying precisely that such ability is exquisitely ours. In this respect, responding by pointing out that learning a language requires both internal schemata and environmental stimuli would flatly miss the mark. In short, there are various, different, partially overlapping ways of determining what does or should count as "human nature." The significance of such classification largely depends on the context at hand and will likely vary across different fields.

Once we have pinpointed, in the circumstances at hand, what it means for something to belong to human nature, the next step is to craft a convincing account. Thus, for instance, suppose that we have identified some form of aggressive behavior as our explanandum. We can then ask under what circumstances a person is more or less prone to display aggressive conduct, how different stimuli affect different people, whether we can find invariant properties across individuals and environments, and so forth. Similarly, after human nature is described as innate cognitive schemata, we may inquire into how exposure to linguistic behavior in early years may or may not affect language learning. Note how an explanation of language learning is likely to be quite distinctive and different from any analysis of aggression or similar kinds of conduct. As Foucault stresses, it would be a mistake— a commonplace blunder made by many, Jaggar included—to think that studying these phenomena is tantamount to providing a theory of human nature per se. What Foucault neglects to tell us is *why* that is.

To address the gap between human nature and its specific subtopics, the considerations developed in the previous section come in quite handy. Once a trait has been described as belonging to human nature, we can then go on to account for it. Depending on the trait in question, the appropriate explanation will be psychological, evolutionary, genetic, sociological, physical, or perhaps a hybrid crossover. Some of these explanations can already be provided in practice. Others still exceed our grasp. We can only bet that we will find them in the future. Yet, in explaining cognitive schemata, aggressive behavior, or regulatory genes, we are not explaining human nature tout court. Human nature is not merely a multiply realizable and miscellaneous collection of traits. It is further an overarching organizing principle, a mode of classification, an epistemological indicator, as Foucault dubs it. We can reduce human nature to more precise concepts. By doing so, we gain the opportunity of explaining the phenomena in question. At the same time, we also lose something significant: we end up altering its defining feature, that is, its intrinsic purpose and generality. In this respect, by analyzing human nature we thereby dissolve it.

In sum, we can surely provide an explanation of traits that, in some situation or other, are classified as human nature. Nevertheless, this is not the same as studying the overarching label. Providing a scientific explanation of who we are is tantamount to giving up human nature in and of itself. Explaining our nature explains it away. Human nature is a scientific concept. But it is not the target of scientific explanation. We cannot study it directly. All we can do is analyze its various, context-dependent proxies. Before moving on to our final summary and farewells, there is one final chore to attend to. We must distinguish my present characterization of human nature from other proposals in the literature, emphasizing some key advantages and limitations.

Let me begin by distancing myself decisively from two extremal views. On the one hand, there are authors who view the quest for human nature as a straightforward empirical inquiry. Echoing Wilson, they argue that science and science alone has the resources to unveil the great mystery of who we are. On the other hand, there are those who view human nature as lying strictly beyond the purview of the sciences. Whether the key lies in philosophy, theology, literature, the arts, or elsewhere, a scientific account of human nature is an oxymoron. Both positions strike me as myopic. One theme that has consistently emerged throughout our joint venture is that science by itself cannot provide all the answers. But to dismiss the wealth of discoveries provided by the enterprise of modern science is equally shortsighted. Shedding light on who we are requires a skillful blend of natural

318   THE QUEST FOR HUMAN NATURE

sciences, social sciences, and humanities. The buzzword is *et* not *aut*, *and* not *or*.

Foucault's position is subtler. To be sure, by contrasting epistemological indicators with "scientific" concepts, Foucault seems to place life and human nature outside of science's domain. At the same time, my own elaboration of indicators explores a different path. Human nature, I have suggested, plays a seminal role in science. But it does not set up an explanandum. It is a placeholder, a preliminary scaffolding standing in for more perspicuous objects of explanation posed at a different level. Is this what Foucault really had in mind? In all honesty, I am not quite sure. And truthfully it doesn't matter all that much. If this is not what the French intellectual was thinking, I'll leave it to someone else to provide a more accurate exegesis. What I do contend is that the present conception of human nature constitutes a promising avenue which overlaps and fits in nicely with the concept of secondary categories as *organizers* (Strevens 2019) and the concept of a *black box* (Nathan 2021). In short, approaching human nature along these lines provides an interesting, fecund, original, and progressive research program. Why not give it a shot?

The suggestion that human nature sets up an explanation without explaining is admittedly not completely novel. The general intuition has been floating around in the relevant literature. For instance, Sterelny (2018, p. 116) mentions—but swiftly brushes off—a proposal that bears some resemblance to mine: "One might, of course, take human nature to be the target of . . . evolutionary explanations, rather than as an explanatory resource. On that proposal, 'human nature' is just a name for the very distinctive features of our lineage that require special explanation." While Sterelny notes that there is nothing wrong with the idea, he dismisses it as "not the most helpful way of framing the explanatory agenda" (2018, p. 116) because the most puzzling features of human evolution are not individual traits but aspects of our social life and population structure. Why is Sterelny so rash in slighting the insight that human nature is the target of an evolutionary explanation as opposed to an explanatory resource? My preliminary diagnosis is that the net may be cast too narrowly. Sterelny is right, of course, that some of the most intriguing facets of evolution do not involve individual traits but require a broader focus. Nevertheless, there seems to me to be no reason for restricting human nature as picking out distinctive features of our lineage. Human nature, as we have seen, may stand in for a much wider range of explananda, from innate traits to genetic toolkits, from social life to population structure, and then some. This makes for a much richer and substantive endeavor, legitimizing the key role of human nature in all fields of knowledge. Placeholders are cheap; why use them so sparingly? Another view that bears resemblance to mine stems from a philosophical analysis of material culture:

> In any discipline or subdiscipline, it can be observed that it is precisely the central and most important concepts that resist definition and occasion the most controversy. . . . There is a reason for this. These concepts orient the more specific questions and problems in the field. So a psychologist, for instance, might ask how to measure intelligence or whether nonhuman animals are intelligent, an epistemologist might ask how we justify our knowledge claims or whether nonhuman animals know things, and so on. Now the problem with strict definitions of these central concepts is that they can invalidate some interesting and significant questions and/or foreclose the possibility of certain answers to them. (Preston 2013, pp. 6–7)

Unsurprisingly, I deeply sympathize with Preston's suggestion that some of the most pivotal scientific concepts orient specific questions and problems in the field. At the same time, it seems to me that the main culprit is not definitions per se but an undue and exaggerated fetishization of explanation as the be-all-end-all of science and philosophy thereof. We should not overlook the importance of definitions, which set up precise explananda. The point is that some concepts, like *regulatory gene* and *core knowledge,* are amenable to definition and explanation. Others, like *human nature* and *innateness*, have an altogether different job to do. And there is nothing wrong with that.

Let me compare my proposal with one final stance. Over the past few years, it has become increasingly fashionable to advocate for the outright eschewal of human nature from our scientific, philosophical, and sociopolitical agenda. The difficulties of providing a viable definition of human nature have prompted various authors to advocate for an eliminativist stance, which questions whether we really need

320 THE QUEST FOR HUMAN NATURE

a robust concept of human nature at all. For instance, developing an insight pioneered in the 1980s by Hull and Ghiselin, Lewens (2015b, p. 79) states: "It is far from clear that any form of scientific enquiry would be impoverished if we were either to endorse a thoroughly libertine conception of human nature, or if we were to get rid of the concept entirely." Kronfeldner (2018, p. 231) takes it a step further: "All things considered . . . it is better to prevent human nature talk as much as possible. The price of such a linguistic elimination is low, and the risk of damage (in terms of dehumanization) will be too high if human nature is not eliminated."[9]

My long rejoinder to this suggestion was developed throughout the entire second half of this book. The price of eliminating human nature from our everyday and technical vocabulary is much higher than it may appear at first blush. To be sure, the threat of dehumanization is a real and pressing concern. But it seems to me that getting rid of human nature tout court is not a viable option. As Jaggar forewarned us four decades ago, some conception or other of human nature is presupposed across the natural and social sciences as well as the humanities. The problem is that this concept eludes strict definition. The solution is to distinguish between explananda and epistemic indicators. Human nature and cognate concepts are scaffolding. Like scaffolding in construction, they may be disposable but only after the edifice has been erected. Once the explanation has been provided, they can be disassembled, moved to a new construction site. After the project is completed, it is easy to dismiss the role of scaffolding. Yet, try building without it . . .

In conclusion, human nature should be understood as an epistemological indicator, an explanandum that is itself only explainable by shifting to a different epistemic level. This reconciles the apparent tension between the claim that human nature is an essential presupposition and the observation that a clear analysis is still wanting. In elucidating the vague notion of an epistemological indicator, I have helped myself to an array of metaphors, from black box to placeholder,

---

[9] Authors who flirt with similar eliminativist approaches to human nature include Griffiths (2002), Keller (2010), Laland and Brown (2011, 2018), Prinz (2012), and Sterelny (2018).

from scaffolding to frame, from tool to pattern. This choice of images is not casual. In *Black Boxes* (Nathan 2021), I draw a contrast between two kinds of black boxes. "Frames" are placeholders that set up an object of explanation without explaining it, whereas "difference makers" are part of a causal explanation. Hence, indicators, frames, and scaffolding all point in the same direction. The idea of a scientific concept that lacks an explanation has been generally neglected in contemporary philosophy of science, where explanation has—somewhat unduly—received a much bigger share of attention than description, prediction, or any other epistemic inference. Unraveling the relations between my closely connected similes is a task that I set aside for a different occasion. The crucial point, for our present purposes, is that human nature, understood as an indicator, is a key normative presupposition across several domains. Focusing only, or even mainly on its explanatory function is to miss its distinctive, sui generis theoretical role, which helps account for its prominent place in the history of thought.

§10.6 Ten Answers to Ten Questions

We've reached the tail end of our journey. It is high time for some final remarks before bidding farewell. Our ventures into the vagaries of human nature began with deceptively simple issues, namely, whether there is a human nature and, if so, what it may turn out to be. This led us down a rabbit hole. Have we found any resolution? Well, no. Conclusive answers are a rare commodity across scientific, historical, philosophical, or other substantive inquiries. Still, here is my best attempt to wrap up the discussion by providing ten succinct answers to our ten guiding questions.

(i) *What's at stake?* There are several compelling reasons why generations of researchers, in the sciences and the humanities alike, have spilled rivers of ink on the hallowed topic of human nature. We've concentrated on one, inspired by Chomsky. Without an underlying conception of human nature, there is no meaningful discussion of who we are and strive to be as a biological species as well as a society. If this is not enough

322 THE QUEST FOR HUMAN NATURE

to get your neurons firing on all cylinders, then I'm not quite sure what will.

(ii) Do we currently have *a science of human nature?* If there is a science of human nature, new or old, we'd sure love to learn what it has discovered. Sociobiology was the first systematic attempt to take human nature out of the dusty offices of philosophers and into the aseptic environment of scientific laboratories. Evolutionary psychology has followed in the footsteps of its intellectual predecessor, purporting to capture the nuances of our "stone age mind." Bordering on half a century after the publication of Wilson's incendiary manifesto, the debate over sociobiology and evolutionary psychology rages on. Bang or bust? Revolution or red herring? Feel free to make up your own mind. Either way, it seems only fair to demand that any true science of human nature at the very least clarifies what it sets out to explain. And in this department not much success can be boasted. Perhaps it would be better to stick with the label "the science of the mind," although the concept of *mind* may well turn out to be yet another epistemic indicator—an intriguing conjecture that I set aside for another occasion.

(iii) *Is there a human nature?* This question is much more loaded and less straightforward than it appears at first blush. Long story short, the answer depends on what we mean by "human nature." Understood, as many non-specialists still do, as a human essence, a set of necessary and sufficient partially intrinsic properties for belonging to *Homo sapiens*, then, no, there ain't no human nature. Period. *Qua* natural state model, human nature becomes a regulative ideal of sorts, although it is not a straight-up empirical construct since the underlying notion of *normality* cannot be naturalized. Finally, conceived along the lines of a field guide—a purely descriptive inventory of our most typical or most salient traits—or as a snapshot of our evolutionary history then, yes, there surely is a human nature. But it is rather doubtful that any of these "thin" characterizations will be substantive enough to underwrite any "thick" substantive theory or normative hypothesis

CAN SCIENCE EXPLAIN HUMAN NATURE? 323

as to who we are and strive to be. Serious ornithologists look past field guide depictions. Humanists worth their salt should follow suit.

(iv) It is commonplace to identify human nature with a set of traits that are innate or genetically determined. Two follow-ups invite us to clarify these notions. For starters, *what makes a trait innate?* Biology and psychology have identified several ways in which features and capacities can be broken down into "innate vs. acquired." These range from species-typicality to developmental fixity, from monomorphism to genetic determinism, from mental modularity to core knowledge. All these concepts shed light on our cognitive profile. But it appears rather questionable whether any of these characterizations transcend their specific domain, deserving the label of "innate" tout court and, derivatively, characterizing our human nature. Innateness appears to work fine as a particular property of traits within the technical confines of a scientific theory, paradigm, or framework. Understood in a broader, absolute context, it becomes vague, slippery, unhelpful. Innateness, perceptive readers will note, starts to look suspiciously like an epistemological indicator no less than human nature itself. This analogy, which legitimizes our pre-theoretical intuitions, is hardly haphazard if I'm on the right track.

(v) Moving on to the second candidate proxy, we can ask whether human nature can be characterized in terms of genetic determination. *Are we genetically determined?* Short answer: no, at least not in any sense worthy of national headlines. There may well be a handful of biochemical properties that follow invariably from the possession of specific genes. But these traits will typically only interest geneticists or other strands of molecular biologists. In order to develop a notion of genetic influence broad enough to capture significant phenotypic conditions that remain invariant across a variety of contexts and circumstances—opposable thumbs, eye color, Huntington's Disease, and the like—one needs to relax the strict sense of determination to include environmental

324   THE QUEST FOR HUMAN NATURE

interactions with genotypes. The underlying insight is captured by norms of reaction depicting the relation between genotype, phenotype, and environment. In principle, it may well be possible to provide a notion of heritability that quantifies the genetic contribution to development. But, as we speak, we are very far from any such meaningful quantification. Right now, high-sounding claims of "genetic determination" appear misleading at best. At the same time, much remains to be learned by posing the right questions. In studying the development of complex creatures such as us, can we meaningfully apportion the role of genotype vs. environment, nature vs. nurture, biology vs. culture? If so, which traits and features should we inquire about? And how do we overcome current methodological limitations? If not, can we find better explanatory strategies? We're better off focusing on these issues rather than hopelessly struggle to quantify a vague notion based on drastically incomplete evidence. Slice the pie any way you like, heritability and determinism do not get to the heart of human nature. Nothing in science apparently does. Perhaps, it is time to put our quest for human nature to rest, for good?

(vi) It turns out that life after human nature is not quite as rosy as we might have expected. Consider, for instance, the pressing issue of race. *Are there human races?* At first blush, it seems hard to conceive of a more straightforward empirical query. Are races real or are they not? Are they more like atoms or like phlogiston? Upon further scrutiny, this question becomes less clean cut than it initially appeared. Facts alone hardly settle it. Phenotypic characters tend to co-vary with genetic traits. This is hardly shocking news. So is the platitude that variation is clinally distributed, that is, gradually sloped. But there are pros and cons to constructing races as natural kinds, social kinds, and eliminating them outright. The answer partly depends on what we want races to do. Conceiving human nature as an epistemic indicator—a placeholder for explananda framing a more precise scientific issue—does not directly suggest how to address racism, sexism, ableism, and other kinds of discrimination. Nevertheless, it pinpoints what all these forms of marginalization have in common and what is problematic about all of them. At root, discrimination is a form of dehumanization, depriving an individual of their status as a human being, a full member of our species. In short, it strips us of our human nature. This suggests that while human nature is confronted by a "dehumanization problem," an analogous challenge is also faced by eliminativists.

(vii) These considerations point to a more general question: *Is human nature inherently oppressive or emancipatory?* Some feminists consider human nature an essential component of their framework, whereas others have come to view it as a hurdle to be overcome. Is human nature part of the dehumanization problem or part of the solution? It is neither. Human nature is a tool, a powerful conceptual tool. As such, it can be put to good use or to bad use. What we do with it is up to us. But the very insinuation that we can have meaningful discussions of the marginalization of certain groups, and related reflections on emancipation and social justice, without some underlying conception of human nature and human rights is a chimera. We need some notion of shared humanity in order to pursue racial justice, gender equality, and other pressing items in our sociopolitical agenda. The challenge is finding the appropriate one. Again, this is a task that will require a subtle blend of science and politics, facts and values.

(viii) On this note, we saw that normality is a pivotal constituent of any thick account of human nature. *Is normality grounded in facts or politics?* Both. Sociopolitical strategies must be deep-rooted in empirical truth. There is no science without normality, just like there is no politics without normality. Normality and human nature, thus conceived, are two sides of the same coin. To determine where we want to be as a society, we must simultaneously assess where we currently are. But the idea that any meaningful notion of nature or normality can be straightforwardly inferred from our physical, biological, or psychological profile is utterly misguided. It is as wrongheaded as the absurdity that normality and nature are

326 THE QUEST FOR HUMAN NATURE

straight-up political notions. Normality is not the outcome of scientific or political inquiry. It is a point of departure. And to start off on the right foot, we'll need a skillful hybrid blend of "is" and "ought," description and prescription. This is admittedly neither novel nor especially controversial. The value-ladenness of scientific concepts is a staple of feminist philosophy of science, at least since the seminal work of Helen Longino (1990). The original point that emerges from the present discussion is that concepts such as human nature may well evolve as inquiry moves along, but they never become bona fide objects of explanation. In this respect, Foucault's contrast between scientific concepts and epistemic indicators is misleading. It makes it sound as if indicators are not scientific concepts at all. Indicators play a prominent role within the enterprise of science. They are just neither explanantia nor explananda. They are general patterns pointing to where explanation is to be sought.

(ix) The absurdity of eschewing the notion of human nature from normative discussions emerged with the most clarity while examining the issue of transhumanism. *Should we be concerned about enhancing our nature?* Should we be excited? These questions are plainly meaningless without adopting a preliminary firm stance on what we take our nature to be. Bioconservatives fear the possibility of rejecting the shackles of own nature. Bioliberals cherish its prospects. But what is it that we need to conserve or transcend? Enhancement and therapy do not explain our nature. Once again, they all but presuppose it.

(x) Our quest for human nature led us to the following final fundamental question: how are we to study this nature? Can an empirical approach get us out of the quagmire? *Can science explain human nature?* No. Far from discovering it, science presupposes a notion of human nature. But what exactly is the alternative? Philosophy? History? Politics? All these disciplines fall prey to precisely the same objections. They presuppose a human nature no less than science does. And just like that we are back to where we started. We are stuck in a circle. But this circle may not be a vicious one but a virtuous one. There sure are plenty of researchers who take themselves to be pursuing the study of human nature. A science of human nature. A philosophy of human nature. A history of human nature. A politics of human nature. Everyone tries to explain human nature or explain it away. I've offered some skeptical considerations to the effect that human nature, after all, may not be a concept amenable to explanation, scientific or otherwise. It should hopefully be crystal clear by now that this absolutely doesn't mean that science, history, or philosophy have nothing of interest to say about human nature. On the contrary, characterized as an epistemic indicator, a placeholder, it becomes clearer why the notion itself is so elusive. It also shows why all the struggles in capturing this pesky concept hardly undercut its importance. Human nature is going nowhere. It is here to stay, although it may end up looking quite a bit different from what we initially assumed.

Some readers may remain unmoved. If human nature functions as an epistemic indicator, a mere placeholder, then it plays no part in explanation. Wouldn't we be better off getting rid of it entirely and concentrating on other concepts more central to science? Why not focus on what we *can* explain? Allow me a final laconic rejoinder. The idea that only the concepts that can be explained scientifically matter for scientific practice embodies a callous and myopic preconception. Even if human nature, understood as an epistemological indicator, does not contribute directly to any explanation, it still plays a crucial role by directing our attention to biological, psychological, and political aspects that are worth our while. And what if, contrary to what I have suggested, it directed our attention to nothing further? The naturalist Stephen Jay Gould elegantly denounced the pernicious tendency of contemporary science to privilege explanation at the expense of everything else. He pleaded the case for *exultanda*, phenomena, like unique behaviors of species, that should be cherished for their beauty without having to be accounted for at all costs:

328 THE QUEST FOR HUMAN NATURE

> Shall we regret the solitaire's passing [extinction] because its unique behavior might have suggested new generalities in the currently "hot" field of adaptive strategies in mating behavior? Or shall we simply mourn the lost opportunity for watching something so fascinating and so different? We had best cherish exultation and explanation with equal tenacity, though I myself would trade several good generalities for the chance to witness such a spectacle. (Gould 1987, p. 188)

In addition to its role as an epistemological indicator, human nature could also be an *exultanda*, in Gould's sense, a spectacle to be witnessed in all its magnificence. Perhaps not all of Darwin's endless forms most beautiful are there to be explained. Would there be anything wrong with that? Paraphrasing, one final time Pico's insight, what a great miracle human beings truly are!

In the end, how successful was our venture into the mysteries of human nature? This is not for me to judge. Some readers will be impressed by the amount of ground covered and all we've discovered. Others will bemoan the lack of conclusive answers. What I can say for certain is that we started off with an apparently straightforward question which spawned ten hefty chapters that barely scratch the surface of a deeper ocean. By the time we were done, we ended up with several additional, less clean-cut, more puzzling inquiries. I will not be apologetic about this. This is how any intellectual inquiry worth its salt should go. It is a sign that something has gone deeply *right*.

References

Albrecht, Gary L. and Patrick J. Devlieger (1999). "The Disability Paradox: High Quality of Life against All Odds." *Social Science and Medicine* 48(8), 977–88.

Alcock, John (2013). *Animal Behavior: An Evolutionary Approach* (10th ed.). Sunderland: Sinauer.

Alcoff, Linda M. (2005). *Visible Identities: Race, Gender, and the Self.* Oxford: Oxford University Press.

Amundson, Ron (2000). "Against Normal Function." *Studies in History and Philosophy of Biological and Biomedical Sciences* 31(1), 33–53.

Anderson, Michael L. (2014). *After Phrenology: Neural Reuse and the Interactive Brain.* Cambridge: MIT Press.

Andreasen, Robin O. (1998). "A New Perspective in the Race Debate." *British Journal for the Philosophy of Science* 49, 199–225.

Annas, George J., Lori B. Andrews, and Rosario M. Isasi (2002). "Protecting the Endangered Human: Toward an International Treaty Prohibiting Cloning and Inheritable Alterations. *American Journal of Law and Medicine* 28(2–3), 151–78.

Antony, Louise M. (1998). "'Human Nature' and Its Role in Feminist Theory." In J. A. Kourany (Ed.), *Philosophy in a Feminist Voice: Critiques and Reconstructions*, pp. 63–91. Princeton: Princeton University Press.

Antony, Louise M. (2000). "Natures and Norms." *Ethics* 111, 8–36.

Appiah, Kwame A. (2007). "Does Truth Matter to Identity?" In J. J. Gracia (Ed.), *Race or Ethnicity? On Black and Latino Identity*, pp. 19–44. Ithaca: Cornell University Press.

Appiah, Kwame A. (2013). *Lines of Descent: W. E. B du Bois and the Emergence of Identity.* Cambridge: Harvard University Press.

Ariew, André (1996). "Innateness and Canalization." *Philosophy of Science* 63, S19–S27.

Ariew, André (1999). "Innateness Is Canalization: In Defense of a Developmental Account of Innateness." In V. G. Hardcastle (Ed.), *Where Biology Meets Psychology: Philosophical Essays*, pp. 117–38. Cambridge: MIT Press.

Ásta (2018). *Categories We Live By: The Construction of Sex, Gender, Race, and Other Social Categories.* New York: Oxford University Press.

Bamshad, Michael J., Steven Wooding, W. Scott Watkins, Christopher T. Ostler, Mark A. Batzer, and L. Jorde (2003). "Human Population Structure

330   REFERENCES

and Inference of Group Membership." *American Journal of Human Genetics* 72, 578–89.

Barclay, Linda (2016). "A Natural Alliance against a Common Foe? Opponents of Enhancement and the Social Model of Disability." In S. Clarke, J. Savulescu, C. Coady, A. Giubilini, and S. Sanyal (Eds.), *The Ethics of Human Enhancement: Understanding the Debate*, pp. 75–86. Oxford: Oxford University Press.

Barker, Gillian (2015). *Beyond Biofatalism: Human Nature for an Evolving World*. New York: Columbia University Press.

Barker, Matthew J. (2010). "Specious Intrinsicalism." *Philosophy of Science* 77, 73–91.

Barker, Matthew J. and Robert A. Wilson (2019). "Well-Being, Disability, and Choosing Children." *Mind* 128(510), 305–28.

Barnes, Elizabeth (2016). *The Minority Body: A Theory of Disability*. Oxford: Oxford University Press.

Barnes, Elizabeth (2020). "Gender and Gender Terms." *Nous* 54(3), 704–30.

Barnes, Elizabeth (2022). "Gender without Gender Identity: The Case of Cognitive Disability." *Mind* 131(523), 838–64.

Baron-Cohen, Simon (2003). *The Essential Difference: Male and Female Brains and the Truth about Autism*. New York: Basic Books.

Basalla, George (1988). *The Evolution of Technology*. Cambridge: Cambridge University Press.

Bateson, Patrick (2001). "Behavioral Development and Darwinian Evolution." In S. Oyama, P. E. Griffiths, and R. D. Gray (Eds.), *Cycles of Contingency: Developmental Systems and Evolution*, pp. 149–66. Cambridge: MIT Press.

Bateson, Patrick and Peter D. Gluckman (2011). *Plasticity, Robustness, Development and Evolution*. Cambridge: Cambridge University Press.

Bedau, Mark A. (1991). "Can Biological Teleology Be Naturalized?" *Journal of Philosophy* 88, 647–55.

Bettcher, Talia. M. (2009). "Trans Identities and the First-Person Authority." In L. Shrage (Ed.), *You've Changed: Sex Reassignment and Personal Identity*, pp. 98–120. New York: Oxford University Press.

Block, Ned (1995). "How Heritability Misleads about Race." *Cognition* 56, 99–128.

Bolnick, Deborah A. (2008). "Individual Ancestry Inference and the Reification of Race as a Biological Phenomenon." In B. Koenig, S. Lee, and S. Richardson (Eds.), *Revisiting Race in a Genomic Age*, pp. 70–85. New Brunswick: Rutgers University Press.

Boorse, Christopher (1976). "Wright on Functions." *Philosophical Review* 85, 70–86.

Boorse, Christopher (1977). "Health as a Theoretical Concept." *Philosophy of Science*, 44(4), 542–73.

REFERENCES 331

Boorse, Christopher (1997). "A Rebuttal on Health." In J. Humber and R. Almeder (Eds.), *What Is a Disease?*, pp. 1–134. Totowa: Humana Press.

Boorse, Christopher (2002). "A Rebuttal on Functions." In A. Ariew, R. Cummins, and M. Perlman (Eds.), *Functions: New Essays in the Philosophy of Psychology and Biology*, pp. 63–112. Oxford: Oxford University Press.

Bostrom, Nick (2005). "In Defense of Posthuman Dignity." *Bioethics* 19(3), 202–14.

Bouchard, Thomas J., Jr. (2004). "Genetic Influence on Human Psychological Traits: A Survey." *Current Directions in Psychological Science* 13(4), 148–51.

Bowlby, John (1969). *Attachment and Loss, Vol. 1: Attachment.* New York: Basic Books.

Bowlby, John (1973). *Attachment and Loss, Vol. 2: Separation, Anxiety, and Anger.* New York: Basic Books.

Boyd, Richard N. (1991). "Realism, Anti-Foundationalism, and the Enthusiasm for Natural Kinds." *Philosophical Studies* 61(1), 127–48.

Boyd, Richard N. (1999). "Homeostasis, Species, and Higher Taxa." In R. Wilson (Ed.), *Species: New Interdisciplinary Essays*, pp. 141–85. Cambridge: MIT Press.

Boyd, Robert (2018). *A Different Kind of Animal: How Culture Transformed Our Species.* Princeton and Oxford: Princeton University Press.

Boyd, Robert and Peter J. Richerson (1985). *Culture and the Evolutionary Process.* Chicago: Chicago University Press.

Boyd, Robert and Peter J. Richerson (2005). *The Origin and Evolution of Cultures.* Oxford: Oxford University Press.

Briggle, Adam (2010). *A Rich Bioethics: Public Policy, Biotechnology, and the Kass Council.* Notre Dame: University of Notre Dame Press.

Broadbent, Alex (2019). *Philosophy of Medicine.* New York: Oxford University Press.

Brock, Dan W. (1993). *Life and Death.* Cambridge: Cambridge University Press.

Buchanan, Allen (2009). "Human Nature and Enhancement." *Bioethics* 23, 141–50.

Buchanan, Allen (2013). *Beyond Humanity? The Ethics of Biomedical Enhancement.* Oxford: Oxford University Press.

Buller, David J. (1998). "Etiological Theories of Function: A Geographical Survey." *Biology and Philosophy* 13, 505–27.

Buller, David J. (2005). *Adapting Minds: Evolutionary Psychology and the Persistent Quest for Human Nature.* Cambridge: MIT Press.

Burge, Tyler (1979). "Individualism and the Mental." *Midwest Studies in Philosophy* 4, 73–121.

Buss, David M. (1994). *The Evolution of Desire.* New York: Basic Books.

Buss, David M. (2019). *Evolutionary Psychology: The New Science of the Mind* (6th ed.). New York: Routledge.

Campbell, Anne (2002). *A Mind of Her Own: The Evolutionary Psychology of Women.* Oxford: Oxford University Press.

332 REFERENCES

Campbell, Donald T. (1974). "Evolutionary Epistemology." In P. Schilpp (Ed.), *The Philosophy of Karl Popper*, pp. 412–63. La Salle: Open Court.

Carey, Susan (2009). *The Origin of Concepts*. New York: Oxford University Press.

Cashdan, Elizabeth (2013). "What Is a Human Universal? Human Behavioral Ecology and Human Nature." In S. M. Downes and E. Machery (Eds.), *Arguing about Human Nature: Contemporary Debates*, pp. 71–80. New York: Routledge.

Cavalli-Sforza, Luca L. and Marcus W. Feldman (1981). *Cultural Transmission and Evolution*. Princeton: Princeton University Press.

Cavalli-Sforza, Luca L., Paolo Menozzi, and Alberto Piazza (1994). *The History and Geography of Human Genes*. Princeton: Princeton University Press.

Chomsky, Noam ([1976] 2006). "A Philosophy of Language." In *The Chomsky-Foucault Debate on Human Nature*, pp. 117–39. London and New York: The New Press.

Chomsky, Noam and Michel Foucault ([1971] 2006). "Human Nature: Justice vs. Power. A Debate between Noam Chomsky and Michel Foucault." In *The Chomsky-Foucault Debate on Human Nature*, pp. 1–67. Cambridge: The New Press.

Chomsky, N. and M. Foucault (2006). *The Chomsky-Foucault Debate on Human Nature*. London and New York: The New Press.

Coady, C. A. J. (2016). "Reason, Emotion, and Morality: Some Cautions for the Enhancement Project." In S. Clarke, J. Savulescu, C. Coady, A. Giubilini, and S. Sanyal (Eds.), *The Ethics of Human Enhancement: Understanding the Debate*, pp. 27–42. Oxford: Oxford University Press.

Collins, Francis (2004). "What We Do and Don't Know about 'Race', 'Ethnicity', Genetics, and Health at the Dawn of the Genome Era." *Nature Genetics* 36, S13–S15.

Collins, John M. (2005). "Nativism: In Defense of a Biological Understanding." *Philosophical Psychology* 18(2), 157–77.

Compton, Elizabeth, Michael Bentley, Sharon Ennis, and Sonya Rastogi (2013). *2010 Census Race and Hispanic Origin Alternative Questionnaire Experiment*. Washington: US Census Bureau.

Cooper, Rachel (2002). "Disease." *Studies in the History and Philosophy of Biological and Biomedical Sciences* 33, 263–82.

Cosmides, Leda and John Tooby (2013). "Evolutionary Psychology. A Primer." In S. M. Downes and E. Machery (Eds.), *Arguing about Human Nature*, pp. 83–92. New York: Routledge.

Cowie, Fiona (1999). *What's Within? Nativism Reconsidered*. Oxford: Oxford University Press.

Cronk, Lee, Napoleon A. Chagnon, and William Irons (Eds.) (2000). *Adaptation and Human Behavior: An Anthropological Perspective*. New York: De Gruyter.

Cummins, Robert (1975). "Functional Analysis." *Journal of Philosophy* 72, 741–765.

REFERENCES   333

Cuvier, Georges (1813). *Essay on the Theory of Earth*. Edinburgh: Blackwood.

Daly, Mary (1978). *Gyn/Ecology: The Metaethics of Radical Feminism*. Boston: Beacon.

Daly, Martin and Margo Wilson (1988). "Evolutionary Social Psychology and Family Homicide." *Science* 242, 519–24.

Daniels, Norman (1987). "Justice and Health Care." In D. Van De Veer and T. Regan (Eds.), *Health Care Ethics: An Introduction*, pp. 290–325. Philadelphia: Temple University Press.

Darwin, Charles ([1859] 2008). *On the Origin of Species*. New York: Oxford University Press.

Darwin, Charles (1871). *The Descent of Man, and Selection in Relation to Sex*. London: John Murray.

Darwin, Charles (1872). *The Expression of the Emotions in Man and Animals*. London: Murray.

Davidson, Donald (1970). "Mental Events." In L. Foster and J. Swanson (Eds.), *Experience and Theory*, pp. 79–101. London: Duckworth.

Davis, Angela Y. (1981). *Women, Race & Class*. New York: Random House.

Dawkins, Richard (1976). *The Selfish Gene*. Oxford: Oxford University Press.

Dawkins, Richard (1982). *The Extended Phenotype*. Oxford: Oxford University Press.

Dawkins, Richard (1986). *The Blind Watchmaker*. New York: Norton.

de Beauvoir, Simone ([1949] 2009). *The Second Sex*. New York: Vintage Books.

Dembroff, Robin (2020). "Beyond Binary: Gender Queer as Critical Gender Kind." *Philosophers' Imprint* 20(9), 1–23.

Dembroff, Robin (forthcoming). *Real Men on Top: How Patriarchy Weaponizes Gender*. Oxford: Oxford University Press.

Dennett, Daniel C. (2017). *From Bacteria to Bach and Back: The Evolution of Minds*. New York: Norton.

Devitt, Michael (2008). "Resurrecting Biological Essentialism." *Philosophy of Science* 75, 344–82.

Devitt, Michael (2010). "Species Have (Partly) Intrinsic Essences." *Philosophy of Science* 77, 648–61.

Devitt, Michael (2023). *Biological Essentialism*. Oxford: Oxford University Press.

Dobzhansky, Theodosius (1962). "Genetics and Equality: Equality of Opportunity Makes the Genetic Diversity among Men Meaningful." *Science* 137(3524), 112–15.

Douglas, Thomas (2013). "Human Enhancement and Supra-Personal Moral Status." *Philosophical Studies* 162(3), 473–97.

Downes, Stephen M. (2010). "The Basic Components of the Human Mind Were Not Solidified during the Pleistocene Epoch." In F. J. Ayala and R. Arp (Eds.), *Contemporary Debates in Philosophy of Biology*, pp. 243–52. Malden: Wiley-Blackwell.

334 REFERENCES

Dupré, John (2001). *Human Nature and the Limits of Science*. Oxford: Oxford University Press.

Dupré, John (2003). *Darwin's Legacy: What Evolution Means Today*. New York: Oxford University Press.

Dworkin, Ronald (2000). *Sovereign Virtue*. Cambridge: Harvard University Press.

Edwards, A. W. F. (2003). "Human Genetic Diversity: Lewontin's Fallacy." *BioEssays* 28(8), 798–801.

Elton, Charles S. (1927). *Animal Ecology*. London: Sidgwick and Jackson.

Engels, Friedrich ([1884] 1902). *The Origin of the Family, Private Property and the State*. Chicago: Charles H. Kerr & Co.

Ereshefsky, Marc (2010). "What's Wrong with the New Biological Essentialism?" *Philosophy of Science* 77, 674–85.

Evans, Nicholas and Stephen C. Levinson (2009). "The Myth of Language Universals: Language Diversity and Its Importance for Cognitive Science." *Behavioral and Brain Sciences* 32, 429–92.

Fausto-Sterling, Anne (1992). *Myths of Gender* (2nd ed.). New York: Basic Books.

Fausto-Sterling, Anne (2000). *Sexing the Body: Gender Politics and the Construction of Sexuality*. New York: Basic Books.

Firestein, Stuart (2012). *Ignorance. How It Drives Science*. New York: Oxford University Press.

Firestone, Shulamith (1970). *The Dialectic of Sex: The Case for Feminist Revolution*. New York: William Morrow.

Flanagan, Owen (1991). *The Science of the Mind* (2nd ed.). Cambridge: MIT Press.

Fodor, Jerry A. (1981). *The Present Status of the Innateness Controversy*. Cambridge: MIT Press.

Fodor, Jerry A. (1983). *The Modularity of Mind: An Essay on Faculty Psychology*. Cambridge: MIT Press.

Foot, Philippa (2001). *Natural Goodness*. Oxford: Oxford University Press.

Foucault, Michel (1976). *The History of Sexuality*, Volume 1. Paris: Gallimard.

Fraser, Nancy and Linda Nicholson (1990). "Social Feminism without Philosophy." In L. Nicholson (Ed.), *Feminism/Postmodernism*, pp. 132–36. London and New York: Routledge.

Friedman, Milton. (1962). *Capitalism and Freedom*. Chicago: University of Chicago Press.

Fukuyama, Francis (2002). *Our Posthuman Future: Consequences of the Biotechnology Revolution*. New York: Farrar, Straus and Giroux.

Garson, Justin (2015). *The Biological Mind: A Philosophical Introduction*. New York: Routledge.

Garson, Justin (2016). *A Critical Overview of Biological Functions*. Dordrecht: Springer.

REFERENCES   335

Garson, Justin (2019). *What Biological Functions Are and Why They Matter.* Cambridge: Cambridge University Press.

Garson, Justin and Gualtiero Piccinini (2014). "Functions Must Be Performed at Appropriate Rates in Appropriate Situations." *British Journal for the Philosophy of Science* 65(1), 1–20.

Gazzaniga, Michael S. (2008). *Human: The Science behind What Makes Us Unique.* New York: Harper Collins.

Gheaus, Anca (2023). "Feminism without 'Gender Identity.'" *Politics, Philosophy & Economics* 22(1), 31–54.

Ghiselin, Michael T. (1997). *Metaphysics and the Origin of Species.* Albany: SUNY Press.

Gilbert, Scott F. and David Epel (2009). *Ecological Developmental Biology: Integrating Epigenetics, Medicine, and Evolution.* Sunderland: Sinauer Associates.

Gilligan, Carol (1982). *In a Different Voice: Psychological Theory and Women's Development.* Cambridge: Harvard University Press.

Giubilini, Alberto and Sagar Sanyal (2016). "Challenging Human Enhancement." In S. Clarke, J. Savulescu, C. Coady, A. Giubilini, and S. Sanyal (Eds.), *The Ethics of Human Enhancement: Understanding the Debate*, pp. 1–24. Oxford: Oxford University Press.

Gladwell, Malcolm (2008). *Outliers: The Story of Success.* New York, Boston, and London: Little, Brown and Co.

Glannon, Walter (2001). *Genes and Future People.* Cambridge: Westview.

Glasgow, Joshua (2019). "Is Race an Illusion or a (Very) Basic Reality?" In J. Glasgow, S. Haslanger, C. Jeffers, and Q. Spencer (Eds.), *What Is Race? Four Philosophical Views*, pp. 111–49. New York: Oxford University Press.

Glasgow, Joshua, Sally Haslanger, Chike Jeffers, and Quayshawn Spencer (Eds.) (2019). *What Is Race? Four Philosophical Views.* New York: Oxford University Press.

Godfrey-Smith, Peter (1994). "A Modern History Theory of Functions." *Nous* 28, 344–62.

Godfrey-Smith, Peter (2007). "Innateness and Genetic Information." In P. Carruthers, S. Lawrence, and S. Stich (Eds.), *The Innate Mind, Vol. 3: Foundations and the Future*, pp. 55–68. New York: Oxford University Press.

Godfrey-Smith, Peter (2014). *Philosophy of Biology.* Princeton and Oxford: Princeton University Press.

Godman, Marion, Antonella Mallozzi, and David Papineau (2020). "Essential Properties Are Super-Explanatory: Taming Metaphysical Modality." *Journal of the American Philosophical Association* 3, 1–19.

Godman, Marion and David Papineau (2020). "Species Have Historical Not Intrinsic Essences." In A. Bianchi (Ed.), *Language and Reality from a Naturalistic Perspective: Themes from Michael Devitt*, pp. 355–65. Cham: Springer.

336 REFERENCES

Goodman, Nelson (1955). *Fact, Fiction, and Forecast*. Cambridge: Harvard University Press.

Gould, Stephen J. (1977). *Ontogeny and Phylogeny*. Cambridge: Belknap.

Gould, Stephen J. (1980). "Sociobiology and the Theory of Natural Selection." In G. Barlow and J. Silverberg (Eds.), *Sociobiology: Beyond Nature/Nurture?*, pp. 257–69. Washington: American Association for the Advancement of Science.

Gould, Stephen J. (1987). "Exultation and Explanation." In *An Urchin in the Storm*, pp. 180–88. New York: Norton.

Gould, Stephen J. (1996). *The Mismeasure of Man* (2nd ed.). New York and London: Norton.

Gould, Stephen J. and Richard Lewontin (1979). "The Spandrels of San Marco and the Panglossian Paradigm: A Critique of the Adaptationist Program." *Proceedings of the Royal Society of London* 205, 281–88.

Gowaty, Patricia A. (2008). "Reproductive Compensation." *Journal of Evolutionary Biology* 21(5), 1189–200.

Gowaty, Patricia A. and Stephen P. Hubbell (2013). "Bayesian Animals Sense Ecological Constraints to Predict Fitness and Organize Individually Flexible Reproductive Decisions." *Behavioral and Brain Sciences* 3, 215–16.

Griffin, Susan (1978). *Woman and Nature: The Rearing inside Her*. New York: Harper and Row.

Griffiths, Paul E. (1993). "Functional Analysis and Proper Function." *British Journal for the Philosophy of Science* 44, 409–22.

Griffiths, Paul E. (1999). "Squaring the Circle: Natural Kinds with Historical Essences." In R. A. Wilson (Ed.), *Species: New Interdisciplinary Essays*, pp. 209–28. Cambridge: MIT Press.

Griffiths, Paul E. (2001). "Genetic Information: A Metaphor in Search of a Theory." *Philosophy of Science* 68, 394–412.

Griffiths, Paul E. (2002). "What Is Innateness?" *The Monist* 85(1), 70–85.

Griffiths, Paul E. (2008). "Ethology, Sociobiology, and Evolutionary Psychology." In S. Sarkar and A. Plutynski (Eds.), *A Companion to the Philosophy of Biology*, pp. 393–414. Malden: Blackwell.

Griffiths, Paul E. (2009). "Reconstructing Human Nature." *Arts* 31, 30–57.

Griffiths, Paul E. and Russell D. Gray (1994). "Developmental Systems and Evolutionary Explanation." *Journal of Philosophy* 91(6), 277–304.

Griffiths, Paul E. and Robin D. Knight (1998). "What Is the Developmentalist Challenge?" *Philosophy of Science* 65, 253–58.

Griffiths, Paul E. and Karola Stotz (2013). *Genetics and Philosophy: An Introduction*. Cambridge: Cambridge University Press.

Gyngell, Chris and Michael J. Selgelid (2016). "Human Enhancement: Conceptual Clarity and Moral Significance." In S. Clarke, J. Savulescu, C. Coady, A. Giubilini, and S. Sanyal (Eds.), *The Ethics of Human Enhancement: Understanding the Debate*, pp. 111–26. Oxford: Oxford University Press.

REFERENCES   337

Habermas, Jürgen (2003). *The Future of Human Nature*. Oxford: Blackwell.

Hacking, Ian (1999). *The Social Construction of What?* Cambridge: Harvard University Press.

Hamilton, William D. (1964). "The Genetic Evolution of Social Behavior, I and II." *Journal of Theoretical Biology* 7, 1–52.

Harden, Kathryn Paige (2021a). "'Reports of My Death Were Greatly Exaggerated': Behavior Genetics in the Postgenomic Era." *Annual Review of Psychology* 72, 37–60.

Harden, Kathryn Paige (2021b). *The Genetic Lottery: Why DNA Matters for Social Equality*. Princeton and Oxford: Princeton University Press.

Hardimon, Michael O. (2003). "The Ordinary Concept of Race." *Journal of Philosophy* 100(9), 437–55.

Harris, John (2007). *Enhancing Evolution: The Ethical Case for Making Better People*. Princeton: Princeton University Press.

Haslanger, Sally (2012). *Resisting Reality: Social Construction and Social Critique*. New York: Oxford University Press.

Haslanger, Sally (2019). "Tracing the Sociopolitical Reality of Race." In J. Glasgow, S. Haslanger, C. Jeffers, and Q. Spencer (Eds.), *What Is Race? Four Philosophical Views*, pp. 4–37. New York: Oxford University Press.

Held, Virginia (1990). "Feminist Transformation of Moral Theory." *Philosophy and Phenomenological Research* 50, 321–34.

Henrich, Joseph (2016). *The Secret of Our Success: How Culture Is Driving Human Evolution, Domesticating Our Species, and Making Us Smarter*. Princeton and Oxford: Princeton University Press.

Henrich, Joseph (2020). *The WEIRDest People in the World: How the West Became Psychologically Peculiar and Particularly Prosperous*. New York: Farrar, Straus and Giroux.

Henrich, Joseph and Robert Boyd (1998). "The Evolution of Conformist Transmission and the Emergence of Between-Group Differences." *Evolution and Human Behavior* 19, 215–41.

Henrich, Joseph, Steven J. Heine, and Ara Norezan (2010). "The Weirdest People in the World?" *Behavioral and Brain Sciences* 33(2–3), 61–135.

Herrnstein, Richard J. and Charles A. Murray (1994). *The Bell Curve: Intelligence and Class Structure in American Life*. New York: Free Press.

Heyes, Cecilia. (2018). *Cognitive Gadgets: The Cultural Evolution of Thinking*. Cambridge: Harvard University Press.

Hirschman, Albert O. (1991). *The Rhetoric of Reaction*. Cambridge: Belknap.

Hobbes, Thomas (1651). *Leviathan or The Matter, Forme and Power of a Commonwealth Ecclesiasticall and Civil*. London: Crooke.

Holmstrom, Nancy (2013). "Is Human Nature Important for Feminism?" In S. M. Downes and E. Machery (Eds.), *Arguing about Human Nature: Contemporary Debates*, pp. 543–56. New York and Abingdon: Routledge.

338 REFERENCES

Hull, David L. (1986). "On Human Nature." *Proceedings to the Biennial Meeting of the Philosophy of Science Association* 2(PSA 1986), 3–13.

Hume, David ([1738] 2000). *A Treatise of Human Nature*. New York: Oxford University Press.

Hutchinson, G. Evelyn (1965). *The Ecological Theater and the Evolutionary Play*. New Haven: Yale University Press.

Irons, William (1979). "Natural Selection, Adaptation, and Human Social Behavior." In N. A. Chagnon and W. Irons (Eds.), *Evolutionary Biology and Human Social Behavior*, pp. 4–38. North Scituate: Duxbury Press.

Izard, Carroll E. (1991). *The Psychology of Emotions*. New York and London: Plenum.

Jablonka, Eva and Marion Lamb (2005). *Evolution in Four Dimensions. Genetic, Epigenetic, Behavioral, and Symbolic Variation in the History of Life*. Cambridge: Bradford, MIT Press.

Jacob, François (1977). "Evolution and Tinkering." *Science* 196, 1161–66.

Jaggar, Alison M. (1983). *Feminist Politics and Human Nature*. Lanham: Rowman and Littlefield.

Jaggar, Alison M. (2006). "Reasoning about Well-Being: Nussbaum's Method of Justifying the Capabilities." *Philosophical Topics* 14, 301–22.

Jeffers, Chike (2019). "Cultural Constructionism." In J. Glasgow, S. Haslanger, C. Jeffers, and Q. Spencer (Eds.), *What Is Race? Four Philosophical Views*, pp. 38–72. New York: Oxford University Press.

Jenkin, Fleeming (1867). "The Origin of Species." *The North British Review* 46, 277–318.

Jenkins, Katharine (2016). "Amelioration and Inclusion: Gender Identity and the Concept of Woman." *Ethics* 126, 394–421.

Jensen, Arthur R. (1969). "How Much Can We Boost IQ and School Achievement?" *Harvard Educational Review* 39, 1–123.

Jonas, Hans (1985). *Technik, Medizin, und Ethik: Zur Praxis des Prinzips Verantwortung*. Frankfurt: Suhrkamp.

Jorde, Lynn B. and Stephen P. Wooding (2004). "Genetic Variation, Classification, and 'Race.'" *Nature Genetics* 36, S28–S33.

Kant, Immanuel ([1798] 2006). *Anthropology from a Pragmatic Point of View*. Cambridge and New York: Cambridge University Press.

Kass, Leon (1985). *Toward a More Natural Science: Biology and Human Affairs*. New York: Free Press.

Kass, Leon (1997, June 2). "The Wisdom of Repugnance: Why We Should Ban the Cloning of Humans." *The New Republic*, 17–26.

Kass, Leon (2002). *Life, Liberty, and the Defense of Dignity: The Challenge for Bioethics*. San Francisco: Encounter Books.

Kass, Leon (2003). "Ageless Bodies, Happy Souls: Biotechnology and the Pursuit of Perfection." *The New Atlantis* 1, 9–28.

REFERENCES   339

Kass, Leon (2008). "Defending Human Dignity." In A. Schulman (Ed.), *Human Dignity and Bioethics: Essays Commissioned by the President's Council on Bioethics*, pp. 297–331. Washington: US Government Printing Office.

Keller, Evelyn Fox (2010). *The Mirage of a Space between Nature and Nurture*. Durham and London: Duke University Press.

Khalidi, Muhammad Ali (2007). "Innate Cognitive Capacities." *Mind and Language* 22(1), 92–115.

Khalidi, Muhammad Ali (2016). "Innateness as a Cognitive Natural Kind." *Philosophical Psychology* 29(3), 319–33.

Kingma, Elselijn (2010). "Paracetamol, Poison, and Polio: Why Boorse's Account of Function Fails to Distinguish Health and Disease." *British Journal for the Philosophy of Science* 61(2), 241–64.

Kitcher, Philip (1985a). "Darwin's Achievement." In N. Rescher (Ed.), *Reason and Rationality in Natural Science*, pp. 127–89. Lanham: University Press of America.

Kitcher, Philip (1985b). *Vaulting Ambition. Sociobiology and the Quest for Human Nature*. Cambridge: MIT Press.

Kitcher, Philip (1993). *The Advancement of Science*. New York: Oxford University Press.

Kitcher, Philip (2001). *Science, Truth, and Democracy*. New York: Oxford University Press.

Kitcher, Philip ([2001] 2003). "Battling the Undead. How (and How Not) to Resist Genetic Determinism." In *In Mendel's Mirror*, pp. 283–300. New York: Oxford University Press.

Kitcher, Philip (2007). "Does Race Have a Future?" *Philosophy and Public Affairs* 35(4), 293–317.

Kitcher, Philip (2011). *Science in a Democratic Society*. New York: Prometheus Books.

Kitcher, Philip (2023). *What's the Use of Philosophy?*. New York: Oxford University Press.

Koon, Justis (2022). "The Medical Model, with a Human Face." *Philosophical Studies* 179(12), 3747–70.

Kourany, Janet A. (2010). *Philosophy of Science after Feminism*. New York: Oxford University Press.

Kronfeldner, Maria (2018). *What's Left of Human Nature? A Post-Essentialist, Pluralist, and Interactive Account of a Contested Concept*. Cambridge: MIT Press.

Laland, Kevin N. and Gillian R. Brown (2011). *Sense and Nonsense: Evolutionary Perspectives on Human Behavior*. Oxford: Oxford University Press.

Laland, Kevin N. and Gillian R. Brown (2018). "The Social Construction of Human Nature." In E. Hannon and T. Lewens (Eds.), *Why We Disagree about Human Nature*, pp. 127–44. Oxford: Oxford University Press.

Lamarck, Jean-Baptiste ([1809] 1914). *The Zoological Philosophy*. London: Macmillan.

340 REFERENCES

Lee, Patrick and Robert P. George (2008). "The Nature and Basis of Human Dignity." In Edmund D. Pellegrino, Adam Schulman, Thomas W. Merrill (Eds.) *Human Dignity and Bioethics*, pp. 409–33. Washington: US Government Printing Office.

Leslie, Sarah-Jane. (2013). "Essence and Natural Kinds: When Science Meets Pre-Schooler Intuition." In T. Szabo Gendler and J. Hawthorne (Eds.), *Oxford Studies in Epistemology, Vol. 4*, pp. 108–65. Oxford: Oxford University Press.

Levins, Richard and Richard C. Lewontin (1985a). *The Dialectical Biologist*. Cambridge: Harvard University Press.

Levins, Richard and Richard C. Lewontin (1985b). "What Is Human Nature?" In Levins and Lewontin, *The Dialectical Biologist*, pp. 253–65. Cambridge: Harvard University Press.

Levy, Neil (2013). "There May Be Costs to Failing to Enhance, as Well as to Enhancing." *American Journal of Bioethics* 13(7), 38–39.

Lewens, Tim (2012). "Species, Essence, and Explanation." *Studies in History and Philosophy of Biological and Biomedical Sciences* 43, 751–57.

Lewens, Tim (2015a). *The Biological Foundations of Bioethics*. Oxford: Oxford University Press.

Lewens, Tim (2015b). *Cultural Evolution: Conceptual Challenges*. Oxford: Oxford University Press.

Lewens, Tim (2016). *The Meaning of Science: An Introduction to the Philosophy of Science*. New York: Basic Books.

Lewens, Tim (2018). "Introduction: The Faces of Human Nature." In E. Hannon and T. Lewens (Eds.), *Why We Disagree about Human Nature*, pp. 1–17. Oxford: Oxford University Press.

Lewontin, Richard C. (1970). "Units of Selection." *Annual Review of Ecology and Semantics* 1, 1–13.

Lewontin, Richard C. (1972). "The Apportionment of Human Diversity." *Evolutionary Biology* 6, 381–98.

Lewontin, Richard C. (1974). *The Genetic Basis of Evolutionary Change*. New York: Columbia University Press.

Lewontin, Richard C. (1978). "Adaptation." *Scientific American* 239, 213–30.

Lewontin, Richard C. (1979). "Sociobiology as an Adaptationist Program." *Behavioral Sciences* 24, 5–14.

Lewontin, Richard C. (1991). *Biology as Ideology: The Doctrine of DNA*. New York: Harper.

Lewontin, Richard C. (2000). *The Triple Helix: Gene, Organism, and Environment*. Cambridge: Harvard University Press.

Lewontin, Richard C., Steven Rose, and Leon J. Lamin (1984). *Not in Our Genes: Biology, Ideology, and Human Nature*. New York: Pantheon.

Linquist, Stefan (2018). "The Conceptual Critique of Innateness." *Philosophy Compass* 13(5), e12492.

REFERENCES 341

Lloyd, Genevieve (1984). *The Man of Reason: 'Male' and 'Female' in Western Philosophy*. Minneapolis: University of Minnesota Press.

Longino, Helen E. (1990). *Science as Social Knowledge: Values and Objectivity in Scientific Inquiry*. Princeton: Princeton University Press.

Lopson, Peter (2006). *Theories of Human Nature* (3rd ed.). Peterborough: Broadview.

Lumsden, Charles J. and Edward O. Wilson ([1981] 2005). *Genes, Mind, and Culture: The Co-Evolutionary Process* (25th Anniversary ed.). Singapore: World Scientific Publishing.

Machery, Edouard (2008). "A Plea for Human Nature." *Philosophical Psychology* 21, 321–30.

Machery, Edouard (2012). "Reconceptualizing Human Nature: Response to Lewens." *Philosophy and Technology* 25(4), 475–78.

Machery, Edouard (2017). *Philosophy within Its Proper Bounds*. Oxford: Oxford University Press.

Machery, Edouard (2018). "Doubling Down on the Nomological Notion of Human Nature." In E. Hannon and T. Lewens (Eds.), *Why We Disagree about Human Nature*, pp. 18–39. Oxford: Oxford University Press.

Machery, Edouard and H. Clark Barrett (2006). "Debunking *Adaptive Minds*." *Philosophy of Science* 73, 232–46.

MacKinnon, Catharine A. (1989). *Toward a Feminist Theory of the State*. Cambridge: Harvard University Press.

Mahowald, Mary B. (Ed.) (1994). *Philosophy of Woman* (3rd ed.). Indianapolis: Hackett.

Mallon, Ron (2003). "Social Construction, Roles, and Stability." In F. F. Schmitt (Ed.), *Socializing Metaphysics: The Nature of Social Reality*, pp. 327–53. Lanham: Rowman and Littlefield.

Mallon, Ron and Jonathan M. Weinberg (2006). "Innateness as Closed Process Invariance." *Philosophy of Science* 73, 323–44.

Malthus, Thomas R. (1798). *An Essay on the Principle of Population, as It Affects the Future Improvement of Society*. London: Murray.

Mameli, Matteo (2008a). "On Innateness: The Clutter Hypothesis and the Cluster Hypothesis." *Journal of Philosophy* 105(12), 719–36.

Mameli, Matteo (2008b). "Sociobiology, Evolutionary Psychology, and Cultural Evolution." In M. Ruse (Ed.), *The Oxford Handbook of Philosophy of Biology*, pp. 410–33. New York: Oxford University Press.

Mameli, Matteo and Patrick Bateson (2011). "An Evaluation of the Concept of Innateness." *Philosophical Transactions of the Royal Society of London*, B 366, 436–43.

Marecek, Jeanne (1995). "Psychology and Feminism: Can This Relationship Be Saved?" In D. C. Stanton and A. J. Stewart (Eds.), *Feminisms in the Academy*, pp. 102–32. Ann Arbor: University of Michigan Press.

Marx, Karl (1867). *Das Kapital: Kritik der Politischen Ökonomie*. Hamburg: Verlag von Otto Meisner.

342 REFERENCES

May, Joshua (2016). "Repugnance as Performance Error." In S. Clarke, J. Savulescu, C. Coady, A. Giubilini, and S. Sanyal (Eds.), *The Ethics of Human Enhancement: Understanding the Debate*, pp. 43–57. Oxford: Oxford University Press.

Maynard Smith, John (2000). "The Concept of Information in Biology." *Philosophy of Science* 67, 177–94.

Mayr, Ernst (1959). "Typological versus Population Thinking." In *Evolution and Anthropology: A Centennial Appraisal*, pp. 409–12. Washington: The Anthropological Society of Washington.

Mayr, Ernst (1982). *The Growth of Biological Thought*. Cambridge and London: Belknap Harvard.

Mayr, Ernst (1983). "How to Carry Out the Adaptationist Program?" *American Naturalist* 121, 324–33.

McConnell, Doug and Jeanette Kennett (2016). "Reasons, Reflection, and Repugnance." In S. Clarke, J. Savulescu, C. Coady, A. Giubilini, and S. Sanyal (Eds.), *The Ethics of Human Enhancement: Understanding the Debate*, pp. 58–74. Oxford: Oxford University Press.

McKibben, Bill (2003). *Enough: Staying Human in an Engineered Age*. New York: Henry Holt.

McLaughlin, Peter (2001). *What Functions Explain: Functional Explanation and Self-Reproducing Systems*. Cambridge: Cambridge University Press.

McSwiggan, Sally, Bernice Elger, and Paul S. Appelbaum (2017). "The Forensic Use of Behavioral Genetics in Criminal Proceedings: Case of the MAOA-L Genotype." *International Journal of Law Psychiatry* 50, 17–23.

Mehlman, Maxwell J. (2003). *Wondergenes: Genetic Enhancement and the Future of Society*. Bloomington: Indiana University Press.

Mehlman, Maxwell J. and Jeffrey R. Botkin (1998). *Access to the Genome: The Challenge to Equality*. Washington: Georgetown University Press.

Mikkola, Mari (2016). *The Wrong of Injustice: Dehumanization and Its Role in Feminist Philosophy*. Oxford: Oxford University Press.

Mill, John Stuart ([1869] 1989). *The Subjection of Women*. In S. Collini (Ed.), *On Liberty and Other Writings*, pp. 1–116. Cambridge: Cambridge University Press.

Millikan, Ruth G. (1984). *Language, Thought, and Other Biological Categories*. Cambridge: Bradford, MIT Press.

Millikan, Ruth. G. (1989). "In Defense of Proper Functions." *Philosophy of Science* 56, 288–302.

Mills, Charles. W. (1997). *The Racial Contract*. Ithaca: Cornell University Press.

Mills, Charles W. (1998). *Blackness Visible*. Ithaca: Cornell University Press.

Nanay, Bence (2010). "A Modal Theory of Function." *Journal of Philosophy* 107, 412–31.

Nathan, Marco J. (2012). "The Varieties of Molecular Explanation." *Philosophy of Science* 79(2), 233–54.

REFERENCES   343

Nathan, Marco J. (2021). *Black Boxes: How Science Turns Ignorance into Knowledge*. New York: Oxford University Press.

Nathan, Marco J. and Jeffrey M. Brown (2018). "An Ecological Approach to Modeling Disability." *Bioethics* 32, 593–601.

Nathan, Marco J. and Joel Cracraft (2020). "The Nature of Species in Evolution." In S. M. Scheiner and D. P. Mindell (Eds.), *The Theory of Evolution*, pp. 102–22. Chicago: University of Chicago Press.

Neander, Karen (1991). "Functions as Selected Effects: The Conceptual Analyst's Defense." *Philosophy of Science* 58, 168–84.

Nielsen, L. Witthøft (2011). "The Concept of Nature and the Enhancement Technologies Debate." In J. Savulescu, R. ter Meulen, and G. Kahane (Eds.), *Enhancing Human Capacities*, pp. 19–33. Chichester: Wiley-Blackwell.

Niezen, Ronald (2003). *The Origins of Indigenism: Human Rights and the Politics of Identity*. Berkeley and Los Angeles: University of California Press.

Noddings, N. (1984). *Caring: A Feminine Approach to Ethics and Moral Education*. Berkeley and Los Angeles: University of California Press.

Northcott, Robert and Gualtiero Piccinini (2018). "Conceived This Way: Innateness Defended." *Philosophers' Imprint* 18(18), 1–16.

Nozick, Robert (1974). *Anarchy, State, and Utopia*. New York: Basic Books.

Nurse, Paul (2020). *What Is Life? Five Great Ideas in Biology*. New York: Norton.

Nussbaum, Martha C. (1995). "Human Capabilities, Female Human Beings." In M. Nussbaum and J. Glover (Eds.), *Women and Human Development: A Study of Capabilities*, pp. 61–104. Oxford: Oxford University Press.

Nussbaum, Martha C. (2000). "Aristotle, Politics, and Human Capabilities." *Ethics* 111, 102–40.

Odling-Smee, F. John, Kevin N. Laland, and Marcus W. Feldman (2003). *Niche Construction: The Neglected Process in Evolution*. Princeton: Princeton University Press.

O'Hagan, Timothy (1999). *Rousseau*. London and New York: Routledge.

Omi, Michael and Howard Winant (1994). *Racial Formation in the United States*. New York: Routledge.

Oyama, Susan (2000). *The Ontogeny of Information* (2nd ed.). Durham: Duke University Press.

Oyama, Susan, Paul E. Griffiths, and Russell D. Gray (Eds.) (2001a). *Cycles of Contingency. Developmental Systems and Evolution*. Cambridge: Bradford, MIT Press.

Oyama, Susan, Paul E. Griffiths, and Russell D. Gray (2001b). "What Is Developmental Systems Theory?" In S. Oyama, P. E. Griffiths, and R. D. Gray (Eds.), *Cycles of Contingency. Developmental Systems and Evolution*, pp. 1–11. Cambridge: Bradford, MIT Press.

Persson, Ingmar and Julian Savulescu (2012). *Unfit for the Future: The Need for Moral Enhancement*. Oxford: Oxford University Press.

Peters, Ted (2002). *Playing God? Genetic Determinism and Human Freedom*. New York: Routledge.

344 REFERENCES

Piantadosi, Steven T. (2023). "Modern Language Models Refute Chomsky's Approach to Language." lingbuzz.net.

Pinker, Steven (2002). *The Blank Slate: The Modern Denial of Human Nature.* New York: Viking.

Pinker, Steven (2008, May 8). "The Stupidity of Dignity." *The New Republic.*

Pinker, Steven (2018). *Enlightenment Now: The Case for Reason, Science, Humanism, and Progress.* New York: Viking.

Plomin, Robert (2018). *Blueprint: How DNA Makes Us Who We Are.* Cambridge: MIT Press.

Pojman, Louis P. (2006). *Who Are We? Theories of Human Nature.* New York: Oxford University Press.

Polderman, Tinca J., Benyamin Beben, Christiaan A. de Leeuw, Patrick F. Sullivan, Arjen van Bochoven, Peter M. Visscher, and Danielle Posthuma (2015). "Meta-Analysis of the Heritability of Human Traits Based on Fifty Years of Twin Studies." *Nature Genetics* 47(7), 702–9.

Powell, Russell and Allen Buchanan (2011). "Breaking Evolution's Chains: The Promise of Enhancement by Design." In J. Savulescu, R. ter Meulen, and G. Kahane (Eds.), *Enhancing Human Capacities*, pp. 49–67. Chichester: Wiley-Blackwell.

Preston, Beth (2013). *A Philosophy of Material Culture: Action, Function, and Mind.* New York: Routledge.

Prinz, Jesse J. (2012). *Beyond Human Nature: How Culture and Experience Shape the Human Mind.* New York: Norton.

Putnam, Hilary (1975). "The Meaning of Meaning." In *Mind, Language, and Reality*, pp. 215–71. Cambridge: Cambridge University Press.

Ramsey, Grant (2013). "Human Nature in a Post-Essentialist World." *Philosophy of Science* 80, 983–93.

Ramsey, Grant (2018). "Trait Bin and Trait Cluster Accounts of Human Nature." In E. Hannon and T. Lewens (Eds.), *Why We Disagree about Human Nature*, pp. 40–57. Oxford: Oxford University Press.

Ramsey, Grant (2023). *Human Nature.* Cambridge: Cambridge University Press.

Rawls, John (1971). *A Theory of Justice.* Cambridge: Harvard University Press.

Raz, Joseph (1986). *The Morality of Freedom.* Oxford: Oxford University Press.

Reich, David (2018). *Who We Are and How We Got Here.* Oxford: Oxford University Press.

Reid, Vincent M., Kirsty Dunn, Robert J. Young, Johnson Amu, Tim Donovan, and Nadja Reissland (2017). "The Human Fetus Preferentially Engages with Face-Like Visual Stimuli." *Current Biology* 28(5), 824.

Rich, Adrienne (1976). *Of Woman Born: Motherhood as Experience and Institution.* New York: Norton.

Richerson, Peter J. (2018). "The Use and Non-Use of the Human Nature Concept by Evolutionary Biologists." In E. Hannon and T. Lewens (Eds.),

REFERENCES   345

Why We Disagree about Human Nature, pp. 145–69. Oxford: Oxford University Press.

Richerson, Peter J. and Robert Boyd (2005). *Not by Genes Alone: How Culture Transformed Human Evolution*. Chicago: Chicago University Press.

Ridley, Matt (2003). *Nature via Nurture: Genes, Experience, and What Makes Us Human*. New York: Harper Collins.

Rosenberg, Noah A., Jonathan K. Pritchard, James L. Weber, Howard M. Cann, Kenneth K. Kidd, Lev A. Zhivotovsky, and Marcus W. Feldman (2002). "Genetic Structure of Human Populations." *Science* 298, 2881–85.

Ruddick, Sara (1989). *Material Thinking: Towards a Politics of Peace.* Boston: Beacon Press.

Rushton, J. Philippe and Arthur R. Jensen (2005). "Thirty Years of Research of Race: Differences in Cognitive Ability." *Psychology, Public Policy, and Law* 11(2), 235–94.

Sahlins, Marshall (2008). *The Western Illusion of Human Nature.* Chicago: Prickly Paradigm Press.

Samuels, Richard (2002). "Nativism in Cognitive Science." *Mind and Language* 17(3), 233–65.

Samuels, Richard (2004). "Innateness in Cognitive Science." *Trends in Cognitive Sciences* 8(3), 136–41.

Samuels, Richard (2012). "Science and Human Nature." *Royal Institute of Philosophy Supplement* 70, 1–28.

Sandel, Michael J. (2007). *The Case against Perfection: Ethics in the Age of Genetic Engineering.* Cambridge: Harvard University Press.

Savulescu, Julian and Nick Bostrom (Eds.) (2009). *Human Enhancement.* Oxford: Oxford University Press.

Savulescu, Julian, Anders Sandberg, and Guy Kahane (2011). "Well-Being and Enhancement." In J. Savulescu, R. ter Meulen, and G. Kahane (Eds.), *Enhancing Human Capacities*, pp. 3–18. Chichester: Wiley-Blackwell.

Savulescu, Julian, Ruud ter Meulen, and Guy Kahane (Eds.) (2011). *Enhancing Human Capacities.* Chichester: Wiley-Blackwell.

Schiebinger, Londa (1989). *The Mind Has No Sex?* Cambridge: Harvard University Press.

Schlosser, Gerhard (1998). "Self-re-Reproduction and Functionality." *Synthese* 116, 303–54.

Schwartz, Peter H. (2007). "Defining Dysfunction: Natural Selection, Design, and Drawing a Line." *Philosophy of Science* 74(3), 364–85.

Segato, Rita L. and Pedro Monque (2021). "Gender and Coloniality: From Low-Intensity Communal Patriarchy to High-Intensity Colonial-Modern Patriarchy." *Hypatia* 36(4), 781–99.

Selgelid, Michael J. (2014). "Moderate Eugenics and Human Enhancement." *Medicine, Health Care, and Philosophy* 17(1), 3–12.

Sen, Amartya K. (1980). *Equality of What?, Vol. 1.* Cambridge: Cambridge University Press.

346 REFERENCES

Shae, Nicholas (2013). "Inherited Representations Are Read in Development." *British Journal for the Philosophy of Science* 64, 1–31.

Silvers, Anita (1998). "Formal Justice." In A. Silvers, D. Wasserman, and M. B. Mahowald (Eds.), *Disability, Difference, Discrimination: Perspectives on Justice in Bioethics and Public Policy*, pp. 13–146. Lanham: Rowman and Littlefield.

Simpson, George G. (1969). *Biology and Man*. New York: Harcourt.

Slater, Matthew H. (2013). *Are Species Real? An Essay on the Metaphysics of Species*. New York: Palgrave Macmillan.

Smith, Adam ([1776] 2000). *An Inquiry into the Nature and Causes of the Wealth of Nations*. New York: Random House.

Smith, David L. (2011). *Less Than Human: Why We Demean, Enslave, and Exterminate Others*. New York: St. Martin's Press.

Smith, Eric A. and Bruce Winterhalder (1992). *Evolutionary Ecology and Human Behavior*. New York: De Gruyter.

Smith, Subrena E. (2019). "Is Evolutionary Psychology Possible?" *Biological Theory* 15(1), 39–49.

Sober, Elliott (1980). "Evolution, Population Thinking, and Essentialism." *Philosophy of Science* 47, 350–83.

Sober, Elliott (1999). "Innate Knowledge." In E. Craig (Ed.), *Routledge Encyclopedia of Philosophy*, vol. 4, pp. 794–97. New York: Routledge.

Sober, Elliott (2000). *Philosophy of Biology* (2nd ed.). Boulder: Westview.

Sober, Elliott and David S. Wilson (1988). *Unto Others: The Evolution and Psychology of Unselfish Behavior*. Cambridge: Harvard University Press.

Spelke, Elizabeth S. and Katherine D. Kinzler (2007). "Core Knowledge." *Developmental Science* 10(1), 89–96.

Spencer, Quayshawn (2004). "A Radical Solution to the Race Problem." *Philosophy of Science* 81(5), 1025–38.

Spencer, Quayshawn (2019). "How to Be a Biological Racial Realist." In J. Glasgow, S. Haslanger, C. Jeffers, and Q. Spencer (Eds.), *What Is Race? Four Philosophical Views*, pp. 73–110. New York: Oxford University Press.

Sperber, Dan (1996). *Explaining Culture: A Naturalistic Approach*. Oxford: Blackwell.

Sterelny, Kim (2012). *The Evolved Apprentice: How Evolution Made Humans Unique*. Cambridge: Bradford, MIT Press.

Sterelny, Kim (2018). "Sceptical Reflections on Human Nature." In E. Hannon and T. Lewens (Eds.), *Why We Disagree about Human Nature*, pp. 108–26. Oxford: Oxford University Press.

Stevenson, Leslie, David L. Haberman, and Peter M. Wright (2013). *Twelve Theories of Human Nature*. New York: Oxford University Press.

Stiglitz, Joseph E. (2012). *The Price of Inequality. How Today's Divided Society Endangers Our Future*. New York: Norton.

REFERENCES 347

Stone, Sandy. (1991). "The *Empire* Strikes Back: A Postranssexual Manifesto." In J. Epstein and K. Straub (Eds.), *Body Guards: The Cultural Politics of Gender Ambiguity*, pp. 280–304. New York: Routledge.

Strevens, Michael (2019). *Thinking Off Your Feet: How Empirical Psychology Vindicates Armchair Philosophy*. Cambridge and London: Belknap Harvard.

Sundstrom, Ronald R. (2002). "Race as a Human Kind." *Philosophy and Social Criticism* 28(1), 1025–38.

Symons, Donald (1979). *The Evolution of Human Sexuality*. New York: Oxford University Press.

Systma, Justin and Jonathan Livengood (2016). *The Theory and Practice of Experimental Philosophy*. Peterborough: Broadview.

Tabery, James (2014). *Beyond Versus: The Struggle to Understand the Interaction of Nature and Nurture*. Cambridge: MIT Press.

Taylor, Paul C. (2004). *Race: A Philosophical Introduction*. Cambridge: Polity Press.

Thompson, Michael (2008). *Life and Action: Elementary Structures of Practice and Practical Thought*. Cambridge: Harvard University Press.

Tomasello, Michael (2019). *Becoming Human: A Theory of Ontogeny*. Cambridge and London: Belknap Harvard.

Tomasello, Michael (2022). *The Evolution of Agency: Behavioral Organization from Lizards to Humans*. Cambridge: MIT Press.

Tooby, John and Leda Cosmides (1992). "The Psychological Foundation of Culture." In J. H. Barkow, L. Cosmides, and J. Tooby (Eds.), *The Adapted Mind: Evolutionary Psychology and the Evolution of Culture*, pp. 19–136. New York: Oxford University Press.

Trivers, Robert L. (1971). "The Evolution of Reciprocal Altruism." *Quarterly Review of Biology* 46, 35–57.

Trivers, Robert L. (1972). "Parental Investment and Sexual Selection." In B. Campbell (Ed.), *Sexual Selection and the Descent of Man: 1871–1971*, pp. 136–79. Chicago: Aldine.

Trivers, Robert L. (1974). "Parent-Offspring Conflict." *American Zoologist* 14, 249–64.

Turkheimer, Eric (2000). "Three Laws of Behavior Genetics and What They Mean." *Current Directions in Psychological Science* 9(5), 160–64.

Wakefield, Jerome C. (1992). "The Concept of Mental Disorder: On the Boundary between Biological Facts and Social Values." *American Psychologist* 47, 373–88.

Wason, Peter C. (1966). "Reasoning." In B. M. Foss (Ed.), *New Horizons in Psychology*, vol. 1, pp. 135–51. Harmondsworth: Penguin.

Waters, C. Kenneth. (2007). "Causes That Make a Difference." *Journal of Philosophy* 104(11), 551–79.

Webb, Alexandra R., Howard T. Heller, Carol B. Benson, and Amir Lahav (2015). "Mother's Voice and Heartbeat Sounds Elicit Auditory Plasticity in the Human Brain before Full Gestation." *PNAS* 112(10), 3152–57.

348 REFERENCES

Weber, Marcel (2005). *Philosophy of Experimental Biology*. Cambridge: Cambridge University Press.

Weckert, John (2016). "Playing God: What Is the Problem?" In S. Clarke, J. Savulescu, C. Coady, A. Giubilini, and S. Sanyal (Eds.), *The Ethics of Human Enhancement: Understanding the Debate*, pp. 87–99. Oxford: Oxford University Press.

West-Eberhard, Mary Jane (2003). *Developmental Plasticity and Evolution*. New York: Oxford University Press.

Wilkinson, Sue (1997). "Still Selling Transformation: Feminist Challenges to Psychology." In L. Stanley (Ed.), *Knowing Feminisms: On Academic Borders, Territories, and Tribes*, pp. 97–108. London: Sage.

Williams, Bernard (1985). *Ethics and the Limits of Philosophy*. Cambridge: Harvard University Press.

Williams, George C. (1966). *Adaptation and Natural Selection*. Princeton: Princeton University Press.

Wilson, Edward O. (1975). *Sociobiology: The New Synthesis*. Cambridge: Harvard University Press.

Wilson, Edward O. ([1978] 2004). *On Human Nature* (2nd ed). Cambridge: Harvard University Press.

Wilson, Margo and Martin Daly (1992). "The Man Who Mistook His Wife for a Chattel." In J. H. Barkow, L. Cosmides, and J. Tooby (Eds.), *The Adapted Mind*, pp. 289–322. New York: Oxford University Press.

Wimsatt, William C. (1999). "Generativity, Entrenchment, Innateness, and Evolution." In V. G. Hardcastle (Ed.), *Where Biology Meets Psychology: Philosophical Essays*, pp. 137–79. Cambridge: MIT Press.

Wollstonecraft, Mary ([1792] 1975). *A Vindication of the Rights of Women*. London: Penguin.

Woltereck, Richard (1909). "Weitere experimentelle Untersuchungen über Artveränderung, speziel über das Wesen quantitativer Artunterschiede bei Daphniden." *Verhandlungen der deutschen zoologischen Gesellschaft* 19, 110–73.

Woodward, James (2010). "Causation in Biology: Stability, Specificity, and the Choice of Levels of Explanation." *Biology and Philosophy* 25, 287–318.

Wright, Larry (1973). "Functions." *Philosophical Review* 82, 139–68.

Young, Iris M. (1990). *Justice and the Politics of Difference*. Princeton: Princeton University Press.

Zerilli, John (2019). "Neural Reuse and the Modularity of Mind: Where to Next for Modularity?" *Biological Theory* 14(1), 1–20.

Index

For the benefit of digital users, indexed terms that span two pages (e.g., 52–53) may, on occasion, appear on only one of those pages.

acquisition, 102–3, 107–8, 124, 307
adaptation, 27–28, 31–32, 37–38, 42, 47, 49–50, 54–57, 59, 62, 64–65, 65n.2, 72–74, 96–97, 109, 149, 239
adaptationism, 37–38, 54–57, 59, 62, 96–97, 149
Adorno, Theodor, 218–19
Aeschylus, 293–94
allele. *See* genetics
altruism, problem of, 28, 31–32, 98
amino acids, 132–33
Amundson, Ron, 246–53, 255–56, 263
ancestry, 10, 15–16, 90–91, 113–14, 167–68, 170, 179n.9, 180–83, 187–88, 189, 192n.18, 195–97, 201, 228–29
Annas, George J., 287–88
anthropology, 8–9, 19, 61–62
Antony, Louise, 203–6, 218–19, 223, 230–31
Aquinas, Thomas, 21
Aristotle, 7–8, 19, 21, 57–58, 76, 177–78, 194, 202–4, 205, 207, 215–16, 219–20, 221–22, 295
artificial intelligence, 49, 271
atomic number, 65–66, 178
atomic structure. *See* atomic number
Augustine, 21, 57–58

Baldwin, James M., 30, 44
Bamshad, Michael J., 181–83
Baron–Cohen, Simon, 216–17
Bateson, Patrick, 107n.8, 110n.10, 146–49, 163–64, 249n.5
behavior, 6–7, 9, 22, 28, 30–59, 61–65, 70, 85–86, 91–92, 105, 109, 114–15,

118–21, 128, 130, 132–37, 142–54, 157–62, 167–68, 170–71, 195, 202, 225, 233–34, 248, 301, 304, 307–8, 316, 327–28
animal behavior studies, 31, 62, 115, 119
behavior genetics, 109, 142–50, 156–57, 161–62, 168–69
totality of human behavior, 63–64
behavioral ecology. *See* ecology: human behavioral ecology
bell hooks, 231n.14
Bernard, Claude, 240
BiDil, 169
bioconservatism, 17–18, 267–72, 275, 280–81, 286–89, 290–91, 293–94, 296–97, 326
bioliberalism, 17–18, 267–71, 272, 280–82, 285–89, 290–91, 293–94, 296–97, 298, 326
biological function. *See* function
biological species. *See* species
biostatistical theory of health, 240–46, 247–48, 253, 255–56
biotechnology, 17–18, 266–71, 272–75, 278–79, 287–88, 291, 292–93
bipedalism, 85, 147–48, 248–50
black box, 29–30, 318
blank slate, 6–7, 55–56, 58, 100, 118, 125
blending inheritance, 26–27, 28–29
Blumenbach, Johann F., 167–68
Bolnick, Deborah, 179–83, 183n.13
Boorse, Christopher, 237–48, 253, 261–63, 274
Bostrom, Nick, 268–69, 286–91

350 INDEX

Bouchard, Thomas J. Jr., 142–43, 146, 157–58
Boyd, Robert, 45, 59–60, 64n.1
Brock, Dan W., 251–52
Brown, Jeffrey M., 253–62
Buchanan, Allen E., 276n.8, 276n.9, 282n.12, 287n.14
Buffon, Georges L., 167–68
Buller, David J., 51n.20, 53–54, 64–65, 72–74, 81n.12, 82–83, 243n.2
Buss, David M., 24n.2, 32, 38n.13, 45–48, 53–54, 57–60
byproduct. *See* spandrel

Campbell, Anne, 45n.16, 55
capabilities. *See* human capabilities approach
capitalism. *See* economics
catastrophism, 23–24
causal mechanism. *See* mechanism
causal parity thesis, 152–54
Chodorow, Nancy, 212n.7
Chomsky, Noam, 2–7, 11–12, 15, 21, 62–63, 92–93, 94, 128–29, 164, 165, 228–29, 230–31, 294, 298–303, 306–9, 316, 321–22
clade. *See* cladistics
cladistics, 171, 172, 184
cloning, 78–79, 157–58, 271, 287–88
cognitive mechanism. *See* mechanism
common ancestry. *See* ancestry
conceptual vs. empirical questions, 99–102
constructionism, 15–16, 115, 166, 177, 184, 185–90, 197, 200–1, 207–8, 217–19, 247
core knowledge, 13–14, 99, 117–25, 126–27, 197, 233–34, 301–2, 319, 323
Cornaro Piscopia, Elena Lucrezia 204–5
Cosmides, Leda, 45–46, 48n.19, 49, 55n.24, 59–60, 72n.7
Cowie, Fiona, 107–8
creationism 10, 27
cultural evolution. *See* culture
culture, 3–4, 5, 9, 10–11, 19, 22–23, 33–35, 38–39, 41, 42, 44–46, 54–56, 58–59, 61–62, 64–65, 84n.13, 86, 88, 90, 94, 98, 99, 110–11, 114–15, 119–22, 128, 150, 158, 173–74,

186, 188–89, 195, 196, 197, 200–1, 211n.6, 212–13, 216–18, 220–21, 276, 287, 318–19, 323–24
Cummins, Robert, 242
Cuvier, Georges, 23–24, 167–68

Daly, Martin, 38n.13, 57n.26
Daly, Mary, 217
Daniels, Norman, 241n.1, 250, 251n.6
Darwin, Charles, 9–12, 19, 21–30, 32, 37, 38–40, 43–46, 57–58, 59, 61–62, 70, 74, 91–92, 100, 112–14, 118, 170–71, 328
Darwin, Erasmus, 25–26
Darwinian anthropology, 10–11, 12, 40, 43–44, 59, 62
Darwinism, 26, 30, 61–62, 74, 88–89, 112, 113, 233–34, 239
Davidson, Donald, 310–11n.7
Dawkins, Richard, 27n.5, 31–32, 153n.15, 250
de Beauvoir, Simone, 210–11, 212, 215–16
dehumanization, 17–18, 75, 84, 88–89, 92, 199, 222, 231–32, 268–70, 284–87, 307–8, 319–20, 324–25
Democritus, 177–78
Descartes, René, 7–8, 21, 100, 103–4, 151, 207
design, 27, 37, 47, 48, 49, 72, 80, 82, 110, 124–25, 241, 242–43, 244, 248–50
development. *See* developmental processes
developmental processes, 36, 37, 58–59, 75–77, 82–83, 88, 100–1, 103–4, 105–6, 108–9, 110, 111–12, 113, 115, 120–21, 122–24, 128, 136–38, 149, 150, 152, 154, 156, 158–59, 162–63, 248–49, 258–59, 305, 323–24
developmental fixity, 110, 111–12, 115, 323
developmental noise, 37, 152, 154
developmental plasticity, 77–78, 82, 84–85, 248–49
developmental psychology, 13–14, 99, 108, 109
developmentalism, 14, 88–89, 130, 134–35, 137–38, 149–54, 156, 159, 160, 161, 162–63, 258–59
normal development (*see* normality)
developmental systems (*see* developmentalism)

INDEX 351

Dickens, Charles, 21
dignity. *See* human dignity
Dinnerstein, Dorothy, 212n.7
disability, 16–17, 227–28, 234–35, 239,
    250–51, 253–62, 263–64, 274, 282,
    292, 294, 297, 298
  disability paradox, 251–52
  ecological approach to, 258–62
  interactionist model of, 256–58, 259–60
  medical model of, 254–55, 259–60
  social model of, 255–56, 259–60
discrimination, 15–16, 75, 94, 150, 195,
    197–98, 200–2, 204, 205–6, 213, 217,
    220–21, 223–25, 228, 233–34, 246,
    256, 259–60, 263–64, 286–89, 291,
    324–25
disease, 79, 114–15, 139–40, 142, 170,
    235–41, 244–45, 262–64, 266–67,
    270–71, 273, 274, 284, 286–87,
    296–97, 305–6
  Huntington's Disease (HD), 139–40,
    142, 143–44, 149–50, 238, 323–24
  Tay-Sachs disease, 261
DNA, 68–69, 98, 101, 105, 128, 131–35,
    140–41, 160, 162–64, 170, 172–73,
    180–81, 190
  forensic applications of, 170
Dobzhansky, Theodosius, 132, 136–37
doping, 277–79
dualism. *See* Descartes
Du Bois, W.E.B., 19, 165, 188, 295
Dunedin Multidisciplinary Health and
    Development Study, 159n.19
Dupré, John, 29n.7, 51n.20, 53–57

ecological niche. *See* niche
ecology, 22, 32–33, 36, 175, 235, 258–62,
    263
  human behavioral ecology, 10–11, 12,
    22–23, 28, 30n.11, 31, 32, 43–44,
    45–46, 48–50, 59, 62, 125
economics, 2, 5–7, 77, 108–9, 131, 135,
    163, 185–86, 209–10, 212–13, 223,
    227, 228–29
ecosystem, 260, 261–62
Edwards, Anthony W.F., 180
Elton, Charles S., 260
empirical vs. conceptual questions,
    99–102

empiricism, 19, 100, 118, 124–25, 126
Engels, Friedrich, 209–10
enhancement, 17–18, 265, 267–70,
    272–75, 276–82, 285–86, 287–89,
    293–94, 297, 326
enhancer. *See* enhancement
environment, 14, 24, 26, 27, 33–35, 36, 43,
    44, 49, 51–53, 64–65, 73, 75, 77–83,
    98, 103–12, 115, 122, 132, 134–64,
    207, 209–10, 212–13, 214–15,
    229–30, 239, 241, 245, 250, 254–63,
    280, 316, 323–24
  environment of evolutionary
    adaptedness (EEA), 52–53, 81–82
  environmental determinism, 55–56
  environmentalism (*see* environmental
    determinism)
  normal environment (*see* natural
    environment)
  natural (normal) environment, 81–83,
    161, 254–55
epigenetics, 26
epistemological indicator, 18, 232, 298,
    302–21, 322–28
essence. *See* essentialism
essentialism, 12–13, 19, 63–70, 75–95,
    96–97, 110–15, 128–29, 178–79,
    180–81, 185, 188, 190, 196–97, 202–
    3, 207–9, 212, 213, 214–17–, 218–19,
    220–21, 228, 229, 233–34, 250,
    295–96, 301, 314–15, 322–23, 325
  causal essence, 76
  folk essentialism, 112–15
ethnicity, 15–16, 75, 118–19, 122–24, 169,
    172–73, 176–77, 191, 202, 212–13,
    223–24
ethnobiology, 171
ethology, 22, 30–31, 32–33, 36
evolution by natural selection, 6, 9–12,
    19, 21–60, 61–62, 64n.1, 69–71, 72,
    73–74, 81–82, 84, 85–86, 87–90,
    91–92, 93, 96–97, 108–9, 110, 111,
    113–14, 115, 118, 128, 147–48,
    154, 158–59, 162, 167–68, 170–72,
    179–80, 183, 192–93, 229, 233–34,
    242, 244, 292–93, 310, 312, 314–15,
    316–17, 318–19, 322–23
  evolutionary advantage, 36, 38–39, 48,
    50, 52–53

352 INDEX

evolution by natural selection (*cont.*)
  evolutionary explanation 10, 22–23,
    36–38, 40, 45–46, 50, 54, 55, 61–62,
    81–82, 118–19, 158–59, 310, 314–15,
    316–17, 318–19
  gene-eye view of evolution, 31–32
  natural selection vs. artificial selection, 79
  objections to evolution, 26–28
evolutionary biology. *See* evolution by
  natural selection
evolutionary psychology, 12, 22–23,
    30n.11, 40, 45–60, 62, 65n.2, 73, 74,
    83, 84, 93–94, 118, 122–23, 124–25,
    128, 158, 295–96, 322
evolved psychological mechanism. *See*
  mechanism
existentialism, 212, 215–16

feminism, 16, 187n.16, 200–32, 265, 298
  cultural feminism, 216–17, 218,
    220–21
  feminist humanism, 220–27
  liberal feminism, 206–9, 210, 211,
    213–14, 230
  Marxist feminism, 206, 208–14, 215
  radical feminism, 206, 210–14
  socialist feminism, 212, 213
field guide conception of human nature,
    12–13, 62–63, 74, 83–89, 93–95,
    96–97, 128–29, 295–96, 301–2,
    322–23
Firestone, Shulamith, 211n.6
fitness, 25–26, 29–30, 31–49, 81–82, 239,
    244, 310, 312
  classical vs. inclusive, 31–32
Flax, Jane, 212n.7
folk biology, 85, 112–15, 126
folk essentialism. *See* essentialism
folk physics, 99–100, 312
folk race. *See* race
Foucault, Michel, 18, 298–309, 313–18,
    325–26
Fox, Robin, 34–35
Freud, Sigmund, 295, 306
Friedman, Milton, 5n.3
Fukuyama, Francis, 276n.8, 289, 291
function, 52–53, 73, 76–82, 118, 216–17,
    221–22, 236–37, 240–53

causal-role function, 240–46
etiological function, 80–82, 242, 261,
    263
functional design, 37, 241, 244
functional determinism, 246–53
  level vs. mode of, 246–47, 248–51
  normal function, 16–17, 92–93, 94,
    110, 212, 234–35, 240–53, 262–65,
    267, 294, 296–97

Galen, 240
Galilei, Galileo, 77
Galton, Francis, 100
gametes, 39–40
gender, 16, 41, 92–93, 118–19, 122–23,
    166, 187n.16, 199, 200–32, 233,
    252–53, 294, 296–97, 324–25
gene-eye view. *See* evolution by natural
  selection
gene. *See* genetics
genetics, 12, 19, 22, 26–27, 28–29, 31–36,
    40, 43, 45, 47, 50, 52–53, 54, 58–59,
    60, 61–62, 64n.1, 68–69, 71–72, 75,
    77–78, 82–83, 84, 89–90, 96–97, 98,
    101–2, 105, 106, 108–9, 110, 128–64,
    168–69, 179, 185, 190, 191–93, 195–
    96, 198, 233, 248, 261, 266–67, 273–
    74, 287–88, 289–90, 292–93, 297,
    301–2, 310, 312, 316–17, 318–19
  allele, 83, 111n.11, 133–34, 138, 139–
    40, 153–54, 159n.19, 175
  genetic code (*see* DNA)
  genetic determinism, 13–14, 22, 34–35,
    47, 95, 96–97, 102, 104, 105, 108,
    117, 126, 127, 128–64, 165, 230–31,
    233, 258–59, 272, 290, 295–96,
    301–2, 314–15, 323–24
  genetic diversity (*see* genetic variation)
  genetic drift, 29, 81–82
  genetic engineering, 266–67, 278, 279–80
  genetic profiling, 271
  genetic variation, 15–16, 70, 106, 116,
    166, 169, 170–77, 178, 179–84,
    196–97, 233–34, 324–25
  genome, 14, 68–69, 104, 130, 131–35,
    162, 170, 172, 173, 182, 184, 248–49
  genome-wide association studies
    (GWAS), 144, 145n.8, 148

INDEX **353**

genome. *See* genetics
genotype, 14, 29n.8, 35–36, 47n.18, 77–
  83, 98, 105–6, 129–30, 131–35, 142,
  144–46, 149–53, 156–57, 160–61,
  163–64, 173, 181, 189
  natural genotype, 77–83
Ghiselin, Michael T., 69–70, 319–20
Gladwell, Malcolm, 278n.10
Glasgow, Joshua, 194, 197n.22
Gould, Stephen Jay, 24n.2, 37–38, 54n.23,
  158n.18, 327–28
gravity, 77, 123, 205, 307–8
Gray's Anatomy, argument from, 62–63,
  71–74, 76, 84, 93–94, 229–30, 295–96
Gray, Henry, 72, 74
Gray, Russell D., 150n.12, 153–54
Griffin, Susan, 217
Griffiths, Paul E., 30n.11, 43n.14, 67n.5,
  87n.16, 88n.17, 105n.4, 110–17, 126,
  150n.12, 153–54, 243n.2, 312n.8,
  320n.9
group selection, 31–32
GWAS (genome-wide association
  studies). *See* genetics

Habermas, Jürgen, 289
Hamilton, William D., 31–32
Haslanger, Sally, 186–89, 192n.18, 193–
  94, 217n.10
Health, 16–17, 132, 159n.19, 222, 227–28,
  234–48, 250, 253, 255–56, 262–64,
  271, 274, 275, 284–85, 289–90, 292,
  294, 296–97
  health care, 246, 250
  practical vs. theoretical, 237
Hegel, Georg W.F., 207
Henrich, Joseph, 45–46, 64n.1, 92n.19
heritability, 14, 106, 108, 117, 130, 142–
  50, 151, 156–57, 161–64, 323–24
  heritability studies, 134, 149–50, 161,
  163–64
Hippocrates, 240
Hobbes, Thomas, 3–4, 6, 21, 227, 302
Holmstrom, Nancy, 219, 223–27, 228,
  229–31
homeostasis, 240
homosexuality, 15, 34–35, 42, 53, 75, 202,
  223–24

hubris, 292–93
Hull, David L., 69–72, 74, 78n.11, 82–83,
  84–86, 91–93, 94, 228, 287n.14, 297,
  319–20
human behavioral ecology. *See* ecology
human capabilities approach, 221–24,
  226–27
human dignity, 166–67, 198, 221, 228–29,
  268, 269–70, 289–91
human races. *See* races
human rights, 15, 16, 92–93, 166–67, 198,
  202–3, 207–8, 210, 221–24, 226–27,
  228–29, 230, 240, 281–82, 284,
  287–88, 297, 325
Hume, David, 8–9, 19, 21, 64–65, 207, 295
Huntington's Disease (HD). *See* disease
Hutchinson, G. Evelyn, 260
Huxley, Aldous, 287
Huxley, Julian, 32–33
hydrocephaly, 248–49
hypergamy, 36, 61–62

illness. *See* disease
impairment. *See* disability
incest taboos, 34–35, 36, 61–62, 110–11
inertia, principle of, 77
inheritance of acquired characters, 23–24,
  26, 28–29
innateness, 13–14, 19, 56–57, 60, 96–127,
  129–203, 208, 230–31, 233, 272,
  295–96, 300–2, 306, 308n.5, 314–15,
  316, 318–19, 323
  biological definitions of, 104–6
  commonsensical definitions of, 102–4
  eliminativism (about innateness),
  109–17
  psychological definitions of, 106–9
intelligence, 43, 45, 99–100, 125, 126–27,
  142, 145, 153–54, 158–59, 273, 319
intelligent design. *See* creationism
interactionism, 33–35, 130, 136–38, 150,
  151–54, 155–63, 256–59, 261
invariance, 105–6, 108
  developmental invariance, 105

Jacob, François, 292–93
Jaggar Alison, 206–14, 223, 231–32, 265,
  314–16, 320

354 INDEX

James, William, 30, 44
Jeffers, Chike, 188
Jenkin, Fleeming, 26–27
Jonas, Hans, 289

Kant, Immanuel, 8–9, 19–20, 21, 167–68,
  202–5, 207, 215–16, 219–20, 295
Kass, Leon, 275, 276n.8, 279n.11, 280–85,
  286–87, 291
Keller, Evelyn Fox, 64n.1, 110n.10, 148,
  320n.9
Kelvin, Lord William Thompson, 27–28
Khalidi, Muhammad A., 100n.1, 106n.6,
  107n.8, 108n.9, 110n.10, 117n.14
kind, 19, 65–68, 91–92, 167, 169, 177–79,
  185–86, 190, 196–97, 201–2, 203,
  324–25
  Aristotelian kind, 178, 190
  homeostatic property cluster theory
    of, 178–79
  Lockean kind, 178–79, 190
  natural kind, 67–68, 169, 177–79, 185–
    86, 190, 196–97, 217–18, 295–96,
    324–25
  social kind, 169, 177, 185–86, 190,
    196–97, 200–1, 217–18, 324–25
Kingma, Elselijn, 245
Kinzler, Katherine D., 118n.15, 119,
  122–23, 124–25, 301–2
Kitcher, Philip, 25n.3, 51n.20, 52n.21,
  53–55, 78n.11, 135n.2, 138–41, 149–
  50, 151, 155–56, 158–60, 158n.18,
  197–98, 243n.2, 271n.5
Kronfeldner, Maria, 64n.1, 75n.9, 88–89,
  110n.10, 231–32, 287n.14, 319–20

Lamarck, Jean-Baptiste, 23–24, 26,
  28–29
language acquisition. See acquisition
laws vs. accidents, 66
Lesch-Nyhan syndrome, 36
Levins, Richard, 6, 151
Lewens, Tim, 43n.14, 44–45, 64n.1, 67n.5,
  86n.14, 88n.17, 92n.20, 94n.21,
  222n.12, 273n.6, 307n.4, 319–20
Lewontin, Richard C., 6, 7, 25n.3, 37,
  38n.12, 54n.23, 78n.11, 92–93,
  150n.12, 155–56, 158n.18, 159–60,

164, 172–77, 179–80, 186–52, 191–
  92, 198, 230–31, 260
liberalism, 2, 135, 207–11, 213, 230
linguistic ability, 90–91, 99–100, 107, 143,
  248–49, 298–302, 306, 307, 316
linkage, 134, 179
Lloyd, Genevieve, 215
Locke, John, 55–56, 100, 103, 118, 178–
  79, 185, 207
Lorenz, Konrad, 30–31, 32–33, 104–29
Lyell, Charles, 10

Machery, Edouard, 64n.1, 65n.2, 85–89,
  214n.8
Madison, James, 19
Malthus, Thomas, 25
marginalization. See discrimination
Marx, Karl, 2, 5–6, 21, 208–14, 215–16,
  227, 230, 295, 302
Marxism. See Marx
Marxist feminism. See feminism
mating. See sexual behavior
Maynard Smith, John, 104–5
Mayr, Ernst, 24n.1, 38n.12, 113–14
McDougall, William, 30
McKibben, William E., 276n.9
mechanism, 23, 30, 38–39, 40, 42, 47–49,
  50, 52–53, 59, 75–76, 84–85, 93, 111,
  118, 146, 178–79, 240, 305
  cognitive mechanism, 40, 47–49, 50,
    54, 59, 62, 71–72, 75–76, 118, 311
  evolved psychological mechanism,
    47–49, 52–53, 71–72, 111
medical positivism, 238
Mendel, Gregor, 28–29, 131, 155, 161
Mill, John Stuart, 207–8, 215–16
mind-body problem, 8, 307–8, 310–11n.7
Mitchell, Juliet, 212n.7
Modern Synthesis, 28–29, 84
modularity. See module
module, 44, 48–49, 55–57, 59, 62, 73, 109,
  119, 121–22, 124–25, 323
monomorphism, 110–11, 115, 323
Morgan, C. Lloyd, 30, 44

natural kind. See kind
natural selection. See evolution by natural
  selection

INDEX 355

natural state model, 12–13, 62–63, 74, 75–83, 84–86, 87–88, 89, 93–94, 96–97, 113, 128–29, 229, 235, 250, 262–64, 281, 293–94, 295–96, 322–23
nature vs. nurture, 100, 150, 154–55, 161, 188–89, 258–59, 323–24
neuroscience, 30, 32, 107–8, 158–59
Newton, Isaac, 77, 115–16, 307–8
niche, 259–61, 263
   niche construction, 152n.14
Nietzsche, Friedrich, 1
norm of reaction, 14, 77–82, 105, 106n.7, 130, 140–42, 144, 148–54, 156–62, 164, 323–24
normality, 12–13, 16–17, 62–63, 75–85, 87–89, 92–94, 96–97, 105–6, 108–10, 113, 128–29, 140, 146, 149–50, 159n.19, 161, 174n.4, 202–4, 208, 227–28, 229, 232, 233–65, 273, 274–76, 281, 289, 295–97, 301, 322–23, 325–26
   critiques of, 246–53
   normal development, 75, 77, 80–81, 82, 105, 108–9, 110, 249
   normal function, 16–17, 76, 79–81, 82, 92–93, 94, 234–63, 240–53, 255–56, 261–63, 274, 281, 294, 296–97
   statistical normality, 79, 81, 87–88, 94, 114, 202, 238–39, 240–46
normativity, 5–6, 62–63, 85–86, 87–91, 93–95, 98–99, 110, 113, 114–15, 164, 166, 189–90, 202–4, 206–7, 215–16, 217–18, 219, 223, 224, 228–29, 230–32, 233, 236–37, 257–58, 263, 271, 273, 293, 295–96, 298, 310–11n.7, 322–23, 326
Nussbaum, Martha, 221–24, 226–27

oppression, 15–16, 166, 200–1, 208–10, 211n.6, 212, 224–25, 233, 296–97
optimality models, 44
Oyama, Susan, 135n.2, 150

panculturalism, 110–12, 115–16
pangenesis, 29–30
pathology. *See* disease
phenotype, 14, 24n.1, 35–36, 44, 70, 75–85, 91–92, 93, 98, 105–6, 110–11,

124, 129–30, 136–44, 146–51, 152–64, 167–71, 174n.4, 189, 190, 233–34, 244, 250, 258–60, 323–256
   extended phenotype, 250
   natural (normal) phenotype, 75–85, 93
physiology, 19, 32–33, 72, 90, 239, 240, 247–48, 310
Pico della Mirandola, Giovanni, 1
Pinker, Steven, 6–7, 45–46, 55n.24, 58, 59–60, 92–93, 125, 164, 267n.1, 291n.16
Plato, 7–8, 19, 21, 57–58, 63, 65, 100, 107, 207, 272, 295
Plomin, Robert, 142n.6, 145n.8, 157–58
population thinking vs. typological thinking 113–14, 168
pornography, 41–42
postmodernism, 218–19
poverty of stimulus argument, 299–302
prenatal learning, 103–4
Preston, Beth, 319
Prinz, Jesse, 132, 320n.9
promiscuity. *See* sexual behavior
proto-naturalistic analyses of human nature, 8–9, 21, 61
psychological mechanism. *See* mechanism
psychological primitivism, 107–9

quality of life, 222, 237–38, 246, 251–52, 282, 284
   subjective vs. objective, 252

race, 15–16, 164, 165–99, 200–2, 217–18, 219, 227–28, 233, 247, 248, 294, 296–97, 298, 324–25
   folk concept of, 168–69, 186, 191–93, 194, 197–98
   race constructionism, 15–16, 166, 177, 184, 185–90, 196–99, 200–1
   race eliminativism, 15–16, 166, 169, 177, 190–99
   race naturalism, 15–16, 166, 169, 177–84, 185, 189–90, 194, 200–1
   racial skepticism, 166–69, 200–1
   racialism, 166, 167–69, 196–97, 200–1
   racism, 13–14, 15, 97, 123, 126–27, 166–67, 194–95, 202, 225–26, 227–28, 252, 286–87, 324–25

356 INDEX

Ramsey, Grant, 65n.3, 86–89
random effects, 37
rationalism, 19, 100, 126
rationality, 58–59, 100–1, 203, 207–9,
 214–15, 221, 230, 308–9, 310–11n.7
Rawls, John, 221–22, 229n.13
reason. *See* rationality
reference class, 39, 241, 243–44, 246–47
religion, 46, 97, 189, 199
Rich, Adrienne, 216–17
Richerson, Peter J., 45n.16, 58n.27, 64n.1,
 84n.13
Rosenberg, Noah A., 180–83
Rousseau, Jean-Jacques, 3–4, 6, 21, 202–5,
 207, 215–16, 219–20, 227, 295
Rubin, Gayle, 212n.7

Samuels, Richard, 87n.16, 100n.1, 102,
 105n.5, 106n.6, 107–9
Sandel, Michael, 273n.6, 293
Sartre, Jean-Paul, 212
Savulescu, Julian, 270n.4, 273n.6, 276n.7,
 285n.13
scientific explanation, 18, 60, 117n.14,
 232, 286, 302–21, 325–26, 327
semantic externalism, 192–93
Sen, Amartya, 221–22, 228–29
sex, 16, 31–32, 36, 40–43, 50–57, 103–4,
 166, 187n.16, 199, 200–32, 233, 238,
 241, 244, 247, 252–53, 294, 296–97
sexism, 15, 202, 252, 286–87, 324–25
sexual behavior, 36, 39, 40–43, 50–57,
 115
sexual selection, 9, 31–32, 49, 271
Shakespeare, William, 57–58, 233
shared ancestry. *See* ancestry
Siddhartha Gautama, 57–58
sign language, 248–49
Simpson, George G., 10
Slipjer's goat, 248–49, 250
Smith, Adam, 2, 5–6, 21, 207, 227, 295,
 302
Sober, Elliott, 28n.6, 66n.4, 76n.10,
 106n.6, 114n.13, 310
social constructionism. *See*
 constructionism
social contract, 3, 4
social kind. *See* kind

sociobiology, 10–11, 12, 22–23, 30–36,
 37–60, 61–62, 84, 96–97, 98, 118,
 129, 205, 217, 295–96, 302, 322
Socrates, 272, 297
soft inheritance. *See* blending inheritance
soul, 7–8, 281–84, 292
spandrel, 37, 80, 214–15
species, 7–8, 9–10, 12–13, 16–17, 19,
 21–28, 33–39, 43, 45–60, 64–93,
 96–97, 105–6, 109–14, 119–20, 128–
 29, 138, 145–48, 158, 166–73, 175,
 178–80, 183, 197–98, 207–8, 215–16,
 220, 223–24, 226–27, 228, 229–30,
 233–35, 241, 244, 247–48, 250, 251,
 260, 267–68n.2, 286–87
species design, 248–50, 321–22, 323,
 327
speciesism, 26
Spelke, Elizabeth S., 118n.15, 119, 122–
 25, 301–2
Sperber, Dan, 45n.16, 57
state of nature, 3–5
Sterelny, Kim, 45n.16, 45n.17, 67n.5,
 88n.17, 318–19, 320n.9
Stich, Stephen, 107n.8
Stotz, Karola, 312n.8
Structure, 181–83
superability, 250–51, 257–58
supervenience, 310–11n.7, 311
Symons, Donald, 40–43
systematics, 70n.6

Tay-Sachs disease. *See* disease
theory of evolution. *See* evolution by
 natural selection
therapy, 269–70, 272–75, 276, 281–82,
 285, 293–94, 326
thick vs. thin concepts of human nature,
 62–63, 89–95, 226–27, 233, 295–96,
 322–23, 325–26
Tinbergen, Nikolaas, 30–33
Tomasello, Michael, 44n.15, 45
Tooby, John, 45–46, 48n.19, 49, 55n.24,
 59–60, 72n.7
transhumanism. *See* bioliberalism
Trivers, Robert, 31–32, 36
Turkheimer, Eric, 142n.6
Turner's syndrome, 36

typological vs. population thinking, 113–14

United Nations Declaration of Rights, 221
United Nations Educational, Scientific, and Cultural Organization (UNESCO), 168
universality, 1, 38–39, 50, 51–52, 69, 90–91, 105–6, 110–11, 115, 142n.6

variability, 54–55, 69–70, 91–92, 93–94, 106n.6, 121, 156–57, 233–34, 248–49
variation, 6, 9, 14–16, 25–30, 44–45, 51–52, 53, 58–59, 68–70, 75–76, 78, 80–81, 82–83, 91–92, 106, 109, 111–12, 113–14, 130, 133–34, 136–37, 141, 143–44, 147–50, 156–57, 161, 168–72, 174n.4, 175–77, 179–84, 196–97, 215–16, 220, 222, 224, 227, 229–30, 233–34, 236, 238–39, 246–48, 255, 260, 262–63, 300
violence, 13–14, 97–98, 126–27, 142, 153–54, 163, 221
Voltaire, 167–68
von Frisch, Karl, 30–31, 32–33

Wallace, Alfred R., 9, 10, 91–92
Wason selection task, 56
Wason, Peter C., 56
Weisman, August, 29n.9
wheelchair, 248–49, 250–51, 254–55, 256, 257, 259–60
Williams, Bernard 90n.18
Williams, George C., 31–32
Wilson, David S., 28n.6
Wilson, Edward O., 10–11, 12, 22, 32–37, 38, 43, 45–48, 45n.16, 49–50, 51, 58–60, 61–62, 71–72, 84, 96–97, 98, 110–11, 125–27, 129, 136, 137, 139, 140, 142–43, 153–54, 160
Wilson, Margo, 38n.13, 57n.26, 295–96, 316, 317–18, 322
Wollstonecraft, Mary, 57–58, 200, 207–8, 215–16, 295
Woltereck, Richard, 78n.11
Woolf, Virginia, 19, 295
Wright, Larry, 80, 242

xenophobia, 12, 38, 43, 47
XXY male, 36

The manufacturer's authorised representative in the EU for product safety is Oxford
University Press España S.A. of El Parque Empresarial San Fernando de Henares,
Avenida de Castilla, 2 – 28830 Madrid (www.oup.es/en or product.safety@oup.com).
OUP España S.A. also acts as importer into Spain of products made by the manufacturer.

Printed in the USA/Agawam, MA
August 8, 2025

891696.004